D0417395

Routes, Roots

and Wings

Maggie Wynton

Published and printed by

FTRR Printing and Publishing, 38-40 Grant St

Inverness, IV3 8BN

ISBN: 978-1-912270-07-1

Other books by same author:
Granny Maggie's funny stories

Dedications

For those I love and have loved. In memory of my Mum, Annie Campbell (nee Fotheringham), who died when I was two-years-old. My Dad, Bob Campbell and my Aunt Margaret. This is also for my wonderful family.

This book tells my story of growing up without my Mum and of preparing my disabled daughter for life without me "The greatest gifts you can give your children are the roots of responsibility and the wings of independence." (Denis Whaitley, writer).
Maggie Wynton

Foreword by Linsey Wynton

Time Flies

Since I was a little girl, my Mum has wanted to write about her life. On the surface, this life of hers may seem fairly conventional, but it is far from ordinary. Her Mum died of cancer when she was just two years old. After that she was brought up in her native Fife and Edinburgh by a series of family friends and aunties as well as her Dad and ageing Grandpa. When she was almost 10 her Dad remarried. But her relationship with her Stepmother was often difficult.

She left home at seventeen and moved to Dundee to train as a primary school teacher. That is where she met my Dad, dancing in the Students' Union. Back then, aged just twenty one, my Mum taught classes of more than forty pupils, even taking them to the swimming pool on her own on the public bus in mid-winter.

My parents moved to the Highlands just before I was born and they had three children: myself, my brother Andrew and our sister Eilidh, who was born very prematurely. When she was about a year old, Eilidh was diagnosed with cerebral palsy. This was devastating for both my parents. As any family who has experienced disability knows, this affects the whole family. Sadly during our early childhood my Mum lost her Dad and Stepmother. She also lost her very best fried Liz to cancer.

Eilidh

Andrew and Linsey

In 1985 my Mum watched a documentary that changed our lives. It was about a little boy and his family who travelled to Hungary to receive seemingly groundbreaking therapeutic treatment to help him learn to walk. My Mum and sister followed in his footsteps and our community kindly donated money to help my sister try to achieve her dream of walking. Sadly Eilidh had problems with one of her hips, which meant she could not achieve that goal. However at that time there was a marked improvement in her balance and she made progress walking with support. My Mum was able to use her experience as a parent of a disabled child to work with pre-school children with disabilities for almost two decades. She helped their parents teach them at home through play, work out the best route for them in terms of schooling and she supported these parents through the strain of raising a child with additional needs. She still occasionally works as a supply teacher in a special school.

My brother and I have long since flown the nest and my sister has gone on to live a fairly independent life thanks to some very amazing carers who are almost a surrogate family to her. My parents have often had to argue for my sister's basic needs to be met, which is unfair, as it is tough enough having a disabled child, who still depends on their family in ways other children and adults do not.

My sister's experience in Hungary inspired me to become a journalist, to tell stories that I believe other people have the right to know, stories that can change people's lives for the better. My Mum's need to tell her story is part therapeutic, and part to share those experiences with others who can empathise, because when you lose your Mum, or have a disabled child, you can feel very alone.

I hope this book will do two things: one, inspire others to record their family history for their children and grandchildren and those around them who share similar experiences; and, two, to speak to others who have sadly lost a parent in childhood, who have coped with having a child with a disability or who simply grew up through the same era as my Mum. I am sure it will be of interest to many teachers, parents and those familiar with Fife, Edinburgh and the Scottish Highlands.

For me, reading this transports me back to my Mum's time – a time when life was simpler and less pressured. I love the references to the music, the food, the clothing and landscape and even the Archers as well as some of the very colourful characters my Mum met along her route. For me two images sum up my life with my Mum: her taxiing us around in her orange Fiat Mirafiori listening to B J Thomas's Raindrops Keep Fallin' on my Head; and the Angel Delight and Ruskoline Years of my Mum juggling eggs as she danced round the kitchen to Robbie Shepherd's Scottish Country dancing programme on the radio. This is not only a poignant read, it is also nostalgic and funny.

People in this book

My Mum's family
My Mum
Ann Campbell (nee Fotheringham)

My maternal Grandparents
Frank Fotheringham and Margaret Scott (Frank's 2nd wife)

My Aunts and Uncles
Aunt Janet – Frank's daughter from first marriage to Elizabeth Beveridge who died. Aunt Janet was married to Bobby Lawson
Aunt Kit (Katherine) was married to Jim Love and they had two sons, Billy and Frank
Uncle Frank (junior) was married to Hilda and they had two daughters Jean and Ann
Uncle David (died as a young man)

Maternal cousins
Mary Fotheringham was married to John Copping

My Dad's family
My Dad
Robert Campbell

My Paternal grandparents
Robert Campbell (senior) and Elizabeth McPherson. After Elizabeth died, my grandfather married Margaret Boag.

My Aunts and Uncles
Uncle Angus was married to Jessie and they had a daughter Shona and a son Iain
John (died in adolescence)
Jean (died in adolescence)

Paternal Cousins
Angus McPherson was married to Nessie Stirling

My Paternal Great Aunts and Uncles
Meg was not married
Susan was not married
Nan was married to James Young and they had a son James (who died in infancy) and two daughters Nancy and Margaret ie my Aunt Margaret Young
Jean was married to George Morrison – they had a son George (known as Sonny)

Tib (Isabel) was married to Bob Brownlee – they had a son Fred
John Campbell was married to Elspeth

My Stepmother
Margaret Ferguson

My Step Aunts and Uncles
Nancy
John
Ben (he died in his thirties)

Family friends
Connie and George Middleton and their children Daphne, Jean, Avril and
Kathleen
Lizzie and Andrew Gibb – they had a son called John
Willie Paris

Others
John – the elderly man who helped my Mum with the garden
Mrs Somerville – a neighbour of my Mum and Dad who lived at 1
Kinneddar Park
Tommy Philbin and Bob Paterson – work colleagues of my Dad
Jimmy and Isabel Knox – friends of My Aunt Nan and Aunt Margaret who
had a son named Henry
Rev Robert Dollar – minister of Dunfermline Abbey Church – my Grandpa
looked after his garden
Celia Graham and her family – upstairs neighbours of Grandpa Campbell in
Moodie Street, Dunfermline
Mr Nelson – my Mum's Headmaster
Dr Russell and Mr Jardine – my Mum's doctors at Edinburgh Royal
Infirmary
Miss Leonard, Miss Halpin, Miss Struthers, Miss Gemmell, Miss McKenzie,
Miss Bonniman,
Miss Letts, Miss MacLean – my primary school teachers

My Stepmother's family
Margaret Ferguson, my Stepmother
Nancy Mazzoni, Margaret's younger sister was married to Dave and they
had a son named Lewis
John Ferguson, Margaret's older brother was married to Betty

My Dad and Margaret's friends
George and Isa Brown
Peter and Margaret Torley
Jim and Mary Hunter
Hector Aird

Margaret's shop assistants
Isa Tatters
Maureen MacGregor

Other local people
Geordie Tatters, Isa Tatter's brother, who was a fruit and vegetable seller
Dougie the milkman
Mr Reekes the dentist

My school friends
Liz
Adele
Doreen
Jean, my cousin, who was my uncle Frank's daughter
Dennis, my first boyfriend

Teachers at Foulford Primary
Miss Moffat
Miss Letts
Miss MacLean

My piano teachers
Bert Livingstone & Alice Calder

Aunt Margaret's cousins
George Morrison who was married to Bunty
Fred Brownlee

Chapters

Introduction

Life is made up of a series of memories – happy, sad, frightening and exhilarating to name but a few. If I've learned anything at all in life, it has been to expect nothing, to work hard, to try to be kind, helpful and cheerful and – most important of all – on no account to live life on regrets.

In 1979 I gave birth to my third child, Eilidh, who was born very prematurely. As a consequence she was critically ill. She had also suffered brain damage. During her early years I was fuelled by a desire to commit to paper the plethora of experiences we shared as a family in coming to terms with a disabled child.

Over the years I had also tried to find out more about my Mum, whom I lost as a young child, and in piecing together this information I came to write about my life. While I was growing up, I usually tended to give consideration to things that I thought were important at the time, but were in fact, transitory. So, unfortunately, I didn't seek answers to the questions that I now wish I had asked all of these years ago.

After my Dad died I found a small, brown, battered case among his personal possessions – inside which was an amazing miscellany of keepsakes. There were photographs, my tonsillectomy bills, the card my Mum received from church when she became a member, my Mum and Dad's work references, some of the notes from my Dad's accountancy course, letters – many of which they'd written to each other when my Mum was in hospital, sympathy cards and the newspaper announcing my Mum's death. My parents' letters unquestionably illustrate the very strong and loving relationship that existed during their 10-year marriage; something I never knew about. That small case was definitely my Dad's memory box, and now it belongs to me.

I would like to thank my elder daughter Linsey for her unstinting encouragement and countless constructive suggestions during the decades I have wanted to write this. I am grateful for her professional journalistic skills in re-drafting and editing this tirelessly over the months and years, often in the wee small hours. I would also like to thank my sister-in-law Moira for putting her professional proof-reading skills to such invaluable use. Thanks also go to my son Andrew for jogging my memory regarding lots of incidents and for suggesting the title. Without my younger daughter Eilidh I doubt if I'd ever have been motivated to do this, so I thank her for changing my life so much – it has been incredibly hard but I feel I have evolved into a much more rounded person as a result. I would also like to thank my husband of almost half a century, Ron, for all his help, support and advice, particularly with the technology. Thanks also go to my friend Sheena Munro for her help advice and encouragement.   And my appreciation goes posthumously to my Dad's cousin, my Aunt Margaret, who was a constant support and a wonderful mentor to me.

I have included all of my Mum and Dad's letters at the end and in their entirety because they are so special to me.
Maggie Wynton

Chapter 1: This Girl Margaret's Early Memories

"My goodness your Grandpa was Frank Fotheringham. He was the fattest man in Kelty," said Mr Watson, my High school music teacher.

Grandpa Frank and family

I'd no knowledge of this since Grandpa Frank had died a long time before I was born. Many years later I discovered that Frank really was very fat. I found this out from a photograph of Frank with two of his grandsons. I also discovered that he had died of a heart attack because of obesity. He was only 57. I learned this from an extract of deaths that occurred in 1928 in Kelty. His occupation was a Master Baker and he obviously had sampled too many of his wares. He died leaving his second wife Margaret Scott and five children. Her eldest child was Annie, my Mum.

1948: The Open Window

I have only one vague memory of my Mum. I was standing on the sill of an open upstairs window. I know that it must have been open because down below someone was shouting and waving their arms. Years later, my Aunt Janet (who was Grandpa Frank's oldest daughter from his first marriage and my Mum's half sister) told me that it was an elderly man called John. He used to help in our garden.

I remember it being sunny and warm, which meant that it was probably summertime, and so I would have been about nineteen months old. I also remember being gathered up, lifted down and cuddled for a long time. Later my Aunt Janet told me that it was my Mum who had rescued me. She said my Mum had left me playing with my toys while she put away the laundry in the linen cupboard next door. I had climbed up onto the small wooden chest that was under the windowsill so that I could look out. My Mum had told her that I was alone only for a few minutes. She'd been completely distraught when she thought about what might have happened.

Just a few months later my Mum died. It was February 1949. She went to Edinburgh Royal Infirmary at the beginning of January with severe stomach pains. She never came home.

Maggie's Mother is second from left - a
young girl working at the Buttercup Dairy

I don't remember anything about that period. I guess that my young mind found the memory too painful and simply shut it out. I was only two and a quarter.

My Mum had twice been a patient in the Infirmary. The first time was in May and June 1944, during the Second World War, when she was treated for mastoiditis, a complication of middle ear infection. From reading her letters written during her second period in hospital just before she died, I discovered that she'd had a very good idea of how ill she was and she realised only too well the strong likelihood that she wouldn't get better.

Above the main entrance to the hospital that has since been rebuilt were carved the poignant words: *"I was a stranger and ye took me in"* and *"I was sick and ye visited me"*.

During her final stay in hospital my Mum wrote a letter to my Dad nearly every day. This was because he was only able to visit her on Saturdays as he couldn't take time off work during the week to travel from our home in Saline in Fife by bus and train. My Mum had lots of visitors including her sisters Janet and Kit, her friend Lizzie, and my paternal

Grandpa Robert's second wife Margaret (nee Boag). They would often bring cards, letters and food, such as scones and cake that friends and relatives had made. Although my Mum was always pleased to have their company she would tell my Dad: *"I miss you and Margaret [me] so much."* In a letter to my Dad she says: *"I keep wishing it was Saturday again as I always seem to have more to tell you than any of the others."*

She wrote the first of this series of letters on 9th January 1949. It was a very frank one, but it was never sent. It was written to a neighbour called Mrs Somerville, who also lived in our street at number 1 Kinneddar Park. Each Friday my Dad would collect fish from Mrs S. When my Mum was rushed into the Infirmary he completely and understandably forgot to collect the fish and I believe that Mrs S. had remonstrated with him. My Mum writes: *"Will you please cancel our fish? I may be away from Kinneddar for quite some time. If I'm spared to come home, I'm going to live with friends."*

In a letter to my Dad dated 13th January 1949, my Mum asks him how he got on with Mrs S. when he went to see her to explain and apologise. In that same letter she asks my Dad: *"How's our wee lamb getting on?"* And then: *"It brings tears to my eyes when I think of the wee soul."* Further on in that same letter she writes that I tell her to: *"Hurry home from the Infirmary mummy."* My Mum replies, *"be a good girl darling"*, and I say, *"yes"*. My Mum goes on to say that she was, *"glad I slept with her the night before, I must have kissed her all night, kissed and cried time about"*, and then: *"That's enough I'm going all sentimental."*

When my Mum was admitted to hospital that second time, with severe stomach pains, she had blood tests and writes that she, *"told the sister about the pain and she told the doctor"*. She was then asked: *"Ever been abroad?"* And: *"Are you sure you never had malaria?"* She describes it as, *"the same talk as last time"*. She must have been referring to her previous time in hospital.

My Dad's letters cheered her up immensely at that time – I wish that these had been in the case too, but I guess that they must have been either lost or left in the Infirmary because of his grief after she died.

In another letter she tells my Dad about, *"my old pal Dr Russell"*, who was a young house doctor when she had her operation in 1944. Dr Russell immediately remembered her and said he'd look back through her old records. He told her that, *"he'd have to have me put right"*, and he goes on to say: *"I remember that night when I brought in the other doctors – you know Mrs C you were very, very ill."* She told my Dad that Dr Russell was now, *"next to the Chief"*, and I can almost hear her accent jumping off the page when she writes, typically missing out the word "got" as we do in Fife, *"he's now a moustache which makes him older looking"*.

Despite the pain, for me reading these letters brought my Mum to life. It also connected me to her in a way I couldn't have imagined before, when I read her loving words. Later in this same letter she tells my Dad that she had a Pakistani doctor who was with her from 9am till 1.30pm. This was part of the exam he was doing in order to become a professor. He had to explain her X-ray plates to the *"Chief"*, and, *"Oh you should have heard him Bob, he certainly knew his stuff."* When he was finished, my Mum told him that she'd, *"kept my fingers crossed for him"*, and he replied: *"Thank you very much Mrs C."*

A few days later my Mum had more X-rays taken. This procedure took more than two hours. When she returned to the ward she was exhausted. Despite that she was determined to let my Dad know what had happened and so she wrote the following letter while lying on her back:

"Dear Bob,

This will be some letter as I'm on my back to write it. I'm back from X-ray 5 o'clock and I've been there since 2.30pm. Believe me Bob I'm exhausted. They took my chest as well as my tummy. Oh God I pray there is nothing wrong with my lungs too. There is definitely something wrong with my liver. I don't like to write this Bob, but I've cried for Margaret and you (the only two people I've got to live for) all day. I do wish we were together again. Please pray for me to get well soon as I pray as hard as I know how."

She goes on to ask him if his friend Willie Paris "was up visiting" and that they'd have a "grand pow wow." Then she tells him about the weather and the scanty tea she's been given, "the first since last night half a slice of toast and a cup of tea it's awful." She tells my Dad: "Don't bother about what I've written as I've taken such a shaking. I feel awful and can only pour my heart out to you. Roll on Saturday." This is when she hopes that decisions will be made. She continues: "I believe that all this wondering is having a bad effect on me. I've pictured myself with all sorts of trouble. Silly eh? Funny, I feel brighter even now."

Having written all of that to my poor Dad she tells him not to worry and wonders if after reading it she should post it. I guess like me, writing was a cathartic process for her.

She wrote only two more letters after that one and in the first of these says that she is *"writing just now as I feel in a sort of good humour"*. She then apologises for baring her soul in the last letter, then goes on to describe the barium enema she'd had when she had her X-rays taken. I guess that she did this to cheer my Dad up, as he pictured her *"trot off in her wee shirt 3 inches above her knees, and socks to the lavy."* After the X-rays had been taken she writes: *"That's when I was silly enough to write you, but I knew if I'd waited, I wouldn't have been able to write you and that would have worried you."*

She went on to tell Dad that: *"Dr Russell was in at me last night again. I wish I saw more of him as he gives me such a lot of confidence. He gave me a good examination but wouldn't tell me what he thought. He said:*

"We'll wait till the plates come back."'

She continues that Dr Russell went on to ask her: *"Why are you letting this temperature of yours go up and down?' I said, "I couldn't understand it." Then he smiled and said, "Tell me do you remember what your temperature was like last time you were in?" Of course I said: "No".' He said: "I'll tell you it was right off the chart altogether and that's over 106 [41 Celsius]."*

The last letter she wrote to my Dad was on the 25th January. She has no idea that it would be her last letter. She tells my Dad that it's, *"just going to be a short scribble"*, and that she'd *"had the surgeon in yesterday with 6 of his henchmen"*. She was thoroughly examined and was to have another X-ray before the decision was made as to whether or not to operate. She seemed more concerned as to whether or not she was to have another barium enema. She goes on to tell my Dad that she was told by a nurse that Mr Jardine, the surgeon, was one of the best in the country and that he was a principal in the Royal College of Surgeons. He'd given her so much confidence that, if he'd said *"come and I'll operate now"* she'd have *"gone gladly"*.

She continues telling Dad that the lady opposite has been christened *"Hungry Horace"* by another lady, because of the amount of food she eats. My Mum says: *"It chaws me with the helpings I get, bet Margaret gets more."* She finishes by saying: *"All my love to my two darlings. Keep praying."*

Although Mr Jardine was one of the best surgeons in the country, not even his great skills could save my Mum's life.

Many years after, my Aunt Margaret – Margaret Young, who was my Dad's cousin, told me that my Mum had had bowel cancer and had undergone major surgery. I had always believed that she had died from pneumonia – cancer was NOT talked about in those days. But when I, as an adult, saw her death certificate, cancer was recorded as the cause.

Aunt Margaret also told me that the September before she died, my Mum had a baby boy who only lived for a day. My future Stepmother Margaret Ferguson later told me that the cancer should have been discovered when she'd had her baby, but sadly it wasn't. Baby Campbell was never named and he is buried beside my Mum and my Grandpa Campbell in Beath Cemetery, which lies between Cowdenbeath and Kelty. I am sure that his name would have been Robert, after my Dad and my Grandpa. I have always wondered what he would have been like and thought about the things we might have done together, things that sadly only ever happened in my imagination.

My guess is that my Mum had secondary cancer and as a result was terminally ill. Maybe after that dreadful news she lost all of her very strong will to live. Annie died on Saturday 12th February 1949 at 12.10am. She was just 36 years old. My poor Dad was utterly devastated and my Grandpa Campbell was inconsolable. No one could believe it and many of her friends and family said *"only the good die young!"* I don't really believe that. I just wish that she'd been there for me during all of the times in my life that I've needed her, as a child and an adult, and these were very many.

Losing his young wife must have been indescribably difficult for my Dad. Aunt Janet later told me that his heart was broken. But at that time, I don't think that it was considered acceptable for men to show such emotions as grief, so consequently these feelings were suppressed. Whilst other men would offer sympathy, they were often very uncomfortable, awkward and unable to show their true feelings for fear of being considered effeminate. Instead many men were raised to be tough, whereas when women were widowed, most had lots of support from the sisterhood – the womenfolk in their family as well as their friends and could weep openly, thus giving vent to their emotions. So my poor Dad having lost my Mum would certainly have felt utterly alone.

Years later, in 1978, my Dad told me his biggest regret in life: *"I wasn't with your Mum when she died."* She was unconscious at the end, and his Aunt Susan had persuaded him to go back to her house to rest. All that I could say to him was: *"But Dad she was unconscious and wouldn't have known that you were there. Please don't blame yourself!"*

During this profound conversation, which I treasure with every fibre of my being, he then said: *"Margaret, I lost you when your Mum died. I should have married Margaret Ferguson earlier."* The inference was that we would all have had a home together sooner, because after my Mum died I lived with various extended family members and friends until my Dad remarried seven and a half years later. This was largely because men were the breadwinners in those days. Time off work was extremely restricted and employers were not as sympathetic towards employees then as they are today.

I think about my Mum every day, and now that I have turned 70, I wish that she'd had her three score years and ten at the very least. I am sure that she'd have been my very best friend.

When I held Linsey, my own first baby daughter in my arms, it evoked very powerful memories of when I was rescued from the windowsill and I fervently wished that she'd been there to share in my happiness. The mere thought of being unable to look after my baby and see her grow up seemed unbearable.

Over the years, I tried to find out as much as I could about my Mum and her relationship with my Dad from family and friends. This is what I learned.

My Mum and My Dad

My Mum, known as Annie, was born on 1st October 1912 to Frank Fotheringham and his second wife Margaret Scott. Annie had an older half sister Janet, her father having been widowed, and was the eldest of her father's second family. She had a sister Katherine (Kit) and two brothers, one was Frank while the other, David, died as a young man. I know from all of her photographs that she had strawberry blonde hair, grey eyes and a smile that would light up any room.

In October 1926, she was selected for interview for a job in Kelty Buttercup Dairy having, *"acquired the required percentage of marks entitling you to be included in the short leet for the situation of Dairy Assistant".*

I well remember that shop with its lovely blue tiled entrance with the picture of the pretty little girl holding a buttercup under her chin. These tiles have been preserved to this day.

Mr R E Nelson, the Headmaster of Oakfield Higher Grade School, wrote a reference for her in June 1927 that stated: *"Miss Ann Fotheringham has been a pupil in regular attendance at this school for almost three years; that she has now practically completed her three years course of study, and that she has been presented for examination in each of the required subjects."*

He continued: *"The group of subjects for Examination for the Certificate are: English, History, Geography, Arithmetic, Algebra, French, Science, Book keeping, Shorthand, Typewriting.*

"Miss A. Fotheringham has been a careful and conscientious student; and her school character is an excellent one."

Annie Fotheringham married Bob Campbell in September 1938. I don't know how or where they met. But my Stepmother Margaret Ferguson later told me that they'd got engaged secretly, and at first instead of wearing her white gold and diamond solitaire ring on her finger she wore it on a chain around her neck. Margaret told me that she'd said to her: *"How can you do that! If that had been me I would have had to wear it on my finger!"*

What I was told by my Aunt Janet was that my Dad, his Dad, my Mum, her sisters Kit and Janet and brother Frank were very close. My Dad's dad Robert Campbell, my Grandpa, just loved her to bits. He often spoke about her and called her *"a good woman"*. Sometimes when he spoke about her, his eyes would fill with tears. He told me that my parents were soul mates in the true sense of the word and consequently were very happy. He told me that Annie was a real live wire, sociable, welcoming, helpful, a good cook and baker.

I also know from talking to my Aunt Janet, Aunt Kit and looking at photographs, that my Mum had lots of friends and included in that circle were Lizzie Gibb, Nancy Ferguson and her sister Margaret, who was later to become my Stepmother. Margaret Ferguson had been engaged to my Mum's brother Frank, but later broke it off. When my Dad and Mum got married, Margaret Ferguson was the bridesmaid, and because my Dad's brother Angus was unable to have time off from his police duties, his maternal cousin Angus McPherson was the best man.

My Mum was also an accomplished musician. She enjoyed taking part in the Kelty Operatic Society productions of Rodgers and Hammerstein and Gilbert and Sullivan. My Dad's cousin Angus, told me that my Mum played the piano well – I have some of her piano certificates – and she sang beautifully. His wife Nessie, said that when I sat on my Mum's lap she would often teach me nursery rhymes and sing the Skye Boat Song, the Londonderry Air, Brahms Lullaby and the Eriskay Love Lilt. Nessie said this last one would often make me cry.

Eriskay Love Lilt

Chorus
Bheir me o, horo van o
Bheir me o, horo van ee
Bheir me o, o horo ho
Sad am I, without thee.

Thou'rt the music of my heart;
Harp of joy, o cruit mo chruidh;
Moon of guidance by night;
Strength and light thou'rt to me.

Chorus

In the morning, when I go
To the white and shining sea,
In the calling of the seals
Thy soft calling to me.

Chorus

When I'm lonely, dear white heart,
Black the night and wild the sea,
By love's light, my foot finds
The old pathway to thee.

Chorus

My Dad, Bob Campbell, was the youngest of four children. His oldest sibling was Jean then three brothers, John and Angus. Sadly both Jean and John died in adolescence, she aged 14 from meningitis, he aged 15 from pneumonia, and their mother, my Granny Elizabeth Campbell nee McPherson, like my Mum, died in the Royal Infirmary in Edinburgh at the early age of 48. She'd had surgery to remove fibroids and had died as the result of shock. Aunt Margaret told me that it was a great loss to all of the extended family. My Grandpa was utterly devastated.

My Dad was a quiet thoughtful man. I know this from

conversations with his brother Angus's wife Nessie. He was scrupulously honest, kind, had a keen sense of duty and was also diligent and punctual – a reference letter writer comments: *"Robert Campbell is a diligent worker, who as far as I know, has never been late for work".* My Dad began his working life at the pithead, in Kelty, though soon progressed to become the colliery cashier.

My Mum always joked that he was addicted to his work. In a reply to one of his letters she writes: *"I've just got your letter and feel very happy about it. We'll go out in the Spring Ha Ha! I know you mean Margaret and me might, but I can't see daddy, he'll always have either office or canteen work to do, and well you know it Robin."* Robin must have been her nickname for my Dad.

Grandpa told me that Annie and Bob complemented each other and as a result were eminently compatible. Perhaps it was their positions in their respective families that marked their personalities. Maybe it was because Annie was the eldest of her Dad's second family that she had such an outgoing personality and maybe my Dad was reserved because he was the youngest of his family. I don't remember him ever talking about his Mum, his sister Jean or his brother John. He was only a wee boy when Jean and John passed away.

I loved my Dad with all of my heart and sincerely wish that I'd have been able to spend more quality time with him. Oh if only circumstances had been different. When I close my eyes I can picture his kind face, his ready smile, his green eyes and his black wavy hair with the threads of silver running through it and those 1950s style glasses that are so fashionable again.

My parent's first home was a flat in Fotheringham's Buildings at the bottom of Cocklaw Street in Kelty. They shared their home with a little black Scots terrier called Scotty. My Aunt Janet and her husband Bobby Lawson lived further up at number 104 Cocklaw Street, in the bottom half of a house named Beverson, on the other side of the road. It is now home to Russell's Bagpipe and Reed Maker's business.

In May 1944, the year before the war ended, and two years before I was born, my Mum contracted mastoiditis and so was rushed to Edinburgh Infirmary. Mastoiditis is a complication of middle ear infection and in severe cases, like my Mum's case, an abscess may be formed in the mastoid bone, leaving the infection to spread to the interior of the skull, perhaps leading to meningitis. I know from her letters to my Dad all about that anxious time – how she suffered after the abscess was drained and her ear was packed with dressings. This was when her *"old pal"* Dr Russell later told her that her temperature was over 106 degrees Fahrenheit or 41 degrees Celsius! I know from her letters that some of her lovely hair was cut from around her ear. Her dressings were changed regularly – when they weren't it was *"a relief"* and though she kept her composure during this excruciating treatment she would weep uncontrollably after the sister had finished. She writes: *"Sister said when she started, 'well dear I'll try not to hurt you' so I knew what to expect."* And then: *"Oh boy she didn't let me down."*

Both my parents found the separation very difficult and since my Dad could only visit at weekends – my Mum found it particularly difficult. She writes: *"I miss you so much whenever I see you I could start."* Mrs. Murphy, who was another patient, advised her to *"keep weeping"* and *"the more I wept the sooner I'd get over it"*. My Mum also said that when the theatre nurse saw her crying *"it started her too, her mother is very ill"*.

I have all of these letters including the nine that my Dad wrote to her during that time. These were written on Lumphinnans No. XI Colliery Pithead Baths notepaper! My Dad must have had some sheets of this at home left over from the time during which he'd been the secretary of that organisation. In one of them he begs: *"Don't give me a row for using the Bath paper"*. He adds: *"Everybody's asking about you. I'm thinking of posting a daily bulletin on Meg McCluskey's window to let the folks know how you're progressing each day."* Meg McCluskey owned a sweet shop in Kelty Main Street.

In another – ever the practical – he asks: *"What about your ration book, they get changed next week?"* He too misses her desperately: *"I wish it was Saturday at 3pm with you and I blethering."* He closes one letter encouraging her to: *"Keep your chin up in the grand old Fotheringham manner."* Poor Dad confesses to be running out of spaces in his diary for all of the folk that wanted to visit and writes: *"You must be very happy to know that so many people are interested in you but none as much as me."*

Their letters really bucked each other up. On the 22nd May my Dad wrote: *"Dear Ann I pray for you every night and please don't get fretful if you think they're keeping you too long. I want you to come home full of beans."*

At this time there was still a blackout and so when the sirens went off everyone had to go to the air raid shelter [known as *"the post"*] until the all clear sounded. He writes: *"I hope you're not frightened because the sirens have just sounded in Kelty at 11.26pm. I expect they'll have gone in Edinburgh. After your experience I don't think the sirens will alarm you. Hurrah the all clear has just sounded at 11.53pm. Glad I didn't waste my time going over to the post. How everybody wishes it were the last all clear don't you and then we could get down to living in peace and comfort."*

My Mum did darning for the Infirmary and cut swabs too. I guess that this was to keep her busy. She didn't suspect this because she felt a bit aggrieved saying: *"Mrs. Thomson's never asked to do anything."* She was bedbound for the first three weeks and then sister asked: *"How long since this girlie came in?"* When my Mum told her *"she ignored me and counted the days on the chart, three weeks!"* Initially my Mum was allowed up for 10 minutes and then, when it was sunny, she was able to sit outside. Though she missed Dad, she joked to him that: *"I'll shed tears when I leave."*

When she went home in June 1944 my parents donated some money to the hospital fund, gave hand knitted socks to the doctor, cigarettes to the *"Chief"* and stockings to the nursing staff. Dad wrote: *"Received a nice letter of thanks and receipt for our donation to the Infirmary funds. Makes you feel good when you read it."*

Although my parents got married in 1938, they delayed starting a family till the Second World War ended. A family friend Daphne Middleton has always sent our family Christmas cards. Over the years I have visited her several times in London and she was able to tell me a little about my Mum, whom she met when my Mum was expecting me.

During the war Daphne was evacuated with her sister Jean to the rectory at Staplehurst in Kent. Her parents George and Connie were good friends of my Mum's cousin Mary and her husband John. Interestingly Mary was cook in the house of the Honorable Lettice Bowlby and her husband John was the chauffeur. Mrs Bowlby was the widow of Captain Geoffrey S V Bowlby (he'd been killed at Ypres in 1915 – his father was a soldier at the Battle of Waterloo). After his death, Lettice Bowlby became Lady-in-Waiting to Elizabeth, Duchess of York, who later became Queen consort then Queen Mother.

Immediately after the war Mary and John invited Daphne and her sister Jean to stay with them in Kelty the summer before I was born. During this time Daphne met my parents and sampled my Mum's shortbread, which she described as being *"out of this world"*. My Dad and my Mum's brother Frank took them to the seaside and also for a visit to the longest mineshaft in the area. Daphne told me that they had had a wonderful fortnight's holiday.

I know from the letters that they wrote to each other when she was in hospital that my Mum and Dad loved each other very much for the ten years that they were married. I sincerely believe that no matter how long they'd have been together, they'd always have been soul mates. The following letter illustrates this. It was written on 4th August 1946 when she was expecting me, and he was having a last week of *"freedom"* camping in Inverness with her brother Frank.

Kelty
Sunday 4th August 1946

Dear Bob

How are you now? I hope you landed safe and sound. This morning it was pouring buckets of rain and this lasted well into the afternoon. I thought if it was like that in Inverness you'd not get the tent down, however maybe it wasn't like that there.

Tommy Philbin and Bob Paterson came up for the urns around eleven. You might have heard Philbin up there. Kept saying "Did you ever see it any better for the Peewit Gala Day" [the Peewit was a coal mine and all of the mines had a Gala Day for the families of those who worked for them] then he asked how I was keeping so he must know.

Well honey enjoy yourself as much as possible for it will be a long time before you get away on your own again. Hadn't I a carry on yesterday when you were leaving. I just couldn't help myself then I was quite mad at sending you away and me with tears in my eyes. I'm a big bubble. I bawled

27

for ages after it, but was ok when Lizzie came. Today Sunday we've been out and in bed all day, we've had a holiday alright.

    Well goodnight my darling try to come home Saturday or at latest early Sunday. Funny Bob, I think I must be more in love with you than ever. I miss you so very much. Kept saying to myself all day, that's one sleep over maybe just another six now. I hope so anyway.

    We went to Kelty Goth [the cinema] last night, just to pass the time that was all it did. All going well you'll take two people for a nice fortnight next year so make the most of your freedom.

All my love

Ann xxxxx

Ps Tell brother [Frank] *I'll post on a post card to him also to behave himself and not promise any more rings.* [This must have been when Margaret Ferguson, who was later to become my future Stepmother, and he ended their engagement.]

Scotty [the dog] *is missing you both a whole lot. She slept in the bedroom last night and didn't go to her chair until I took her at 2.20am. Poor wee soul when I was bawling yesterday, she laid her head on my knee and kept staring at me with her big eyes. Then she brought her ball for me to play with she couldn't understand what was wrong. 11 o'clock.*

Ann xxxxxx

    I was part of the post-war baby boom generation: I was born on 7th November 1946 in Dunfermline Maternity Hospital. As it was, I do know that I was a very much wanted and loved baby, because Aunt Margaret and Aunt Janet told me. I was christened Margaret Scott after my maternal Granny, whose name I saw on my Mum's birth certificate.

My Third Home: Staying with Lizzie

While my Mum was in hospital the second time I'd been looked after by Lizzie Gibb, a family friend. Her home in Kelty was the third of six that I would live in before the age of ten. (the first being Fotheringham's Buildings in Kelty and second being 11 Kinneddar Park in Saline) Lizzie had been engaged to my Mum's brother David. But after David's early death, she had married Andrew Gibb. They had a grown-up son called John, who had arranged emigration to New Zealand. So she was the natural choice to look after me. My Aunt Janet told me that Lizzie had always wanted a little girl, so I suppose I fulfilled that longing. At that time it was very difficult for widowed fathers to look after their children however much they wanted to. The Welfare State was in its infancy, and consequently there were few of the benefits available today. Although it was commonplace for widowed mothers to look after their children, widowed fathers did not. Instead motherless children were often looked after by grannies, maiden aunts or even put in orphanages if no other help could be found.

After my Mum's funeral, my Dad could no longer bear to live in our spacious four-bedroom family house at Kinneddar Park in Saline. This T-shaped cul-de-sac of houses had been built for the employees of the National Coal Board. He went to stay with his Dad at Glebe Cottage, 31 Moodie Street, Dunfermline.

He visited me regularly at Lizzie's and I guess that I just accepted that fact because young children are surprisingly resilient. I certainly don't remember being unhappy or missing my Mum, but as I grew older, I must have asked about her because I clearly recall being taken back to our old house by my Dad – I later learned that this happened at my Aunt Margaret's instigation. I'm not sure how we got there and I don't quite know what I expected, but I sincerely believe that I thought my Mum would be there.

As we walked up the path, a lady nearby called over and my Dad spoke to her for a short time. Then he opened the door and we turned right into the living room. I clearly remember standing looking around. I remember the piano with its music book and stool all set out just waiting for someone to play, the two china faces that hung on the wall above, and the big free standing radio. My Mum was not there. I can't remember looking for her in any of the other rooms, I can only recall the living room. I must have asked my Dad where she was and, at this, he began to cry. I'd never seen him cry before and on seeing this, I started to cry too – he held me so very tightly and sobbed. I have no idea of how long we stayed, or of us leaving. But I do know that it must have been a cathartic experience, the catalyst that encouraged him to give up the house, store the furniture and try to move on with his life.

I don't remember exactly how long I lived with Andrew and Lizzie Gibb. Soon after I went to stay with them, their son John emigrated to New Zealand and this must have been extremely sad for them because it was very unlikely that he would ever return.

I remained a well-loved child. I guess that people felt sorry for me and did lots to help my Dad and me. It must have been dreadful for him, though at my young age, I had no notion of this and simply accepted it as the norm that he visited me regularly at Lizzie and Andrew's house, sometimes bringing me presents. I still have Winkie, the pink plastic dog-shaped torch whose eyes lit up when its tail was pressed. My Dad would stay awhile playing and reading with me before getting the bus back to my Grandpa's.

Andrew was like a second Dad to me and made me a dolls' house. It was illuminated by small lights that worked at the press of a switch fixed to the gable wall. The front opened to reveal four rooms – two up and two down and a small staircase to access the upper floor. I loved it and played with it regularly for years after.

I vividly remember going to the rag and bone man as he and his horse trotted down Lizzie and Andrew's road collecting unwanted items. One day I was given a balloon tied to a stick in exchange for some old clothes. I also remember sometimes going to Boni's chip shop for fish and chips. Mmm! I think that the owner was called Romelo. One day Lizzie took me to the circus, but had to take me out as I cried inconsolably when the clowns' car made a loud noise. I remember being so upset that I flatly refused to go back into the circus big top!

During this time, my Aunt Margaret made me pretty frocks, some with smocking on the front and I had a siren suit for the winter. I was also asked to be a flower girl at a family friend's wedding

and so my Aunt Margaret made me a lovely long pink dress. As a present, I was given a gold locket, which I wore on the day of the wedding, and inside was a picture of my Mum. I still treasure this locket.

I used to often visit my Aunt Janet. She and her husband Bobby, who worked in the rubber factory, had no children and so I suppose that I was very special to them. I remember my Aunt Janet's wool winder that Uncle Bobby had made for her and the smell of her wonderful ginger wine. Uncle Bobby used to always refer to his wife as Mrs Lawson – just like Mr and Mrs Bennett in Jane Austen's Pride and Prejudice. They were both very good to me as I grew up and both of them lived well into old age.

My Fourth Home: Staying with Aunt Margaret in Dunfermline

I can't remember exactly when but, not long before I started school, I went to stay with my Aunt Margaret and her mother, my great Aunt Nan, in their very grand house in Venturefair Avenue, Dunfermline. I did not know at the time, but years later, my Aunt Margaret told me that I went to stay with her and Aunt Nan because Lizzie and Andrew wanted to adopt me.

I simply accepted the fact that I was going to a new home and I really enjoyed myself there. There were lots of rooms to explore, interesting cupboards and contents, a big garden to play in, plus I got lots of attention. Aunt Margaret continued to make me lots of pretty dresses. The house was full of wonderful cooking aromas. Aunt Margaret made lots of jam, pancakes and tomato and vegetable soup with alphabet pasta. I used to spoon up the liquid and keep the vegetables and pasta till last.

Aunt Margaret was a cuddly lady with an ample bosom and an apple-shaped tummy. She had rosy cheeks and wavy hair and wore those 1950s supra spectacles that curled up. She worked as a civil servant and followed the stock market, making smart investments in shares. She loved the outdoors, was very sociable and loved playing cards and board games.

Aunt Margaret smoked Du Maurier cigarettes, named after the actor Sir Gerald Du Maurier and father of the author Daphne du Maurier. Though he didn't smoke them himself, he gave his name to the brand. The idea was to raise some money after being pursued by the Inland Revenue for non-payment of the tax bills that he'd ignored over the years. These cigarettes were in a burnt orange-red square box, with a border of gold lines and a hinged lid. To access the cigarettes, you had to lift up a layer of white tissue paper that was attached to the back of the box. They were very classy! (Later in life, when I was a student, I sometimes smoked them out of respect for my wonderful Aunt.)

Aunt Margaret and Aunt Nan made real coffee. They ground the beans then put them in a percolator attached to a stand and heated by a little flame underneath the glass. When I think about it, I can still hear the sound of beans like hailstones being poured into the blender and then ground. I can even still smell the glorious aroma that pervaded the kitchen, as the coffee percolated.

Another bonus of life with Aunt Margaret and Aunt Nan was that their friends Isabel and Jimmy Knox came to visit regularly from Glasgow. They had a son called Henry who was a couple of years older than me. Sometimes when they visited, Aunt Nan would make Henry and me each a picnic of different kinds of sandwiches, cake, apples and water, then she'd put everything into two tea towels that she then tied onto two walking sticks. We would then go down to the bottom of the big garden, or into the woods across the road to eat, drink and play hide and seek. Henry and I loved what we called our "*Dick Whittington adventures*".

Aunt Margaret and Aunt Nan's house was in a quiet avenue and faced south. On the east side was Canmore Golf Course and to the west was the busy main road. One day, while returning from a Dick Whittington expedition, I crossed that road without looking and was knocked over. I wasn't badly hurt, but was taken to hospital all the same, carried on piggyback by Henry's Mum. What a fuss everyone made of me!

My Aunt Margaret was dearly loved by me for all of my life. She was the younger daughter of Aunt Nan and her husband James. She had an older brother called James who died as a baby; my three children all wore his beautiful christening dress made by Aunt Nan and many years later, two of my grandchildren Iona and Callum also wore it when they were christened. Aunt Margaret also had an older sister called Nancy whom I never knew existed until many years later. Although Aunt Margaret spoke about James, she never mentioned Nancy.

Despite that she was a marvellous aunt to me. She was a civil servant and worked at Rosyth dockyard where, at Christmas time, parties were held for employees and their families. She took me several times with another two little girls who lived nearby. I always wore a pretty dress that she'd either made or bought me for the occasion. It was great fun, with lots of party food, games and lovely presents – I remember Santa Claus giving me a doll.

Aunt Margaret was known as a maiden aunt, someone who was not married. After the immense death toll among young men in the war there were many women in her situation, who were sometimes referred to as unclaimed jewels. To me Aunt Margaret was my surrogate mother. Looking back she was the one person who understood intuitively that what I needed most was unconditional love and security. She taught me to knit, to sew, to embroider, to cook simple things, to recognise types of trees and wild flowers, and to spot the difference between weeds and flowers in the garden. She took me on trips to the theatre – I remember once we went to the King's Theatre in Edinburgh to see Cinderella. I was given money to get some theatre glasses that were available to the audience if a coin was put into the slot of a container between the theatre seats. After the performance I accidently trapped her handbag along with the glasses when I was putting them back and she had to put more money in the slot to retrieve her bag. She wasn't very happy, but quickly forgave me.

Aunt Margaret encouraged me to become interested in history. She took me to Linlithgow and Falkland Palaces, Edinburgh Castle and various museums. She devoted lots of her time and attention to me. When I was growing up, I often wished that she'd been my Mum: not so that she'd have taken my real Mum's place; but because I know in my heart that my Mum would have been so happy knowing that she was looking after me.

My Fifth Home: Staying with My Dad and My Grandpa

In August 1951 I was due to start school and so I returned from Aunt Margaret's home in Venturefair Avenue to stay with my Dad and Grandpa. Aunt Margaret told me later that this happened because I'd said that I didn't want to go to the school near her house. Why, I do not know.

My Grandpa's house was also in Dunfermline and very near the Abbey (see below). Each Sunday, as I recall, its carillon of bells would peal out the hymn Immortal Invisible God Only Wise. This splendid sound filled the airand could be heard over quite a distance.

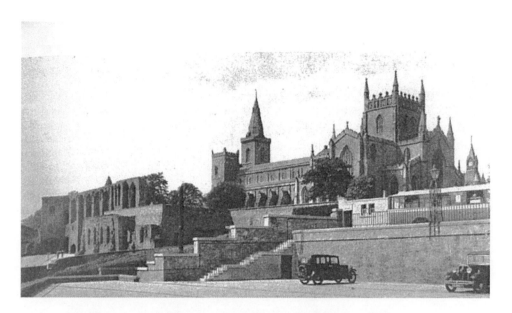

To this day it is one of my favourite hymns. Grandpa was a wonderful gardener. I can still picture his beautiful garden and smell the fragrant wallflowers, Nancy Pretty or London Pride, antirrhinums or snap dragons and a stupendous variety of vibrant dahlias. These formed a border along the gable of the house and there was a path beside the wall on the left hand side. At the front was a manicured lawn, gravel paths, sweet peas, roses and a vegetable patch. At the bottom was a green shed where he kept his tools, a barrow, my doll's pram and my little black Triang trike, complete with a boot compartment: I loved cycling this trike around the garden. After Grandpa retired from his job as a miner he also looked after the adjacent garden belonging to the Rev. Robert Dollar, who was the minister of the Abbey Church.

Grandpa's house overlooked Dunfermline Glen and the building was divided into three houses. He occupied the ground floor, which had four rooms: two at the back and two at the front. A corridor ran between the front door and the toilet was at the end. I loved sitting on the heavy substantial wooden seat and when I'd finished, standing on tiptoe to flush it by pulling the chain that dangled from the high cistern.

The small scullery was accessed from the living room. The two front rooms faced south and were light and airy in contrast to those at the back. We all slept in the front bedroom. I had a single bed, and my Dad and Grandpa shared a double bed. Sometimes I'd take my Grandpa breakfast in bed and I often played in the back room behind the bedroom.

The two upper flats were accessed by an outside stairway. An elderly lady called Celia lived in the flat on the left hand side. I would regularly visit Celia, always getting a barley sugar sweet from her tin. I well remember that I calculated, with help, that she would be 100 years old when I reached my 17th birthday. Mr and Mrs Graham and their two children occupied the flat on the right hand side. There couldn't have been room in there to swing a cat.

Access to my Grandpa's house was from the main road, a steep hill with tenement blocks and cottages on either side. At regular intervals and built into these blocks were passageways or "closes" as we call them in Fife. These led into spacious cobbled yards behind and housed the laundry facilities for the occupants – clothes poles, washing lines and wash houses. The latter contained sinks, boilers and mangles. Families had to share these facilities. It must have been an all day job to do the laundry, with few washing machines at the time and certainly no tumble driers.

The street lights were powered by gas and were lit each night by the lamplighter. I never knew his name, but I well remember learning Robert Louis Stevenson's poem – Leerie the Lamplighter about a character whom a sickly wee boy used to watch from his window each night.

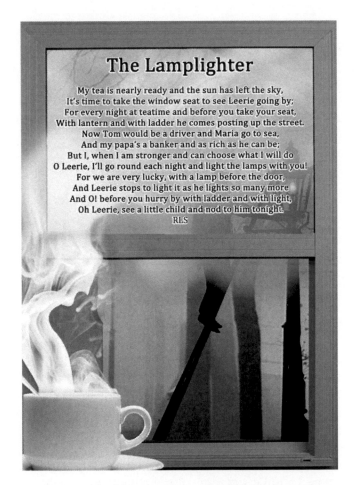

The Lamplighter

My tea is nearly ready and the sun has left the sky,
It's time to take the window seat to see Leerie going by;
For every night at teatime and before you take your seat,
With lantern and with ladder he comes posting up the street.
Now Tom would be a driver and Maria go to sea,
And my papa's a banker and as rich as he can be;
But I, when I am stronger and can choose what I will do
O Leerie, I'll go round each night and light the lamps with you!
For we are very lucky, with a lamp before the door,
And Leerie stops to light it as he lights so many more
And O! before you hurry by with ladder and with light,
Oh Leerie, see a little child and nod to him tonight.
RLS

Grandpa's house was powered by gas too and the light from the gas mantles together with the flames from the coal fire gave a warm comforting glow to the room.

I distinctly remember the nearby chemist's shop with its distinctive gold mortar and pestle sign above the entrance, the brown shelves neatly packed with a miscellany of toiletries, scissors, nail files, medicines, and the array of glass bottles full of the most wonderful colours of liquid.

Halfway up the road was Stephens the baker or Step Hen as I imagined it was called – *"hen"* being a common Fife expression of endearment. My Grandpa often called me *"hen".* He'd often ask me to fetch his slippers saying: *"Wull ye fetch ma baffies hen?"* Grandpa loved a roll for his breakfast and I was allowed to go to the shop for these. It wasn't too far, no road to cross and there was little traffic in those days. On one occasion while leaving the shop clutching the bag of rolls, I saw Lizzie Gibb. I hadn't seen her since I'd gone to live first with Aunt Nan and Aunt Margaret. She gave me a great big cuddle and a dolly. I well remember the dolly because it had white knickers, a dress, socks and pink shoes made of soft rubber, with little straps that fastened onto tiny buttons. I can't remember what she said but I remember her crying. I wondered why she didn't come back to Grandpa's with me. When I returned to my Grandpa's and told him that I'd seen her, I got a big row for talking to her, though I think that I was allowed to keep the dolly.

My grandpa Robert Campbell and his
second wife Margaret at Glebe Cottage

My Dad must have been so distressed about the prospect of Lizzie and Andrew wanting to adopt me. This probably explained the cause of his terrible headaches that Aunt Margaret told me he suffered. He was worried that he was going to die and that I'd be left an orphan. The headaches may also have been caused by the stress of him working so hard to save money for me. As he explained to Aunt Margaret: *"Somebody will look after her if she has a pound or two."* But it also must have been a heart-breaking situation for Lizzie and Andrew, who clearly loved me and had formed a strong bond with me.

I loved my Dad very much. He was always a very good and caring Dad who loved me unconditionally. He tucked me up in bed each night when we stayed in the same house and heard my prayers. When I was sick he'd hold my head for me, while I vomited in a bowl. He very rarely gave me a row or even raised his voice. I think of him often and can hear him whistling Mascagni's Cavalleria Rusticano, humming Brahms Lullaby or singing snatches from There is a Lady Sweet and Kind:

There is a lady sweet and kind,
Was never face so pleas'd my mind;
I did but see her passing by,
And yet I love her till I die.

Her gesture, motion, and her smiles,
Her wit, her voice, my heart beguiles,
Beguiles my heart, I know not why,
And yet I love her till I die.

Her free behaviour, winning looks,
Will make a lawyer burn his books;
I touch'd her not, alas! not I,
And yet I love her till I die.

I think that his favourite lyrical song was Softly, Softly Come to Me by Ruby Murray. After I had been playing the piano for a year or two, I was given Offenbach's Barcarolle to practise. My Dad was delighted and told me that that was his favourite piece of instrumental music.

Grandpa was the chief cook and bottle washer. He'd worked as a miner down the pit and became a fireman: the miner who sets the charges at the coalface to blast and release the coal from the seam. Mining was and still is a dirty and highly dangerous job, despite better safety standards. Grandpa's two and a half missing fingers were testimony to that. He was determined that neither of his two sons would go down the pit. My Dad's older brother Angus joined the police and became a sergeant in Bellshill, in Glasgow, while my Dad worked for a time at the pithead, before becoming the colliery cashier. He enjoyed accounting and did courses and exams, eventually qualifying as a chartered accountant. Sadly I didn't share his love of figures. I found some parts of arithmetic very difficult to understand. When my Dad helped me with my sums, he would get very exasperated because I *"didn't get it"* and I would start to cry.

Grandpa's culinary skills were limited and he cooked out of necessity. Despite being widowed twice, he had a very small repertoire of menus: Scotch broth, mince and tatties, stew, fish and chips, scrambled and boiled eggs are all that I can remember. The kitchen was tiny. In fact, it was a scullery and comprised a small sink, shelves, a meat safe, table and a cooker with shiny brass taps and no grill pan. As a substitute my Dad got two 6 by 4 inch pieces of wood on which Grandpa grilled toasted cheese that tasted great! I sometimes marvel at the great escape that we had from food poisoning, splinters and house fires.

Grandpa was tall and slim and sported a moustache and, most of the time, a tweed cap. He spoke in very broad Scots in contrast to his sister my Aunt Nan, who was very proper and most particular. He'd often call me a *"braw bairn wi broon een"* – a pretty child with brown eyes and, when making a pot of tea, he'd *"sine oot"* the teapot; rinse it with boiling water. He teased me mercilessly about Aunt Nan's coffee percolater, referring to it as a *"perambulator"*. He'd often take me on his knee and give me a *"beardie"* by rubbing his unshaven face against my poor cheek. The Scottish folk songs Silver Threads Among the Gold and The Old Rustic Bridge by the Mill were two of his favourites. He'd often, like many of his peers, recite a parody of Felicia Dorothea Hemans' Casabianca poem about the Battle of the Nile, *"The boy stood on the burning deck whence all but he had fled."* Grandpa's version was: *"The boy stood on the burning deck selling tatties at tuppence the peck."*

I think that he'd been quite a lad in his time. Apparently he'd once picked up a cat, tucked it under his arm and then asked Aunt Nan if she'd like to hear the bagpipes! I imagine that she was probably so horrified, that she would have fainted and have had to be revived with smelling salts!

Another incident that comes to mind is when Grandpa was moving house. He'd installed a nice fireplace in the house from which he was moving and wanted to take it to the new place. The landlord refused to allow this, so when Grandpa knew he was out at a wedding, he and some friends went back to the house and removed the fireplace. I'm not sure if the landlord ever came after him.

Aunt Margaret told me that as a very young child I'd had whooping cough and as a consequence was very ill. I also had several bouts of tonsilitis and my Grandpa told me that because this had made me so ill, my Dad was advised that I should have my tonsils out. He had to pay privately for this. I remember going with my Grandpa to the Royal Hospital for Sick Children in Edinburgh to have this done. We went by train and sat facing forwards. I wore a wee pink cotton dress and navy jacket. In the lapel of my jacket was pinned a pink plastic Astor flower brooch. I think that I may have unpinned it and my Grandpa got jagged. He was really cross with me and took my brooch away. I don't recall seeing it ever again.

The Royal Hospital for Sick Children in Sciennes Road is still there. I remember going up in a lift with open mesh metal doors. There were lots of children in bed in the ward and I soon joined them. Then my Grandpa went away and I was left with no one familiar. I remember going down to the theatre on the trolley. I was cosied up in a red blanket and was given a pill with jam on it; that must have been the pre-med. The only other part I remember is eating ice-cream afterwards and the child in the next bed to me crying and being sick. I don't remember being unhappy, frightened or lonely. I think that I must have simply accepted that that was how things were. My Dad came to visit me and before he took me home I stayed at St

Mary's Convalescent Home in Edinburgh in order to completely recover. My Dad had to pay for the doctor, the anaesthetist and the surgeon and the convalescent home separately.

GP - 5 shillings (25p)
Anaesthetist - 4 guineas (£4.4shillings or £4.20)
Surgeon – 15 guineas (£15.15 shillings or £15. 75)
Queen Mary Nursing Home - 6 guineas for board (£6.6 shillings or £6.30) and 1 guinea for the theatre fee (£7.7 shillings or £7.35)

I don't remember being consciously lonely as a child despite having no siblings. My brother, who had only lived for a day, was born one month early in September 1948 and so was 22 months younger than I was. I don't think that he was christened because on the grave interment certificate he was referred to as Baby Campbell and that makes me feel very sad.

A Holiday in London

I loved my Dad very much and enjoyed being with him. Before I started school, we were invited to London to stay with the Middletons – George and Connie and their four daughters, Daphne, Jean, Avril and Kathleen.

My Dad packed our clothes into a brown leather suitcase and we boarded the Flying Scotsman. I loved the smells, the steam and watching the platform guard who blew his whistle and waved us off with his red flag at every station. Dad and I played games, drew pictures and read books to pass the time. One of my favourite stories was The Little Red Hen. Sometimes when he read it he'd deliberately miss a page, but I always noticed and I'd make him read it again.

The Middletons lived in South East London in Abbey Wood. They were the first owners of a lovely red brick end of terrace house in Willrose Crescent. Until a few years ago this was still occupied by Daphne. The house had suffered major damage during the London Blitz, but thankfully none of the family was injured, having made it to the air raid shelter in the nick of time. It was after that scare Connie and George decided that Daphne, then aged 10 and her younger sister Jean, should be evacuated till the war was over. Daphne told me that although they missed their family, they loved living in the rectory at Staplehurst in Kent.

At the time of my visit to London with my Dad I was four-years-old, Daphne was 22, Jean, 21, Avril 16 and Kathleen 13. The dining room had a French window that opened out into the back garden, which George lovingly tended. I clearly remember Connie having the loaf of bread on the table and spreading it with butter, before cutting a slice, then repeating the process. Dad and George took me on the tube. I marvelled at the doors that opened and closed by magic. At that time, lots of people, particularly men, smoked and they were allowed to do it everywhere, including on the tube. I remember getting my hand accidentally burned on George's cigarette and him getting a big row from Connie when we got back.

We went to see Buckingham Palace and Trafalgar Square – my Dad was born on 21st October or Trafalgar Day, which marks Nelson's defeat of the French and Spanish fleets in 1805. I remember the huge fountains and the flocks of pigeons. We also saw the Changing of the Guard and the Tower of London. Everything was so very big. I seem to remember getting some new clothes and George teaching me the rhyme Two Little Dickie Birds. And I recall having a straw put in my tea. Funnily enough, it didn't work.

Starting School

In August 1951, I started school at Pittencrieff Primary School in Dunfermline – the first of four primary schools that I would attend. My Grandpa took me and I remember that we were able to walk part of the way there through Dunfermline Glen, which could be seen from the bottom of his garden. I remember writing with chalk on a slate and having a wee duster to wipe it clean. Although I was left handed, thankfully no one forced me to write with my right hand.

At school most of the teachers wore buttoned up overalls and I don't think that any of them were married. At that time women had to give up work when they married. My Primary 1 teacher was Miss Leonard. She always wore a flowery button-up overall. In contrast, Miss Halpin, who was my Primary 2 teacher, generally wore a maroon costume – a skirt and jacket and a string of pearls.

My first school Pittencrieff Primary

The classes were very big. I remember one day in particular when I desperately needed to go to the toilet and was refused permission. Eventually I was allowed to go but just as I reached the classroom door, my sphincter muscle failed because of the pressure and I wet the floor and myself. That awful feeling has stuck in my mind and as a teacher I have always been sympathetic to those children in similar need.

I vividly remember my vain attempts to knit and, oh, how I struggled to master the knack. Eventually after many tears, failed attempts and great encouragement by both my Aunt Margaret and Aunt Nan, I managed. Now six decades and the wool of several flocks of sheep later, I believe that I could knit in my sleep. I am utterly addicted and knit almost every day. All my family and friends have had myriads of knitted jumpers, socks, hats, scarves, gloves, blankets and I have even sold children's clothes or Knit Pickings as I like to call them.

Anyway, I digress. Back to my first primary school and I also remember going to the school dentist and being given a new toothbrush. The toothpaste that I used was called Gibb's Dentifrice. It was a hard block, pink in colour and contained in a small round tin. In order to use it, you had to wet the brush then rub it over the surface. My Dad used Euthymol toothpaste that was in a tube and which can still be bought today. It has a wonderfully distinctive flavour. Grandpa had *"wallies"* [false teeth] and so used Sterident to clean them. Each night before going to bed, he removed them and soaked them in the glass of clean water, which he kept by his bed. I used to see them smiling at me when I woke up in the morning!

One day, my Grandpa was late in coming to collect me and so I decided to walk home from school by myself. I felt really proud of myself, but that was short lived when I met him en route and he gave me a big row for not waiting for him.

It was good living with my Dad and Grandpa, despite the gaslight, no plumbed in bath and lack of variety of meals. I loved going through the close – the passageway between houses – to meet my Dad when he returned home after work. He always wore a trilby hat, a gaberdine overcoat and carried a briefcase. As soon as I saw him coming, I ran to meet him and we hugged each other. I was very happy and settled and well-loved.

As well as my beloved doll's pram trike and doll's house, I had a wind up Snow White dancing with her Prince and lots and lots of books. We also regularly listened to the radio – I liked the MacFlannels, who were a fictitious family from Glasgow.

My Grandpa's brother John and his wife Elspeth lived across the road and we saw them quite regularly. My Aunt Kit, my Mum's sister, kept me supplied with cosy hats, mitts, twinsets, Fair Isle cardigans and jumpers. She smoked constantly and I well remember her washing the dishes with her cigarette dangling from her lips. (Years later my husband Ron used to do this before he was banned from smoking in the house!) Aunt Kit's husband Uncle Jim used to encourage me to play football with his two boys, my cousins Billy and Frank, when we visited.

   I found out much later from Aunt Margaret that my Grandpa and Aunt Nan weren't on the best of terms. My Dad's Mum, who was Grandpa's first wife, died at the age of 48. My Grandpa remarried a good while afterwards. Just before his second wedding, he had bumped into Aunt Nan in the town, told her that he was getting married, and suggested that she come to meet his future wife. Aunt Nan was taken by surprise and said that she'd come later, but never did. Aunt Margaret told me that she was very fond of my Granny, Grandpa's first wife. Families!

   In those days it was accepted that children at that time were *"seen but not heard"*. And looking back on my early years when I was at school in Dunfermline I became well used to amusing myself. But I guess the huge responsibility of raising a small girl was a great worry for both my Dad and Grandpa. When I was born, my Grandpa was 66. Although he was a strong healthy man, he was probably considering the perils of a teenager and possibly a tear away one. I don't remember either of them talking about it either between themselves or with me.

My Sixth Home: Staying with Aunt Meg and Aunt Susan

Great Aunts Susan, Meg and Jean

My Dad and my Grandpa gave my upbringing a great deal of thought. When I was almost 7 years old, they decided that I should go to live with my Aunts Meg and Susan in Edinburgh. I don't remember anything about how this decision was reached. All that I do recall is the journey with my Dad on the train over the Forth Bridge and then by bus. Aunts Meg and Susan were known as the Misses Campbell and they lived at 31 Briarbank Terrace. Their home was a spacious upstairs flat in a quiet terrace behind busy Slateford Road. There were several terraces of these houses with pretty names – I remember reading them as my Dad and I walked along: Alderbank Terrace, Almondbank Terrace, Hollybank Terrace and Hazelbank Terrace.

Much later I discovered that these terraces were part of the 19th century housing development which is laid out like a fishbone, known as Shaftsbury Park Colonies and situated in North Merchiston in an area known as Shandon. These colonies' houses were specifically designed by the Edinburgh Co-operative Building Company to provide housing which, unlike tenement developments,, gave families their own front door and garden. This is now a conservation area.

I clearly remember Great Aunts Meg and Susan and my Dad and I being in the sitting-room where I became fascinated by a small round footstool that had a tapestry design of a cottage and garden on top. I traced the forefinger of my left hand around the paths and flowerbeds while my imagination conjured up pictures of the family who lived there. I don't remember much about my Dad leaving. But when he did another chapter of my life began and so it was that for the next four years I became an Edinburgher.

I just loved the house. There was a large back garden where the washing could be hung out and a small neat front garden with two pretty evergreen trees in brown wooden tubs at either side of the front door. The railway line was quite close and I soon got used to hearing the trains as they rattled and rushed along the line.

I remember the spacious hall, the cream panelled doors, the magnolia walls, the bathroom with its frosted glass panelled door, the big front room with the bay window and the small cosy sitting room with its three doors. One led into the hall, one led into a small scullery fitted with shiny maroon kitchen units while another was the door of a large shelved cupboard and where my sweets and treats that my Dad brought me on his Saturday visits were kept on the topmost shelf. I vividly remember one occasion when Aunt Meg fainted as she was reaching up to get me something from that shelf. I watched in amazement as she fell, then quickly ran for my Aunt Susan. Aunt Meg soon recovered.

Aunt Meg was the eldest of Grandpa's sisters. Not surprisingly, given the popularity of the name Margaret in my family, her actual name was also Margaret. Aunt Susan was ten years younger than Aunt Meg. They were both spinsters or unclaimed jewels, though Aunt Margaret told me that at one time Susan had been engaged to a detective, but Aunt Meg had *"put a stop to it"*. She didn't elaborate further about that but went on to say that Aunt Meg would give the orders and poor Aunt Susan would just carry them out. They had once owned a house in Chalmers Street and made their living providing board for university students.

When there was baking to be done, Aunt Susan would cream the margarine and sugar for the cakes by hand and in a big mixing bowl while Aunt Meg would sit and watch her. Aunt Susan smoked Players, which were unfiltered cigarettes. She used to fiddle the housekeeping money in order to buy them. They were in a flat packet with a picture of a lifebelt framing the face of a bearded sailor. The packet was made up of two rows of ten and didn't have the modern day flip top.

Aunt Meg, who was born in 1876, was a tall well-made woman and exactly four years older than my Grandpa. Her snow-white hair was worn in a tight bun and secured with hairpins. She had round spectacles and when she was at home, which was most of the time, always wore a crossover apron to keep her clothes clean when she was doing the housework. By contrast, Aunt Susan was a small plump woman who always seemed to be bustling about. Her hair was salt and pepper in colour and worn rolled up along the back and secured with hairpins. I clearly remember her humming The Toreador's Song from Bizet's Carmen and at other times she'd sing snatches of the Neapolitan song O Sole Mio. I don't remember Aunt Meg ever singing – maybe she was tone deaf. The pair of them always seemed to be cleaning, polishing and cooking. I don't remember either of them playing with me or reading to me. But they were pretty ancient I suppose.

My Dad came to see me every Saturday and, like my Mum before me, I lived for his visits. He always carried a medium sized brown leather suitcase packed with goodies; mainly for his aunts. I think that he brought luxuries such as biscuits, sweets and suchlike because after the war some of these things continued to be rationed. I was so pleased to see him and really looked forward to his weekly visits. My Dad would sometimes take me on visits to the zoo, to the Camera Obscura, to the museum, the Castle and once or twice we took a tram along Princes Street and climbed up to the top of Scott's Monument. Sometimes I had my photographs taken at my Dad's cousin George's studio. His Dad, also called George, had also been a photographer and was married to Grandpa's sister Jean. He had retired and George, his son, had taken over the business. Yet another of Grandpa's sisters, Isabel, was known as Tib,. She was married to Bob who worked as both a photographer and optician. Their only son was called Fred.

Fred who was about 24 at the time, enrolled me in Primary 3 at Craiglockhart Primary, the local school, which was quite nearby. This was a large Victorian building surrounded by a tarmac playground, shelters for when it rained and outside toilets that were very cold. Each morning when the bell rang, everyone lined up and, if I remember correctly, at different entrances – boys at one door and girls at the other. My classroom was upstairs, and the teachers some wearing in flowery overalls, stood on the landing awaiting our arrival and clapping their hands in time to the music that played from a loudspeaker on a shelf above the classroom doors.

I have vivid memories of my Primary 3 teacher. Her name was Miss Struthers. She was tall, wore a black twinset, a single strand of pearls and she shouted a lot. I remember getting the strap from her several times for making mistakes with my work. I did not like her, though I think that the feeling was mutual. (When, years later, I trained as a teacher I vowed never to use my strap, even though it was still legal.)

Craiglockhart School, Edinburgh.

Despite my misgivings about Miss Struthers, at Christmas I decided to make amends and give her a present – some other children had bought gifts. I didn't have any money and so I looked around for something useful. I found a comb that belonged to one of my aunts. It had a missing tooth, but nevertheless I washed it and was just about to wrap it in a bag and put it in my school bag when Aunt Susan pounced and I had to confess, then I got a big row. I guess that it was just as well – Miss Struthers wouldn't

44

have wanted a second hand comb and she'd probably have given me the strap again.

I recall Christmas at Briarbank Terrace. My Dad and his cousin Fred came. They made up two of the jigsaws that I'd been given as presents. I also had a Polly Perkins hand puppet, a selection box and lots of books. My Dad also decided that I could have sixpence a week pocket money – that's two and a half pence nowadays.

During the summer holidays I spent some of the time with my Dad and Grandpa at their house in Dunfermline. I really enjoyed this, not least because I was allowed stay up a bit later at nights. I also spent time with my Aunts Margaret and Nan in their new bungalow in Aberdour in Fife. My Dad spent a lot of his time there digging over the earth in what was to become a lovely garden. I well remember the day that I was told to go outside to play and get as dirty as possible. I stared at Aunt Margaret in amazement and for a few moments, remained rooted to the spot. Aunts Meg and Susan always scolded me if and when I got a bit grubby. So once I recovered from the shock I needed no second bidding because at that time I was a fairly obedient child. I believe that I got extremely dirty.

In June 1953, after the death of her father, Princess Elizabeth was crowned Queen. I went to stay with my Dad's brother Angus, his wife Jessie, and my cousins Shona and Iain in Bellshill in Glasgow for part of the holidays because my Dad had to do his accountancy exams at Newbattle College near Edinburgh. They were lucky enough to have a television so we were able to watch the magical ceremony.

Before he left, my Dad gave me a square box with a Union Jack design. Inside and wrapped in tissue paper was a lovely chocolate crown that had been made for the occasion. It was beautiful and I really wanted to keep it forever. Shona and Iain had other ideas and though I hid my precious box, they bullied me into giving it to them. Since they were a few years older than I was, I felt that I'd no choice. I don't remember if they shared it with me. I do remember that when my Dad returned he brought me a table and chairs for my doll's house. I loved them.

I lived at 31 Briarbank Terrace for a year, then my aunts bought a new modern house at 104 Craigcrook Road in Blackhall in Edinburgh. My Dad, Grandpa and Fred dug the garden and Aunts Meg and Susan cleaned the house and arranged the furniture, pictures and ornaments. There were five rooms plus a box room altogether; three downstairs and two upstairs. The two rooms at the front had fireplaces on the gable walls. Both of these front rooms had built-in cupboards on either side of the fireplaces and the top halves of these had glass doors to display family heirlooms and tea sets. The room on the right of the front door was the parlour and only used on special occasions. The room at the back was the guest bedroom and sometimes used by my Dad and Grandpa.

The kitchen had an alcove that housed the blue and white enamel gas cooker and a little black stove that burned anthracite. There was a hatch in the wall into the front room that was used as both a sitting and dining room. An enormous table with carved legs stood in the centre, with six heavy dining chairs on castors placed around it. On the back wall was an organ, although I don't remember anyone ever playing it. On either side of the fireplace were two armchairs. In the corner on a small table sat a wooden radio. Each weeknight, at 6.45pm my aunts, without fail, would tune in to the Home Service to listen intently to The Archers and woe betide anyone who interrupted this ritual. I guess this is where my addiction to this radio soap opera began. But in those days I was more interested in listening to Children's Favourites hosted by Uncle Derek most Saturday mornings.

In the hall on a wall near to the front door was a wonderful Grandfather clock with a painted face. I just loved the friendly comforting tick, the mellow chimes and the clicking sound of the key when Aunt Meg wound it up each week. As in Briarbank, the décor was magnolia.

Sometimes Aunt Susan would take me up town to Princes Street to buy me new Clarks shoes, a nap coat for the winter, a blazer, or gaberdine mac for wet days, liberty bodices, navy knickers with wee pockets and colourful ribbons for my hair – I hated these ribbons and sometimes would deliberately lose them. Aunt Susan, who like my Grandpa also spoke in Broad Scots, would ask in exasperation, *"Margaret, whaur's yer ribbon?"* I would confidently reply: *"The wind blew it away."* This would be greeted with a black look, a sigh, or sometimes a clip around the ear.

My Dad's cousin Fred's parents lived in a bungalow in nearby Strachan Road. However, Fred came to live at Craigcrook Road with us. He had one of the upstairs bedrooms and shared it with a couple of budgies. He was the apple of Aunt Susan's eye; she just loved him to bits and he could do no wrong.

I shared the other upstairs room with my aunts, though if truth were told I'd have preferred to sleep in the small box room at the top of the stairs that had a small skylight window on the roof and a pretty raindrop patterned glass panel on the door. My two abiding memories of sharing the bedroom are of the chamber pot that was kept under the bed to save my aunts going downstairs to the toilet during the night and Aunt Meg sitting up in bed belching. She had dreadfully noisy wind that she referred to as politely as possible as *"flatulence"*!

Edinburgh 1953 – 1956

Once a week Aunts Meg and Susan's sister Jean and her husband George came for afternoon tea. They lived in a lovely flat, which I occasionally visited, in Falcon Gardens, Morningside; a very desirable part of Edinburgh. Aunt Jean spoke very properly, just like her sisters Meg and Nan. She and George arrived in a big black car. He was a quiet and pleasant man, but she, who always wore black, reminded me of a large black crow. During the winter she kept her neck cosy with a fox fur – the beast's head and feet were clearly visible and I used to often wonder why on earth anyone would want to have a dead animal around their neck. Years later a friend of mine told me that when she was a small girl she was severely scolded for laughing in church after her Mum, who'd been offering Pandrops around, accidentally offered one of these sweets to the fox fur around the neck of the lady in front.

Anyway, Great Aunt Jean took great delight in scolding me for small misdemeanours that had taken place during the week and for which I'd already been punished. On one visit, it was too much for me and I retaliated by calling her *"an old goat"*. There was a stunned silence and then I was banished to the bedroom.

I vaguely recall being told that my Great Granny had twins. Much later, after my own daughter Linsey had identical twin boys, I found out from family records that Jean was one of my Great Granny's twins. From the family photograph there are two girls who seem very alike, and are dressed very similarly. I believe Jean's twin Janet may have emigrated to America or Canada. Maybe to escape from the old goat. I think that Aunt Margaret and Aunt Nan visited her when they sailed to the US and Canada on holiday. I still have a Maple leaf brooch that they brought back with Toronto engraved on it.

For the next three years I lived at 104 Craigcrook Road. Next door lived a boy and girl – Alexander and Anne, and we used to play together. Two doors along at number 108 lived Winifred and Sylvia Rose. I remember their Mum and Dad were called Phyllis and Arthur. One day Winifred teased me mercilessly – I can't recall why. I had a towel in my hand – we must have gone swimming or paddling – and I punched her nose. Her Dad gave me a big row and threatened to tell my aunts. Thankfully he didn't as that saved me from a smacking.

I went to Blackhall School when I was seven. I did the remainder of Primary 3, Primary 4, and most of Primary 5. This, like Craiglockhart Primary, was a large stone building with a tarmac playground, shelters and outside toilets. It has since been demolished and a new one has been built at the end of Craigcrook Road. It couldn't accommodate all of the pupils and so the children, including myself were schooled in a prefabricated classroom beside the school. During my time there, I had three teachers – Miss Gemmell in Primary 3, Miss McKenzie in Primary 4 and Miss McKenzie and Miss Bonniman in Primary 5 – they must have job shared. I liked all of them, even Miss McKenzie who gave me the strap for either chatting or making mistakes. Miss Bonniman seemed to have a soft spot for me. I guess that she felt sorry for my situation.

I was trusted to walk to the school, a distance of about a mile, and back twice a day because I went home for lunch. It was a pleasant walk and I used to enjoy looking at all the houses and gardens. Luckily there was only one main road to cross. Often on the way home I'd play by myself in the park that was halfway along the road. There was a fairly high stone wall around the park and behind this at the back was a flooded quarry with a high cliff on one side. Although I was very scared of the dark murky water, I was always drawn to peer over the wall and look at it for a few minutes most times when I was in the park. I later discovered that it was Ravelston Quarry and the stones from it had been used not only to build houses but also in the construction of Holyrood Palace and St Giles Cathedral.

Often I'd meet Mrs Smith with Campbell her baby. They lived near the park and she always let me push the pram along to her house. I also had a little friend who lived nearby and we often enjoyed each others' company en route to school. Her name was Rosemary Brown and she wore such pretty cardigans that her mum knitted for her. I had pretty dresses, made by Aunt Margaret, though my aunts, who were quite Victorian, didn't like knees showing and so often let the hems down, much to the despair of Aunt Margaret and Aunt Nan. I also had to wear woollen stockings rather than ankle socks; I'm not sure why, though I suspect my aunts considered it immodest to do otherwise.

Sometimes if it was really wet I was allowed to get the bus. But much to my disappointment it never seemed to rain much in those days. There was a sweet shop near the bus stop and I remember being able to buy sweets for farthings. I loved the small copper coin that was the size of a sixpence and had the picture of a tiny wren on the front.

Each Saturday after tea, when my Dad left to catch the bus that would take him to Waverley Station and home, I was allowed to accompany him along part of Craigcrook Road towards the bus stop. Sometimes I'd walk along the whole of the way and get a row from my aunts for doing so when I returned. I really loved that time when I could hold his hand and share stories as we walked along. I wished the walk would never end, but it always did and it was really sad waving goodbye. I honestly cannot remember what we talked about while we walked. I only know that I treasured that precious time with him. Our Saturdays passed all too quickly.

At that time I went to a weekly dance class where I learned the steps for country dancing. At the end of the season we had a concert in the Little Theatre at the Pleasance. My Dad came to watch me. I remember wearing a green skirt and dancing the Irish Washerwoman, the Cumberland Reel and the New Rigged Ship with other children. Afterwards my Dad had to rush off to catch the train. Other children's Mums and Dads took them home. Ah c'est la vie.

Just before the summer holiday of 1956, my Dad told me that he was going to get married to Margaret Ferguson, whom I'd already met a few times when my Dad had taken me to visit. I'd previously suspected that she'd carried a candle for him. He told me that I was to stay at her house in Cowdenbeath until the wedding in August. He had previously thought about enrolling me at James Gillespie's School in Edinburgh, but after much discussion, it was decided that I'd leave Edinburgh. I clearly remember Miss Bonniman sitting with me and putting her arm around my shoulders. Her eyes seemed moist. I suppose it was for the best because by that time Aunt Meg must have been 80 and though Aunt Susan was younger, a girl of nearly ten was a big responsibility. And so it was that in May 1956 I went back to my roots in Fife.

Chapter 2: A New Beginning

"If you've got to go you've got to go," I would tell myself as I opened the chocolate brown painted door of Grandpa's toilet cubicle. To be honest it *was* the colour of excrement. Taking a deep breath I would switch on the light and try hard not to look up into the dark recesses where spiders lurked behind their intricate webs awaiting their prey. BUT however hard I tried, as soon as I sat down on the heavy mahogany seat, I could not resist looking, feeling as if I myself might be the spider's prey

I dreaded the experience and I remember thinking: *"I'm sure there are more than yesterday. They must have brought their friends along."* In a wavering voice I would quietly sing the rhyme of Incy Wincy spider and try to conjure up a picture of that friendly creature. Years before, when I first learned the Nursery Rhyme, I pitied the bedraggled Incy Wincy. But when it came to his arachnid friends in Grandpa's lavy cubicle, the cold fingers of fear crept over me and I would shudder as if I were Miss Moffat.

1956: A step back to my roots

One sunny April morning in 1956, my Dad told me we would be spending the day with his new fiancée, Margaret Ferguson. It was the school Easter holidays and I was staying with him and my Grandpa in Dunfermline. Margaret lived five miles away in the town of Cowdenbeath.

Cowdenbeath was both a town and a burgh inland in west Fife. It grew up around the extensive coalfields of the area during the pre-Thatcher days of our thriving coal industry. In 1890 it became one of many Police Burghs in Scotland. These essentially local burghs or municipalities were created under the Burgh Police (Scotland) Act in 1833.

Margaret's address was 257 Stenhouse Street. As we walked up the street, it seemed so very long and steep. With hindsight, it was a metaphor for my relationship with Margaret, my future Stepmother.

Back then, at the naïve age of 9 and a half, it felt like a great adventure. To make our route more interesting, my Dad and I counted the house numbers as we walked uphill. We passed three schools on the way there: St Bride's Primary and St Columba's Catholic Secondary on one side of the road and Beath High School, with its northern gable propped up by strong metal girders, on the other side. Dad told me that this precaution had been taken because of the subsidence caused by the numerous coalmines in the area. Fife was Scotland's coalmine capital at that time.

Eventually we arrived at number 257. I remember Margaret answering the door when my Dad rang the bell and smiling warmly at both of us. She had wavy black bobbed hair and glasses and appeared to me to be quite small. First she gave my Dad a peck on the cheek and then hugged me tightly. I can't remember what we had to eat, but I felt very welcome. I really liked Margaret's gate leg table, the frilly napkins, the doilies, the pretty china and the shiny cutlery. There were lots of dainty ornaments on the shelves and shiny brasses on the tiled mantelpiece.

Margaret's house had been the Ferguson family home and after the death of her parents she continued to live there. I felt very happy and looked forward to living there.

Just a month later in May 1956 I moved 18 miles north from my Aunt Meg and Aunt Susan's home in Edinburgh to live at Margaret's house. The plan was for my Dad to continue living with my Grandpa in Dunfermline until his wedding to Margaret in August that year.

Margaret's house was semi-detached and had a garden at the front and back. A wooden fence and gate enclosed the front. Margaret told me that originally there had been metal railings, but the Government had requisitioned these, like the decorative iron railings that surrounded the many civic spaces, during the Second World War to manufacture armaments and more Spitfire aircraft.

Behind the back gardens was a row of wooden lock ups (garages). Margaret had the one nearest her house and in this she kept her small blue Hillman Minx MFG 471.

Margaret's solid front door was painted a shade of moss green and had a shiny brass handle and letter box. Between that and the sun ray patterned inside door was a small vestibule with a tallboy (a small wardrobe for hanging coats and jackets) against the wall. Diagonally opposite the inside door was the bathroom, which had a shiny, black, ceramic modern splash back panel above the wash hand basin, complete with holder for a tumbler and toothbrushes. To the right was the living room, with a window at either end of the room and two doors, one of which led into the kitchen. This was a far cry from Grandpa's tiny scullery. There was a sink for general purposes as well as a Belfast sink and mangle for the laundry. Margaret also had a washing machine. It was a Hotpoint – a large round metal container on three legs. What absolute luxury.

From the hall, a staircase led to the three rooms on the upper floor. The first two steps led to a small landing which was just big enough for a fashionable fifties formica topped table and a huge, heavy black bakelite phone. Margaret's telephone number was 2188. Another ten steps led to another turn and the final four steps to the upper floor. These turns made it difficult to manoeuvre furniture, such as my Mum's piano, into a second living room directly above the one downstairs.

The other two rooms upstairs were bedrooms; a medium sized one and a very small one. Both still had fireplaces – wooden and tiled surrounds respectively – though neither was used while I lived there. Often on a winter's night, I used to wish that I could have had a fire because there was no central heating at that time and the only fire that was used was downstairs in the living room.

Because my Dad worked for the NCB (National Coal Board) he used to get concessionary coal. This was delivered a ton at a time and stored in a coalbunker that had been especially built under the back living room window. All the houses had coal fires, so it was essential to have lots of fuel. The only other heating in the house was a small, bronze oil filled radiator in the bathroom.

Margaret slept in the medium sized bedroom overlooking the back garden and I was given the small one facing the side. It had a really large shelved cupboard that was big enough to accommodate all of my books and toys. I had my own wardrobe, dressing table and even a double bed. There were feather pillows, a quilt and a primrose yellow candlewick bedspread (cotton material into which loops of yarns are hooked and then cut to give a tufted pattern). Margaret had put a few pretty dresses in the wardrobe. I loved them. She also put both white ankle and three quarter length socks in one of the dressing table drawers. I was delighted as they were much nicer than the woollen stockings that Aunts Meg and Susan insisted that I wore.

She had good taste in clothing and décor. She would typically wear pleated skirts with fine woollen jumpers or twin sets. Before she married my Dad, Margaret told me that she regularly went on wonderful Mediterranean cruises during her summer holiday. She must have travelled first class because she told me that a member of staff would run her bath. Lots of her ornaments, such as her musical trinket box and Swiss cuckoo clock, were holiday souvenirs.

Margaret enrolled me at Foulford Primary School. This was about a mile from our house. It was built with bricks from the local brickworks at the nearby village of Hill of Beath. I spent the last few weeks of Primary 5 there and this gave me time to make some friends before the summer holidays started at the beginning of July. Luckily, as at my three previous primary schools, I did not have to wear a uniform. I would typically dress in a floral blouse and pinafore and have my straight brown bobbed hair parted to the side with a hairclip.

My teacher's name was Miss Moffat. She always wore a two string pearl necklace and heavy framed spectacles and she had black hair that matched her black twinset. I soon settled in and quickly made friends with my classmates. One of the girls had very long hair, which she wore in plaits. Her name was Elizabeth and she soon became my very best friend: we were inseparable. We sat together and we played together, both in and out of school.

The months before my Dad and Margaret got married were some of the happiest of my young life. I had a new home and my Dad would be coming to live with us soon. My Grandpa was still very fit and active at 76 and was going to move into the little flat above one of the two shops that Margaret owned in Cowdenbeath High Street.

Margaret's shops

Margaret was the first daughter of Agnes Laird and Richard Torley Ferguson. She had a sister called Nancy and brothers named Ben and John. Tragically Ben died in his 30s leaving a wife and a son and daughter.

Margaret told me that her Dad had been a really hard worker and had started his business from scratch. He had bought a handcart and called at houses selling drapery and hosiery. He was a shrewd businessman, who worked assiduously to support his growing family and over the years had built up a thriving business, eventually owning two nearby shops both named R T Ferguson & Co in the bustling little town of Cowdenbeath.

Margaret had inherited her father's business acumen and quickly learned the ropes. Nancy, John and she had shares in the shops although Nancy sold her share to Margaret and John when she married her husband Dave. The business continued to thrive. Two ladies worked in the small shop in the High Street that sold drapery and wool; Isa Tatters and Maureen MacGregor. There was a window on either side of the front door and the items there were regularly changed. A few plaster mannequins modelled the skirts, tops and trousers and, in addition, some underwear, hosiery and wool were attractively displayed. One wall was lined with shelves for wool and in front there were two solid wooden counters fitted with drawers for items of underwear, hosiery and haberdashery. One had a 60 inch brass ruler attached for measuring various items.

The cash from the sales was kept in a long wooden container with a money tray divided into sections for coins and notes. On the front of the drawer was a lovely brass cup shaped handle and on the top of the box was a small perspex window, where the shop assistants wrote down the name and cost of the purchases on a roll of paper, that was fixed on a roller near the top of the box. On the back wall and opposite the front door was a small storeroom, and a door on the left hand side led to the dimly lit staff toilet.

Opposite that, another door led out into the yard and to the other bigger shop in Foulford Street that provided employment for four ladies. It was a building on three levels and the ground floor at the time was divided into two flats. One of them was rented to tenants, while the other was used as a storeroom. This was later converted into a medical practice after Margaret's brother John married a GP called Betty from Yorkshire, whom he'd met on a Mediterranean cruise. They lived in Foulford Road with Dollar, their golden Labrador.

John, the youngest of the Ferguson four, was blessed with a cheerful disposition and infectious smile. Like my Dad, he too smoked Embassy cigarettes and enjoyed playing golf. He whistled very tunefully and sang a variety of songs in his fine tenor voice; I clearly remember one of his favourites being Willie Nelson's Let the Rest of the World Go By. His favoured headgear was either a cap or a bowler hat, while heavy black spectacles framed his jolly round face. Whenever he came into the shop he'd tell jokes that often reduced everyone to laugh until their sides ached and caused Margaret to come out of the office to see what was going on. When this occurred, the laughter quickly subsided and the former order was restored.

Access to the shop was by an outside stair that had been built nearer the right hand side of the building. Opposite the entrance was a counter that ran along three quarters of the length of the wall and had a glass screen on top. This was where the customers paid either for items they'd just bought or made payments for items that they'd bought on credit. Behind this screen was a glorious old cash register where the money from the sales was kept. It had lots of knobs with numbers on them and these were pressed when the final sale's total was reached. It made a wonderful pinging noise when the drawer opened revealing lots of pound and ten shilling notes, half crowns, florins, sixpences, three-penny pieces, pennies and halfpennies.

There were note pads for the assistants to add up the sales if they couldn't count everything in their heads. If the sales were large there was a grey plastic adding machine with a huge keypad of numbers on its front and a handle on the right hand side. My favourite was a very heavy Imperial black typewriter that I was sometimes allowed to use. The paper was fed over a metal roller and secured. A coloured ribbon that was impregnated with ink was attached behind the rollers. The Qwerty keyboard was fashioned of metal keys whose bases had the imprint of the letters on the bottom of them. As the keys were struck they hit the ribbon, the type appeared on the blank paper and the roller moved to the right. When the roller couldn't move any further a bell pinged and the typist had to manually push it back to its original position. It was a very noisy activity. Whenever I hear Leroy Anderson's composition of Typewriter, which is used as a signature tune to Radio 4's The News Quiz, I think of this magnificent Imperial typewriter. Sadly it was eventually superseded in favour of a smaller and lighter Olivetti model that my Dad regularly used. I still have it in its original red case in our loft.

On the other two sides of the shop, the walls were lined half way up with glass fronted drawers that contained pyjamas, nightdresses, ties, shirts, gloves, hats and scarves. In front of them stood three more large, dark wood counters one of which had a brass ruler fixed to its top. This was for measuring out curtain material and rufflette tape. These items along with pillows, bedcovers, quilts, towels, sheets and pillowcases were kept above the drawers, so the shop assistants needed a ladder to access them. There were more drawers with glass fronts and trays in these counters too for baby items, underwear and hosiery.

Three quarters of the way along the other wall was a passageway that led to an office, a compact shoe department that stocked an amazing amount of good quality footwear and a small kitchen where on six days a week, Margaret would cook lunch.

Opposite the front door was an inside stair leading to the upper floor which was one enormous room illuminated by two skylight windows. There were rails upon rails of coats, jackets, trousers, skirts and dresses for men, women and children. There was a curtained area for changing, one large mirror fixed to the wall and one full-length portable mirror on castors.

Margaret worked very hard in her shops. I guess she was a workaholic. Like her father, she was an extremely shrewd businesswoman who seemed to know instinctively exactly what type and amount of stock to keep. I don't remember her buying any white elephants.

In addition to the six shop assistants for both shops, Margaret employed three commercial travellers, or sales reps in modern day parlance. Her brother John was one of them. It was their job to go to outlying areas and sell goods to the people who lived there. They were provided with vans so that they could do this.

Later, because the business was growing fast, a fourth commercial traveller was employed to help. When he came to work I recognised him. It turned out he had been the manager of the Lochgelly cinema. Margaret's sister Nancy lived in Lochgelly and one time when I went for tea with her and her son Lewis, we were allowed into the cinema free to see *Pinocchio*, much to my amazement.

Nancy's husband Dave Mazzoni owned a plumber's business and their son Lewis was about eighteen months younger than I was. Nancy was always great fun and I regularly took the bus by myself to Lochgelly where she lived. Like her brother John, Nancy also smoked Embassy cigarettes and enjoyed a regular game of golf.

Wedding bells

Before my Dad and Margaret got married I remember she would sometimes come into my bed in the morning and we'd chat and sing. She taught me songs from musicals such as Oh Rosemarie I Love You, Ramona, Under the Bridges of Paris, I'm Forever Blowing Bubbles, Apple Blossom Time and Mademoiselle from Armentieres.

My Dad took Margaret to Glasgow to buy her engagement and weddings rings from Hamilton Laidlaw, the jewellers near St Enoch Square. Since she was in business, she was able to buy things at cost price. Her diamond engagement ring was designed with five diamonds in a row and her wedding ring was octagonal in shape.

My Dad's cousin Fred got married in June of that year and my Dad was asked to be his best man. I went with my Aunts Meg, Susan, Nan and Margaret, as well as Margaret Ferguson. I wore a cream silk dress that had a lace trimmed collar and pearl button fastenings. It was gathered at the waist and tied in a bow at the back with 2 broad ribbons of the same silky material.

Fred's was the first wedding that I have any memory of and the best part was the ceilidh and dancing after the meal. When I was very tiny I had been to my Mum's brother's wedding. I do not remember this unfortunately, though my Aunt Janet told me that during the ceremony I pulled my Mum's crystal necklace and it broke scattering the beads all over the floor of the church! Later I was a flower girl at a family friend's wedding but even the studio photograph of me in my lovely long dress, which I believe was pink, doesn't prompt my memory.

I don't remember much about my Dad and Margaret's wedding arrangements other than it was to be on Wednesday 8th August 1956. I do remember wedding presents such as a Kenwood Chef mixer – I still have it and it's still working after nearly sixty years of good use, a Hotpoint ironer – a heated electric mangle that made a great job of sheets, pillow slips and hankies, and a glorious new Hotpoint washing machine. It was a large cream, rectangular, appliance with Hotpoint spelt in chromium letters in the middle near the top. The washing was loaded in the top, the two wash buttons were on the right hand side and the lever to start the programme was on the left. A temperature gauge was in the middle.

On the morning of the wedding Margaret, Nancy and I went to Mitch, the local hairdresser's shop, to have shampoo and sets. It was the very first time that I'd experienced this luxury and I clearly remember singing Apple Blossom Time while I was under the drier. I didn't realise that anyone could hear me until I saw people looking at me then clapping when I'd finished.

I wore a lovely shaded lilac dress, made of taffeta with a sweetheart neck. A tiny posy of rosebuds nestled at the left hand side of the waistband between the lacy bodice and the net overskirt. Aunt Kit knitted me a little bolero in case it was chilly on the day. My gold locket with the photo of my Mum inside and a pair of lovely cream shoes completed the outfit.

Margaret's sister Nancy, who was the Matron of Honour, wore three quarter length turquoise lace and net dress. After she'd got ready she took one of my dad's cigarettes out of his box, put her finger to her lips and whispered: *"Don't tell."* As if I would have. My Dad, his brother Angus, who was his best man, and Margaret's brother John wore morning suits and Margaret wore a pretty white lacy three quarter length wedding dress. She told me later that when my Dad saw her he whispered: *"You look beautiful."*

It was not a grand affair. There were around forty guests and Maureen MacGregor, one of the shop assistants, played the organ. After they were married and had posed for photographs, we all boarded a single-decker bus that had been hired for the occasion and went to the Green Hotel in Kinross for a celebratory meal. I was disappointed to discover that there was to be no dancing as there had been at Fred's wedding. Later we boarded the bus again and went to Strathyre where we had tea. The only two things that I clearly remember are my lovely new shoes pinching my toes and Margaret's friend Hector from Bishopbriggs, who was quite tipsy, walking up and down the bus and singing at the top of his voice.

I can't remember my Dad and Margaret leaving; they went to Dublin for their honeymoon. For the next two weeks my home was to be with my Dad's brother Angus, Aunt Jessie and cousins Shona and Iain – the chocolate crown thieves. It was not a particularly happy holiday for me. I don't think that anything terrible happened but because I was the youngest, I got bossed around and I didn't like it. I fervently wished that the honeymooners would return and each night after I'd said my prayers, I counted the remaining sleeps.

The honeymooners duly returned by car. We said our goodbyes to the Bellshill branch of the Campbells and set off on the journey back to Cowdenbeath. I tried to tell them how I'd been, but they didn't seem all that interested, so in the end I gave up and went to sleep.

There's an old Scot's saying: *"It's back tae auld claes and parritch."* Literally translated to mean the return to old clothes and porridge – when the gilt wears off the gingerbread then it's really back to reality. And so it came to pass that I learned that very hard lesson at the hard school of knocks. My Dad and Margaret returned to their respective jobs while I went back to school – a new session in Primary 6 and a new teacher called Miss Letts – my friend Liz and I agreed that she didn't live up to her name. It should have been Miss Letts-not: she was very, very strict.

At that time the Government decreed that all children should partake of one third of a pint of milk in order to promote good health, so each morning the milkman would deliver metal crates of these small foil topped bottles to every school. Our teacher kept a box of straws in her cupboard and every day appointed two children to pierce each lid with the straws. Just before the bell rang for playtime we were instructed to line up and drink our milk before going outside. After break the same two children would carry the crate to the wash hand basins and rinse them out. Liz and I loved this job and when our turn came round, we'd hurry along to where the basins were, remove the straws and the foil tops then rinse the bottles before throwing their contents at the tiled wall whilst chanting: *"I baptise these walls!"* We laughed heartily as we watched the water cascade down the tiles. Thankfully we were NEVER caught during this activity and the bottles were always well rinsed out.

Life as *"Miss Ferguson's daughter"*

After the wedding, Margaret told me, instead of calling her Auntie Margaret, as I had been, I should call her Mum. Looking back on it I wasn't asked, I was simply told. At that time children were *"seen and not heard"*. So I did as I was told and she was Mum from then on. However, she remained Miss Ferguson while at work and I was known as Miss Ferguson's daughter! Although single mums were stigmatised at that time, as were *"bidie ins"* (unmarried partners who lived together), to my knowledge no one ever cast aspersions in her case. I always thought it strange and at times felt resentment well up inside because I was *not* her daughter and I sensed intuitively that the feeling was mutual.

After the wedding, my Dad came to live with Margaret and me in Stenhouse Street. He also *"kept the books"* behind the glass screen in one of Margaret's shops after he got back from his day job at the wages accountant for the NCB. I believe that after he took over this duty, these books were never out by as much as a penny. If they were, he wouldn't rest until he found the error, so that they balanced. These books were quite small. Some of the covers were made of ox blood coloured leather while the others that were covered with green material had a shabby appearance. They opened from the bottom and the cards inside, which contained the credit customers' details could be flipped over, rather like modern ring binders. I don't remember him using the adding machine for this duty.

The New Beginning had started very well; it was almost too good to be true and I hadn't realised it. In sharp contrast to her siblings Nancy and John, Margaret seemed to find it hard to laugh and joke, at least with me. There was no more chatting or learning of new songs in the morning – not even on Saturdays.

Saturday was a really busy day in the shops and then it was all hands on deck. Though I didn't serve any customers till I was a few years older, I had to help to refold and tidy up the trays of underwear in the wooden units that lined the walls, help to arrange clothes on the rails and help to tidy up the shoe department.

On occasions I'd sneakily model some of the large knickers that had elastic at the bottom of the legs. They looked like knickerbockers. Once Liz and I climbed inside a pair and pranced madly around until gravity triumphed and we fell in a heap. Thankfully we weren't caught, the knickers remained undamaged, were duly folded and returned in their pristine state, back to the drawer to await someone of the size of my Aunt Margaret. Sometimes I swept the floor when I returned from school. At other times I'd sneak off to go to my Grandpa's wee upstairs flat that was above the small shop and just across the yard from the other shop and hope that no one noticed.

Sundays were sacrosanct. No housework, no sewing or knitting though I was allowed to read. Still it wasn't like in my Grandpa's day. He told me that his family had to walk to church twice and in all weathers. The sermons were long, loud and often terrifying. I considered myself lucky since we went to church by car and our minister was a kindly man whose sermons were of a reasonable length. I quickly learned to make the two pandrops (mint sweets often called pepperies) that Margaret would slip into my hand last during that time.

The Pepperies!

It's Sunday again the rain's pooring doon.
There's dubs an' glaur a' ower the toon.
But on the Sabbath wi darenae shirk
Fae gangin tae oor parish kirk.

Frae aff the shelf Pa taks the Book.
He fixes us a wi a stern look.
Ma gies us sillar frae her purse.
Oh my, the rain is gettin worse!

Wearin raincoats and wellies we gang ootside.
Methinks at hame A'd raither bide.
We arrive at kirk like drookit rats.
An aon the hallstand hing oor hats!

We troop doon till we reach oor seat,
An at oor neighbours nod tae greet.
The organ music's vera dour.
An oan the pew there's lots o stoor.

The Meenister fixes us wi a stare.
An me, a jist look at the flare.
He drones on in an awfu voice.
Bein at hame wis ma first choice.

Ma slips something in tae ma hand
A peppery! Oh boy it tastes just grand.
Ane'll last me fur a while.
Ma mooth it braks intae a smile.

The Meenister announces the final hymn.
Ootside the weather is still grim.
Then it's hame to the fire and some meat.
Pepperies are sic a minty treat.

According to James VI, the county of Fife was a *"beggar's mantle fringed with gold"*. Wonderful towns such as St Andrews and pretty little fishing villages including Leven, Largo, Aberdour, Anstruther or Crail with their lovely beaches form the golden fringe. After Sunday lunch we would often go for a walk in one of these fishing villages. Sometimes Liz came with us and these occasions were always the most enjoyable.

Grandpa's flat

After my Grandpa downsized to a flat in Cowdenbeath, we would all eat lunch together. My Dad would come home from work at the NCB and Margaret would cook in the small kitchen at the back of the big shop. Then it would be carried downstairs, across the yard and up the stair leading to my Grandpa's wee flat. We usually had either mince or round steak followed by rice pudding or custard and tinned fruit; all of this on account of my Grandpa's *"wallies"* (false teeth).

Grandpa's flat was reached by an outside stair. It had a metal railing and handrail for part of the way up and once it turned towards the green door at the top there was a handrail on the wall. The flat comprised two rooms, a tiny scullery and a toilet cubicle. Despite its size the scullery boasted two sinks, one being a Belfast sink and alongside them was an old Belling cooker. I think that it probably came from my parents' house in

59

Kinneddar Park. Grandpa's old geriatric gas appliance with the home-made wooden grill pan would likely have been left behind in Moodie Street, Dunfermline for obvious health and safety reasons.

I think that that floor was stone. Inside the scullery was a brown painted toilet cubicle. It would not have looked out of place in a horror film. I hated using it as there was no window, the ancient toilet bowl had a heavy wooden seat and on the right hand side of the high cistern was a chain flush with a wooden handle.

There was a shelf above for cleaning materials but it seemed so terrifyingly dark and dreich (dreary) there that I never looked up. I knew exactly where the chain to flush it was and so closed my eyes before reaching out for the solid wood handle at the end. I always heaved a sigh of relief when I came out into the daylight because there were always spiders of varying sizes lurking in the shadows. Even though their webs were removed, these arachnids were extremely determined and spun more before my next visit. I was convinced that they lay in wait for me and sometimes my dreams turned into nightmares with these creatures chasing me. Their presence never seemed to bother anyone else but it triggered my lifetime fear of spiders. Though I have tried hard to overcome this over the decades, remaining calm when my children were small, I was always relieved that my elder daughter Linsey, who loved all creatures great and small, would always remove them for me.

Grandpa's toilet was so terrifying that after lunch I would often wait to use the toilets at school. And they were pretty unsavoury – until I was in 4th year of secondary school, everyone had to use the outside facilities: *"the bogs"* as they were fondly known. But these at least had windows. I rested safe in the knowledge that I could always use the toilet in the small shop after school. There was no toilet in the other shop and unfortunately the shops were closed for an hour at lunchtime.

From Grandpa's scullery a door led into the living room and at either end of that wall were two smaller windows which provided some daylight, though not as much as the one in the bedroom. The wooden framed fireplace was tiled inside and on either side of the fire was a hob for kettles or pots. Above the mantelpiece was a very shiny picture of Sydney Harbour Bridge. The background was green and the bridge was outlined in black. Underneath the window near the fireplace was an easy chair and a walnut cabinet that housed the black and white television set which my Dad had bought for my Grandpa. Opposite the television cabinet was a two-seater moquette settee. At one end there was a lever and when that was pulled the arm would flatten out. My Grandpa would usually sit on the settee smoking his pipe with the silver cap. I used to buy his tobacco for him at the local Co-op. No one batted an eyelid about children purchasing tobacco in the 1950s. The tobacco was wrapped in a silver foil rectangular shaped packet and on top was a pink and white label bearing the words of his preferred brand Union Black Cut. When my Grandpa smoked the smell was quite overpowering and would often make my eyes water if I was nearby: no one thought about the dangers of children passive smoking then.

Other furniture in that room included my Dad's light oak sideboard, his free standing radio, square table and four matching chairs with brown leather covered seats, as well as a dark wood three-cornered cupboard for *"the good china"* and a wonderful old Grandfather clock that had the most comforting steady tick and mellow sound when it struck the hour. It was my Dad's job to wind it each week and pull up the brass weights that made a lovely whirring sound. I was given it after I was married but sold it as it had woodworm holes and I didn't want our new furniture to be affected. Now I regret this and wish instead that I'd thought to treat the casing with Rentokil fluid.

Grandpa's bedroom faced the High Street. Opposite the door was a large window underneath which stood his *"kist"*. This was a large chest that my Grandpa had made before he married my Granny for the sole purpose of storing bedding. My Aunt Margaret had made a similar one at a woodwork class. However, after my Grandpa moved to Cowdenbeath, various knick-knacks and other mementos were kept inside. Sometimes I'd lift the heavy lid and peer cautiously into the depths hoping that no spiders were lurking therein. Once I found my Granny's rose gold wedding ring and to my delight was allowed to keep it. Unfortunately I lost it and I simply couldn't remember where that happened. I felt both sad and very ashamed of myself for being so careless and stupid.

In the middle of the wall to the right of the door was a wooden framed fireplace with a high mantelpiece and to the right of that was a very large shelved cupboard. The doll's house that Andrew Gibb had made for me was stored there along with other books and toys, so that if I was at Grandpa's flat then I'd be able to amuse myself. My Grandpa's double bed, my single bed, and a small cabinet stood against the wall opposite the fireplace and a dressing table and wardrobe were on either side of the door.

Two vivid memories of that room remain with me. The first one is of my poor Grandpa being confined to bed for quite some time due to an acute attack of bronchitis and the second is of me aged twelve being thrashed on my bare bottom by Margaret. I can't recall what crime I'd committed but the thrashing, one of several, was excruciatingly painful and, unlike these poor adults like Raif Badawi, who are flogged in countries like Saudi Arabia, despite my best efforts, I cried out several times. When she'd vented her spleen on me I quickly pulled up my knickers and ran out past my Dad and Grandpa wondering why on earth neither of them had made any attempt to intervene. I made my way back to school, my poor bottom stinging and throbbing and tried hard to compose myself and stop the tears that were pricking my eyes from flowing down my cheeks. I was too ashamed to confess what had happened even to Liz. To this day I can still feel the pain and humiliation that I felt afterwards. It is probably why I hardly ever smacked my three children and on the odd occasion I did it was just a small single tap on the hand or a fully clothed bottom.

Daily life

Every morning, except for Sundays, the milk was delivered to most of the people in our street by Dougie the milkman and Jock his huge, brown Clydesdale horse who pulled the cart. Dougie, a stocky man, whose face was expressionless and weather beaten, always wore a donkey jacket and carried a leather moneybag over his shoulder. An old tweed bunnet covered his bald pate and a pair of tackety boots completed his ensemble. The musical medley of Jock's hooves clip clopping along the road together with the rattle of milk bottles used to waken me up. Sometimes I'd peep through my curtains to watch Jock stop at each house, munching on the oats in his nosebag and waiting patiently till Dougie took the full bottles out of the crates, before trudging up the garden paths. Once he'd put them on the doorsteps he'd collect the empty ones and trudge back to the cart to put them in the crates. The horse never moved until Dougie told him to.

I remember one morning when Margaret went outside to take in the milk she noticed Dougie pouring milk into an empty bottle. She ran down the garden path and remonstrated with him, saying that this wasn't allowed, the bottles had not been sterilised and that if he ever did it again she'd report him to his boss. I believe he did this because a lady's milk bottle had broken and she was unable to pay for it. I never did see him do it again. This was probably the first time that I'd ever seen one grown up giving another a dressing down. In my limited experience, it always was children who were scolded. I began to realise that Margaret was quite feisty.

It wasn't just the milk that was delivered by horse and cart. Most Wednesdays Geordie Tatters delivered lovely fresh vegetables to regular customers. He had a beautiful black and white Clydesdale horse called Wullie. Like Jock, he was a very patient animal who did exactly what Geordie asked him to do. I think that Geordie had a small shop on the High Street where his dad and brother worked. The horse lived in a field nearby. I think that Geordie really preferred to be outside rather than working in the shop. His sister Isa was one of my stepmother's shop assistants. Both of them went about their business quietly.

There were no supermarkets at that time and so Margaret used to buy fish from the fishmonger, meat from the butcher, bread from the baker and the papers were delivered by the paper-boy. The weekly shopping was ordered and bought from Cuthill, the grocer's store at the Fountain end of the High Street, and delivered to Margaret's house on Wednesday afternoons when her shops closed for a half-day: this was the modern version of online shopping for working women! That part of the High Street was so called because the fountain to celebrate Queen Victoria's Diamond Jubilee had been donated to the burgh in 1897 by Henry Mungall, who was elected Provost at the first meeting of the Town Council in 1891.

The Fountain remained the focal point until it was removed in the mid 1940s because the ornate cast iron panels and stone base were showing all of the effects of the mining town's smoky atmosphere.

Margaret was extremely house proud. When my Dad and I went to live with her, the house had no fitted carpets. Instead, all of the rooms had linoleum floor covering, with a carpet on top. When the carpet was in place there was a two to three foot border of lino around the outside of the room. This was generally highly polished and if you weren't careful you could slip. The carpets and rugs were taken out regularly, hung over the clothes line where they were then beaten with a carpet switch until all of the dust flew out. Each morning, the brass front door handle, letterbox and keyhole plate were polished and the back and front door steps were swept. The china ornaments were washed regularly and every Friday evening it was my job to polish the brass ornaments, silver jam spoons and the silver fish cutlery. As a consequence I chose to only polish the few brass things I inherited a couple of times a year and to keep Margaret's silver fish cutlery in the loft. Life is too short to polish!

After Grandpa moved to the little flat above the small shop, he no longer had a garden to look after, so he regularly cut Margaret's grass, tended the flowerbeds and planted vegetables. He must have missed his beautiful garden in Dunfermline so very much. But over time and by dint of his green fingers, he lovingly transformed Margaret's garden into one bursting with a stupendous array of flowers and prize-winning vegetables.

My Dad was a keen football supporter and on Saturdays he always went to watch Dunfermline Athletic, known as The Pars, play their home games at East End Park. His friend George, whom I think was a work colleague too, always went and sometimes I would go along too with my football rattle. I loved to stand on the terracing cheering on the Pars and revelling in the hilarious banter. It was so different to going to a game today with the commercialism of football and the seated stadiums.

George and his wife Isa lived nearby and had been friends of Margaret's for many years. We regularly visited each other's houses for tea. I particularly enjoyed going there because Isa always bought lovely cakes and I was allowed to watch some television. They had no children of their own and so always made a fuss of me. I went to their house each Wednesday evening. George would always give me some money to buy sweets from the small shop nearby and we'd share them while we watched the game show Take Your Pick hosted by Hughie Green. We often played Ludo, Snakes and Ladders or Happy Families and sometimes we had quizzes. I really looked forward to these times.

Other regular visitors and good friends were Peter and Margaret Torley – I am not sure if they were distant relatives of Margaret's father. They lived in the village of Cardenden and were really nice people. Peter was a barber who used to cut my Dad's hair when he visited and Margaret was an infant school teacher. They didn't have children and that was a great pity because they'd have made wonderful parents. In fact, I sometimes wished that Margaret Torley could have been my stepmother instead of Margaret Ferguson.

My best friend Liz

I loved visiting my best friend Liz and her family. She lived with her parents and older sister Isabel in a prefab. These simple houses were constructed after the war because of a critical shortage of housing and builders. Prefabs were relatively cheap to build, easy to erect and used less manpower to construct than conventional brick houses. In fact, I discovered that as early as 1944, Winston Churchill had begun work on a temporary housing programme. The Housing Temporary Accommodation Act of that year had a fund of £150 million committed to that project and the factories that had once manufactured aircraft parts were then put to great use manufacturing these prefabs. Anyway, Liz's home was a very nice compact little house and her Dad once won the local competition for the Best Kept Garden.

Most Saturday mornings Liz and I went on the bus to the Carnegie Swimming Baths in Dunfermline.

SWIMMING POND, CARNEGIE BATHS, DUNFERMLINE.

After we'd paid and got our tickets, we went through the turnstile to the cubicles that were around three sides of the pool. My swimsuit was sky blue with ruffles at the front that looked like bubbles. Although the water was cold it didn't deter us, for once we'd changed we just leapt or belly flopped into the pool then practised and honed our developing diving and swimming techniques. When the lifeguard blew her whistle and held up her number board, we knew that it was time to come out. Then, after getting dried and dressed, we bought hot blackcurrant juice and ate our *"shivery bites"* (these were snacks that we'd brought) before catching the bus back.

On wet Saturdays we'd be given money to go to the pictures. We'd go through the door into the huge darkened room where an usherette would scrutinise our tickets and guide us to our seats by torchlight. The same lady would patrol the aisles. If she heard any undue noise she'd shine her bright torch in that direction and sternly warn the offenders. At the intermission, she and another usherette would appear with illuminated trays of ice cream and very quickly queues of cinemagoers would form. Liz and I loved these tubs and our fingers very quickly would feel for the small tab on the lid, peel off the small wooden spatula that was stuck to the underside before tucking into the vanilla or chocolate ice cream. Though we were happy to watch most films our particular favourites were Westerns, Carry On films, or ones starring Jerry Lewis. In fact we'd often hide so that we could watch a bit more once the performance was over. More often than not we were unsuccessful!

On other Saturdays we'd go to the local Palais de Danse where we'd hire roller skates and whizz around the dance floor to the rock 'n roll music of Elvis that blared from loud speakers high above. It was great fun and both of us became very proficient at this sport. However, I was to find out later that the skills needed for roller-skating are so very different from those required for ice skating...

I sometimes went to Liz's house after school. Her parents were very liberal and made me feel very welcome. I enjoyed the relief of not having to return to the shop to do chores. Sometimes we experimented with cooking and I well remember the time we toasted some digestive biscuits sprinkled with custard powder under the grill!

Liz's Dad worked as a manager organising the ambulances for the local area. He was a true socialist, a real people person who really *did* speak up for the rights of workers and I have him to sincerely thank for influencing my political beliefs. My Dad and Margaret always voted Conservative but they'd never tell me why. Maybe it was because of Margaret's business. I don't recall any political debates or discussions such as the ones at Liz's house. I do remember always thinking that what her Dad said made perfect sense because he explained everything so clearly.

Liz and I were members of the local Girl Guides Association and each Thursday evening we went to the group where we participated in a variety of activities, games, crafts and songs. One night, on the way home, Liz and I decided to play *"chap door run"* ie ringing someone's doorbell, then running away as fast as possible, hiding and watching the reaction of the occupant of the house when they answered the door. Near Margaret's house lived a lady who was so particular and house proud that, as well as brushing and scrubbing her outside steps, she even got down on her hands and knees to scrub her garden path. Well, one night we snuck up her path and took it in turns to ring the doorbell, before Liz uttered the words *"run frit"* Burglar Bill style. However, before we reached the gate, the front door

65

was flung open and an angry voice yelled: *"Stoap, whit are ye daeing?"* Of course, as good Girl Guides, we obediently did as we were bid and then hung our heads in shame as we received a stern lecture about what would happen to us next time. Duly chastened, we apologised profusely and made our way down the garden path. However, as soon as we got round the corner and out of sight, we collapsed on to each other and giggled uncontrollably. We never did ring that particular doorbell again, but it didn't stop us doing it elsewhere. Sincere apologies to all of those folk whose evenings we interrupted – this was the forerunner of unwanted phone calls to people with unusual surnames, which I believe *my* children made, or the mobile phone addictions of today's pre-teenagers.

Liz and I went to Guide Camp on a couple of occasions. To everyone's horror we discovered that there were no toilets! I found that I had to relieve myself in what was a ditch! We were informed that this was a *latrine*. I don't remember whether we had to dig these ditches ourselves or whether it had been done for us before we arrived. I would almost have preferred Grandpa's toilet with the spiders!

The food was pretty awful. Liz and I affirmed that it tasted more *"boaking"* (sickening) than the school dinners smelt. I had been given some pocket money and I put it in my favourite little red soft leather purse that had two ladybirds on its front. Sadly it disappeared along with the contents and though I searched everywhere I could think of, I never did find it. Nevertheless it was quite an adventure going to sleep in a sleeping bag on a bedroll and under the canvas of a Bell tent. other side the sky was beautiful. I think that I very much enjoyed the experience, despite being a bit sick during the descent.

After we left the airport we went to the train station at Basle and I was sick again. I don't recall getting much sympathy though. We hired a taxi to the Hotel Esplanade. It was just beautiful, as was the weather. The hotel was situated in lovely surroundings and had lots of palm trees nearby. The high snow capped mountains and the pretty little houses with their colourful painted shutters were just like the ones I'd seen in books and on chocolate boxes. All of the staff in the hotel spoke very good English and that was just as well since we were all monoglots.

I vividly remember going in the bus over the border and into Italy. The travelling didn't seem to agree with my poor tummy and though I was never sick again, I often felt a bit queasy during the next few days and got rows from Margaret for spoiling her holiday. One thing I do recall about the journey to Venice was a toilet stop. I went with Margaret into a small and foul smelling room. There was no free standing toilet rather what is best described as a vitreous enamel draining board with a hole in the centre. The hole was full of unmentionable stuff and there was no toilet paper. Even though my bladder needed to be emptied, I was too scared to squat over that hole in case something horrible emerged and that fear seemed insurmountable. I found that I couldn't manage so climbed back aboard the bus, crossed my legs and hoped that Venice wasn't too many more miles.

Primary 7

Maggie class at Foulford Primary
3rd row from bottom fourth from right

I very much enjoyed my time at Foulford Primary School, especially the English exercises from First Aid in English, learning words from Schonell's spelling book and stories from Scottish history. At that time it was customary to regularly read round the class and recite our tables. Woe betide anyone who made an error – some poor souls were punished daily with the strap for committing this crime. Much later I realised that this was because they had reading difficulties.

My Primary 7 teacher was called Mary MacLean and was commonly known as *"Spitfire"*. This was because when she shouted, and this was a regular occurrence, she showered the unfortunate victims with spray. Thankfully neither Liz nor I were ever recipients of these outbursts.

I dreaded the weekly needlework lessons. The visiting teacher who taught us to sew and knit was called Mrs Kean and I still have the lap bag that I made in Primary 6 in which to keep my needlework and knitting. It is bright pink cotton and has my initials M C embroidered on the front. During the first term of Primary 7 I made a blouse and really struggled to sew the obligatory French seam. It took me many weeks to complete this article. The turquoise thread turned grey and eventually black from my constant unpicking of squint stitches, but I finally mastered the art of sewing both evenly and neatly in a straight line. During the second term we made white aprons and hats to wear in our cookery classes when we went to secondary school. When my Dad and Margaret went to a Primary 7 parents' evening and spoke to Mrs Kean about my work, she just burst out laughing uproariously. I was really embarrassed when my Dad told me.

That same year Margaret arranged for me to have piano lessons with Mr Livingstone and once a week after school I'd walk round to his house. He lived in a street of miners' *"raws"*. These were rows of small cottages that had been built for the miners. I used to enjoy this excursion and soon learned both bass and treble clefs. With practice I became quite proficient at scales and arpeggios and amazed myself when I mastered the art of playing with both hands simultaneously.

I recall that in Primary 7 we were given application forms to take home for elocution lessons. Margaret and my Dad thought that it seemed a splendid idea and Liz thought that she'd like to go too. They were held in one of the rooms in the Carnegie Hall in Dunfermline and once a week after school we went along. I've little memory of the actual lessons though at the end of the term I remember that there was a production of Rumpelstiltskin. I was given the part of the peasant girl who said she could spin flax into gold, then married the King and was threatened with the loss of her baby. My Aunts Kit and Janet came to the Production in Carnegie Hall as well as my Dad, my Grandpa and Margaret. I believe that I delivered my lines well and in a perfect Edinburgh accent. I wore a long green dress and clearly remember the lines: *"Round and round my wheel goes flying. None to see me but the moon."*

During the summer term, we sat the *"quali"* or eleven plus exam to determine which secondary school we'd attend. At the annual prize giving Liz was first in the class and I was third. After the summer holiday Liz and I together with several others would go on to Beath High School.

High School and High Jinx

The first time I had to wear school uniform was when I started secondary school. It consisted of a navy blue pleated skirt and a white blouse. Liz always used to call round for me when we were at Foulford Primary and we would walk there together and I am glad that we did the same things when we started at Beath High School.

H.G.SCHOOL AND STENHOUSE STREET, COWDENBEATH

I remember walking down Stenhouse Street and into the school playground. In comparison to our primary school, Beath High School was immense and looked even more so once we were in the playground.

Beath High School was founded in 1910 as a grammar school mainly for the children of the local mine executives. It was an imposing building of red sandstone and stood on our road, Stenhouse Street. Unfortunately the original building suffered subsidence as a result of its proximity to the No 7 pit. The huge steel girders that supported the northern gable of the school reminded me of those that supported the Forth Rail Bridge.

The walls were punctuated at regular intervals by large windows and, right in the middle, a flight of stone steps led up to the front entrance porch that was for the sole use of the rector, his staff and visitors. The pupils' entrances were at either side – the girls' door was beside the art block while the boys went in by the end that was supported by girders. Liz and I often imagined that if the school fell down (when no one was there of course) we'd have an extended holiday.

The school campus housed a number of buildings and huts, since it couldn't accommodate the growing number of pupils. To the right of the front of the school was the art room block. To the left and right of the front entrance and near the wall were two modern huts that housed the History and Geography departments. To the left of these were two very ancient huts where some maths classes were taught and where our school assemblies were held. At the back were the toilets for the juniors and more ancient huts for maths and the Home Management department as well as the dinner hall.

Neither Liz nor I ever stayed for the school lunches that were delivered daily in huge metal containers. They always smelt the same – indescribably *"boaking"*. We always opted to go home despite the long walk and the limited menu I was offered.

I vividly remember that first day entering the vast school hall with Liz. It was right in the middle and had lots of doors leading from it. The ceiling went all the way up to the school roof and wall bars were fitted on three of the walls: this was where we'd have our PE lessons. In those days we simply did PE in our navy knickers. A gallery ran the length of the back wall and so when you went to the upper floor you could look down into that room, meaning the boys could spy on us.

That first day it all seemed very overwhelming. One wall had a board on which were written the names of the school duxes and proxime accessits (runners up). One of the duxes was Jennie Lee, later to become Baroness Lee of Asheridge. She was a devoted socialist who went on to become the youngest member of the House of Commons and was a minister in Harold Wilson's government of 1964. She was influential in the setting up of the Open University and was married to Aneurin Bevan who had been instrumental in setting up both the Welfare State and tackling the housing programme after the Second World War.

Another notable pupil was the distinguished pharmacologist Sir James Black who later, in 1988, received the Nobel Prize for his work leading to the development of the drugs propanolol, which is used to treat cardiac conditions, and cimitidine, which is used to treat gastro-intestinal conditions. Jim Baxter, the footballer who played for both Rangers and Scotland, was also educated at Beath High.

Liz and I stood nervously with all of the other first years who had come from the other towns and villages in the catchment area. Then we were put into our first year classes and given timetables – a plethora of information to absorb. There were four first year classes: 1A, 1B, 1C and 1D. Liz was put in 1A while I went to 1C – quelle misere. Well, we'd just have to make the best of it. 1A studied French and Latin, 1B studied German and Latin, 1C studied French and 1D studied German. There were four school groups known as houses namely Adam, Moray, Scott and Stewart. Each house had a coloured metal badge; red, yellow, green and blue. I was in Adam. If you had siblings then you were all put in the same house to avoid competing against other members of the family. Pupils always got into trouble if they were late for class, but once Liz and I familiarised ourselves with our timetables and the layout of the school we always managed to arrive on time.

One teacher who would have been very grateful had his whole class been late was Mr Duff – we used to call him *"Plum"*. I vividly remember the day when he was struggling to teach us some geometric theorem or algebraic equation. In sheer exasperation he asked: *"What class is this?"* He was told that we were 1C. Silence followed while he thought for a moment, no doubt remembering that there was also 1D, then he said, *"Don't tell me that there's a class worse than this!"* I do remember some of the class sniggering quietly, but don't think that anyone's feelings were hurt or that either confidence or self-esteem was affected.

I hated Maths and although I can still measure angles correctly, recite some theorems and name the different types of triangles, I found the concept really difficult and gratefully dropped the subject after two years. Phew! In those days Arithmetic was a separate subject. I found the mechanical side very straightforward but intensely disliked the problem side and it took me three attempts to pass the O Grade.

All of the teachers except for those who taught PE, Home Management or Homecraft and Art wore black gowns, which must have kept the wearers snug in the draughty building during the cold winters. But as far as Liz and I were concerned they made the occupants of these habits seem like crows, especially when some were seen hurrying or striding along the corridor with their gowns flapping behind. Mr Henry Philip, the head of the Classics department, known as the *"Wamp"*, bore testimony to that thought. He was very tall and acquired that name because he insisted on pronouncing the letter *"v"* as *"w"*. For some reason the tune of the Ride of the Valkyries was always hummed in relation to the Wamp.

William Eadie the rector, known as *"The Beak"*, was an imposing middle-aged man. He always wore shiny black shoes and under his gown wore a dark suit and white shirt. He had heavy horned rimmed spectacles, a moustache and a head of iron grey hair neatly parted at the left hand side. I don't ever remember him laughing, smiling or sharing a joke with anyone. But he commanded great respect and whenever he entered a classroom everyone, including the teacher, would stand up. His office and those of his two secretaries were behind the double glass doors opposite the galleried wall of the school hall. The senior staff comprised the Rector, the Depute and the Heads of Department. There were no guidance teachers then, only a lady superintendent called Miss Dowson who was one of the music teachers: she dealt with *"girls' matters"*.

I recall that one of the girls came to school with a headscarf on. She'd had a perm and still had the rollers in because her hair hadn't quite set properly. When the bell summoned us to line up she was spotted, given a dressing down, sent home and warned not to return till her hair was sorted. That same girl was later sent home to remove some nail varnish that she'd been seen wearing and also to change into *"sensible shoes"*. On reflection *"girls' matters"* seemed to be concerned with image at that time. I don't know to whom the boys turned if *they* had any problems.

Those pupils in our Primary 7 class who had not passed the *"quali"* were destined for junior secondary. The girls went to Moss-side School which was quite nearby. Both Margaret and Nancy had been former pupils. There they were taught the core subjects of English and Arithmetic and the other subjects such as shorthand, typing and book keeping.

The boys on the other hand were nevertheless educated at Beath High. Their timetable also comprised English and Arithmetic and they were taught in classrooms on the ground floor and *"Techi"* in the workshops in the basement. On reflection, they were probably considered to be at the bottom of the pecking order and where their classrooms were sited reflected this; the basement with its cold stone floor was only visible from the back of the school. There were windows only along that wall, so as a consequence the classrooms were very dim. The *"Techi"* teachers who taught metal work, woodwork and technical drawing were mainly recruited from men who had been joiners, builders, electricians and plumbers. They were all very fierce, shouted a lot and one in particular used to patrol the corridor in his beige coloured dustcoat looking out for miscreants so that he could either give them a row or hone his belting skills.

I clearly remember many of my teachers and also others who didn't teach me. Bizarrely in all of my six years of secondary education I don't remember any of them appearing to age.

The *"Wamp"* AKA Henry Philip was Head of Classics. Every time I saw him striding along the corridor with his black gown flapping I'd hum a few bars of Wagner's Ride of the Valkyries.

"Wee Louis" AKA Mr Marshall was Head of French and he was of small stature. Our French lessons were taught in a room that boasted a trap door. We had a very young teacher, Miss Scott, who found it difficult to keep order. When she turned to write on the blackboard some of the boys – it was always the boys – lifted the trap door lid and disappeared down below. Of course when she turned back to talk to us she noticed that several of them were missing. *"I'm going for Mr Marshall,"* she'd say and, gathering her gown round about her, she'd scurry off. Of course, when she returned with *"Wee Louis"* everyone was back in their seats and writing diligently in their jotters. *"Wee Louis"* occasionally took the lesson. For more than half the period he'd regale us with boyhood tales of fishing from Rothesay pier during his holidays and for the rest of the lesson he taught us French. We actually seemed to learn more that way.

"Ma Broon" was one of the French teachers. Before we left for pastures new some of the boys tacked a kipper under her chair. I'm not sure how much time elapsed before she discovered the shrivelled piscine! But it must have reeked.

Mr Scott taught French and German. He was a kindly man who was very tall with spectacles and a mop of dark wavy hair. He was commonly seen smoking a pipe.

Mr Orr, known as *"Old Joe"*, was the Depute Rector who taught English. He must have had regular ear problems because he always had a piece of cotton wool lodged in one of his ears. One day he came into our class during a reading of Julius Caesar. We'd just reached the part where someone says: *"Oyez, oyez!"* *"Old Joe"* looked around, echoed *"oyez, oyez,"* scratched his head and walked out of the room.

Mr Summers known as *"Scratchie"* was a science teacher. Rumour had it that he had a metal plate at the back of his head. I never discovered the origin of his nickname. Although he was both kind and an entertaining teacher, I abandoned science after two years.

Sybil Wilson taught us geography in one of the huts near the front wall. One day when it was hot and she was looking for something in the cupboard, some of the boys climbed out of the window and crossed the road to the shop on the other side returning later with crisps and ice poles. I don't think that she noticed either the missing boys or the confectionary they had with them on their return.

John Watson was Head of Music. He was a very inspiring man who encouraged all of the pupils he taught. He organised a school choir made up of 4th, 5th and 6th year pupils and a small choir of those doing O' Grade and Higher music. The large choir gave a performance of Gounod's Faust in the Carnegie Hall in Dunfermline and the small choir visited all sorts of places singing excerpts from Die Fledermaus, The Merry Widow, The Gondoliers and many other pieces.

Mrs Winchester taught Homecraft and Home Management. She was very kind and during 6th year when we had a free period we would often go to her room to make scones to have with a cup of tea.

Mr MacNaughton taught History and made the subject come alive. Our Higher group were few in number and so were often in classes with the younger pupils. Once we'd finished off our work he didn't mind us doing other things. I sometimes used to do my sewing or knitting. Ann Brown, the maths teacher, was called *"Annie Broon"*.

The *"Techi"* teacher who patrolled the bottom corridor was known as *"Chinky Chan"*; I can't remember either his real name or how he'd come by that name.

The kindly RE teacher was nicknamed both *"Holy Joe"* and *"Hallelujah Harry"*. I remember being shocked on one occasion when someone had written something unkind about him on the blackboard. He didn't get angry or even ask who did it, he just quietly taught his lesson and I believe afterwards that the culprit apologised.

My school years at Beath High were wonderfully memorable even though I found some subjects impossible. I really enjoyed English, History, Geography and Music. Most weeks Liz and I went regularly to the Youth Club in the local church hall. Margaret, who was a keen Scottish Country dancer, decided that I should learn to dance too. So once a week we went down to a dance class held in the Masonic Hall near the bottom of Stenhouse Street. I think that I was the only teenager there. I asked Liz, but she declined that invitation. The teacher was a very tall man called Charlie Farrell and like *"Plum Duff"* he stood no nonsense. If we failed to carry out his instructions, he'd shake his head despairingly and pass some comment. None of us took offence and we all tried a bit harder. At that time there were neither tapes nor CDs and so the music was provided by a callow youth who played his piano accordion flawlessly. I was truly amazed at the sight of this instrument and struggled to comprehend how anyone could play a keyboard with their right hand and depress buttons with their left and while engaged in this, not even looking at what they were doing.

At the end of second year I opted to take Music as one of my subjects and so it was jointly decided that I should take piano lessons in Dunfermline in one of the rooms at the Carnegie Hall. My teacher was Alice Calder who had at one time studied at the Conservatoire in Vienna. She was a small dynamic lady whose company I really enjoyed. After a few lessons it was decided that my Mum's piano ought to be replaced and Miss Calder was invited to accompany us to Muir's music shop in Dunfermline. A small Challen piano was bought and duly delivered to Stenhouse Street. I loved playing it and practised very hard indeed. I have it to this day though regrettably I don't play much now and am truly ashamed when I think of some of the music that I played all of those years ago.

The rival Margarets

After my Dad and Margaret got married, my relationship with her got more fraught. Although Margaret did her best for me in terms of arranging social activities, buying me nice clothes and cooking my meals, I always felt she talked down to me. I guess this was because she was not my birth mother and she had not had children of her own. She was quite harsh and not very loving. I guess also as an only child and typical teenager I may have seemed ungrateful for all she did for me – and she could not love me unconditionally because she was my Stepmother. Plus she was not really one of those women who cooed over children – she was a businesswoman and she was possibly quite occupied with the responsibility of running her shops.

I also suspect her philosophy of child rearing was twofold, firstly *"spare the rod and spoil the child"* and, like my Aunts Meg and Susan in bygone years, *"children should be seen and not heard."* When I first lived with Margaret, she took a half day off work on Wednesday and used that time to clean the house. Eventually she decided that she'd benefit from some extra help, so she asked one of her regular customers Hetty if she would come to *"do"* at 257 Stenhouse Street.

Hetty was a tall statuesque woman who was great fun and had a wealth of stories to tell. I thoroughly enjoyed her company. She was so easy to talk to and I felt that I was treated as an equal. Hetty would tell me stories about the war, the boyfriends she'd had, the scrapes that she'd got into and lots more. When she'd finished cleaning the house sparkled and so did I.

I remember the day that Margaret went to have all her teeth extracted because she already had a partial denture and the others were beginning to cause some problems. I had gone with my Dad as we were having dental checkups. Mr Reekes, the dentist, put Margaret to sleep with the gas and set to work. The peace was shattered by an assortment of very unusual noises emanating from Margaret in the dental chair and when he'd finished, Mr Reekes immediately fitted her with *"wallies"* (dentures). She spent the rest of the day in bed with her *"wallies"* on the bedside cabinet beside her. I was assigned to make tea that night as cooking was not my Dad's forte. I ought to have felt sorry for her, but instead there and then I resolved to try to keep my own teeth for as long as I could for I had absolutely no desire for *"wallies"*. Lots of people of my generation did have lots of extractions because dental care was not the priority that it should have been.

Margaret's dental health may not have been perfect, but her house was immaculate. It took me a long time to accomplish cleaning the brass and silverware to her satisfaction and there were quite a lot of things to polish. One evening when I was doing this, Margaret scolded me for not doing it properly. I think that I was cleaning a spoon at the time and was really doing my best, however the more she scolded me the more nervous I became as I didn't understand what I was doing wrong. Eventually exasperation got the better of her and she slapped my face soundly with her open palm. My Dad, who had been quietly reading his newspaper stood up and smacked her hand. I clearly remember him telling her: *"Remember she's someone you're bringing up!"*

Stunned and with my poor face stinging, I turned to see two shocked adults, one of whom looked furious while the other appeared very contrite and obviously ashamed of what he'd done. My Dad was a gentle person who never cursed or swore and I had never seen him lose his temper, far less hit anyone. He'd never ever smacked me and while I felt glad that he'd intervened since it cancelled out his non-intervention during the times when I was previously thrashed, and there were quite a few, a guilty feeling slowly spread over me because I felt responsible for having caused the situation in the first place. After what felt like an eternity Margaret turned, went out of the room, took her coat out of the tallboy in the hall and left the house banging the front door behind her. I went out of the room too and my Dad followed. *"Where are you going Margaret?"* he asked me. *"To the toilet,"* I replied. He must have thought that I was going out too. I sat on the storage box that held the bathroom towels for quite a while and thought about what had happened before going back into the living room and finishing off what I'd been doing. I remember hugging my Dad tightly then making him a cup of tea before going off to bed. Margaret did not come home before I fell asleep but she was there in the morning. I simply kept my head down and only spoke when asked a question. I deduced that if I did that, I couldn't get into any more trouble.

The other occasion I vividly recall getting into severe trouble and, this time, it was justified, was when I decided to experiment with my Dad's cigarettes. He carried a packet in his jacket pocket together with his lighter and kept a supply in a cigarette box on a shelf in the living room. I sometimes took one and smoked it, though it made me splutter and cough

– practice makes perfect was my philosophy. Quite a number of people at school smoked too and I guess that I just wanted to try as well. The little shop at the bottom of Stenhouse Street sold *"penny singles",* single cigarettes, but I thought that I'd keep my money and just help myself now and again. After all Nancy had taken one on the morning of my Dad and Margaret's wedding. Unfortunately for me that was my downfall for unbeknown to me, my Dad had noticed that some cigarettes had gone missing, so he kept a tally and did a bit of detective work. One dinnertime, when I went home, Margaret tackled me. I got such a row from her and later from my Dad. Even my Grandpa joined in. I never smoked again until I left home and even then it was only a few and for a limited period.

Once I do remember running away to Aunts Margaret and Nan's house in Aberdour after getting a row from Margaret. I'd no money for the bus fare, so I walked all of the way from Cowdenbeath to Aberdour, a distance of around 6 miles. Aunt Margaret and Aunt Nan were quite shocked, but told me not to worry. They phoned my Dad and he and Margaret came for me later on. Aunt Margaret explained the dangers of walking all of that way on the country roads, but also had a quiet word with my Dad and Margaret. I remember that Aunt Margaret asked me to apologise to them for causing them to worry and I know that, when she talked to me later, she had told them that I needed to know that I was loved so I would feel secure. I don't know how well that went down though and although no more was said about it, I suppose that I hoped that Margaret would have been worried about me and so relieved that I was none the worse for the experience. Instead it felt as if she blamed me for spoiling their Sunday afternoon.

I vividly remember my Dad's golfing friend Jim Hunter getting on to Margaret because of the way she spoke to me. Jim, who worked as a painter and decorator, was a tall, jolly, well-built man with a ruddy complexion and lots of grey curly hair. He put new wallpaper on our living room walls not long after I started at Beath High and after that his wife Mary began visiting too – they were both very funny and they had a daughter Moira who was in my year and who was extremely clever.

One time after Jim heard Margaret scolding me as she often did for something or other he told her in no uncertain terms that she shouldn't speak to me the way she did and that if he heard her doing it again then he wouldn't do any more work for her. It was kind of him, though it really didn't make any difference. Though as I became older my confidence grew and I cautiously began to challenge her.

I eventually took revenge on one occasion when Margaret was changing the winter curtains for summer ones. She put a bucket of water on the floor, together with a chamois leather for cleaning the twelve tiny window panes that made up each frame. A ladder was necessary to reach the top windows and as she stepped down she missed the last rung and her foot ended up in the bucket. Despite my Herculean effort, I couldn't suppress my laughter. After extracting her soaking foot she made to slap me, but this time I was ready for her and ducked. Her second attempt almost succeeded in reaching the target but I got in first and struck her. She reeled in shock, muttered something and handed me the bucket telling me to dispose of the contents. Never again did she ever attempt to strike me.

My teenage years

I remember one particular Christmas as clear as day – I was 13 years old: It's Christmas Eve and the tree stands in the corner, its fairy lights and decorations twinkling brightly. Ever hopeful, I am about to place my stocking carefully on top of a big square box that has been wrapped up in shiny paper. The label on it reads: "To Margaret with love from Aunt Nancy and Uncle Dave." I pick it up, gently shake it, feel it, listen out for any sounds that will identify the contents and then succumb to temptation and carefully open part of one end just enough to see what's inside. It's a Max Factor gift set! There is lipstick, mascara with two tiny brushes, a powder compact, face cream and some clear nail polish. I'm deliriously happy. Aunt Nancy always buys great presents. I carefully re-stick the parcel and put it back where it was and now with my stocking on top. Maybe this year my stocking will be full. Usually most of it is stuffed full of newspaper and when this is removed there's an apple, tangerine and either a halfcrown or a two shilling piece. Hope springs eternal.

I continued to enjoy school and tried my hardest. I recall one evening that my Dad and his friend George went out to visit one of his relatives. When they returned my Dad said that he'd seen a wonderful school report card and had given the owner of this masterpiece half a crown because it was so good. In comparison my report card was not wonderful and while I'd good marks for English, Music, History, Geography, Domestic Science and Home Craft and average for French, my marks for Maths, Science and Arithmetic were abysmal. *"Oh well,"* I thought to myself, *"you can't make a silk purse out of a sow's ear."* I know that in this world there are some people who seem to be good at everything and there were a few of these people at school. They just seemed to grasp concepts so easily and how I envied them at the time. When I told my Aunt Margaret she simply said: *"Well Margaret you can't be good at everything and I love you just the way you are."* I returned this compliment by giving her an enormous hug. This took some doing because my Aunt Margaret was a BIG woman.

When I was fourteen Margaret arranged for me to have a Saturday job in Cuthill's grocery shop. I was allowed to keep what I earned and once it was added to the existing pocket money I was given for drying the dishes, setting the table, polishing my Dad's shoes and cleaning Margaret's brasses and silver fish cutlery, I considered myself to be quite well off.

I remember my days there as if they are happening right now…

It's 8.30am on Saturday and as I open the door of the shop the small brass bell jangles to announce my arrival. *"Mornin' Margaret,"* says Mrs Cuthill from behind the dark polished counter where she's weighing out Demerara sugar into strong brown paper bags, using the shiny brass weights on the balance scales. *"How are ye the day hen?" "Fine",* I reply, as I stand for a few seconds imbibing the wonderful aromas of coffee, cheese and smoked bacon. I hang up my coat on a brass peg in the back room and wash my hands in the small sink. I take my clean blue and white striped apron from the drawer, tie it securely and put my pencil and notepad in the large pocket at the front. Mr Cuthill is already there, collecting cardboard boxes for the grocery orders. *"Hello hen,"* he says. *"Will ye tak some o' they boxes ben the shop and ye can start makin up the oarders?"*

Mr Cuthill packs these into his van and delivers them to the customers who either phone or come in to the shop with a list. One of my jobs is to collect the items, pack them in the boxes and add up the total cost which Mrs Cuthill checks. I nod and carry several through, my gaze lingering over the walls lined with shelves that are packed with tins of soup, vegetables, ham and sock eye salmon, bottles of vinegar, sauces, juices, and jars of preserves and a cornucopia of sweets.There are already six orders and if I'm quick I'll be able to do the first one before the shop opens at 9am. Now let me see: Poonakandy tea, ground coffee and I'm allowed to grind the beans – I love the sound they make; like hailstones as I pour them into the blender, Heinz Tomato soup, Baxters Royal Game soup, Keillor's Orange Marmalade, a Plain half loaf, carrots, cabbage, a neep (turnip), Kerr's Pink potatoes, thick cut bacon, eggs, cheese, Hampden wafers – I wonder if there'll be any broken ones because I'm allowed to eat them – tomato sauce, a packet of "Spangles" (sweets), Lux soap flakes for washing woollies, Rinso washing powder, Wright's coal tar soap, Izal toilet paper, which I hate because it's so smooth, slippy and uncomfortable, and 40 Senior Service unfiltered cigarettes.
By 8.55am I have everything in the box, except for the cheese and bacon. I'm not allowed to use either the cheese wire or the bacon slicer in case I cut myself and I shudder when I think of my Grandpa's missing fingers.

The job is both interesting and fascinating because of the variety of tasks. I ensure that there is an adequate stock of a variety of paper bags in which to put foods including rice, sugar and the loose biscuits that are kept in tins with clear glass lids. I sweep the floor, replenish the shelves from the storeroom at the back, pack bags and help to serve the customers. Their bills are totalled on notepads because the large brass coloured cash register at the end of the counter doesn't have an addition facility. At the end of each Saturday my heart is full of pride when I receive the wee brown envelope containing my wage.

I had that job for a year until my Dad and Margaret decided that I should help my Grandpa on Saturday mornings because his health had begun to deteriorate. A lifetime of working in the mines had left him with silacosis – a lung condition caused by the continuous inhalation of silica dust that causes massive fibroids in the lungs and leads to breathing difficulties. In addition, he was showing early signs of dementia and, because of this, he now had a Home Help each weekday morning. Although I was disappointed to leave Cuthill's, I didn't really mind for I loved my Grandpa dearly and we'd often sit together on the moquette settee while he sang and told me lots of stories, all of which I'd heard many times before.

In the autumn of 1961 and, not long after we'd started our 4th year, Liz became very ill. She caught a cold from which she'd found it impossible to recover and was rushed to hospital. There after some painful lumbar punctures, pleurisy was diagnosed. With rest and medication she slowly began to recover, but it was many weeks before she was allowed home. I was really worried about Liz because she'd never been ill before. I don't think that she'd ever been in hospital until then. I missed my very best friend so much and went to visit her with her Mum and Dad as often as I could. I'd also call at her house after tea and spend some time talking to them and so it was that I went to the youth club by myself and, though there were other friends who went there too, I really missed not having Liz's company there and back, and *"chap door run"* was impossible to carry out as a singleton. In November of that year and just a few days before my 15th birthday, the accordionist from the dancing class came to the club. We found ourselves chatting to each other during the evening and when it was time to leave he walked all of the way home with me and shook my hand at my gate. During the evening I discovered that he'd been the recipient of my Dad's half crown. I felt amazingly happy and really looked forward to seeing him at school. He was in a different class for English, French, Geography and Arithmetic and in neither of the other subjects for which I'd opted – Music and History – because he was taking Maths, Greek and Latin. His name was Dennis Deas and over the next few years our friendship grew and blossomed and we spent a great deal of time together.

Another good friend was Adele. We'd got to know each other from being in the same class for English. Adele lived in the nearby village of Kelty with her parents and younger brother Alan. Her Dad was Italian and owned the local garage and her two uncles had the café in the Main Street. It sold the most delicious fish and chips and Italian ice cream. When she was better Liz and I sometimes went to visit at the weekend. Her mum and dad Mary and John were always very pleased to see us and made us very welcome.

When she was sixteen, Adele was given a scooter and she often used this mode of transport to come to school rather than the bus. One day when she was returning home, she had an accident with an oncoming car and broke her femur. Poor Adele was in plaster for weeks. I don't remember how long she was absent from school but it seemed a very long time.

The School Trip

Towards the end of 1961 all of the 4th year pupils were given the opportunity to go on a school trip to Italy during the Easter holidays. We were to travel to Dover, take the ferry to Calais and then travel to Italy by the type of train that had couchettes (sleeping bunks) on board. Quite a number of us were allowed to go including Liz, Adele and Dennis, my new boyfriend. It was a very exciting prospect and would give us all a welcome break from studying for the new O' Grade exams that the Scottish Exam Board had introduced. Our classes of 1962 were to be the guinea pigs.

There must have been about seventy pupils on the school trip and I recall the presence of *"Wee Louis"*, Mr Scott, *"The Wamp"* together with his wife and six-year-old daughter. I remember her being extremely knowledgeable and thinking to myself that, just like Mozart, she was a child prodigy!

We travelled to London by train and spent our first night in a hostel. Dennis took me to Penge to meet his oldest brother Tom, his wife Catriona and Vicky, their new baby girl. It was a lovely evening. Liz and I shared a room with Adele and a girl called Gillian. Before Liz went to bed she washed her socks and knickers in the sink. We all fell asleep quite quickly and I dreamed of waterfalls. All of a sudden I woke and jumped up in bed still hearing the water. Liz had left the tap on and the water was almost at the top of the sink! I turned it off and breathed a sigh of relief. Had I not woken up there definitely would have been a waterfall. Liz never did that again – at least not on that holiday.

The next morning after breakfast we set off for Dover. I don't remember how we travelled there, but the short ferry journey was unforgettable. The weather was cold, squally and rainy. Quite a number of girls and boys had by this time become couples, so sat on the deck holding on to each other tightly and not just because they were experiencing young love! Rather it was from a basic sense of self-preservation because, unlike Liz and I, they didn't have good sea legs and consequently suffered quite badly from mal-de-mer. Their once happy excited faces became chalk white as they shivered in the cold, clutching their sick bags and desperately scanning the horizon for a glimpse of the French coast.

From Calais we took the train to Rome, where we were to be based. A local bus had been booked to take us on tours of both the city and other sightseeing places. Our accommodation was in a pension and I remember having ham and cheese for breakfast. On our first evening there, Adele was given permission to go out by herself. I believe that she lost her way and returned much later and in tears.

Each morning we'd all board the bus and set off to different places. In Rome we went to Vatican Square and into St Peter's Cathedral. I marvelled at the sight. It was so big and breathtakingly beautiful. Never before had I been in such a huge church. I remember the markings on the floor to show how big it was in comparison to Westminster Abbey, St Paul's Cathedral and Notre Dame. I thought of Paul Gallico's fictional story, The Small Miracle, a story of Pepino, the wee boy, and his donkey Violetta, who became dangerously ill. He wanted to take her into the tomb of St Francis of Assisi – the Patron Saint of animals because he firmly believed that if he did that she'd get better and regain her lost smile. No matter how many times he was rebuffed by the authorities he didn't give up and eventually managed to be granted an audience with the Pope. The thought of this small ragged village boy finding his way to this enormous city and to the Pope himself filled me with awe.

We also went to see the white Victor Immanuel Monument or the Wedding Cake as it is known, the Forum or the Roman market place of ancient Rome and the enormous Colosseum where contests between Christians, lions and other contestants were held. As I stood in the middle of the arena, I thought about the terrifying experience that awaited the combatants as they emerged from underground and into the light to the cheers and jeers of the spectators. It was a horrific thought.

Later our route took us down the Amalfi coast where we marvelled at the turquoise blue water that looked so inviting. We went to Capri where we met Gracie Fields.

She was a famous singer who'd also sung for the troops during the Second World War. Some of the class were photographed with her, but unfortunately neither Liz, nor Adele or I were. We visited the ruins of Pompei, the small town near Naples. It was buried under thousands of tons of ash from the volcano Mount Vesuvius when it erupted in AD79.

Gracie Fields

Although Vesuvius has not erupted since 1944 it is said to be the world's most dangerous volcano and three million people now live within 20 miles of it.

One day on our travels, we stopped at a factory that made and sold distinctive cameo jewellery, Dennis bought me a cameo pendant that sadly, I no longer have. On another day we went shopping and I bought Margaret a large brown leather bag which she used for years afterwards. I bought myself a wee leather duffel bag that I also used for years afterwards.

We had a fantastic time and all too soon the trip ended and we travelled back home. The sea crossing was calm this time and when we reached the train station we all said our goodbyes to each other knowing that the next time we met we'd be back at school and soon in the exam room. Margaret met me from the train. Despite everything, I was so very pleased to see her and gave her a big hug. She seemed very pleased to see me too. I secretly hoped that she'd missed me. It had been a lovely holiday, but it was so nice to be home especially as my Dad and Grandpa were delighted to see me.

The weekend before the O' Grades began, Margaret rented a caravan that was berthed at Leven. I think that the first exam was on the Monday morning and that was a Bank Holiday. It was the dreaded Arithmetic, my least favourite subject, and my Dad took me there and brought me back. I didn't enjoy the experience. Exams have always made me extremely nervous and I often wonder how I managed to pass those that I did. I guess that they have to be given to test the candidate's ability under pressure. Anyway I coped with the five other exams and crossed my fingers for the results.

Liz took five exams instead of seven because she had missed so much school due to illness. She passed them all and her Dad was so proud. Dennis passed all seven of his, of course. And I passed four of my six subjects and had to carry Arithmetic and French into 5th year. I was pleased that I'd passed English, History, Geography and Music, and decided that I'd do Higher English and History in 5th year along with the two resits of French and Arithmetic. My plan was to then do Higher Music, Higher Geography and O' Grade Home Management in 6th year.

Dennis

Dennis and I spent lots of time together and he greatly helped me with my schoolwork. His parents, Ina and Tom, made me very welcome. They were really lovely people who seemed genuinely interested in others and his dad, who was a skilled slater and plasterer, kept a wonderful prize-winning garden, rivalling Liz's Dad's garden. Dennis bought me a copy of Chaucer's Canterbury Tales for my 16th birthday. He copied out *all* of my Higher History notes for me – there were no photocopiers or printers then and it was no mean feat to copy out two fat jotters of Mr McNaughton's notes, one of Scottish history and one of European. In 6th year, he copied excerpts for me on manuscript paper for my Higher Music. I still have them.

One Christmas he gave me a large rectangular box that at one time might have contained a shirt or similar article. I opened it to find that it was crammed full of goodies. I can't recall everything but distinctly remember there was a ceramic bracelet, which I still wear, a pair of seamed stockings and a small chocolate umbrella. Once for a birthday he bought me a bottle of Chanel no 5. I felt really special.

One summer Margaret, my Dad and I spent a week at Stonefield Castle Hotel in Argyll. It certainly lived up to its name and looked like a picturesque castle in beautiful grounds. Dennis bought a special pen and wrote two letters in lovely italic handwriting, which he posted to me there. It was wonderful to go down to breakfast and find a letter addressed to Miss Margaret Campbell, Stonefield Castle Hotel, Loch Fyne, Tarbert, in the green baize letter rack.

One day during the holidays Dennis came to the house. Hetty was cleaning and so we stopped for a cup of tea and a chat. Quite by chance Margaret's car drew up and she got out. I suspected that I would get into trouble because I was supposed to be helping Hetty. Then I had a bright idea. *"Go upstairs,"* I said, *"and hide under my bed!"* Well Dennis took to his heels and ran as fast as he could and just made it in the nick of time! Margaret bustled in and started giving me a row for something or other then stayed for a bit talking to Hetty. Eventually she left, although poor Dennis had no idea. So when Hetty crept upstairs and looked under my bed he got such a fright that he nearly fainted. We had such a good laugh afterwards. These are memories that remain undimmed.

These school years were great fun and I have so many happy memories, like the time the buttons on my suspenders flew off causing both of my nylon stockings to roll down to my ankles. There was the time when it was raining heavily so we couldn't play hockey and Miss Nicolson the PE teacher wasn't there. Somehow I found myself at the front of the class telling them the story of Goldilocks in an American accent. I recall that it was well received and when Miss Nicolson returned just towards the end she seemed to also enjoy it. There was the time Mr Watson's whole school choir was practising Gounod's Faust for the Christmas concert in the Carnegie Hall. While he was conducting or beating time he would always sing: *"Ya pa pop a."* He would repeat this several times. However, on this occasion he sang what should have been: *"Sitting at ease there we abide."* But instead he sang: *"Shitting at ease there we abide."* There was silence followed by sniggers, then uproarious laughter. Some things are never forgotten.

An unexpected phone call

One Saturday night in 1963 and not long after I'd gone to bed I heard the phone ring. It was unusual to have a late call and I heard my Dad answer it. About ten minutes later he came into my room and told me that he and Margaret were going over to her brother John's house because he had become very ill. I think that was the first time that I had been left in the house by myself at night. I assured him that I'd be fine and settled back to read the next chapter of my book. Half an hour later Dave and Nancy came to the door. She was crying hysterically. I told them that Margaret and my Dad had already left. I found out the next morning that John had a heart attack and died very suddenly. He was only in his mid-forties. It was very sad because he was well loved by everyone who knew him.

There were lots of visits to his house because Betty, his widow, needed support to help with the arrangements. One day before his funeral, I went over with Margaret and my Dad. The sitting room door was ajar and John's coffin was on the floor by the front window. Although I must have been sixteen at the time, I had never seen a coffin before. For some reason I was not upset by this sight. Margaret, however, was quite shocked. She shut the door and told me very sharply to go into the wee sitting room at the back of the house. I guess that it was her way of trying to protect me, although it was unnecessary. I do think that at that time many adults tried to shield their children from the inevitable cycle of life. Given the circumstances, it was inevitable that I wasn't allowed to go to his funeral. I believe it was very well attended because he had a wide circle of friends.

And of course I wasn't privy to any information concerning his will, but as far as I can remember his widow Betty was the main beneficiary. At the time of his death John owned a half share of the business and therefore Betty was entitled to this. I recall my Dad and Margaret discussing the terms of his will. Margaret had seven years in which to repay his share to Betty. My Dad who was aged 53 then made the decision to take early retirement from the National Coal Board. Although he had very secure employment as the area wages accountant, he joined Margaret's business to help repay this money. I don't think that he made the decision lightly but it coincided with talk about his department being scheduled to transfer from Lochgelly to Alloa. This town was quite some distance away and would have involved a great deal more travelling.

At his retiral event he was presented with lovely cards and gifts, one of which was a screen for showing cine films. He had recently bought a cine camera and so this was a perfect gift. When he returned home and showed us he was clearly upset by the occasion, the kind words, the cards and genuine tributes paid to him for, though he was a quiet unassuming man, he was very well liked and could always be depended upon. I always remember that Margaret seemed very non-plussed about it, simply giving the gifts a cursory glance before going into the kitchen to make tea.

Aunt Margaret and Aunt Nan

I was always curious to know about Aunt Margaret's sister Nancy, of whom she never spoke. I once met her by chance when I was about twelve or thirteen. I was with my Stepmother, and my Great Aunt Susan, with whom I'd stayed in Edinburgh. She had come to visit us all; she was very fond of my Grandpa, and we had walked from Leven over the dunes to Lundin Links. As we passed all of the beautiful stone built houses, I noticed one that had peeling paint on the windows and a garden gate that needed attention. I can't remember walking up the path but I do recall a lady rushing out of the gate towards us. As she got nearer, I thought that it was Aunt Margaret and I wondered why she was there. I was ignored as the lady ran into the outstretched arms of Aunt Susan and the pair of them hugged each other tightly. I fleetingly wished that Aunt Susan had shown that level of affection to me when I stayed with her. I can't recall how my Stepmother and she greeted each other, but what I do remember is being sworn to secrecy with the stern words from Aunt Susan: *"Dinnae tell yer Auntie Margaret"*. And I didn't until many years later.

During my teenage years I enjoyed visiting Aunt Margaret and her Mum, Aunt Nan, in their home in Aberdour. Aunt Nan was often bedridden – I think she had rheumatism and a weak heart. At least her room overlooked the back garden and the rolling hills. Around the time that she died, my Aunt Meg, with whom I had lived in Edinburgh, also died. After this, my Aunt Susan went to stay with Aunt Margaret. From these two bereavements came a new lease of life for Aunts Margaret and Susan.

By 1963 Aunt Margaret learned to drive, passed her driving test at the first attempt, bought a Volkswagen camper van and took early retirement, ready for an adventure. By this time her cousin George had sold his photography business in Edinburgh and moved to Ullapool with his wife Bunty and their two miniature Shetland collies Misty and Blaze, who were amazingly good at dribbling a football with their noses. Sonny and Bunty bought Rivendell, a beautiful house on the shores of Loch Broom with glorious views towards the Summer Isles and Beinn Ghobhlach.

After a visit to George and Bunty, Aunt Margaret decided that she would do likewise and so she sold the house in Aberdour. She bought Tigh-na-Drochaid (meaning house of the bridge). It was a house by the river with an adjoining cottage on Old Moss Road in Ullapool where she offered dinner and Bed and Breakfast as well as renting out the cottage, initially to Patrick and Vernon who worked locally. Later when they married their girlfriends and moved away she rented it out to those guests who wanted to self cater. She also adopted Vernon's golden Labrador called Butch. This greatly surprised me because she had always been very wary of dogs. Aunt Susan's last few years there were some of the happiest of her long life. She passed away peacefully in the Royal National Infirmary by the River Ness in Inverness.

During the summer holidays I'd often spend a couple of weeks in Ullapool with my Aunt Margaret. I really looked forward to and relished these times. In the evenings we'd usually play board games such as Monopoly and Careers. I'd take Butch for a walk while she went to the hairdresser for a shampoo and set. We'd sometimes go out in the camper van for a picnic, sometimes to Conon Bridge to buy fresh raspberries and strawberries for her to make jam and sometimes for a treat we'd have fish and chips from the local chip shop. Aunt Margaret's house was always busy because she had lots of friends and visitors. There was always a lot of clutter and I smile when I remember how she'd simply lift the pile of whatever and put it somewhere else to allow a visitor to sit down.

My last two years in Fife

In May 1963 we sat our Fifth year exams in the school hall of the nearby Ballingry High School and travelled there by bus on exam days. I can't remember the reason for this and can only imagine that Beath High School hall wasn't big enough to accommodate everyone.

Although I had done a lot of preparation I still felt nervous especially about my re sit of Arithmetic. I clearly remember heaving a sigh of relief on the journey home after the English exam and was discussing the literature paper with Dennis. One of the questions I'd chosen was from Chaucer's Canterbury Tales and I related my answer in great detail. To my horror, he told me that I'd answered it wrongly. My euphoria quickly evaporated and changed to extreme worry. Although Dennis did his best to reassure me it was to no avail. To this day I can clearly recall the countless times on which I endeavoured to count up the marks I might have scored hoping that there would be enough to give me a pass mark. After all I'd scored over 60% in the prelim.

After our summer holiday in the Isle of Man, Dennis's sister Betty was married and I went to the wedding. I had a lovely blue and white two-piece costume – a suit in today's parlance. It was the very latest Twist Suit – the skirt was tight to the hips then flared to just above the knee. It was given that name because the latest dance was the Twist. I think that folk expended more energy doing that dance than they perhaps do nowadays at the gym. To complete my outfit I wore a pair of blue patent leather high heels and carried a matching handbag. I bought these myself from saving up my pocket money. I don't remember a great deal about the wedding except for Margaret and my Dad's friend Isa objecting to where she had been seated.

The next day Dennis had an upset stomach. His mum phoned me the following day and asked me to come down to the house. When I arrived she told me that he'd been taken off to hospital because he was so very ill. We were all very upset and when I told my Dad and Margaret, it was arranged that I should go down to stay with Margaret's cousin in Malvern – far, far away. On reflection I think that she arranged this in case anything dreadful was to happen to poor Dennis. I remember not wanting to go, but feeling that I really didn't have the energy for any arguments. As far as I was concerned she'd always win the contest.

When I returned a couple of weeks later Margaret told me that she'd heard that Dennis had passed away. This was completely untrue. He was kept in isolation and I remember one evening going with his parents in his Dad's work lorry to Cameron Bridge Hospital at Windygates, which was quite a distance away. We were not allowed to go inside, but had to content ourselves with standing outside and talking to him from an upstairs window. He was really so pleased to see everyone. Like Liz he was in hospital for quite some time and convalesced at home for a short time after he was discharged.

When the exam results arrived, I found that I hadn't done very well at all. I passed the History but narrowly failed my English; I gained a compensatory O' grade, which meant that I'd scored between 45% and 49%. I felt so ashamed and a real failure. Mr Hunter, my teacher, who'd greatly encouraged me, told me not to worry. He submitted an appeal because I'd scored over 60% in my prelim. I'll never forget his kindness to me on the day he told me that the appeal had been unsuccessful. He sat beside me and put his arm around my shoulders while telling me that it had been rejected; I don't think that would have been possible nowadays. He seemed to me to be doing the thing that came naturally. Although disappointed, I sincerely thanked him for his efforts and said that I'd pass next time. And I did.

It was a relief when Dennis was better. But Margaret began passing remarks about my relationship with Dennis and began to try to discourage it. For a long time I disregarded her. By this time we were in Sixth Year and were busy studying for our second year of Highers and Sixth year Studies. Our small choir went out regularly entertaining people of different age groups and was always well received. I remember that before one concert I twisted my ankle badly when I tripped going down a narrow stair. However, once I'd had it heavily bandaged, I managed to sing quite heartily with the others.

Besides the concerts Dennis and I went regularly to the cinema and sometimes at the weekends visited places in Edinburgh such as the Castle, the Canongate, Scott's Monument and the Planetarium. We shared a common interest in music – classical, jazz, folk and the latest hits from the charts. One time he came to our house for tea and another time we went to Aberdour with my Dad and Margaret and took the boat over to the little island in the Firth of Forth on which Inchcolm Abbey stands. I remember that Dennis was very impressed when my Dad paid for everyone. I think that I must have just taken it for granted that that was what everyone would do.

As well as the accordion, Dennis played the piano very well. Sometimes after school we'd go to the local Italian café and drink hot blackcurrant juice. At Christmas our Youth Club went out carol singing on the cold frosty nights before Christmas, the light from the street lamps illuminating our *"hoary"* breath (breath that looks like steam because of the cold air). Ron Ferguson, who lived further up the street, and who later became the leader of the Iona Community, was part of the group. Another one of our number called Jim played the violin and before we sang each carol someone would say, *"Give us an A Jim,"* and Jim duly obliged.

Liz, Adele and I had girls' nights in when we listened to the latest hit songs from the charts – Liz was quite convinced that she was going to marry Cliff Richard and positively swooned when Living Doll was played on the radio.

Over time Margaret's discouragement about my relationship with Dennis really began to grate.

The elite School Choir Beath High School
Boy friend Dennis is top right top row and I'm in front on the left.

I felt she was pressurising me so I thought that maybe I ought to spend time pursuing other interests. One Sunday night in March 1964 I told Dennis that I wanted to do my own thing. I really did hope that we could still be friends. I remember going over to Liz's house afterwards. I know he was devastated for a very long time as we spent the last few months of 6th year going our separate ways.

After the Easter holidays in 1964 a new Beath High School building was opened and I went there during my last couple of months at school. At this point the school was split, with the old building becoming the lower school and subsequently commonly referred to as Old Beath, whilst the modern school was referred to as New Beath. The old building was demolished in the nineties and in 2003 New Beath itself was closed due to subsidence and a new school funded by PFI was built.

I took the last of my exams in the New Beath building. I was retaking my Higher English and O' Grade Arithmetic (for the third time) and taking Higher Music and O' Grade Home Management. I loved all of these subjects with the marked exception of Arithmetic. Mr Hunter supported me superbly in English, Music was just great, while Home Management was a blessed relief. For the practical part of the exam I recall making a cheese soufflé and a pineapple upside down cake, both of which turned out perfectly. The examiner was a kindly lady, who after tasting both of my dishes, commented: *"Well the folk who are having this will be extremely lucky!"* I was just thrilled.

I went to the new Beath High to take the final four exams except for the practical parts of the Higher Music and Home Management. I took these in the old building. The New Beath High was very light and airy in comparison. This was my last chance. If I didn't pass English and Arithmetic I wouldn't be eligible for the teacher training course that I desperately wanted to do at either Moray House in Edinburgh or Dundee College of Education. I had finally decided that that was the career that I wanted to follow and so before each exam I breathed deeply, read the paper thoroughly then first of all tackled the questions that I was confident about answering before going on to complete the others that I was less certain about. I remembered that advice and many years later passed it on to my own children.

A Fitting End

A break in tradition meant that the last prize giving ceremony was not held at the usual venue of Guthrie Memorial Church, but in the hall of the New Beath High School. Since space was at a premium no parents were allowed to attend. However they hadn't reckoned with Tom Deas, who decided that this rule simply couldn't apply to *him*. After all, his youngest son Dennis was the school Dux and Tom decided that nothing and no one was going to prevent him from attending. Since Tom knew the school janitor well he knew he'd be allowed in. Dressed in his work clothes and with cement dust on his face he drove up to the school in his work lorry. When Dennis went up to collect his awards and looked around at the sea of faces, pupils and teachers he saw his extremely proud Dad beaming broadly. Dennis Deas is the last name on that Dux board.

That summer of 1964 was interesting. The Labour party swept to power with Harold Wilson as the Prime Minister. Liz, Adele and I spent the first two weeks unwinding and then Adele went to help her uncle in his shop, while Liz got a job in the local paper shop. Meanwhile, I decided to go further afield. So along with my friend Doreen, whom I'd got to know in my 6th year English class, I went to work in The Stewart Hotel in Scarborough for the summer. Just exactly how we came to that decision I don't know, but we did and so The Next Great Adventure was about to begin.

Chapter 3: The Next Great Adventure

I slung my bag on my back, took to my heels and fearing for my life ran towards the gate. Glancing quickly over my shoulder I saw the black and white Border Collie, that was gaining on me. My teeth were chattering, my heart was pounding and my fingers were numb with cold. This was not what I had expected when I took a holiday job as a Postie.

Somehow I managed to negotiate the catch on the gate and escape before the dog could pounce and bite into me with its terrifying teeth. Waves of relief swept over me as I took a few deep breaths and went on my way. I had two streets to deliver mail to before my post round was finished for the day. And within 24 hours I had to find a way of evading this terrifying beast...

Summer, Sun and a Job

"Now Margaret, don't you start to smoke!" This was my Dad's warning as he hugged me and put me on a bus in St Andrew's Square in Edinburgh, heading 200 or so miles south to Scarborough with my friend Doreen.

It was the summer of 1964 and we were 17. We had just finished school and were on our first adult adventure – to work at a seaside hotel.

Of course, my Dad's words weren't heeded for long. We'd already mostly surreptitiously experimented with tobacco and we knew that in Scarborough there would be little chance of anyone we knew seeing us engaged in this pastime and mentioning it to our families.

We were young women after all. A few months earlier my school friends had applied for teacher training college. While Liz had been unconditionally accepted for Dundee, Doreen and I received conditional acceptances. My friend Adele had been conditionally accepted for Home Management at Edinburgh's *"Dough School"*. These acceptances were on condition that we passed our Higher English and that I passed my dreaded 'O' Grade arithmetic. There were a lot of limbs and digits crossed. But we must have had great faith in ourselves because none of us had even considered what alternatives there were had we not gained the required results. I have no idea why Doreen and I decided to spend July, August and part of September in Scarborough, though I think that both of us wanted to be far away when the exam results were sent out, just in case.

Doreen had the most incredible blue eyes and wispy strawberry blonde hair. She had a younger sister and twin brothers, who were always referred to as *"the twins"* and the family lived in the nearby pit village of Lochgelly.

Most teachers would have been familiar with the village of Lochgelly for it was here that the belt, otherwise known as the *"tawse"* or even *"the Lochgelly"* was made. Robert Philp, a local ironmonger and saddler, at the request of his son, a local teacher, invented it in 1885. It became the instrument of torture that most teachers kept in their desk drawer. It was regularly used, not only for the punishment of bad behaviour but as a teaching aid, in particular for instances of forgetfulness and inattention.

Many years later two mothers raised an action in the European Court of Human Rights. One of them, Jane Cosens, had a 15-year-old son Jeffrey who attended my old school, Beath High School. He was due to be strapped by the Assistant Headteacher for attempting to take a forbidden shortcut to school through a graveyard. He refused the belt and was suspended from school. In 1982 the court found in favour of the two mothers. After that landmark ruling, the use of the tawse was gradually phased out across Scotland.

Fair Scarborough

I don't remember much about the long journey to Scarborough, though I expect that both of us chatted, read books and magazines, ate and drank and slept fitfully to pass the time – we may even have had a few cigarettes when the bus stopped for comfort breaks. When we arrived it did not take long for us to buy a box of what we considered quite sophisticated Peter Stuyvesant menthol cigarettes. These were tucked away in my green leather handbag to be taken on afternoon outings on the pier and in the odd evening out to a bar.

I don't remember how we got to The Stewart Hotel at St Nicholas Cliff. But I do recall that every building in that street was either a hotel or guesthouse. The Stewart Hotel was a narrow white building that stood in the middle of a terrace. It was directly opposite the Grand Hotel. At the bottom of the short road was the promenade and beyond that stretched the North Sea. The Scarborough air was very breezy to say the least. Baltic is a fine word for it.

Back in 1964 the Stewart Hotel was owned and managed by a middle-aged couple called Clifford and Jessie Poskitt (nee Stewart). We were told that they had named the hotel after her. Initially they seemed a pleasant couple and made us feel very welcome. Although once we started to work, we were often treated very sternly and off-handedly.

On arrival we were shown up to a compact attic room with a low sloping ceiling and a single window facing the imposing brick façade of the Grand Hotel. When I craned my neck to the left, I could see one of the main streets, while the other direction afforded a view down to the promenade and the sea.

The furnishings were sparse. There were two single beds against the back wall with a bedside cabinet and small lamp in between, a small wardrobe for clothes on the wall opposite the window and a large mirror with a shelf underneath on the wall opposite the beds and beside the door. The only other furniture was a small chest of drawers and two rickety chairs.

Once we'd unpacked our cases we went downstairs to be shown round, given our duties and meet the only other member of staff – a plump, middle-aged Spanish lady called Maria. She spoke no English and neither Doreen nor I spoke any Spanish. However, we would all manage to communicate by visual means. Over time Maria, Doreen and I would learn some words and phrases of each others' mother tongue. We had great fun teaching her phrases such as: *"It's a braw, bricht, moonlicht nicht the nicht" (It's a nice bright moonlight night tonight); "Jist a wee deoch an doris" (Just a small drink before leaving);* and, *"Och aye the noo!" (Yes just now)!* Sometimes Maria would come out for walks with us. She was a really homely person and as we got to know her better it felt as if she was a favourite aunt.

On our first day Clifford Poskitt took us to a local shop that sold uniforms for schools, shops and hotels. The interior, with its dark wood counters, shelves and glass trays, strongly reminded me of my Stepmother Margaret's larger shop. In fact, it even smelt similar. He bought us the frilly aprons, caps and sleeve protectors, which we would be required to wear when we were serving meals. Doreen and I had already been told to bring black skirts and white blouses with us.

As far as I can remember, the hotel was on five floors. One of these was a basement where the laundry was done. The kitchen, stillroom and sinks for washing the dishes were on the ground floor along with the reception area, dining room and lounge. There were bedrooms of various sizes on the first and second floors and the attic accommodation comprised our small bedroom and a separate bathroom.

I think that most of the guests booked for full board: breakfast, lunch and high tea. Our various jobs were to set the tables, serve meals, clear away, wash the glasses and cutlery while Maria washed the rest – the crockery, cooking pans and kitchen utensils. I think that she also helped to prepare vegetables while Clifford Poskitt did most of the cooking. He was plump, of medium height and had slicked back iron-grey hair. He wore checked chef's trousers and white jacket. His wife Jessie, as I recall, had a weak heart and so did very light duties such as looking after the dining room, thus ensuring that everything was *"just so"*. She also made small talk with the guests. I vividly remember that she had beautiful platinum coloured curly hair and that her nails which were exquisitely manicured were always painted a bright shade of red.

After we'd cleared away the breakfast things we had to make or change the beds, dust the furniture and clean the bathrooms. We had one day off per week. The remuneration for these labours was £4 per week. However, we were allowed to keep any tips we received from satisfied guests and often these amounted to the same or slightly more than our wages. We thought it only fair to give Maria a share of the money because she worked very hard too and was rarely seen above stairs by the guests. I decided to open a savings account with the Yorkshire Penny Bank, in which I saved my wages. I spent some of my tips. After we'd been working for a month, our weekly wages were increased to £4 and 10 shillings (£4.50 in today's currency)!

Every morning we had to rise very early to serve breakfast and the work seemed unending. Each afternoon we had a few hours grace before it was time to serve tea. Sometimes we went out for walks to the shops, the promenade or the swimming pool. At other times if we were really tired we'd go upstairs for either a nap or to read. The change of work coupled with the sea air meant that we slept really soundly each night.

At the end of July, a family friend of the Poskitts, also called Margaret, came to help as the hotel always became busier in August. She was a few years older than Doreen and me and I think had finished her university course. Margaret helped with cooking and did some housekeeping tasks. She also came out with us regularly.

We'd come to Scarborough as two fairly naive and slim school leavers. But the long hours coupled with walking what felt like miles each day made us feel constantly hungry or, at least think we were. If there were any leftovers from breakfast or cakes from tea-time, then we'd take them. As a consequence we did a great deal of eating and thus gained quite a bit of weight.

Early one August morning, as Doreen and I were coming downstairs to serve breakfast, my Dad phoned. He was very excited and told me that I had passed all of my exams. Then he added: *"Do you remember what I promised you?"* I'd actually forgotten that I'd been promised a record player if I passed everything. It was very exciting and I hugged myself with joy – I'd fulfilled my ambition.

Then I turned round to see Doreen ashen faced and close to tears.

"I've failed," she cried: *"My Mum hasn't phoned me!"* Chastened, I did my best to reassure her, but she was inconsolable. So I offered to serve all of the breakfasts while she went back upstairs. Later in the morning she received the call she'd been awaiting. So after lunch we went out to celebrate and I bought my first LP – the Beatles album A Hard Day's Night. What a relief it was to know that for the time being our immediate futures were settled.

That same day I got a telegram from Alice Calder, my old music teacher. She was absolutely delighted and told me that I was to come in to visit anytime and should play a Chopin waltz for her. How I wish I could still do that as fluently as I used to.

Our summer in Scarborough was quite a useful induction to student life. For the first time in our lives we were responsible for our own actions. Sometimes we went to the local dance hall and twisted and gyrated to the music of the Beatles, the Kinks, the Rolling Stones, Cliff Richard and the Shadows and the Beach Boys, meeting others our age and having a laugh. Although we weren't yet 18, we sometimes went for a drink. I remember that one night I had more than I should have and was very sick afterwards. Doreen was very kind and looked after me. The next day I had a BAD headache. It was a lesson learned.

One afternoon, while in town, we found a sign on a building advertising a fortune-teller. We both went inside and waited our respective turns to have our palms read. I think that it cost each of us half a crown (twelve and a half pence). We were very careful not to give away any information. I was told that I was going to work with either small children or animals, that I was going to marry someone who was tall and with a lean chin and that I'd have two girls and a boy. One of the girls would be good at maths, the boy would be musical while the other girl would not really excel at anything. I can't remember anything else or indeed what she told Doreen but I do remember that I left thinking that if what the lady had told me came true, then my future would be quite exciting.

Shortly after our exam results a boy named Derek whom I'd gone out with a few times before I left school wrote to me and came to Scarborough for a fortnight's holiday with his cousin Billy. He had just left school and had been accepted for an accountancy course. Doreen and I spent quite a lot of our free time going out as a foursome and we had great fun dancing, going to the cinema and to cafes. The fortnight raced past and after they left it was back to the grind again.

The last few weeks went by rapidly and all too soon it was time for Doreen to return home, a week ahead of me. I suddenly realised how much *I* was missing *my* home and felt very alone. I remember really wanting to return to my house, sleep in my own bed, in my own room and meet up with the rest of my friends.

In desperation I phoned home. But there was no answer. So I phoned my Stepmother's sister Nancy. I explained how homesick I was and asked her if she'd give me permission to return because I couldn't get hold of either Margaret or my Dad. To my dismay she said that she couldn't do that but she'd contact them. Margaret phoned me much later and gave me a big row for making such a request. She told me that she and my Dad were going to come down for a short holiday in the hotel before putting me on the train to London where I was going to have a holiday with our family friends the Middletons. She left me in no doubt that she simply couldn't believe that I'd even thought of making such a request.

After Doreen left, I worked for another week. Then I closed my bank account, withdrew my savings and with the accrued interest had the princely sum of over £60.

I was pleased to see my Dad and Margaret when they arrived and I vaguely recall taking them to various places of interest. I do remember my Dad thought that I should have saved more of my money. I just thought: *"Well there's no pleasing some folk."* I wonder if he suspected I had spent some of it on cigarettes...

The End of the Holidays - Before I Uprooted

I'd first visited our family friends the Middletons in London with my Dad in 1951 when I was nearly five. Luckily Daphne and Jean Middleton had sent me a family photograph so I would recognise them when they came to collect me at King's Cross Station. When I arrived, we travelled on another overland train and passed through Woolwich Arsenal and Plumstead before we arrived at Abbey Wood and walked the short distance to Willrose Crescent.

The house seemed much smaller than I remembered it and of course Connie and George, who warmly welcomed me, were thirteen years older. Their other two daughters Avril and Kathleen had married and left home by this time.

Jean and Daphne went to work most days and I pottered by myself. I helped Connie with the housework, cooking and shopping. I also helped George in the garden and sometimes I went exploring by myself.

One day I took the train to Plumstead and went to the Turkish Baths. It was quite an experience and very hot. I seem to remember that no one wore swimsuits and the people there were all sorts of shapes and sizes.

One day Jean took me to Bond Street in Central London where I had my ears pierced and later I bought a Butterick pattern and green boucle material, then helped Daphne to make me a shift dress. On another day we went to visit my Mum's cousin Mary Copping and her husband John at Brackley. Jean and Daphne really did make a supreme effort to make my holiday as full and happy as possible and it truly was. They also took me to the Royal Shakespeare Theatre at Stratford-upon-Avon to see Coriolanus and bought me a book of the play. I also remember going to Hampton

Court Palace to see a wonderful production of Son et Lumiere with Henry VIII in his barge sailing up the Thames.

I really did enjoy my time in London and all too soon it was time to return to Cowdenbeath to unpack, spend time with my family and friends and get ready for life in Dundee.

The last few days of my holiday, before I uprooted to Dundee, were spent mostly with my friends. I remember that I met Dennis and we took the train to Edinburgh for the day. I have always found that journey over the magnificent Forth Bridge truly magical. Dennis was really happy that he had been accepted for Edinburgh University where he was going to study Classics. We agreed to keep in touch and he said that he'd come to visit me in Dundee. By this time he owned a Vespa motor scooter

My Route to Adulthood

Although I had been to lots of places in Scotland, I had never been to Dundee. Yet I was about to move there to go to teacher training college! And so it was that one Sunday at the start of October I packed my belongings into my Dad's denim blue Austin Wolseley. My Dad and Margaret drove me to Mayfield Hostel – the halls of residence for student teachers.

Dundee College of Education. Now the Law School

Liz, Doreen and I had applied to live in the halls for the first year of our course so we could have our breakfasts and evening meals prepared. We hoped this would give us time to become familiar with the town so that we might find a flat to rent later on.

My knowledge of that city was very limited. I knew about the Tay Rail Bridge disaster and William McGonagall's poem about this tragedy – I have included it at the back. I had also learned about Dundee's three "Js" – jute, journalism and jam: the jute mills; the journals and newspaper publications of D C Thomson; and, the Keillor factory that made preserves, including jam and marmalade.

The car journey took longer than it would today because the Tay Road Bridge was still under construction. We passed through the pit village of Kelty, where I'd lived as a wee baby. Then through Kinross, where Margaret and my Dad had hosted their wedding reception. Then on to Milnathort, where Spitfire, my Primary 7 teacher, lived. My favourite village was Glenfarg. I loved the arrangement of garden gnomes on a grassy bank, in front of a small cottage that was surrounded by a beautiful garden and near the corner, just before the village sign. Nowadays the gnomes are no more: they were likely uprooted because they were probably a distraction to the increasing volume of motorists.

As we approached the village of Bridge of Earn I could see the rows of huts that formed the hospital. These huts had been built in 1939 as emergency medical centres for war casualties. Our next stop was the lovely county town of Perth where we parked at the Inch and went for a bracing walk by the River Tay before travelling the remaining 25 miles to our destination.

The first thing that I noticed when we left Perth was that the road was a dual carriageway, so the second part of the journey didn't take as long as the first part had. On the outskirts of the city there was a small roundabout to negotiate, which would take us along the Kingsway. The eastern part of the road had been dualled in the 1930s, but the western part was not.

On the left hand side there were many factories including Timex and NCR (National Cash Register, which later became the manufacturers of ATM cash machines). On the right hand side there were mainly housing estates. I didn't realise this at the time, but 3 years later I would teach the children at a school serving one of these estates. At regular intervals there were roundabouts to enable the traffic to leave the Kingsway to travel to other locations.

The landscape changed as we drove on, leaving the factories and housing estates behind. Then I saw beautiful stone built houses on either side of the road, grassy parks, football pitches, the Ice Rink (where I would later learn to skate) and Kingsway Technical College. At the last roundabout, my Dad took the last exit and drove along the Arbroath Road. I remember passing more mansions, the Eastern Cemetery and vast expanses of playing fields – Cowdenbeath had nothing to compare with this. Opposite this and behind black painted metal railings were the grounds of Mayfield Halls of Residence.

Mayfield Halls had originally been Mayfield House, a mansion owned by William Dalgleish and designed in the 1880s by the architects Peddie and Kinnear. In 1912 it was acquired at a reduced price as a hostel for women students training to be teachers at Dundee College of Education.

The driveway was fairly long, wide and tree lined. The back of the building faced the Arbroath Road, while the front faced the direction of the River Tay. As we drove down, I noticed a modern block, quite ugly in appearance compared to the lovely old mansion. This block had been built to house the increasing number of students who were being trained. I later discovered that many of the teachers who worked in primary schools were unqualified.

The reception area was on the ground floor. The warden, Miss Bickett who had responsibility for all of us girls, checked my particulars. I think that she must have lived in the Morningside part of Edinburgh because her accent strongly resembled that of my Great Aunt Jean (she whom I had referred to as an old goat many years previously). Miss Bickett always wore a two-piece costume – skirt and jacket. I often thought that the item missing from her ensemble was a bunch of keys.

On the ground floor were rooms such as the dining room, lounge, recreation rooms – one had a piano and another a pianola. I'd never seen one of these instruments before and was amazed at how it played music when a metal roller covered in raised dots, like Braille, was inserted onto the bracket in the front of the instrument. In another room was something called an epidiascope. This was a piece of equipment that magnified pictures and was extremely useful to me when I needed to make some visual aids for teaching practice. Drawing from memory has definitely never been my forte.

The bedrooms were all on the upper floor and access to these was by a magnificent wooden staircase. I don't remember how it happened that Doreen and I came to share a room but we did. It must have been because we'd shared a room while working in Scarborough.

Student Life

In 1964 Dundee College of Education was situated halfway up Park Place and next door to the Demonstration School, a primary school known as *"the Dem"* (where singer Edwyn Collins was later educated). The college was used for the training of future teachers, educational experimentation, research and professional development. Since the college was quite a distance from Mayfield Halls of Residence, the bus was the mode of travel.

The college was a red sandstone building that reminded me of the old Beath High School, although luckily it had no need of support from girders. On the opposite side of the road were the Dental School and other buildings that were part of St Andrew's University for those students studying science and medicine.

On my first day, the future teachers of the year gathered in the hall to be issued with timetables. Our days were going to be filled with learning how to teach subjects including English, arithmetic, music, art and PE to youngsters as well as teaching practices. Best of all we were timetabled for teaching practice, each of us being allocated to a local school one day per week.

The dining room was down in the basement and the queue for the cafeteria was very lengthy. There were lots of older women and I later discovered that they were the unqualified teachers. One lady and her daughter were on the same course at the same time. There were also graduates who were taking their teaching course to enable them to teach in either primary or secondary school. In addition, there were a number of men training to be teachers of technical education.

In that basement there were some table tennis tables and often some of the students would play during their breaks. Quite a number played very well indeed. That area was quite cold and many of us, myself included, bought navy worsted gowns similar to those worn for graduation ceremonies, from a local stockist. These kept the wearers very cosy indeed and distinguished us from those students who were studying science and medicine. They wore red ones.

The nearby bookshop on the Perth Road was the supplier of all of the books that were needed for the course. These could be bought either new or second hand, if any were available. I bought some of each. A college scarf was essential for identification and my navy gown certainly kept out the cold because some of the rooms in the college were very draughty. The other thing I did during that first week of the course was to open a deposit account with the nearby branch of the Bank of Scotland, in which I deposited my statutory grant of £50. I was ineligible for a larger student grant. My Dad paid the Hall fees and to supplement the grant I was committed to work every holiday.

Teaching practice and *"crit"*

It's my first day of teaching practice. I dress smartly in a navy flared skirt, a pale blue blouse and a striped tank top, which I've knitted. The ceramic bracelet from Dennis completes my outfit. Balerno Primary School is in a housing estate and involves a 15 minute bus journey. This doesn't cost me anything because I have my student bus pass.

The school is fairly newly built and I quickly find the Headteacher's office. She takes me to the staffroom and introduces me to the other teachers, most of whom smile encouragingly. I am allocated to the infant department. The class teacher is quite young, tall and has brown wavy hair. In contrast, the infants are tiny and obediently line up at the desk with their lunch money.

I notice a pretty little girl with dark blue eyes and black curly hair. Her name is Mary and her Mum's baby is due. When the teacher asks if it has arrived. Mary sadly shakes her head. The teacher says: *"Oh Mary, your Mummy's been waiting a long time hasn't she?"* Mary nods in agreement, her dark curls bobbing all of the while. When I return the following week the baby has arrived – stillborn.

The days in between teaching practice pass quickly. We don't have much free time at all. Evenings are spent reading, doing assignments and preparing things for teaching practice. The lecturers and tutors are very kind, but there's much more emphasis placed on us to complete our work in comparison to being at school and I very quickly adapt to taking the responsibility for this.

Weekends are spent catching up on sleep, doing laundry, shopping and leisure pursuits. This includes exploring the pubs such as The Howff on Constitution Road. Frequented by students, this soon becomes a regular haunt, as does the Students' Union on the corner of Perth Road and Airlie Place. Every Saturday night a group of us, including Liz and Doreen, go there because there is a live band that plays a selection of the popular music by The Beatles, The Rolling Stones, The Troggs, Gerry and the Pacemakers, The Animals, The Shadows and Liz's favourite, Cliff Richard. While we all jive, twist, or gyrate to this, we sing the lyrics at the top of our voices. I think that life is just GREAT! At the end of the night we all walk the three miles back to Mayfield Halls, as by that time the buses have stopped running for the night and taxis are a great luxury.

I really look forward to my weekly teaching practice. *"Aren't those children sweet?"* I remark. The teacher looks at me in amazement and replies: *"Well Miss Campbell, I wouldn't say that."* I feel embarrassed and firmly decide NEVER to utter such a remark in future.

That afternoon she conducts an art lesson with the theme of drawing a flag. I help squeeze colours of poster paint into pallettes and then distribute them among the children together with paintbrushes and sheets of A3 cartridge paper. When everything has been given out the lesson begins. The teacher places an art easel at the front of the class and has fixed a piece of paper to it. Nearby she has a pallette of paint and brush. *"Everyone pay attention,"* she announces. All of the children obediently follow this instruction and watch attentively as she picks up her brush, dips it in paint and draws a diagonal line. *"Now children pick up your brushes and copy what I have done."* I don't really recall how many of these infants managed, but I do remember that after she thought that everyone had completed the line, she painted another from the opposite corner. I am surprised art wasn't a little more creative, especially for such young children.

It is said that excellent lessons or dreadful ones are those we remember. That particular one has remained in my memory for more than 50 years. Even though I was not gifted at art, I decided that I would never teach art or any other lesson in such a military fashion.

At the very end of that first term students had to teach a class lesson while Miss Barbara Smith, the methods lecturer would sit at the back of the class. Afterwards she would offer constructive criticism – *"crit"* for short. This initial lesson was to be a story and we could choose any one that we liked.

The story that I have chosen is The Enormous Turnip and I have selected this because there's lots of repetition, lots of actions and I can involve all of the class. In preparation I buy a large turnip, a piece of plywood, some felt, sandpaper and glue then ask Doreen to help me draw the characters on stiff cardboard, colour them and glue some sandpaper to the back. These will be my visual aids. Then I make a flannel-graph, by covering the plywood with the felt, so that I can stick the story characters onto it as I tell the tale (there was no Velcro at that time). Once I have finished I place everything carefully in a bag – I can use them again and will gladly lend them to anyone else who chooses to do that story.

The following week, Miss Smith arrives promptly and sits at the back of the class. She talks to the children who are sitting nearby and smiles encouragingly at me. I am understandably nervous but after a few deep breaths I begin. When I hold up the turnip and ask if anyone knows what it is, most of the hands go up. Then I forget all about Miss Smith and tell the story. The children smile and laugh as they repeat: *"They pulled, and they pulled but they still couldn't pull it out!"* Miss Smith smiles at me – she seems very pleased and I feel very relieved.

Years later I learned the song that tells the story of The Enormous Turnip. It is sung to the tune of Ten in the Bed and uses signs. I've used this version many times and both children and staff thoroughly enjoy it.

Before we break up for Christmas, we have a diet of exams. Once more I feel the fingers of cold fear beginning to creep over me, but I remember what I did before I took my very last exams at Beath High School and try hard to replicate it. I read the paper carefully then do all of the questions I know the answers to first. It works and my confidence grows. The results are posted on the notice board just before the holidays and to my delight I discover that not only have I passed everything well, I have scored excellent marks in both teaching practice and English. I have also been awarded a very good mark in the Arithmetic exam. Possibly because I fully understood the problems that a number of children would have with some of the teaching methods, I have an insight into how best to teach it.

Christmas 1964

It's the Christmas holiday and Liz, Doreen and I return to Fife on the train. My Grandpa's health is deteriorating and I spend part of each day with him and make him a sandwich for his tea. He continues to have his Home Help and my Dad and Margaret have their lunch with him. My Dad helps Grandpa to bed each night, then he locks him in because Grandpa has recently taken to wandering. He must have had dementia – though nobody really talked about this at the time.

One night, and despite Grandpa's lung condition, he walked the two and a half miles to Lochgelly, where he was picked up by the police and taken to the station. They phoned my Dad, who collected him and took him back home. Over the past few months he has had some respite in Rannoch House, a care home in Dunfermline. This has meant that my Dad and Margaret can have peace of mind when they go on holiday. My Uncle Angus and Aunt Jessie have had Grandpa to stay and refuse to have him again as they say that he is too much responsibility. I tell my Dad that it's probably because Grandpa was in a very unfamiliar place and that would have made him especially anxious. My Dad agrees and arrangements are made for my Grandpa to move to Rannoch House whenever there's an available room. That way he'll be safe and my Dad will not feel worried.

Some months afterwards when a room became available my Grandpa moved in. He quickly settled and spent the last 3 years of his life there before passing away peacefully.

The rest of the holidays pass all too quickly. I catch up on lost sleep, help Margaret whenever she needs me to in the shop and visit my Aunt Kit and my Aunt Janet. Adele and I spend some quality time together. She's met someone she really likes and is enjoying student life. Dennis invites me to go to a concert in Edinburgh. He says that we can stay at his flat and return the next day. I agree and tell my Dad that I'm going to Adele's for the night: I have already asked her to be complicit. The concert is superb, we have fish and chips afterwards and a drink in a local bar. Later we return to Dennis flat, which he shares with his cousin who has gone home for the holidays, so I have his bed. Amazingly Dennis has brought an electric blanket for me. He thinks of everything and so I am very cosy and have a good sleep. Next day after breakfast I show him how to clean around the taps of the washbasin in the bathroom. He is very impressed and I smile smugly knowing that I have knowledge of something that he doesn't.

I go carol singing with Liz and some others from the Youth Fellowship Group that we used to attend. Liz, Adele and I go dancing at the Raith Ballroom in Kirkcaldy and the Kinema Dance Hall in Dunfermline. I don't have a Christmas stocking anymore now that I'm considered to be an adult, but I do get a lovely blue suede jacket. All too soon the holidays are over and it's time to return to Dundee.

College life, in 1965

After we return to college in the New Year, much to my disappointment, there are no weekly visits to school this term. We are told that visits will be arranged for the second term. Life continues much as before with lectures for much of the day and coursework, reading and assignments in the evenings.

My social life is very enjoyable. We continue to go to the Student's Union on Saturday nights and meet lots of interesting lads. I go out to the cinema, Rep Theatre, bars and cafes with them. It's all good fun. One of them, a hirsute art student is known as Scoop. He always wears jeans and an old leather jacket. One night he tells me that he loves me. I say goodnight and resolve not to see him again. It's just not the right time for any sort of commitment.

In March, a letter arrives from Dennis: he wants to come to visit me and suggests coming one Sunday before the Easter break. I write back, arrangements are made and soon after he arrives on his Vespa scooter – they were all the rage at the time. While it was lovely to see him again and hear about his family, his course and student life I didn't feel able to make any commitments at that time.

I've had my long hair cut into a bob because I think that it will be easier to manage. Unfortunately I don't find that that's the case – it needs to be dried and styled when it's washed whereas previously I never really had a bad hair day because when it was long it could just be tied back, or worn in a French roll. Although I am disappointed I console myself with the fact that it will grow again.

I find myself wishing that I had a single room. It's not that I don't like Doreen, rather it's the fact that I always seem to be having to compromise. Being an only child this is not so easy for me. Doreen borrows my suede jacket without asking, wears it to The Howff where some beer is spilled on it! I am not happy. My Tweed perfume is liberally used too – there's hardly any left. In the end, I ask Miss Bickett if I can have a single room the following year and she agrees.

After the Easter break and to my great delight the weekly teaching practice is resumed. I am sent to Charleston Primary in a housing estate at the other end of the town. There the teachers embrace and implement the new teaching methods I have been learning about. I am really impressed. The children no longer sit in rows – their desks are arranged in groups. One thing that strikes me is that there seems to be much more room and the children seem happy.

After the exams we return home for the summer holidays. Liz goes fruit picking and I help look after my Grandpa and when needed, work in Margaret's shops. Adele and I arrange to go hostelling in the Lake District and my Dad and Margaret agree to drop us off and pick us up when they go on holiday to Lytham St Anne's. (I still have the cosy blue duck down hooded sleeping bag that I got for the holiday!) I have vague memories of hitching lifts, which was perfectly safe in those days, sightseeing and sunbathing. I don't think that we did a lot of walking but I remember buying two pairs of earrings - I still have the copper ones.

My second year of college

It's great to be in second year and best of all I have my own bedroom. This is in a flat within the new block at Mayfield. There's a kitchen, two bathrooms, a sitting room, three single and two double bedrooms. Doreen shares one of these with a girl called Mary. Two girls named Annie and Kate occupy the other two single bedrooms.

There are also interesting new subjects like psychology and education, but the books are both heavy and expensive. No teaching practice is timetabled for this term but we'll have a block of three weeks in rural schools after the Christmas holidays.

The throbbing of my upper jaw wakens me. I have ignored the recent intermittent twingeing of my 7th tooth on my left jaw – an upper molar. Now I must address the issue. I bitterly regret that I have been very tardy about going to the dentist, the last time being three years previously when I had an extraction and Dennis came with me. It's a great blessing that the Dental School is directly across the road from the college and so I make an appointment and am lucky enough to get one for later in the morning. In the meantime to ease the throbbing, I buy some oil of cloves from the chemist.

When I return to the Dental School I'm directed to a large room with walls lined with lots of glass fronted cupboards and shelves containing equipment. Several dental chairs are spaced evenly on the floor and are occupied by people in different stages of treatment. There's a buzz of conversation and the sound of drills. Ugh! I'm shown to a seat and a student called Bickerstaffe introduces himself and examines my teeth. He does his assessment and then asks his tutor to confirm his findings then they both withdraw to discuss. They return and tell me that I need six fillings. I am horrified and resolve never to neglect the health of my teeth ever again.

I will always be extremely grateful for the gold star care and treatment I had there. The offending tooth was immediately treated and further appointments arranged for the rest. Over the next few weeks I was a regular patient – my mouth was anaesthetised, the teeth were drilled and packed with temporary dressings. I remember returning to Mayfield after these sessions and going to bed because my mouth was so very uncomfortable.

Towards the end of the Christmas term Mayfield held a Christmas Ball and Adele helped me to make a dress. It had a black satin skirt and a sparkly top with cap sleeves. It was my first long dress. Liz didn't go, though Doreen and her roommate Mary did. We took partners and I invited Chris, who, like Scoop, was an art student. I remember that he hired an evening suit and wore a bow tie – he looked quite smart. We all spent a lovely evening jiving and smooching to the music of the Beatles, Stones, Righteous Brothers and Freddie and the Dreamers.

The Rookie Postie

During the holidays I have a job as a postie delivering the Christmas mail. It's not in Cowdenbeath, but in Crossgates, so involves an early morning bus journey to the local office where I am told which round I have been allocated. Then I'm quickly shown how to sort through the cards, letters and small parcels. I pack everything into the large canvas post bag, cross the heavy bag over my shoulder and trudge through the snow.

Crossgates is a small village and my round begins in the streets nearby. Although initially my bag is very heavy, by the time I reach the end of the first street it seems much lighter.

Halfway down the next street – Manse Road, there is a house that has a long path up to the green front door. As I push the letters through the brass mailbox, I hear the sound of growling from behind the door. I feel very relieved that the canine is inside the house because it sounds very fierce. I imagine it to be a German Shepherd or a Rottweiller, but maybe it's just a Poodle or a Westie.

I finish my deliveries and have a cup of tea with the other posties. They have lots of stories to tell about addresses that are impossible to read, envelopes without stamps, badly wrapped parcels and dogs that bite. My blood runs cold as I think of the growling dog and what fate might befall me. This is most definitely on a par with exams.

Next day I approach the house with trepidation. To my great relief there is no dog outside and I walk down the path confidently. Just as I am about to post the letters through the box, a bloodcurdling sound fills my ears. I look round and, to my horror, see a large Collie bounding towards me. Ignoring the advice to stand my ground, I turn and flee back up the path, somehow managing to negotiate the catch on the gate and reach safety. The Collie bares its teeth and snarls. I am really terrified.

I share this experience with my colleagues. They sympathise and suggest I carry some dog biscuits in my coat pocket. I decide to take their advice and buy a box of Shapes.

Over the next few days there is no sign of the dog and I wonder if he has been kidnapped. I fervently hope so and breathe a sigh of relief each time I deliver the post to his owner's house. However, these feelings are short lived because soon the dog suddenly appears from nowhere. On seeing me he snarls and bares his sharp teeth. Nervously I throw him a biscuit. He jumps and catches it in mid air. As I go to open the gate he glares at me then jumps up and snarls. *"There's no way that I'm going down that path while that animal is out,"* I say to myself and reach in my pocket for the plastic bag that I carry for shopping. I put the letters and cards and leave it on top of the gatepost with a stone on top as a precaution.

I finish my round and return to the Post Office and decide that from now on I am going to leave the letters and cards in a bag on top of the gatepost. I am too ashamed to share my experience with the others.

Unfortunately my plans are to be thwarted by the lady who lives in the house. When she sees me leaving the letters she rushes out of her house and shouts: *"Whit dae ye think that yer daeing? Ye better pit ma post through ma letter box or A'll report ye."* I tell her that I am very scared of her dog because he jumps, chases, snarls and barks noisily. She just laughs and tells me that he wouldn't hurt a fly. Despite her reassurances I have my doubts and ask her if she'll keep him in when the post is due. Thankfully she agrees and I have no further altercations with her pet, although he still barks fiercely when I deliver the letters. I give her the box of biscuits as a peace offering.

Despite this I really enjoyed the job. Sadly I lost some of the money I earned though. Liz and I had been to the Raith Ballroom in Kirkcaldy. On the homeward journey I took my earrings out as they were hurting me – they were a pewter set I had bought on my visit to the Lake District with Adele. I put them in my new leather purse, but when I got home I was devastated to find that my purse wasn't in my pocket. I'd dropped it on the bus. Not only had I lost my earrings, I'd lost my bus pass and some of my earnings. In the morning I phoned up the lost property office at the bus company but no one had handed it in. I hadn't expected anyone to do so.

Sixties Haute Couture and the Wild Thing

Some clothes are well remembered – my bright orange shift dress was one of these. It was knee length, had a round neck and long sleeves. I wore it regularly because it was both fashionable and comfortable and, as there were no shops selling second hand clothes, I made do with my scant wardrobe. Another favourite was a mid-purple moiré silk mini dress. I had a full length black, belted PVC coat, a blue suede three quarter length jacket and a musquash fur jacket – it was a cast off from Margaret and went very well with the purple mini dress.

One Saturday night towards the end of January I dress in the orange shift and fur jacket and walk to the Union with Liz, Doreen and a few others. We find a space on the crowded dance floor and are soon dancing to the music. As I look up I spy a very tall figure leaping madly around to the music. He has a mop of brown curls, black-framed glasses, an amazing patterned jersey and white jeans. What an interesting person I think to myself. I wonder who he is?

Later on he brushes past me and stands on my foot. He apologises and then asks me if I'd like to dance, so I agree. I tell him that he has a very carefree style of dancing – he nods. I find his mode very infectious and soon both of us are dancing quite madly to songs including The Troggs' Wild Thing, The Rolling Stones' Satisfaction and The Kinks' You Really Got Me. In between dances, when we can have a conversation, he tells me that his name is Ron and that he comes most Saturdays with his friends. They call him *"Prof"*. I introduce myself and tell him where I live.

When the band has finished for the night, Ron asks if he can take me back to Mayfield. I hesitate but then he explains that he has a scooter and as this seems a good alternative to walking I agree and tell my friends what I'm doing.

The scooter is parked around the corner. It is a Sunbeam and is 250cc: that's quite a powerful machine and many weeks later Ron tells me that it can do wheelies. It doesn't have any "L" plates and so I assume that Ron has passed his driving test. He gives me his white crash helmet that feels enormous and has two large eyes painted on the back of it. I put it on, climb on the pillion seat, wishing that I was wearing jeans, and off we go.

I had never before ridden on a bike, far less a scooter. It was very noisy. As we whizzed along Perth Road, up Victoria Street and then onto Arbroath Road I became colder and colder. By the time we reached Mayfield I was numb. Somehow I got off the scooter, thanked Ron and said *"goodnight"* before stumbling gratefully into the warmth.

Next morning at breakfast Miss Bickett remarks: *"Someone has got a very noisy bike."* I splutter into my cereal and avoid eye contact.

Revenge, Rattray Primary and Ron

One Sunday afternoon my Dad and Margaret come to visit me at Mayfield and see my new room. I introduce them to the rest of the girls and since others currently occupy the sitting room, I take them downstairs to an area near the stairs where there is a small round table and several comfy chairs, two of which are under the stair well. Margaret sits in one of them. Ron has come to visit and Kate and her boyfriend Mike are there too. We chat and later I make everyone some tea and biscuits. As Margaret stands up to leave she forgets that she's under the stair and clatters her head on the concrete. Kate gasps: *"Are you all right Mrs Campbell?"* Margaret nods, probably still seeing stars. It must have been painfully embarrassing. I have the wicked thought that it's pay back time for the thrashings I got from her all of those years ago.

I am delighted to be sent out for teaching practice in a rural school – Rattray Primary in Blairgowrie. I will spend three weeks here. It's some 15 miles from Dundee and so I need to leave early each morning to catch the blue and white single decker from the Bus Station. The journey from the town centre takes about half an hour and that gives me an opportunity to read my book.

I am going to spend the next three weeks with a Primary 5. Luckily all of the children are well behaved. I help them with their work, listen to reading groups and I am asked to teach some music. I really enjoy playing the piano while these young voices sing lustily. For my *"crit"* I decide to do the musical story of Peter and the Wolf, thus combining the two subjects. I have the story on a long-playing vinyl record.

I buy several large sheets of cartridge paper, new felt pens and borrow a book with illustrations of musical instruments from the library. I'm full of enthusiasm as I set about the preparations and this time I'm determined to do it unaided and I do.

I draw each person and creature in the story and use the epidiascope to magnify the instruments that depict those characters. I carefully draw the five lines of the stave and treble clef, then write the first few bars of the music that heralds the characters as they appear.

Although this task takes me quite a number of evenings, I really do enjoy it and am extremely proud of the end result. The *"crit"* lesson is a success. Even better, some of the other teachers in the school ask to borrow it, as do some of my friends. (In fact, I was so proud of myself I kept this material for about 50 years before I decided it was probably time to recycle it.)

Meanwhile I continue to go to the Union where I dance some of the time with Ron and ride pillion on the back of the scooter. I discover that this machine has a history. Although he has a licence to drive a car, Ron has never passed his motorbike test and so is not allowed to have pillion passengers. Some time previously he had applied to do his motorbike test. He set off in good time, but the scooter broke down. He telephoned a friend, borrowed his bike and arranged insurance for that day.

Unfortunately he didn't have time to collect the necessary certificate to prove this. He was greeted at the test centre by a grim faced examiner, because he was five minutes late. *"You're late,"* he barked, *"You could be failed for this."* Ron apologised and explained the reasons. *"Do you have insurance for this bike?"* Ron replied in the affirmative, but of course couldn't produce the certificate. *"You could be failed for this,"* said the examiner and with his voice growing louder: *"Where are your "L" plates?"* You could be failed for this."* At that Ron turned, jumped onto the bike and drove off leaving the examiner standing probably open mouthed on the pavement outside the test centre.

One night after the Union, Ron asks me if I'd like to go to the cinema during the coming week – Jack Lemmon is starring in the comedy The Great Race. I've finished my assignments, so I agree. The film is hilarious. By the time we come out our jaws are aching with laughter. We buy some chips and eat them on the way back to Mayfield. I feel really happy and glad to be alive.

Sometimes we meet mid week and go to the cinema, the repertory theatre or for a meal. Ron is an apprentice design draughtsman at the NCR and attends the Kingsway Tech where he's doing an Ordinary National Certificate (ONC). He left school, having passed ten O' Grades, when he was 15 years old. It was the first time he'd met the Headteacher, who tried to persuade him to stay on and do some Highers. Ron however had other ideas, having been offered two apprenticeships – one with DC Thomson, the newspaper publisher, and the other with the NCR. He tells me that he hasn't regretted his decision and he is earning money. I consider his circumstances and wonder what I'd have done had I left school when I was 15. I suppose that there was an expectation that I'd stay on at school and go on to further education. But, by his own admission, Ron will only do something if he thinks that there's a point to it.

It is during this time that Liz meets Geoff, who is a medical student. He rents a farm cottage near Alyth with his friends. Liz sometimes spends part of the weekend there, and now and again she and Geoff and Ron and I go out as a foursome. One Saturday night we go for a meal at the Lahore Restaurant in the Perth Road. I have recently been introduced to Indian cuisine and am really enjoying the experience.

The restaurant is quite busy. It is dimly lit and there are flowers and candles on the white tablecloths. The air is infused with a myriad of spices. We order our meals and chat amongst ourselves. Over in the corner a solitary figure is having his dinner. He is quite drunk and is having great difficulty in getting the food from the plate to his mouth. His eyes close, his body gently sways on the chair and then he falls forward, face first into his curry. I wonder if he will suffocate or maybe Geoff will be required to use his medical skills. The waiter notices, goes over and rouses the man. He sits back up, his face covered in rice and curry sauce, wipes himself and after a few moments resumes his meal! We all have a quiet laugh.

The End of Second Year

Bonskeid House is a beautiful old house near Killiecrankie in Perthshire. It is situated in spacious well kept grounds and surrounded by woodland . Until 2001 it was used as a youth hostel and during the Easter term of 1965 an outdoor holiday was organised there for us student teachers. The views up the valley to Mount Schiehallion were spectacular and the weather was absolutely glorious. I remember canoeing on Loch Tummel. I'd never done this previously and found the experience exhilarating. As well as going hill walking, to the little theatre at Pitlochry and visiting Killiecrankie, we went to famous beauty spots such as the Soldier's Leap. Most evenings we had ceilidhs where some of the group would sing and others would play their musical instruments.

After Easter, Liz and I went to Dens Road Primary for our teaching practice. Unlike some of Dundee's other primary schools there were no playing fields, just a tarmac playground: this resulted in pupils having a lot of skinned knees. For the first time, I was left alone with the class on several occasions! Towards the end of term we had exams, which thankfully I passed along with all of my friends. Some poor souls had to re-sit.

Since my Grandpa was now living in residential care I decided that I'd stay in Dundee rather than return to Cowdenbeath for the summer. Before the end of term two of my flatmates, Kate and Annie, and I viewed a second floor two bedroomed flat in Blackness Road. We decided that it would suit us, even though there was only a tiny scullery and no bath. Access to the washing line was via the living room window.

I successfully applied for a holiday job with the Scottish Gas Board. My job was to check the readings and records of the meter readers. I remember being shocked by some of the paperwork being binned. When I asked the reason for this I was told that it was because there was just too much for the staff to deal with. I found this justification really puzzling. There were also some interesting phone calls from customers to deal with, some of them quite irate. At the time I made friends with two of the office staff – Irene, an older lady who was married to a policeman and who had a teenage son – and Stella, a single mum. I would occasionally look after her six-year-old daughter.

Ron and two of his friends decided that they would like to go it alone and rented a first floor flat nearby. It was filthy and so we all set about cleaning it. I took down the curtains and washed them several times in the sink. When they were finally rinsed, wrung out as tightly as possible and hung out on the line they were a completely different colour. But it did not take them long to decide they preferred the home comforts of their respective families.

At this time Ron's maternal Granny, of whom he was very fond, was in the local hospital awaiting transfer to a care home. She had Parkinson's Disease and could no longer look after herself. On several occasions he took me up to hospital to visit her and I well remember her constant tremors that made me feel so sorry for her.. When he went on holiday later with his friends, I went up to visit her and it was there that I initially met his Mum and Dad, Nan and Dave. After the visiting hour they took me to meet Ron's older sister Moira and her husband Douglas in their pretty flat in Garland Place. Both of them worked for DC Thomson. Moira was a proof reader while Douglas was a lino type operator. They were an extremely nice young couple and I didn't feel that I was being scrutinised in the least. They talked about Ron's older brother Graham who at the time was studying for a BSc, and his younger brother Martin, who was an apprentice with BT. Afterwards Ron's parents took me back to my flat in Blackness Road.

Winter Pastimes

Ron and his older brother Graham were both keen skaters. Ron had two pairs of boots – one for figure skating and the other for speed skating. At the end of the public session there was a session for speed skaters to practise whizzing around and after that he and some others would sometimes stay on and play ice hockey.

From September to March the ice rink was open for skating and so, just before the start of the college term, at Ron's suggestion I went there with him and Graham. It was very uncomfortable squashed into a space at the back of Graham's Frogeye Sprite which only had two seats. The skates that I hired pinched my feet and it was very difficult to walk on terra firma. That was nothing in comparison to trying to keep my balance on the ice while everyone else, including people much younger or older than I was, whizzed confidently past.

Ron and Graham each took one of my hands and soon I was gliding confidently to the music. *"This is so easy",* I thought to myself: *"I can skate."* What I had forgotten was that I was being securely held and all that I had to do was move my feet. It was all going so well until we came up behind a family – Mum, Dad and two children. Ron assumed that Graham would hold onto me and steer me round the group, while Graham thought that Ron would. Both let go of my hands. I continued to move forward, crashed into the group and we all fell down. I felt so embarrassed and was thankful that no one was hurt. I was grateful to the family for being so understanding.

For my 20th birthday Ron bought me a pair of white ice skates. Having my own skates certainly helped both my comfort and confidence, though I cannot remember a session without falling over several times.

My foray into winter sports widened and during the winter of 1966 I found myself on the ski slopes. The NCR had a ski club and often in the winter months a busload of employees would head to the hills of Glenshee, then afterwards have a meal and ceilidh at the Angus Hotel in Blairgowrie. Ron was a keen skier and had his own gear. I, on the other hand, had none. In anticipation, Ron bought me a lovely Norwegian sweater (I had it for years afterwards and wore it to death). One Sunday we went to Glenshee on the bus. Ron told me that I could practise on the nursery slopes. I hired skis, poles and boots from the ski shop and headed for the slopes. The hired boots were very uncomfortable but that was nothing in comparison to wearing skis. I spent most of the morning in, rather than on, the snow and felt very miserable. In addition to feeling cold and wet, I was extremely disheartened. However, later in the day I found that I could stay upright for longer and by snowploughing – pointing the skis inwards - I could control my movements, slow down and stop independently.

One man who came on one of these outings was Sid Scroggie. He worked as a telephonist in the NCR factory. Sid had been injured during the war – he was blind, had lost a leg and so wore a metal prothesis. Despite these disabilities, Sid was an amazing person possessed of a remarkable memory and positive mental attitude. He walked the 3 miles from home to work and back every day.

A month before Ron and Sid had gone on the staff hill walking group's walk from Kirkton of Glenisla via Monamenach into Glenshee. As they got off the bus Sid had said to Ron: *"You are the perfect height to be my guide."* Sid would put his right hand on the left hand shoulder of the person who was guiding him and walk half a pace away from them. That way he could tell if they were on the level, or going either up or downhill. All Ron had to do was to give him a constant running commentary as to what he could see and highlight any possible obstructions or dangers to Sid.

As everyone set off Sid became aware of the little stream to the left that could be heard gurgling as they moved up an incline towards a small copse of trees, on the right where birds could be heard chirping as they feasted on the Rowan berries. The track there was covered in loose stones and so Ron cautioned Sid to take extra care lest he should lose his footing. They crossed another burn before coming to several huge slabs of moss-covered stones. Once again Ron warned Sid about his footing. Some two hours later, after they'd stopped by a low wall to have a snack and cigarette, they noticed that mist was rolling down from the hilltops. Since they were only halfway to their destination, they walked on for a little while longer by which time they found that the mist was becoming virtually impenetrable.

Some folk even wondered if they'd find their way back the way they'd come and so they were all astounded when Sid announced: *"I can show you the way back."* He then proceeded to describe in reverse order virtually every step that the group had taken. And so it was that a blind one-legged man led a party of able-bodied walkers safely down the hillside and into the local hotel while someone summoned the bus that had been waiting for them at Glenshee.

Over a few beers Sid asked Ron if he'd be going out again the following month. Ron replied that he hoped that there would be snow because if so then he'd go off skiing. Sid announced that he'd love to try skiing and asked if Ron would be prepared to take him. Sid's wish was quickly granted. How could Ron possibly refuse?

As usual, Ron organised the ski hire. All that was needed were foot sizes for the boots and the heights of people that determined the length of skis, and ski poles. When it came to Sid, he only needed a single right boot. This somewhat flummoxed the shop assistant. Ron explained about Sid's metal leg and how his existing boot would fit into the existing ski bindings. He didn't require ski poles because he was blind and there would be a danger of him inadvertently poking or stabbing someone. Sid was granted the boot and the skis free of charge. They led Sid to the nursery slopes having previously explained what they were going to be doing. There would be one person in front doing the snow plough followed by Sid doing the snow plough immediately behind him and holding onto his waist and Ron doing the snow plough behind Sid and inside his skis, holding him to try to keep him balanced. They told the many youngsters on the nursery slopes what they were up to and warned them to keep well out of the way. All went well as they slithered down 20 yards or so before coming to a stop on the level. Sid was led up a bit higher the next time and the exercise successfully repeated.

A wee while later Sid could hear the children shrieking with laughter and asked why they were so excited. Ron explained that they'd made a big pile of snow and created their own ski jump. Needless to say Sid asked them to ask the children if he could try it. Off set the mad trio towards the jump. Only once they were airborne did they realise that they couldn't maintain contact; the snowplough only works when in contact with the snow. They landed in a tangled heap. Ron asked: *"Is everyone okay? No broken arms or legs?"* Sid's response was" *"I'm fine but I may have crumpled my tin leg."* He went on to say that this was a regular occurrence and that the Orthotic Department kept spares for him. *He added: "I'll get a new one soon enough, although I'm not sure if I'll be up to the dancing tonight!"*

One day in early January of 1967 Alan and Colin, two of Ron's friends, arranged to go skiing at Cairngorm near Aviemore, because Colin's Dad said that he could borrow his car. Alan was slightly built, while Colin would have made a good prop forward. Since there were two spare seats, Ron and I were asked if we'd like to join them and we did. It was snowing when we left, but the ploughs were working hard to keep the A9 reasonably clear of snow. Colin made good progress and we'd nearly reached our destination when he negotiated a corner too sharply. The car skidded and rolled over, coming to rest on its nearside and close to a small loch. *"Is everyone all right?"* asked Colin, and we all replied in the affirmative. *"Open the door will you"*, said Ron and Alan simultaneously. At that Colin, who was still holding the steering wheel, let it go and promptly fell on top of poor Alan – it was nothing short of a miracle that Alan was not crushed by Colin's weight. Somehow we all got out by which time a French tourist and his young son had stopped to ask if we were injured. Thankfully none of us was. He then asked if we'd like a lift to the ski slopes, an offer that we declined. Colin, Alan and Ron managed to get the car back on its four wheels and drove it back to the police station in

Aviemore where it was checked over by the police. He was advised that he could drive it back and so telephoned his Dad to explain what had happened to the car. I was just so thankful that none of us was injured.

The last lap at college

I was really happy sharing with Kate and Annie and we shared the rent, though Kate and I bought our own food for the weekends (Annie used to go home). There was an electricity meter and washing such as bedding and towels was taken to the local launderette then hung out to dry on the outside line. We used to use the bathing facilities at the local swimming pool and sometimes I used the bath in Ron's parents' house. The bathroom wall was decorated with shells of all different shapes and sizes, Ron's Mum having collected these from the beach at Broughty Ferry each time she went there for a walk. His Dad and Douglas made many jokes about buckets of sand and sang songs from the musical The Desert Song.

One weekend I thought that it would be a great idea to organise a party at our flat as Kate and Annie were away for the weekend. However, I soon bitterly regretted my decision. Word of this celebration spread and several unknown visitors gate-crashed! It became very noisy and several of the neighbours complained to me and said they'd report me to the landlord. I managed to ask the revellers to leave before sincerely apologising to all of the neighbours the following morning. Kate and Annie were absolutely furious when I told them and on Monday morning I visited the letting agent's office to explain what had happened and gave them an assurance that this would never again happen.

I thoroughly enjoyed my third year because the end of the course was in sight and I looked forward to putting all that I'd learned into practice and being paid for the privilege.

Subjects such as psychology and education were studied in more depth and I remember selecting drama, as did Kate, from the optional column. I truly loved it and was overjoyed when we did a college performance of sketches, one of which was the handbag scene from Oscar Wilde's The Importance of Being Earnest. I was chosen to be Cecily. I've long forgotten the name of the other sketch I took part in. What I do remember is that my American accent sounded authentic, my small red portable radio was used as a prop and was the subject of the quote: *"Turn that squit off!"* The evening was wonderful. I really enjoyed myself and discovered a great love for amateur dramatics that, to my regret, I never pursued.

The first term's teaching practice is in the school close to our flat. This is excellent. The teacher, called Mrs Carnie, wears a floral overall that reminds me of some of my teachers. The children are age seven, so Primary 3. One of the little girls called Moira is particularly quiet and seems reluctant to join her peers at break times. Mrs Carnie tells me that her Mum died quite recently. She lives nearby with her Dad and older brother. I feel really sorry about this – I guess that it reminds me of my

113

own situation. I do my best to try to include her and spend time talking to her. Then after careful consideration I ask her if she'd like to go to see the animals at Camperdown Park, though only if her Dad agrees. She says that she would and I write a letter to her Dad and give him my contact details. He seems very pleased and so I tell Mrs Carnie. This is something that I ought to have done first. She isn't best pleased and tells me that it's not a good idea to become involved. Of course this wouldn't have happened nowadays because I'd have had to have a PVG (Protecting Vulnerable Groups disclosure).

We go to Camperdown and Moira enjoys seeing the animals and having some juice and an apple on a park bench. I take her on several other outings while I'm at the school – to the beach, the cinema and to Camperdown again because she really liked going there.

It was quite sad when that term ended because after that my studies increased and I found that most of the daytimes at weekends were spent doing things for my course. I lost contact with Moira. It was a hard lesson learned by me: always think about the consequences of your actions.

A Granny's Adventures

Ron and I continued as before. When we went out for long walks, Ron told me several funny stories about his Granny. One of my favourites was about the day his Granny took Ron and his two brothers to the beach at nearby Broughty Ferry. While the boys made sandcastles and paddled in the water, she sat down on a blanket. Reaching in her bag for her magazine she discovered a bag of her favourite toffees. Since toffees and wallies (false teeth) are not compatible she removed both sets of dentures and tucked in.

Everyone had a lovely day and then they packed everything up when it was time to return to Granny's house. She had just started to grill some sausages when a sudden thought struck her, *"Meh teeth!"* she wailed, *"Eh've left thum!"* There was nothing else for it than to catch the next bus back to the beach and hopefully find the missing wallies. A mad dash followed, the posse alighted at the same stop and a search began. By this time the beach was empty apart from a few walkers and some dogs. *"Eh jist hope thit nane o they dugs hiv goat meh teeth"*, a mournful Granny remarked. By good fortune the tide hadn't turned, they soon found the castle they'd built and there beside it were Granny's missing wallies. The boys took them down to the water and carefully washed them. Granny just smiled and put them back in her mouth. *"Well lads, Eh'll buy ye some fish suppers fur yer tea,"* she said.

On another occasion Granny needed Ron and Graham's help to remove her old settee. One of her neighbours, who'd bought a new one, had offered Granny her old one. Its condition was better than Granny's ancient settee the fabric of which had been burned in several places by her cigarettes. Ron and Graham often stayed overnight with her at weekends and were promised some extra pocket money if they'd help. Of course the boys thought this was too good an opportunity to miss. Unfortunately Granny lived three floors up and so, with many stairs to negotiate, the boys thought that this would be too difficult. Instead they decided to manoeuvre the settee over the balcony railings till the fulcrum was reached, then shove and let gravity do the rest.

It took the two youngsters quite a while to achieve this and when they did the settee crashed on the ground with a tremendous bang and broke into several pieces. Ron and Graham hid as they watched people come out of their houses to see what had caused the noise and later, when the coast was clear, they carried the pieces to the bin. They found some coins that had fallen down the sides, then after pocketing them returned for their promised payment. Thankfully no one was injured and no one discovered the source of the bang.

It was Ron's Granny who inadvertently introduced him to his habit of smoking, which he began at an early age. He used to pilfer cigarettes from his Granny, who was partially sighted. He once dared his older brother Graham that he could swim further across the pool than him – after taking a puff of a cigarette. And sure enough Ron won.

Almost there

My penultimate block of teaching practice is with a P7 class in Arbroath Primary. Mr Millar, the teacher nicknamed Dusty by his pupils, wears a black gown. He's a kindly man and I very much enjoy being with this class. I enjoy the daily bus journey along the coast to this lovely wee fishing village and popular seaside resort. Sometimes Ron and I would go there for bracing walks on the cliffs and eat fish and chips out of newspaper.

The end is in sight: only a few more weeks to go. Some lectures are followed by exams and there is a final teaching practice in a local school at home in Cowdenbeath. Liz and I return to Foulford School and the teacher I am with is Miss Letts – my old Primary 6 teacher. We go exploring and find that nothing whatsoever has changed, from the tiled walls and basins in the cloakroom where we rinsed the milk bottles, to the tarmac playground where we skipped and played tag and hopscotch. Miss Letts actually seems quite interested in what both Liz and I have been doing.

Engagement and graduation

After the exams Ron and I decide to get engaged and go to Cowdenbeath for the weekend to tell my Dad and Margaret. They are out for the evening so we wait up and tell them when they return. My Dad seems quite pleased at this news but Margaret seems quite shocked. I also decide to tell both of them that I'll be staying in Dundee after I finish college. That does upset my Dad – he doesn't say anything, but his expression tells me exactly what he's thinking.

The following weekend Adele and her boyfriend take Ron and me to Aberdeen for the day. They go off to visit relatives while Ron and I shop for a ring. I finally choose a second hand one made of 9 carat gold and set with 2 sapphires and a diamond. It costs Ron £35. It is left in the shop to be cleaned and sized then sent to Ron's house in a small heart shaped box. Ron's Mum thinks it is beautiful and I wear it very proudly when I return from teaching practice.

The exam results are posted. Ron comes with me for moral support. I scan the lists of successful students and to my delight, near the top is Margaret Scott Campbell. I am ecstatic and literally jump for joy. Then I look to see if all of my friends have passed. To my relief they have. Liz and a handful of others, including one of the older ladies who'd been working as an unqualified teacher, have merits in curricular studies. Unfortunately there are a fair few who haven't passed so will have re-sits in September: fingers crossed for them.

For those of us who have opted for drama, a trip to Stratford has been arranged and all of our group goes. We travel by bus. Kate and I sit together and admire my ring. Stratford is beautiful in the summer sunshine. We arrive in late afternoon and are booked for the evening performance of Coriolanus. It is a good job that I'm familiar with the play as I am so tired that I keep falling asleep. Later in the week we are given a guided tour backstage and on another evening we go to see Hamlet. It is so fascinating and I marvel at the stage, curtains, flats, scenery and other miscellaneous props. We have lots of free time to explore the lovely little town and relax by the River Avon, eating ice cream.

Adele has decided that she's going to get married in September and has asked me to be her bridesmaid. I go to Cowdenbeath on my own for the weekend. Margaret talks to me about a job and tells me that if I return home I can stay for nothing. Later my Dad takes me over to Adele's house for the night. We talk about my future career and I tell him that although I won't be living at home, *"I love you Dad and you haven't lost me."* His eyes fill with tears as he says, *"Margaret, I lost you when your Mum died."* When we stop at Adele's house I hug him tightly and give him a kiss. I feel really torn and a bit selfish.

"You shall go to the ball Maggie," says Ron and so I buy a double ticket costing £2 for the Graduation Ball. It is held at the Angus Hotel in the city centre on Tuesday 20th June 1967 and is from 8pm until 2am. I buy a long straight dress that has a delicate pattern of flowers printed on

116

the muslin material. It has a big slit up the back that allows free movement for the essential dancing. Long white gloves with pearl buttons, satin sling back shoes and a matching clutch bag complete my outfit. The dress code was formal and to my absolute amazement, Ron hires a dinner suit! We dance into the wee small hours then Ron takes me back to the flat in a taxi because my poor feet are aching.

The graduation ceremony is held in the Caird Hall in City Square on Thursday 22nd June and for the occasion we all hire black gowns and blue, white and gold hoods. Earlier in the week I have a formal photograph taken by JD Brown, the photographer (see below). Ron's Mum comes to the ceremony and has invited my Dad and Margaret for lunch. Ron is not able to get time off work. All the graduates sit in alphabetical order in the seats provided and walk out a row at a time to wait in the wings of the stage until our name is called. I remember George – I can't recall his surname - our English lecturer who arranged the Stratford trip smiling and saying: *"Now give a big Stratford entrance."* And so I do. I have a truly wonderful day and Ron's Mum makes us all very welcome. The Next Great Adventure has not disappointed.

Chapter 4: The Probationer

When I think about it now, I can't quite believe that at 21 years old I was standing on Lochee High Street in freezing January weather with my class of 41 pupils, catching the bus back from the swimming baths. Our first session at Lochee Baths in Dundee was in January 1968. Every Primary 7 pupil did exactly what I said when I stood in the middle of the street, stopping the traffic, and asked them to cross the road smartly without blocking the pavement.

Sometimes the bus took a while to come and the girls had developed icicles in their hair. But they all just got on with it, tucking into their *"shivery bites"* or snacks on the bus back to Dryburgh Primary School.

The Calm Before the Storm

Lyon's Maid was a popular brand of ice-cream products in the 1960s and definitely my favourite. Luckily for me my last holiday job before becoming a teacher was working in the office at the Lyon's Maid factory in Dundee and I was able to eat ice-cream regularly. My favourite products were the mouth-wateringly delicious strawberry Mivvis, with their bright pink shells encasing creamy vanilla ice-cream that oozed out when bitten into. I also loved fruity Orange Maid lollies.

I later learned that the late Margaret Thatcher had once worked for Lyon's Maid also. She was a chemist with the firm, before becoming a barrister and then a Conservative MP. While working there, she helped develop methods for preserving ice-cream.

After we left college, my friends dispersed. My flat-mate Annie had returned to Thornton where she had got a job in a local school. She married Willie her boyfriend shortly afterwards. Kate and Mike got engaged and arranged to get married the following Easter. So she and I agreed to rent a smaller and cheaper flat from the same estate agent – we paid a retaining fee for the holidays. Though smaller it was much nicer and had the luxury of a proper bathroom. After we'd been there for a few weeks we decided that it was still going to be too expensive. Kate discovered that there were two bedrooms for rent in the home of an elderly lady called Clementina Christie who lived in Maryfield Terrace. We went to meet her and thought that she and the accommodation would suit us very well. We would have our own sitting room and the use of the kitchen and bathroom. The estate agent was not best pleased – I had the dreaded task of telling him.

I had my school interview just before the holidays and fervently hoped that I would be able to go to Charleston Primary where I had enjoyed my college placement. However, it was not to be and I was appointed to Dryburgh Primary, which was in the same part of Dundee as Charleston.

In 1967 the probationary period for a newly fledged teacher was two years and during that time the Head Teacher regularly carried out

118

appraisals. If these were satisfactory the teacher received his/ her Parchment (a certificate of competence) and was admitted to the register of the General Teaching Council.

My First Teaching Job

Dryburgh Primary School (above) was an architectural carbuncle of the sixties – an ugly flat roofed box-like construction that was built on three floors. Its front was a geometric arrangement of glass windows and blue painted panels. My first impressions of the school reminded me of a gigantic box made from blue Lego blocks.

The main entrance was at the front of the school on the right and next to that was the block that housed the Primary 1 infant department. There were twelve classrooms in the main block – four on each floor with two staircases to access them. There were two classes in each year group because there were too many children for just one class.

At the other end of the playground was the school janitor's house and Mr Kidd, the *"janny"*, was the first person I met when I arrived. He was a tall well-built man who wore a uniform that closely resembled that worn by a policeman or prison officer. Although he was friendly towards the staff, he brooked no nonsense from any of the pupils.

I arrived very early in order to meet the Head Teacher, the staff and also to explain that my friend Adele was being married mid-week some six weeks later and had asked me to be her bridesmaid. Tentatively I knocked on the Head Teacher's door. There was no reply and so I went into the staff room where a few teachers were drinking mugs of tea and coffee. I was invited to help myself. I'd brought my own cup as I knew better than to inadvertently use one that belonged to another staff member.

Miss Bibb, the infant mistress, explained about the tea kitty. She introduced me to those others and told me that the Head Teacher, Mr George Mechan, would be in later. Everyone seemed very welcoming, especially a pretty young woman whose name was Karen Grant. I liked her from the outset and our friendship has now spanned five decades.

George Mechan arrived at 8.50am, welcomed me, and said that I would have Primary 6 and that my classroom was on the top floor, next door to Karen's. When I explained about Adele's wedding he readily gave me permission. Thanking him, I left for the long walk upstairs.

My classroom was at the opposite end of the building from the main entrance and I got upstairs just before the bell rang. From the window on the landing I watched as the classes lined up at the back of the school – one line of boys and another of girls. Two teachers supervised these lines very closely ensuring that they were straight.

First Impressions

I watch intently as two crocodiles of children enter the building, one behind the other. There is a buzz of conversation from the bottom of the stairs where the cloakrooms are. This is followed by a rumble that grows louder and louder as the children ascend the stairs. Karen, who I discover is a second-year probationer, stands at her classroom door ready to greet her class and smiling. I also stand at my classroom door, only I am rooted to the spot with apprehension. *"Don't worry,"* she says in a comforting tone: *"You'll be just fine!"* I nod and smile wanly. *"Why did I ever choose to do this?"* I mutter to myself, fervently wishing that I'd opted for a job in a library. Then the noise stops as the two classes round the corner and see us. *"Oh dear,"* I think, *"some of these children are almost as big as I am. What am I going to do?"* Somehow they all file into the classroom and find seats for themselves in among the rows of desks and chairs. I quickly do a head count and to my horror find that there are 41 children! I shut the door, walk to the front, take a deep breath, welcome them back to school and introduce myself. As I write my name on the board I overhear someone say: *"She's corry pawed."* This means that I am left-handed. I choose to ignore this remark, turn round and ask them about their summer holiday.

This exercise takes quite a bit of time and affords me the opportunity to discover those children who are quiet, bold, cheeky, thoughtful or disruptive. First impressions indicate that there are quite a few of the latter. From the depths of the cupboard I find paper, pencils, rubbers and rulers and ask them to write a story about themselves. By doing this I reckon that I will quickly judge both concentration and literacy skills. Then I will speak to Mr Mechan and ask if I can be allowed to arrange the desks in groups. Hopefully he'll agree – I cannot think of any reason for him to object. The new primary memorandum has recently been published and group arrangements are actively encouraged.

At interval Karen and I go down to the staffroom and have a welcome cuppa. I learn that there is a duty rota for filling and switching on the kettle and washing up afterwards. That responsibility is given to two Primary 7 children; there were no Health and Safety policies then. Karen has a Primary 7 class, so she is responsible for the rota.

The rest of the morning is spent distributing textbooks such as Holmes Arithmetic, First Aid in English, Fred Schonell's spelling book and jotters for the various subjects. During the afternoon we have singing and I read part of Paul Gallico's story entitled The Small Miracle, then ask my class questions about it – just to make certain that they have been paying attention.

Mr Mechan readily agrees to me rearranging the desks and I do this with Karen's help after school. When we finish, the room looks so much better – it seems roomier. I feel a great deal more positive so afterwards both of us take the bus to the town centre and go to the Val d'Or café in City Square for a Devon slice and a cappuccino. Mmm.

Karen and I decided to make this a tradition. So every Wednesday after school she and I used to go for refreshments because we felt we'd earned them. Mostly we'd go to the Val d'Or café, but when we'd been paid we'd go to Draffens Department Store where we'd have afternoon tea. We both loved the convivial atmosphere of the spacious restaurant with its tables covered in starched snow-white cloths, damask napkins, china tea sets, silver plated cutlery, teapots and hot water jugs. In the corner by a window stood a grand piano on which someone played popular light music – selections from musicals such as Carousel, Oklahoma and South Pacific – while models paraded around displaying the latest fashions that could be bought in store. The waiting staff, who wore black skirts, white blouses, frilly aprons and little caps, served tea or coffee and a delicious selection of scones, cakes and biscuits that were attractively arranged on doilies on cake stands. We also loved watching the other customers, a few of whom were *"the Blue Rinse Brigade"* who wore beautiful clothes and lots of bling.

I loved Draffens because it was so customer friendly. I still have the navy leather gloves that I bought over 40 years ago. One winter I bought a pair of pony skin boots – Liz was aghast when I showed them to her. *"How can you possibly wear these knowing where they've come from?"* I hadn't really considered this and had bought them because they were warm, fitted perfectly and had been in the sale.

At that time Dundee had several other wonderful department stores, all within a short distance of each other and all were flourishing businesses. People would often dress up in their best clothes to go into town to shop in DM Brown, Smith Brothers, Caird and GL Wilson. Sadly these have long gone and retail developments such as Zara, Accessorize, the Body Shop and other chain stores are in their place. But this quote from Gavin Wilson, the proprietor of GL Wilson, one of the city's most prominent department stores of this period, sticks in my mind: *"Memory binds one to something for which there is no legal divorce. It is there: 'for better, for worse; for richer, for poorer; in sickness or in health. Therefore, one might as well contrive by conscious effort to have a good one."*

I well remember the lifts with the folding metal doors in both GL Wilson and DM Brown and the Flying Fox: the metal cylindrical container into which the customer's money was put once the purchase was made. It travelled aloft on a wire to the cash desk where the money was removed and the receipt and change inserted. To a child it must have seemed magical. I simply marvelled that the correct amount of change was always returned.

Interestingly Garnet Wilson, Gavin Wilson's son, was the Provost of Dundee between 1940 and 1946 and was the main player in bringing the National Cash Register (NCR) factory to the town.

My Classroom and My First Class

Maggie's first Class – third row, far right.

Since my classroom was on the top floor, at the far end of the school and consequently at the end of the heating system, it became bitterly cold on winter days and really hot in summer. There was a thermometer on the wall and when the temperature fell below 50 degrees Fahrenheit or 10 degrees Celsius I would take my class downstairs to the cloakrooms so that they could put on their coats for extra warmth. How I longed for a classroom in a rural school from the last century where there would have been a coal fire. At least the toilets were inside the main building and not outside in the playground.

The room was rectangular – the two long walls that faced the back and front playgrounds had four small and large metal-framed windows respectively. These usually ran with moisture during the winter months and I frequently dried them with a chamois leather. The wall at the far end was fitted with a roller board and on either side of that were two large pin boards where pupils' work could be displayed.

In front of that stood my desk and a small freestanding cupboard, where there was a supply of jotters, pencils, rubbers, rulers and pens and a bookcase with a selection of children's books. At each end of the opposite wall were two doors – one leading to the stairs and the other into the walk in cupboard that provided both ample storage and a Belfast sink for the two classrooms. In between the doors was a longer pin board.

The class of 1967 comprised nineteen boys and twenty-two girls aged mainly ten. A few would turn 11 during the course of the year. One of the boys, who later broke into the school and caused damage, would turn 12 years old that school year, having repeated Primary 5. Initially I would tremble when I considered the relatively small difference in ages between them and me – I was only 20.

The children fell naturally into three groups, namely a top, middle and tail, as we would say in those days. During that first term I assessed their abilities and prepared the appropriate levels of work for them. Most weekday evenings were spent making work cards and other materials from the variety of books that I'd bought. My fiancé Ron helped me to cover them with strong polythene because at that time there was no laminator in school.

I have very clear memories of Myra who was a very able girl, though quite shy and nervous. She regularly stammered especially when reading or answering questions. I spoke to her former teachers and found out that Mrs Mackenzie, who had taught her in Primary 1, had encouraged her to sing her reading rather that simply saying it. I decided to do likewise and discovered that it really worked. So later I asked Myra and several others to help some of the less able children by reading with them – I guess that we were unwittingly doing paired reading. Gradually Myra's confidence improved and the stammer all but disappeared by the time she left primary school. The little Hummel figure that Myra later gave me as a wedding present has pride of place in my display cabinet.

Apart from the usual maladies, such as colds or tummy upsets, most children in the class were quite healthy. I remember going to hospital to see one of my pupils, Robert, who'd had appendicitis, and then visiting him once he returned home. The class made Get Well cards and we bought him a new football. Generally, and to my disappointment, it seemed that it was the well behaved pupils who tended to be off sick. I have to confess to a feeling of elation when some of the pranksters were absent.

I took my revenge on two such lads one April Fools Day when two of Karen's boys came in and asked: *"Miss Grant says can you give us a long stand?"* I gave them each a piece of chalk, told them to keep an eye on the class and write the names of any miscreants on the board. I then beckoned Alec and Graeme, the two boys who were regular worthies responsible for disruptions like winding up other pupils, being cheeky and at times downright disobedient. I took them downstairs to the gym hall where I pointed to one of the netball stands. *"Right boys",* I said: *"Let's take this up for Miss Grant."* Now the stand was quite heavy and a bit awkward to take up two flights of stairs, but they managed. By the time they reached the top landing they were puffing. When the boys took this into Karen's room, she and the class fell about laughing. All was well though – her boys had had a long stand and my boys had collected one. I took pity on them and chose another two to return it to the gym.

My own health record was good and I had very few absences during the two years I worked at Dryburgh. However, one morning I woke with flu like symptoms. When I took off my pyjamas, I found that my chest was covered in small red itchy spots. I phoned the doctor who did a home visit and told me that I had contracted German Measles and that I needed to stay off school for at least a week. After he left, I phoned Mr Mechan who sympathised, told me that he hoped that I'd soon be better and assured me that he'd make arrangements for my class – I don't recall supply teachers then. I think that the children were shared out amongst the other classes, though sometimes the Head Teacher would take them.

The Dreaded Admin

The blue register was the bane of my life. It was a large oblong shaped jotter with outside covers made of stiff blue cardboard. There was a white label on the front to identify which class it belonged to. Inside were pages of stiff white paper, two of which were half size for the names of the children to be written on and the rest full size so that attendance could be marked against each name. Each school day comprised two openings – morning and afternoon – so ten for the week. These had to be added and a running total kept at the bottom; by the end of the year this ran into thousands. Every Friday the Depute Head was tasked with checking the registers and woe betide any teacher who made mistakes.

Worse still, all entries had to be done in fountain pen. I always erred on the side of caution and initially used a pencil and then when I was sure of my figures I went over them in ink. Karen and I used to check each other's register after she made an error and rubbed so hard that she made a hole in the page. After that she too used a pencil.

Dinner money was the next administrative priority. Many of the children stayed for the lunches, which were cooked on the premises and were served in the school canteen. The money was generally paid on Mondays. Some youngsters were entitled to a free lunch, while the cost to others was one shilling (5 pence), 11d, or 10d – this cost was worked out as to the number of children in the family. Two teachers supervised meals and this duty was rewarded with a free lunch. The menu comprised mince, dough balls and tatties, fish and chips, Irish stew, toad in the hole, macaroni and cheese, sausage and beans. Though many of those meals were high in calories there were very few overweight children in any class.

This was because at playtime the boys played football on the grass, while the girls played *"peevers"* (hopscotch), tig, and a variety of skipping games. Everyone walked to and from school and there were no fizzy drinks or regular snacks of crisps or chocolate available since the children who took school dinners were not allowed out of the playground at lunch time.

All teachers kept the particulars of what they'd done during their lessons in the blue covered jotter sized Record of Work book. These were written weekly and were checked each month by Mr Mechan.

Lessons and a Surprise at Assembly

Every teacher in school began the day with The Lord's Prayer – each child had learned it by heart. For me, and I hope for them, it was a moment of reflection. Though when we came to the part that states, *"Lead us not into temptation but deliver us from evil,"* I often thought: *"Please help me teach this class of mine and grant me unlimited patience."*

Ron told me that when he was in Primary 7 his teacher used to spend a few minutes on a mental arithmetic lesson each morning in order to help get everyone's brain cells engaged. This lesson had proved to be a success, so I decided to teach a similar one. I gave the class six sums of varying degrees of difficulty at talking speed, for example: *"7 times 2, plus 6, divided by 4, minus 3, equals what?"* It certainly woke them up, and me as well, and soon most of the hands would shoot up into the air.

Each page of Fred Schonell's Spelling Book had lists of words divided into groups of five or six. I graded the spellings to suit these children who had literacy difficulties. Class homework was to learn four groups each week and on Friday mornings I'd test them. Reading was also done in groups and I was very grateful for the graded material from the Science Research Associates (SRA) reading laboratory box.

Every Friday morning I told my class Bible stories and strove to make these as exciting and child friendly as possible. I tried to relate parables such as the Good Samaritan to their daily lives and we sometimes acted them out.

Often on Friday afternoons I would choose two children and invite them to pick one of my topic cards from its box and tell the others about it. This was essentially teaching the children life skills such as how to make a cup of tea, how to make a slice of toast, how to clean shoes, how to cross the road safely, and how to look after a pet.

At that time, most parents had little involvement with the school and generally only visited on parents' evening after the reports were sent home. I thought that it would be a good idea to invite some in to talk about their work and was glad when Mr Mechan agreed to this proposal. I remember three of the Dads who came in and talked about their jobs: one was a fireman, one was a policeman and one was a postman.

Mrs Maxwell, a member of the Blue Rinse Brigade, was Dryburgh's visiting music teacher. Karen and I were delighted because that meant that we would have some time to either mark work or plan lessons during the school day. My delight, however, was short lived, the peace being shattered by a loud rapping on the staffroom door. *"Mrs Maxwell says you've to come back Miss Campbell immediately,"* announced the out of breath rapper. We hurried up the stairs to find a red faced and flustered Mrs Maxwell glaring at some of the boys who were decidedly smirking. Before I could open my mouth she said: *"This is the worst class I've ever had! I was trying to teach them the song "Bonnie Dundee" and they really weren't paying attention. When they came to the last line of the chorus they actually shouted really loudly, "up wi' the bonnets of Bonnie Dundee". You will have to stay in the classroom during the lesson."* It was not as if they had got the words wrong, rather she was not happy with their bellowing. I just sighed and wondered how I could get revenge…

In those days there were some separate lessons for girls and boys. The girls were taught sewing and knitting each week by another visiting teacher, Helen Symington, while I did some craft work with the boys. We made raffia baskets and toast racks with prepared wood and cane and these lessons were very peaceful indeed. It was lovely to have half of the class and good for the children to have things to take home at the end of each term.

As a class we chose a topic for a project each term and I tried hard to incorporate the general curriculum as far as possible into this. We made collages, papier mâché models, mobiles, etc and I would spend time after school making displays of the children's work on the walls.

Among my certificates is one for being able to operate the Bell and Howell projector. I did the course after school over a few weeks. On one occasion someone visited to show the children a film and so I offered to set up the projector. My initial attempt had to be aborted as I put the film in upside down but it served as an ice-breaker and I managed successfully the second time.

Punctuality was not Mr Mechan's forte. The Head Teacher was often late for school. When this happened, he never came in by the front entrance, rather he snuck in by the fire door at the back. Karen and I reckoned that he did this because he wouldn't be so likely to be seen. Every Wednesday morning, after the register and dinner numbers were done, all of the children gathered in the hall to say a prayer, sing hymns and have a talk from the Head Teacher or sometimes the local minister. At one end of the hall was a stage with heavy curtains which were always drawn. The piano was at the front and was played on alternate weeks by Mrs Tait, who taught Primary 3, or me.

One morning, as usual, everyone waited in the hall and I waited at the piano, but there was no Mr Mechan. Then all of a sudden the fire door burst open and a small burly figure dressed in a trench coat and Trilby hat appeared. He glared fiercely around before hurrying up the steps and onto the stage behind the curtains. The curtains rippled from one end to the other as he strove to find the gap and eventually his dishevelled figure appeared to all staff and pupils. Karen and I glanced at each other, trying hard neither to giggle nor to clap. Then the assembly began. From this point on, Karen and I always used to hum the Dance of the Sugar Plum Fairy when we thought of Mr Mechan.

Lochee Baths on the Bus

During my second probationary year at Dryburgh, I stayed with my class as they entered Primary 7. I vividly remember announcing: *"We're going to have weekly swimming sessions at Lochee Baths. So you'll each need costumes or trunks and a towel. You'll also need bus fares and shivery bites."* The latter necessities were snacks to be eaten on the homeward bus journey. Mr Mechan had booked a course of lessons during the second term of Primary 7 and so once a week I single handedly took 41 children to the bus stop where we waited for the service bus. Despite our long procession, I can't recall any drivers ignoring us and driving on as we waited at the bus stop.

We alighted in Lochee High Street where the bus stop was directly opposite the baths – the entrance was in St Mary's Lane. I would stand in the middle of the road and stop the traffic while the children crossed and waited at the other side. Looking back, it was an absolute miracle that everyone listened and learned the routine.

Lochee Baths were both old and compact. The changing room below was communal and known as *"The Dungeon"*. I used to go into the water too so that I could help the few youngsters who couldn't swim. By the time the course of lessons was finished, quite a few children achieved their swimming badges. Others, who'd initially been non-swimmers, managed to swim a few strokes without buoyancy aids.

I don't remember there being any hair driers so afterwards, during the cold weather, damp hair froze. Girls with long hair were transformed into Ice Maidens, with icicles in their hair. I always kept my fingers crossed that we wouldn't have too long to wait for the bus.

The Frogeye Sprite

JKS 700 was a Frogeye Sprite (like the one above) that belonged to Ron's brother Graham. Graham had sold his MG Roadster and bought the Sprite. When Graham decided to buy a Triumph Spitfire, Ron bought the Sprite. He then decided that it would be a good idea if I learned to drive. I agreed with this in principle, but having him teach me was not a good idea. It led to lots of tears and tantrums and finally before my test, I had a handful of lessons in the Sprite with a retired policeman. Ron adapted the offside window so that I could carry out the hand signals that were then compulsory and I applied for my test.

Ron took me to the test centre in Brook Street Broughty Ferry at 4.15pm on 1st April 1969. I had a very pleasant examiner who gave me my pink slip at the end. There was no one more surprised than Ron. He couldn't believe it and I guess he can take the credit. We had many happy times with that car until eventually the cost of repairs escalated and we exchanged it for a Ford Classic. I found out many years later from Karen that the Sprite had originally belonged to Scott, her lovely boyfriend who had tragically passed away at a very young age.

School trips

In early June my Primary 7 went to the Youth Hostel in Aberfeldy for three days. Pete Clunie, who taught Primary 6, and I swapped classes because he was keen to go and I was quite keen to let him. Mr Mechan and a couple of Dads accompanied them and they had a lovely time. Karen and I visited one evening along with Mrs Tait and her husband. We took a modest carry out as a present for the staff but Pete wouldn't allow anyone to have it as he said that that would be setting a very bad example to the children. We smiled politely and shared the contents ourselves once we left. Rather wickedly we also hummed the tune to the Ride of the Valkyries behind Pete's back. This was also the song that had been hummed in relation to my secondary school teacher, the Wamp (AKA Henry Philip).

Karen and I used to always arrive at school before 8.30am in order to ensure that everything was ready for the day ahead. One day we were surprised to find Mr Mechan already in his office. *"Miss Grant and Miss Campbell would you come in please?"* he said, indicating two seats. *"I'm going to offer the P7s the opportunity of a holiday to Belgium during the Easter holidays and so I'll give out the letters at assembly. There will be two chartered buses, we'll sail to Zeebrugge, and we'll have accommodation in Middelkerke. There will be sightseeing trips round Brussels, to the Atomium that was built for Expo '58, the amusement park, to Bruges and the bulb fields in Holland. We'll need seven adults altogether, so are you both willing and able to go?"*

Though we could think of various reasons for not going, we felt we'd no choice. I was halfway through the second year of my probation and didn't want to create any obstacles. We were young, enthusiastic and still possessed boundless energy, plus a misguided sense of adventure. As

I recall all of the Primary 7 children signed up for the holiday and the money for this was collected each week.

When the great day arrived, goodbyes were said and parents stayed to wave us off in the two buses that would be our transport for the trip. The two bus drivers, who were fairly young, were quite jolly fellows besides being good drivers. I don't remember much about the journey except that many of the children consumed quite a lot of sweets, crisps and juice, despite being warned about travel sickness.

When we boarded the ferry, it was quite windy and so the crossing was not the best experience for the youngsters, or indeed most of the staff. Karen and I have good sea legs and I clearly remember spending part of the crossing taking children up onto the deck where they could sit in the fresh air, rather than below deck. Unfortunately some of the hardier pupils sat by the galley window eating roast potatoes. *"Oh Miss Campbell,"* wailed Stella from my class: *"This is the worst moment of my life, I feel so ill."*

The accommodation in the hostel in Middelkerke was basic but comfortable and when we arrived all of the children and most of the staff went for a lie down. Since Pete Clunie, felt rather ropey Karen and I went to look after him.

One of the highlights of the tour of Brussels was the statue of the Manneken Pis, a statue of a small naked lad urinating into a fountain. We also visited the park that had housed Expo '58, the World Fair Exhibition. Another day we visited the bulb fields in Holland; I can still see the carpet of wonderful colours. We visited a lace-making factory in Brugges and did some shopping for souvenirs. I remember going to an amusement park and being asked by my pupils Anne, Linda and Stella to accompany them up the enormous slide because they were too afraid to climb up by themselves. However, once everyone reached the top and Anne slid down, I was told that it was my turn next! Not only was the slide very high, it had several bumps on the surface at regular intervals ALL the way down. Since I didn't want to lose face, I held onto the sides, gingerly sat down, pushed myself off and closed my eyes. As I sped towards terra firma, Stella's words rang in my ears: *"This is the worst moment of my life."* However, when I reached the bottom an enormous cheer rang out. I smiled faintly: after all these children would be leaving school soon.

It was just as well that Karen and I had each other for company because the other adults were quite cliquey. One afternoon when we had a bit of time off we went to have a coffee with the two bus drivers.

Somehow we all arrived back at school in one piece and none the worse for the experience. Both of the bus drivers came to the school a few weeks after we returned to visit Karen and me. We'd not given them any encouragement and explained that while it was kind of them to call in, we were already spoken for. After this there were just a few days grace before the summer term started and my second probationary year came to an end.

Wedding plans

Before our wedding, which was planned for the summer of 1969, Ron and I decided to buy a house. We opted to buy a newly built house rather than one that needed any sort of work done to it because we really didn't want to spend our weekends and evenings doing DIY. We had both been saving regularly towards a deposit and had a total of £1,000. Betts the builders had bought land on the outskirts of Broughty Ferry and were building a variety of designs of houses there. We went to have a look and chose a corner site on which an Isla design was planned. This was a detached house with two bedrooms, a living room, a kitchen/ dining room and bathroom and it even had an under floor gas warm air central heating system. Unbelievably by today's prices the house cost just over £4,200!

The loft space was floored and we arranged for a Ramsay ladder to be fitted: the design allowed for two additional bedrooms to be built upstairs later. We paid the deposit and spoke to the mortgage broker at the Abbey National Building Society. He told us that the maximum amount we could borrow was three times Ron's annual salary: we decided to borrow two and a half times and opted for an endowment mortgage of £3,300 over 25 years. We started making the payments in January 1969. The house was due to be completed by the end of May. Our address was to be 55 Ceres Crescent.

In November 1968 my Dad and my Stepmother Margaret held a party at a local hotel to celebrate two things. One was buying out Margaret's brother John's share in her two shops from Betty his widow. The other was to mark my 21st birthday. I wore the bottle green dress that I had worn as a bridesmaid at Adele's wedding. I remember the ceilidh and the disco and dancing with Ron. It is funny to think that by this young age I had a degree, a job, a house and was engaged to be married. But among my contemporaries, this was pretty much the done thing.

I later discovered that when my Mum had died the money she had was willed to me and that I should receive it when I was 21 years old. My Grandpa had also opened a bank account for me, under the same conditions. I was an heiress receiving £424.51 and £276.15 from my Mum and Grandpa respectively.

With this extra money we were able to do a loft conversion for £500, have an extra window in the living room for £15 and pay £2 extra per door so that all of the doors, including those of the wardrobes and cupboards, could be Sapele instead of plain plywood. There was even enough left over to pay the legal fees.

My Dad and Margaret paid for our living room to be furnished. Ron's parents bought us our dining room furniture – amazingly it is still in daily use and as good as new. We bought our cooker, washing machine, fridge and vacuum cleaner from a local teacher who was emigrating to Canada. My Dad and Margaret bought everything else that we needed at cost price and we repaid them over the next year. We were extremely lucky to have such a good start in life.

I asked Liz and Karen to be my bridesmaids and Karen's mum Marjorie agreed to make their dresses. We agreed on a very simple style and I chose bright emerald green material, Ecru daisy trim and a Butterick pattern. Margaret and I went to Glasgow where I chose my white satin sleeveless dress and matching lace coat, my cashmere camel coloured going away outfit with the box jacket and A-line skirt and a white gold wedding ring. I had decided to wear the engagement ring that Ron bought for me on my right hand and ask Margaret and my Dad if I could have my Mum's white gold wedding and engagement rings. Much to my annoyance Margaret would often wear these on a chain around her neck. Perhaps my Dad had given them to her, though I never asked him that question. At the time it did not occur to me that Margaret was my Mum's friend and she must have missed her in her own way. However, I knew that if I wore her rings I would feel that my Mum would always be with me.

Unknown to me, my Primary 7 class at Dryburgh Primary were collecting money and one morning Anne and Linda came out to my desk and said: *"Miss Campbell, someone's taken £1 from the money that we were collecting for your present."* I didn't want to search anyone for fear of reprisals from the others against the culprit, though I suspected that it was more than likely to be the lad who'd broken into the school the previous year. I spoke to the class and said that whoever had taken it should put it in an envelope and leave it on Joyce's desk – she was the school secretary. I did my best to assure the children that no one would get into trouble. The money was never handed in but I replaced the £1 so nobody apart from the thief was any the wiser. Amazingly, I still have the square casserole that they bought with their money and, though the lid was broken some years ago, the dish is still in regular use.

Just before the summer holidays I had a letter telling me that I was no longer a probationer and this came as a great relief. Unfortunately I needed to be at a school that was nearer my new home and so I applied and got a job at Powrie Primary in Broughty Ferry. It was the twin carbuncle of Dryburgh, the only difference being that the outside was red instead of blue. There was a celebration tea for me at which I was presented with a set of Pyrex dishes from the staff. Miss Bibb gave me an apron and Mr Mechan made a very complimentary speech. I was sad to leave after just two years, but at the beginning of July 1969 I left Dryburgh Primary in pursuit of happiness.

Chapter 5: In Pursuit of Happiness

I had just settled down to sleep when I fancied I heard music coming from the living room. *"It must be my imagination,"* I thought and turned over. No there it was again. Someone was playing the piano. I got out of bed and tiptoed through to the living room and switched on the light. *"Oh Honey,"* I said: *"What are you doing?"* Our newly acquired chocolate brown Labrador looked decidedly guilty.

Honey and me

I guess that she was exploring her new surroundings, had stood on her hind legs and explored the keyboard with her forelegs. As I recall, the sounds were quite melodious and after all this was her very first night in her new home. I closed the lid of the piano, settled her down in her basket in the hall and returned to bed. There was no more music that night although there would be plenty more fun and games to come with this somersaulting canine.

An Exciting Time

My wedding to Ron was to be held on 13 August 1969 in my local church, Beath Parish Church, in Cowdenbeath. At the time we were both 22. Looking back it seems so young, but many of my friends from college were already married or engaged, some were even expecting their first child.

We sent out a hundred and fifty invitations to guests in the middle of June and nearly everyone said they could come – except my Aunt Margaret as she had guests booked into her Bed and Breakfast in Ullapool at that time. I was so disappointed.

Ron had never met my Aunt Margaret. So once the school summer holidays started in July, I decided that it was time he met this marvellous lady who was effectively my surrogate mother. Aunt Margaret was delighted when I phoned to ask her. She and Ron immediately clicked. During the day we went for walks with Butch her dog, collected shopping, helped make meals, weeded the garden and visited Sonny and Bunty, her cousin and his wife who lived nearby in their beautiful house which was called Rivendell.

The exterior was roughcast and painted sunshine yellow, the rooms were large with solid hardwood doors and wonderful parquet floors. Their spacious garden was spectacular. The front garden stretched down to the shores of Loch Broom, where Sonny kept a small boat. There was a huge carpet of grassy lawn and a great variety of shrubs and pretty flowers. Their miniature Shetland collies, Misty and Blaze, were extremely talented canines whose soccer skills had been honed on the front lawn of the garden where they would dribble their football using their noses and front feet.

Our evenings were usually spent at Aunt Margaret's where Sonny, Bunty, Misty and Blaze would join us and we'd play games like Canasta, Bolivia, Scrabble and Contraband. We spent the most wonderful ten days in Ullapool and wept unashamedly for quite a few miles during the drive home.

After my return to Dundee I stayed on in Maryfield Terrace in the room I was renting. The newly built house we had bought in Broughty Ferry needed floor coverings, curtains, blinds, light fittings and furniture. So Ron and I, along with his Mum and my friends Liz and Karen, cleaned it from top to bottom.

Ron's Uncle Jim, who worked for Justice's furniture and carpet store, arranged for the carpet fitter, Peter Gow, to fit our carpets. Peter was a true craftsman who stitched the joins together with very thick thread and stretched them so that they fitted perfectly. Ron and his brother Graham fitted the curtain rails, blinds and light fittings and very soon the house began to take shape. The garden, however, was another matter. When we chose that particular corner site, a large garden seemed a good idea. But as we were to discover, creating one from scratch was a monumental task that was to take us many months to complete.

Back in Cowdenbeath things were just as busy. The flowers had been ordered and Mrs MacGregor, whose daughter Sandra had been in my 6th Year Home Economics class, made the bouquets and buttonholes. Margaret, my Stepmother, asked her friend's husband, who was a baker, to make our traditional rich fruit cake. She provided all of the ingredients and I distinctly remember that 36 eggs were used in the process. There were three square tiers, all decorated with small silver horse shoes, sugar flowers and twelve small sprays of blue flowers and silver leaves. On the top there was a silver bell musical box. When it was wound up I think that it played phrases of Mendelssohn's Wedding March.

The black Bentley cars were ordered from a local car hire firm. Hair appointments were confirmed and everything else was double-checked. The upstairs rooms of the local Co-operative Hall were booked for the Wednesday before the wedding for a showing of the many presents we were given. In the 60s there were no wedding lists, at least not in Cowdenbeath where they'd likely have been frowned upon. Couples would have been expected to be grateful for what they'd been given even if it meant they had four irons and two toasters. I remember Liz and me displaying all of the gifts on trestle tables while the other room was set out for tea, sandwiches and cake. I wore a blonde wig that I'd recently bought. Wigs were all the rage then. Though it looked stylish, it was very itchy, so my new look was not long lived. At the end of the evening everything was packed up and taken back to Stenhouse Street where it was stored together with my *"bottom drawer"* items. These were a collection of useful items made or bought by the bride-to-be for her new home, such as a decent tin opener, good quality bed linen, hand embroidered tray or supper cloths, jam spoons and towels. At the weekend, it was Ron's job to transport everything to our new house.

The night before the wedding, Karen arrived from Broughty Ferry. She was staying at Liz's house and after tea we went up to the church for a rehearsal. I gave them the bridesmaid's gifts I'd bought for them – a silver bracelet for Karen and gold leaf earrings for Liz. Both of them were delighted. Before we returned to our respective homes, I visited the grave in the cemetery across the road where my Mum and my Grandpa were buried. I spent some time there wishing that both of them had lived to share this special time with me because I knew that both of them would have been so proud. When I went to bed that night I lay awake for a very long time thinking about the adventure ahead and how changed my life would be afterwards. I thought about how kind everyone had been to me and how lucky I was. Then I said my prayers and drifted off to sleep.

The Big Day

Ron and my wedding. Dad and Rons Mum to my right Step Mum and Ron's Dad to my left

134

My alarm rings at 8am and at once I'm awake. I yawn, rub the sleep from my eyes, then look at the wardrobe door where my wedding dress hangs. *"Something old, something new, something borrowed, something blue"* fills my mind. I've borrowed Kate's wedding veil, I am wearing my Mum's engagement ring, which she was bought in 1936, and along with my new wedding dress, I have a blue garter.

My wedding is at 12 o'clock and best of all it's not raining. I get up and go through to see my Dad and Margaret, who are awake but still in bed. I tell them that I will have breakfast and go off to the hairdresser to meet Liz and Karen. I walk there and my Dad meets us afterwards and takes us back to our respective houses to get ready.

I do my own make up and complete my mental checklist. Margaret changes into her blue dress and matching lace coat, her navy court shoes, leather handbag and lacy gloves. A blue tulle hat worn at an angle completes her ensemble. My Dad changes into a morning suit but does not want to wear a top hat. I pin their respective buttonholes onto their outfits before I put my dress on. When Margaret sees me she says: *"You look very bonnie Margaret. I hope you'll be happy."* Then the car arrives for her and then it's just Dad and me.

We give each other a huge hug, take deep breaths and leave the house. A crowd of neighbours is waiting at the gate to throw some rose petals over us. Some youngsters gather too and once we're in the car, my Dad rolls down the window and throws a handful of coins to them. This is known as a *"poor-oot"*, the pouring out of all of the small change from the pockets. We get into the car and sit side-by-side holding each other's hands very tightly. Neither of us speaks. I do wonder if he's thinking about his wedding to my Mum and how proud she'd be or if he's thinking about his wedding to Margaret. Maybe he's just reflecting on how different things might have been if circumstances had been different. Oh the *"what ifs"* of life.

In the road outside Beath Parish Church a policewoman stands directing traffic. The Dundee contingent has hired a bus courtesy of Napper Thompson while others, including Ron's sister Moira, husband Douglas and their two-year-old daughter Audrey have come by car. Ron's younger brother Martin is an usher at the front gate while his older brother Graham is an usher inside the church. Karen and Liz and Liz's Mum have already arrived and we all have our photographs taken together before we go into the church.

Organ music fills the air and while we wait to make the long walk down the aisle, Kate, who is expecting a baby in November, and her husband Mike arrive and are shown to a seat. Wagner's Bridal March heralds our entrance and we walk slowly to the front where Reverend Martin, the minister, Ron and Jim, his Best Man, wait for us.

When we reach the front Dad squeezes my hand and leaves me. Ron and I exchange smiles, I give my flowers to Liz and Karen arranges the train on my lace coat. Rev Martin intones: *"Dearly Beloved we are gathered together..."* Some 30 minutes later we are married. We go into the vestry to sign the register then outside where we have our photographs taken and little Audrey gives me a horseshoe – in February of the following year her sister Elaine would be born. My Dad, Margaret and Ron's parents shake hands with everyone as they leave the church. Just before we leave in the wedding cars for the Green Hotel in Kinross, Ron crosses the road and goes into the cemetery where he leaves my bouquet on my Mum and Grandpa's grave.

The Green Hotel is a lovely venue. The gardens are at their best at this time of the year. The trees are stately, the scent from the blossoming shrubs and flowers is heady and the lawns are manicured to perfection. The driveway has been swept clean – I expect that's why the Manager greets us with the stern words: *"No confetti please!"*

We all spend time in these gardens having more photographs taken. My Dad has just bought a new cine camera and is filming everyone. Margaret encourages as many guests as she can to walk towards him – when we played it back later we all had a good laugh because it was so very funny watching everyone slowly walking towards the camera. It looked totally unnatural.

Inside there are toasts to be drunk and a lovely meal – roast turkey or roast beef with all the trimmings and raspberries and ice cream or trifle, followed by tea or coffee. I feel so hungry that I eat absolutely everything and my Dad, usually so quiet and unassuming stands up and holds out my empty plate for everyone to see. He makes a very moving speech. Jim's speech is amusing and Ron's speech is both emotional and very funny – he concludes by inviting people to visit and help dig our new garden.

After we have cut the cake, the tables are cleared, the chairs put around the walls and the band members organise their instruments for the ceilidh. Ron and I dance the Bridal Waltz, while everyone claps. Gradually more and more couples join in until almost everyone is dancing. We hooch to the Eightsome Reel, the Dashing White Sergeant, the Gay Gordons and Strip the Willow and dance and jive to the latest chart music such as the Beatles Hey Jude and I Got You Babe by Sonny and Cher, as well as to old favourites. Some guests who have had a few too many bevies perform party pieces such as Oh Rowan Tree and Annie Laurie. Margaret's sister Nancy balances on one knee and sings Al Jolson's Mammy to her husband Dave. Ron's Dad, who is quite intoxicated, does his party piece Nellie Dean on the return bus journey to Dundee, singing most of the way home.

Luckily I do not have to endure his dulcet tones. I change out of my dress and into my going away outfit. Our suitcases are in the back of Ron's Frogeye Sprite, which is parked outside the garage at the back of my Dad and Margaret's house in Cowdenbeath. My Dad thinks that he can sneak us away in his car, even though it has been tastefully decorated with tin cans and a sign saying: *"Just Married"*. However, it is too late. Jim, the Best Man, and some other friends soon spot our impending departure and once we get into the car they bounce the back of it up and down a few times. We wave to everyone out of the back window and return to Cowdenbeath to collect the Sprite. From there we drive to beautiful Stonefield Castle Hotel in Tarbert on the south west coast of Scotland for our honeymoon.

The last thing I remember before I leave is my Dad in tears shaking Ron's hand and seeking reassurance that he'll look after me. That thought never entered my head. On reflection, maybe that was what he was thinking about when he was so quiet on the way to church. I hug my Dad tightly, give him a kiss and thank him sincerely for being my Dad.

Since the school holidays end the weekend after our wedding and I have to return to work, we only have a four day honeymoon. Nevertheless, the weather is perfect and we go for walks to White Shore, the Pier Road, visit Inverary Castle and take ferry trips to the lovely islands of Arran and Gigha. Here we imbibe the glorious scenery that reminds us of Ullapool in Wester Ross where Aunt Margaret lives.

All too soon the holiday is over and we move into our new home. I start my new teaching job in Powrie Primary and Ron has another week's respite before returning to NCR. I say respite but he spent much of that time digging the garden and tiling the bathroom walls with turquoise tiles that matched the fittings, which were so fashionable back then.

55 Ceres Crescent

Ron and I quickly settled into our new life together and shared the household chores. I cooked the meals because Ron said that I made delicious food. He added that I had an "O" grade in Home Management. We agreed that if I cooked, then he'd wash up. I did the laundry, Ron washed the windows and the car and we both did the shopping. For the first few months we spent part of most weekends digging the garden, whose depths concealed an amazing miscellany of things, including pieces of drainpipes, plastic covers and other plumbing materials. There was the cover of a central heating unit, two doors, a sink top, bricks, screws, nails, broken glass and lots of pieces of wood. By the following summer we had created lovely back and front gardens with help from Graham and my Dad and Margaret when they visited.

The neighbours were all very friendly and would often stop and chat. We regularly crossed town to Ron's parents' house in Dalrymple Terrace in the Balgay area of Dundee for tea. Karen often visited and sometimes at weekends we went out for the day with her and her boyfriend Dave. Liz, was back at college doing the Froebel nursery course to qualify as a nursery teacher. Sometimes she would come for tea and Geoff, her fiancé, would come too when he wasn't on duty as a hospital doctor. We sometimes visited Kate and Mike, who lived in Fife. One time we went to the races at Balcormo where we won money then spent most of it on a lovely meal. When we returned to Dundee we didn't have enough left to pay the bridge toll, but thankfully the cashier waved us on our way.

Powrie Primary

My new place of employment was about a mile and a half from our house. During that first week I took the Sprite and then when Ron returned to work, he either gave me a lift or I walked. This latter option benefited me greatly because by the time I arrived at school I was well exercised and ready to face the day.

Although the staff were very friendly and made me feel extremely welcome I did miss Karen and the quirky sense of humour that we both shared – no more humming of tunes when teachers appeared as we'd done for Pete Clunie and Mr Mechan while at Dryburgh. However, I quickly settled in and soon made friends with Sheila, who had many years of experience, and Hazel, who had been teaching for two years longer than I had.

Hazel and I have remained firm friends to this day. She was, and still is, a petite, dynamic lady brimming full of creative ideas. She sewed, crocheted, painted and encouraged and inspired her pupils to undertake class projects incorporating art, history, science, etc. We were both only daughters and, like me, Hazel had a kindly Dad while her Mum, like Margaret, was feisty and held strong opinions. Hazel enjoyed badminton and at lunchtimes we'd often put up the net and play together or with other teachers who fancied a game.

I worked for three Headteachers during my five years at Powrie: the avuncular Mr Cluckie; then Miss Fraser, whose passion was curling; and lastly the gentle Miss Butterfield, who came from the Demonstration School. Jimmy Marnie, the Depute, was an extremely jocular man. One day he came into the staffroom while the subject of wife swapping parties was being light heartedly discussed. He listened intently as he learned that party guests' keys were put into a dish in the middle of the table then randomly chosen. Then for the next few times he came in to the room, he'd nonchalantly toss his keys onto the coffee table then look around expectantly with a twinkle in his eyes. Needless to say these overtures were ignored.

The janitor, a small, kindly, plump man who patrolled the corridors in his beige dustcoat, was called Mr Hogan. He was usually on hand to help administer first aid, or fix anything that needed mended. When he became aware that I'd just got married, he made up a box of polish, dusters and other cleaning materials.

My Class of 1969 - 1971

Most of the memories of Powrie are very happy ones. My first class was a Primary 6 and had 43 pupils. The next year I taught those children during Primary 7. Unfortunately, they had had three supply teachers during Primary 5. I think that the Headteacher was quite glad that he had got a teacher with some experience, albeit two years, and who was likely to stay there for a few years.

On my first day I didn't quake nearly as much as I had done on my initial morning in Dryburgh. *"Och",* I thought to myself: *"I'm not a probationer any more and so I have nothing to fear!"* I was not wrong. It was a very nice class. Perhaps the children were happy to know that they now had a teacher who'd teach them until they left for secondary school. One other bonus was that, being a fully-fledged teacher, I was sometimes assigned student teachers who were on teaching practice and so had some extra help in class.

Since this class had had so many changes the previous year, I spent some time assessing their abilities and quickly discovered that there was a top of six, a tail of ten, with the remainder of the children somewhere in the middle. I was able to teach lessons to the majority of the children and modify them for those children who were less able. I organised a variety of material that the most able children could work at when they finished their set work.

There were more than enough girls to form two netball teams and I was really pleased when most of them said that they would like to do this for half an hour after lunch a couple of times during the week. They were all very enthusiastic, quickly learned the rules and steadily improved during the course of the year. We entered the inter-schools' tournament in Primary 7 and, to the girls' delight, they reached the quarter final, despite a slight hiccup, in the weeks leading up to it.

Anne, who played Centre, was a lovely girl, but a chatterbox who persistently talked whenever the opportunity arose. One day the class was working reasonably quietly and I was teaching a small group, while Anne was chatting. I asked her twice to stop talking and get on with her work and eventually told her that if she persisted then she'd be suspended from the netball team. She ignored this request and so she was suspended. After lunch Margaret, who was one of the other team members, came to the staff room to see me with Anne and two other members, *"If Anne's not playing then neither are we,"* she told me. I don't quite know what she expected but my reply completely took the wind out of her sails as I called her bluff. *"Well Margaret that's a great pity and as far as I'm concerned then there will be no more netball."* I then closed the door. The quartet obviously considered the consequences because by the end of the day they came and apologised. I told them that I'd let them know my decision the following morning and to their relief netball was reinstated.

On another occasion, while I was working with a group of children, the dreaded words rang out: *"Mrs Wynton! Jackie Hutchison's been seek!"* Indeed poor Jackie had thrown up all over his desk that had a hinged lid, so unfortunately some of his tummy contents had dripped through onto the floor. To add to this, Mr Hogan was not in school, so we had to clean it up ourselves. I cleaned up poor Jackie and sent him with another child down to the rest room. Then I asked a couple of lads to fetch the brush, mop, sawdust and a bucket from Mr Hogan's cupboard. Before long, the room was back to rights.

Sunshine streams through the classroom window and so I walk over to lower the blinds. I survey the scene and smile with satisfaction as I watch my charges at work. As I walk back to my table to begin marking the pile of jotters, I hear snatches of conversation between Nicol and Alastair about Mr Cluckie, the Headteacher. Apparently they've been given a telling off and are feeling somewhat aggrieved. I rise and approach them from behind. They are so deep in conversation that they haven't noticed me. *"Do you boys know that Mr Cluckie is my uncle?"* I enquire and manage to suppress a laugh as shocked looks cross their faces. They are very relieved when I confess that he isn't.

Sometimes I used to take other classes for singing and their teachers in turn would take my class for something else. It was a good arrangement and worked well. Those children who were interested in music had weekly violin lessons from Mr Deuchar, while Kathleen, one of the other teachers, and I taught recorder to a small group of children during Thursday lunch times.

I clearly remember quite a number of the children and George was one of them. He was a quiet and gentle lad who could read and write with minimal difficulty and though he had mastered the process of addition he found the concept of subtraction impossible. I tried really hard using a variety of materials such as blocks, sweets, pencils and methods, such as going up and down the stairs, but to no avail. I was bitterly disappointed and felt that I'd utterly failed him. Mrs McKean, the remedial teacher, was not appointed until after the class of 1969 – 1971 had left for secondary school, so poor George's needs were sorely neglected. Unfortunately he tended to isolate himself from his peers, though they always encouraged him to take part in their games at break times. Despite that George seemed relatively happy. He was always willing to undertake tasks, such as taking the lunch money to the office, or delivering the register to Mr Marnie. I discussed the situation with Mr Cluckie and asked if it would be permissible for George to help Mr Hogan on occasions and he agreed to this. George was delighted.

One morning the first thing I notice when I arrive at school is a police car in the playground. The word spread like wildfire: *"The polis are in school!"* Those rascals who had committed minor crimes like chap door run quaked and kept a low profile. It was the weekly assembly and the policeman stood on the stage beside Mr Cluckie, running a keen eye over the assembled children before he said: *"How many of P7 own bikes?"* Some 20 hands shot up. *"Well I'm coming to school every Wednesday afternoon for the next ten weeks. I'm bringing another policeman with me and we're going to teach you how to cycle safely on the road. At the end of the ten weeks we'll give you a cycling proficiency test that includes questions on the Highway Code. If you pay attention and practise then you'll pass and get a certificate."*

For the next few weeks those children with bikes had lessons with the police and the others came out to the playground to watch. I helped also and in between practical lessons ensured that everyone was really familiar with the Highway Code. The children certainly improved and, at assembly, Mr Cluckie duly presented pass certificates to everyone. There was even one for me. As he presented me with my badge and certificate and shook my hand he announced: *"Mrs Wynton has been certified!"*

The following year, my friend Hazel got married to her boyfriend who was a teacher in Dundee: they had met at the police station when they were doing the Advanced Driving course. They were both into hill walking and he was a good badminton player too. To my delight Hazel asked me to be her Matron of Honour. We made the dresses at my house because her Mum and Dad didn't really approve of her choice of partner. I think that the pattern we used was a "Butterick" type and both dresses were made of the same fabric in different colours: white and orange respectively for Hazel and me. The styles were exactly the same: full skirted, covered buttons from top to bottom, frilled around the neck and down one side of the front. They were cut just above the knee with belts in the same fabric with bows worn around our waists. It was a very quiet wedding. I missed Hazel very much when she and her husband went to live in Perth after the Easter holiday.

"We're going on the school trip during the last week of term," I announced one June day. Each year the P7s had an excursion before they left for secondary school. This time it was to be a visit to Edinburgh – to the castle, the Camera Obscura and Princes Street. We travelled by train and our lunch had been booked at Crawford's restaurant. I knew from past visits that the restaurant used white damask tablecloths and silver-plated cutlery, tea knives and fish cutlery, as well as standard cutlery. In the weeks before we travelled, I taught the children which cutlery to use, how to read the menu and we practised these skills in the school dining room.

Mr Cluckie, together with the female student who was assigned to me, and I had a very interesting day in the capital with the children. Though they thoroughly enjoyed the places of interest, the highlight of the visit was lunch in Crawford's restaurant. Most of the children chose fish, chips and peas AND used the correct cutlery - with minimal prompting and served by waitresses wearing black skirts, white blouses, starched white aprons and small hats. A small notebook and pencil for writing the orders hung from a clasp on their waistbands.

The two years I spent teaching the class of '69 – '71 were very happy and at the end of term I was really sad to see the children leaving for the newly built Craigie High School on Arbroath Road.

Ron's New Route

The new green shoots of the spring flowers we'd planted some weeks previously had just begun to push through the soil when Ron decided that he'd like a change of career. He showed me an advert for a job selling accident insurance. *"I'm wondering about applying for this. What do you think?"* I considered for a moment then replied: *"Well if that's what you'd like to do then go ahead. There's no harm in finding out a bit more."* He applied, had an interview and was offered the job. Nevertheless there was no basic salary and the sales staff had to earn their wages through commission. However, he decided to take it and shortly afterwards left the NCR and the security of a monthly salary.

The job was interesting and took him all over the county and, while he was a good salesman, earnings were variable. However, he enjoyed both the challenges and the encounters with a great variety of people. I remember being told the story of when several of the sales staff met for lunch. No one had any calls for the afternoon and so they decided to go up the main street playing imaginary instruments. I think that Ron pretended to play the drum while someone else snapped castanets. Although they didn't write any new policies, they certainly knew how to pull a crowd as they made their way along the street to loud cheers and applause.

One day while on a visit to a farm, he noticed a lovely chocolate brown Labrador whose name was Honey. The farmer told him that she'd been trained as a gun dog by the local gamekeeper but, because she was terrified of the noise, was going to be shot. He told the gamekeeper that he'd take her and find her a good home – he asked Ron if he'd take her. Ron didn't hesitate and immediately decided that he would. As he was leaving he gently called her name, opened the car door and Honey leapt in.

I was cooking our evening meal when he arrived home. *"Hello Maggie come and see what I've brought home for you."* By now I was well used to these *"surprises"* and assumed that it would be either something such as a bottle of wine or some home made jam he'd got from a person to whom he'd sold a policy, or some plants for the garden. I went outside. *"Open the door Maggie,"* said Ron and so I did. Imagine my surprise when the loveliest dog I'd ever seen came cautiously out. *"I'll take her to work with me,"* said Ron

Honey was a pure bred Labrador. She had beautiful appealing brown eyes, a brown, wet, leathery nose and a tail that wagged vigorously. When I commented on the little marks on her muzzle, Ron explained that they were pellet marks from when she'd been hit by being taken too close to the gun. Although it was sad, we were both very glad that she'd come to live with us. After tea we took her for a walk along the beach. Honey kept very close to heel and when it was bedtime, we gave her a blanket on the living room floor. Just as I was drifting off to sleep, I heard the notes of the piano playing. When I went to investigate, I found her standing on her hind legs, playing the piano with her forelegs. I closed the lid, settled her down and returned to bed. In the morning Honey was curled up on the floor by our bedroom door.

Honey settled well with us. She'd lived with us for some six months before she ever barked and that was at a neighbour's cat that had strayed into the garden. When she went for walks, she covered many times the distance that we did. She loved to run and her speciality was performing spectacular somersaults. Whenever she met another dog, she'd do her very best to involve it in her antics by bounding straight at it as if to say: *"Come on and play!"* When this hilarious spectacle occurred, we'd both laugh uncontrollably till the tears rolled down our cheeks.

The Class of 1971 – 1974

I was ecstatic and the reason was because my new Primary 5 class comprised ten girls and fourteen boys: only 24 children. This was absolute bliss. The other bonus was that, this year, my classroom was on the middle floor instead of right at the top.

"Alan", *"Here"*, *"Ramsay"*, *"Here"*, *"Ronald"*, *"Here"*, Kevin"... there was no answer. *"Has anyone seen him?"* There was a collective shaking of heads. I guessed that Kevin must have had some sort of accident. He was a small, red haired feisty lad who was incredibly healthy, rarely absent and never late. I had just marked the register, with pencil, when the door burst open and a breathless Kevin entered. *"Please Miss, sorry E'm late"*, panted Kevin: *"Meh Mum's in hospital."* We all looked quite shocked. Kevin's Mum had had a baby a few weeks previously: *"Oh dear that's not so good,"* I said. *"It's OK,"* said Kevin, *"she's getting sterilised!"* *"Well she'll be home again very soon,"* I said, not knowing whether to laugh or cry at his lack of discretion. *"Now take out your spelling books children."*

The school gym hall was very well used and we had two sessions per week. I organised my class into five groups and took out equipment, such as climbing ropes, benches, mats, vaulting horse, beanbags and hoops or balls. The other session was used for teaching ceilidh dances such as the Gay Gordons, the Virginia Reel and the Dashing White Sergeant. However, before these dances could be perfected the children had to learn to keep time to the music. Initially instructions were simple: *"Listen to the music, clap in time to the music, walk round to the music, then walk round for eight and stop for eight."* Or: *"Clap for eight and stop for eight."* This could be funny as some children lost count but when they were asked to skip round that was hilarious, because even at the age of ten, many of them, particularly the boys, had yet to master the art of skipping.

The girls were very keen to play netball, but since there weren't enough of them to make two teams, I played a team of boys against them. Initially the girls would panic and bunch up when the ball came towards them, while the boys, who were well used to playing regular football, ran into spaces naturally. However, over time they progressed and eventually reached the semi-final in the interschool's tournament – Miss Fraser, who was the current Headteacher, came to watch and announced their progress at assembly. The following week I took the girls back to my house for a celebration buffet tea: small sausage rolls, ham sandwiches, chocolate cake and orange juice.

June always is a busy month in schools – similar to the run up to Christmas – with Sport's Day, visits, Parents' Night and reports. The small blue books formerly used for reports had given way to single A4 sheets.

There were two copies: one for parents and one for the file. This copy was made by using a sheet of blue carbon paper between the pieces of paper.

I was making great progress with these and words and phrases flowed from my pen as I conjured up a mental picture of each child. When I came to do Ronald Brown's I wrote: *"Ronald is an ebullient boy who usually gives of his best."* I thought no more about it. When his Mum and Auntie came to Parents' Night they both looked decidedly worried. *"Whatever's the matter Mrs Brown?"* I enquired. *"Whit's wrang wi meh Ronald,"* wailed his Mum. *"Why"*, I asked. *"Oh Mrs Wynton ye've sade he's ebu... something or ither!"* I smiled: *"Mrs Brown, your son Ronald is such a lovely, bouncy wee lad and he's a real credit to you."* Mrs Brown sighed: *"Oh meh Goad Eh'm awfa gled."* And with that she took my hand and shook it firmly.

Another New Route for Ron

Despite Ron's best efforts, the job selling accident insurance was a great disappointment. He didn't want to return to NCR and though there were plenty of other available jobs he decided to apply for a place on the technical teacher's course at Dundee College of Education. So in October 1971 he became a full-time student and he received a grant. Obviously our income was less than when we got married and so Ron took temporary jobs. Every year at Christmas he worked on the post. Unlike my time as a postie delivering Christmas cards and avoiding scary dogs, he was lucky enough to work in the sorting office. He also qualified as a driving instructor and worked for a local driving school. I also decided we should rent out one of our bedrooms to a lady called Janice. She was one of Liz's friends and they had met on the Froebel nursery teacher's course. Janice had a job in the Demonstration School, next door to the College of Education, which was regularly used as an exemplar for teaching methods and practices. She stayed at our house for the year before she was married. As for Honey she happily stayed in the hall where she had plenty of room and I returned home at lunchtimes to take her for a walk.

Ron also took a job as a barman in a local hotel. The Ballinard was a lovely old stone built house formerly owned by a jute baron. It was set in spacious well-kept gardens on the outskirts of Broughty Ferry. Two sculptured lions reposed on stone plinths directly in front of the balustrades that bordered the steps leading up to the impressive heavy wooden front door. The ground floor, bedrooms and bathrooms of the hotel were lovely. The function rooms, cloakroom, toilets and bar were situated in the basement, access to which was down a wide flight of stairs.

While many of the local residents were heavily mortgaged and could only afford a modest drink that would last them for most of the evening, the entrepreneurial owner decided to move to a different market. Since there was a huge council estate only a short bus journey away, he advertised attractions such as live music, dancing at the weekends and strippers on Fridays. This proved to be a great success and especially the strippers.

Now Ron's induction to the Ballinard provided him with magnificent opportunities to 'people watch' and he relished these. The first time he saw the stripper he admitted that he watched her, then on subsequent occasions he watched the expressions on the faces of the punters. Occasionally a few would climb onto the tables to get a better view. One evening a middle-aged man put his chair onto the table so that he could watch in comfort. Well, so he thought. Somehow he lost his balance and fell, cutting his chin on the way down. There was so much background noise that this accident went unnoticed until Ron went over with a tray of drinks. He spotted the man, a bit the worse for wear sitting at the table with a hand propping up his chin, from which blood was dripping. The man's friends hadn't wanted to miss anything of the stripper's act! Ron fetched the first aid box and patched him up.

Verbal altercations between folk were a regular occurrence, though physical fisticuffs were fairly rare. One night, however, people were happily dancing to the music when an argument between two women escalated and soon the small dance floor was crowded with squabbling people. Those who'd been dancing joined the fray as did others who'd been happily sitting drinking. Handbags were the premier choice of weapons and used to whack the nearest person. Old scores that had long festered were settled that night. I believe the threat of the police eventually stopped the fracas.

On another occasion the police were called because a young man had been involved in a physical disagreement outside. He arrived at the bar a bit bruised and rather dishevelled, his shirt awry and his jacket torn. *"What happened,"* asked the burly policeman. *"Eh fell!"* came the reply.

Often I'd take Honey to meet Ron after he finished and on the way home he'd regale me with these hilarious stories. Sometimes I'd venture in and wait until all the glasses were washed and order restored, then we'd have a few games of dominoes.

Helen was the lady who helped clear the tables and wash up. Of course not all the glasses were empty. Helen firmly believed in the maxim *waste not, want not* and so she'd often drink the contents of these instead of pouring them away. As a consequence she was frequently inebriated. She would often fall asleep while we were playing dominoes and miss her turn. One time as we were all about to depart, she woke up: *"eh'm chappin',"* she said. Another time she overbalanced outside and fell over one of the stone lions, though thankfully she didn't hurt herself.

Weddings and Babies

The summer after Hazel's wedding, my primary school friend Liz married Geoff at Kirkcaldy Registry Office. She wore a long white dress with her long blonde hair pinned up. A big floppy brimmed hat, which was all the rage, completed her outfit. I wore a suit I had made with Karen. It was a floral print and I also wore a floppy hat, like Liz's to complete the ensemble. Afterwards we had a lovely meal and both Dads made nice speeches. Since several of our friends from our college days were there we had a wonderful time catching up on all of their news.

By this time my Dad and Stepmother had moved from Cowdenbeath to a bungalow in a quite cul-de-sac in Crossgates in Fife two doors down from their friends Anne and Archie Allan.

The following year my friend Karen, AKA Miss Grant, whom I met in my first teaching job at Dryburgh Primary, married her boyfriend Keith. I was her Matron of Honour. Karen's Mum made two lovely full-length A-line floral print dresses; one for me and one for Sandra, another of Karen's friends. We had white sling back shoes while on our heads we wore turquoise close fitting caps made from artificial flowers. After the church wedding we had a lovely meal in a local hotel and a ceilidh.

It was great to see my friends happily settled and in time Hazel's first baby was born. We sometimes visited when we went to Perth for the day and sometimes Hazel and her husband brought him to our house. Honey would lie beside him while he stroked her.

School Pets

"Now remember if you're too noisy you'll frighten the animals," I cautioned the children. Classroom pets had a very calming effect on the children and during my time at Powrie we had two guinea pigs (one at a time), three goldfish and a gerbil. Ron made a hutch and small run for the guinea pigs and I acquired both a cage for the gerbil and a tank for the fish. The children willingly brought in 1p per week to buy snuggle bedding and food and they cared for these creatures very well. There was also a ready supply of newspaper with which to line the cages. The guinea pigs, both of whom were called Snuggles, quickly endeared themselves by cosying in to anyone who cuddled them and by making squeaking and purring sounds. There was a rota for those children who were able to look after the class pet at weekends and holidays. I think that the Snuggles the First died during the first summer holiday while Snuggles the Second was adopted by two of the girls when they left school.

A few weeks before the summer holidays Honey, who was usually so healthy, became unwell. Although she'd never had any puppies she seemed to be producing milk. We took her to the vet, who admitted her and performed a hysterectomy. A few days later she came home with several stitches in her tummy. I was concerned that she'd chew at them and thought it might be a possibility for Honey to come to school. I explained the situation to Miss Butterfield and told her that if I couldn't bring Honey then I would have to take unpaid leave of absence until the stitches came out. She agreed for Honey to join me at school, so long as none of the other teachers objected. No one did and so Honey and her basket came to school to the delight of the children. I put her basket in the corner and there Honey lay quietly until I went to write on the board. She possibly thought that was the signal for her to get up and so she cautiously stepped out of the basket, yawned, stretched and walked towards me to a chorus of *"Aw"* from the children.

We returned to Edinburgh for our Primary 7 school trip and this time it was to the zoo. We travelled in one of Napper Thompson's buses and as it proceeded towards the Windy City with streamers billowing from the windows, choruses such as, *"Ye Cannae shove yer Grannie aff the Bus"*, were lustily sung by the occupants.

This time we had our meal at the zoo. In sharp contrast to my last class trip to Crawford's restaurant, the table tops were covered with formica, instead of snow white cloths, the cutlery was made of plastic rather than silver plate, and it was self service rather being waited on by smartly clad staff.

The penguins and sea lions were the most popular creatures and the children thoroughly enjoyed their day. Customary souvenirs were bought in the shop and taken carefully home in the bus by their proud owners. The bus was much quieter on the homeward journey as most of the children fell asleep.

Soon afterwards the children left for pastures new and *their* next great adventure AND the surviving guinea pig moved on also to *its* new home.

Uprooting North

"I've accepted a job in Inverness Maggie", said Ron when he returned from the interview by the panel that offered new graduates jobs in different places. *"I'm going to work for half of the week in Inverness Royal Academy and in Millburn Academy for the other half."* I wasn't surprised, as there was a lack of jobs in the area for technical teachers, but I was sad. Ron had the choice of this job, or one in Perth but had opted for a complete change. I had been very happy at Powrie Primary and I felt really settled in our home in Ceres Crescent, Broughty Ferry. I would really miss my friends.

With that decision made there was lots to do. Not only had the house to be sold, we had to find somewhere else to live. From having a fairly predictable life, we were going into the unknown and, though it was quite an exciting prospect, I felt apprehensive.

I handed in my notice at school and said my goodbyes to my colleagues. I felt quite sad to leave since I got on very well with all of the staff. But at the same time I'd been there for five years and new opportunities beckoned for both of us. An afternoon tea was held just before the holidays, on which occasion I was presented with a clock. Unfortunately, I sadly have no idea of its whereabouts now, unlike the casserole dish I received from the children of Dryburgh Primary.

Quite a few potential buyers came to view our house. It was not on the market for long and was bought for £11,800 by a couple of teachers who'd amazingly worked in Inverness Royal Academy – they spoke very highly of its reputation. I guess that, once I got used to the prospect of moving north, I was quite excited and, though we'd be leaving our lovely first home, there were definitely more pluses than minuses. I cheered myself knowing that we'd see Aunt Margaret more often.

We initially decided to rent temporary accommodation so that we could find a house in an area that we both liked. We contacted Inverness County Council and were offered a newly built house at 14 Wallace Place in Smithton, Inverness. It was very sad uprooting ourselves and saying our goodbyes to everyone, in particular my Dad, Ron's parents, Karen, Liz and Hazel, but we all promised to keep in touch by letter and telephone and to visit when we could.

Chapter 6: Onwards and Upwards to the Highlands

Mairi Mackenzie

Who is that person on the road
She has no idea of the Highway Code
Paying scant heed to cars and the occasional lorry
One of these days she is going to be sorry.

But Mairi's faith was true and strong
As she bowled along she sang a song
And swung her shopping bag to and fro
As down to the village she would go.

Sporting a trilby hat and stripey stockings
She little cared for the road she was blocking
The local traffic knew her well
By the stockings they could always tell!

And Mairi was very kind
She had great faith in all mankind.
Her lilting voice, her beaming smile
Made visits to her most worthwhile.

Life in Inverness

"That fence looks like a stockade!" I gasped in horror as Ron stopped our little red Fiat 127 outside what was to be our new home. We had spent the morning driving the 130 miles from Dundee to Inverness, passing our Pickfords removal lorry en route through the spectacular Cairngorms mountain range on the A9 north. Despite the incredible natural beauty of our new surrounds in the Highland capital of Inverness, it was hard to leave our first house and garden that we had so lovingly decorated and cultivated behind - forever.

This was the first time I had set eyes on the maisonette we had been allocated – we had not even seen any photographs. After I stepped out of the car, I shut my eyes, fervently hoping that when I opened them I'd see a lovely bungalow like the one we'd left. But when I peered around the gate, taking a deep breath, I stared forlornly at what was to be our new home. It seemed so soulless.

In 1974 the town of Inverness was steadily growing and several new housing estates had been built. When Ron accepted his first teaching job there, we were allocated a property in the Smithton area of Culloden. These homes were built in terraces of four and the exterior was roughcast with grey and white chips. The small front gardens were open plan. Meanwhile high wooden fencing, with gates in the middle, offered the occupants some privacy at the back.

Our maisonette was in 14 Wallace Place and seemed so small in comparison to the detached home we'd been accustomed to. Downstairs was the hall, a living room and a kitchen, while upstairs there were two bedrooms and a bathroom. It would be fine as a stop-gap, but very quickly both of us resolved to spend our weekends searching for a home to buy.

Ron settled well into his new position as a Teacher of Technical Education in two secondary schools – Millburn Academy fairly near the town centre and Inverness Royal Academy, nicknamed the IRA, and a stone's throw from the busy High Street in a quiet residential area called the Crown. The IRA was one of the best secondary schools in the Highlands and its intake included children from the Western Isles – Lewis, Harris, North Uist, Benbecula, South Uist and Barra – who stayed in a hostel nearby during the term time. Doing well at school was their hope of a future on the mainland if they wanted to move away from the crofts.

There were quite a few characters at both schools and one of them was Jack McCall, the IRA janny, or janitor. He often visited the Technical Department at break times and told a succession of anecdotes. A particular favourite that Ron shared with me involved Jack's daughter, who was a police constable in Inverness. One day she took a phone call from a man on her beat and who had reported a commotion coming from a flat directly above his. He asked if the police could come round to investigate, so Jack's daughter and a colleague did. When they arrived they could hear a lot of noise. The door was answered and they went inside and up the stairs. The noise grew louder. The bathroom door was opened to reveal a small black Shetland pony noisily munching a pile of hay that was in the bath. The man explained that he thought the pony, which lived in a field further down the road, was lonely. He always fed it a carrot or apple when he walked by and of course the pony had got to know him and followed him, so he took it home. Although the equine had managed the stairs, professional help was needed to take it back outside to its field.

As yet I had no job. Although I missed the children and the buzz of the staffroom, I hadn't applied for a job yet because I wanted to look around beforehand. I found that I was really enjoying having some free time – an extension of the summer holiday. Each week I bought the local Inverness Courier and eagerly scanned the property section for homes within a 15-mile radius of Inverness, and at the weekends Ron and I would go and view houses together, taking in the most wonderful scenery of hills, lochs and rivers. No wonder the Highlands was such a popular tourist destination – the natural beauty of our new surroundings bewitched us.

During the week I busied myself unpacking our belongings, tidying up the garden and taking Honey for long walks to explore our new environment. Our neighbours were friendly, although many were out working. I was grateful that the lady next door, who was a vet, had a new baby and was at home, so we'd sometimes have coffee and craic together. A small black mongrel lived next door on the other side and she would accompany Honey and me on our favourite ramble to the nearby Culloden Woods. At that time there was a huge grassy field behind the houses and

Honey together with her new friend would bound over it on the way to the forest. We would walk past the stables and the entrance to Culloden House, a stately home, before crossing the railway bridge to the woods. Sometimes I'd stop and watch if I heard a train coming and, as it passed under the bridge, I'd wonder where all of the passengers were going.

The many paths in the woods meandered in a variety of different directions. Honey and I explored them one by one and it was down one of these tracks that I discovered the Clootie Well. I had no idea what it was, but I later discovered that a Clootie Well was a well or spring that had been a Celtic place of pilgrimage. To this day, strips of cloth or rags are left there, usually tied to the branches of the tree as part of a healing ritual. In Scots nomenclature a *"clootie"* or *"clout"* is a strip of cloth or rag. The tradition is generally to wash the affected part of the body with the wet rag and then tie the rag on a branch. As the branch and cloot disintegrate over time, the ailment is supposed to fade away.

The approach to this particular Clootie Well was through a particularly dark part of the woods where the pine trees were very tall and close together. In the distance I could see a circular wall and, as we drew nearer, I noticed some scraps of material tied onto the lower branches of the surrounding trees. As I stepped through the opening in the wall, to my amazement, I saw the well – it was sunk into the flagged-stone floor. The water was very dark and still. Honey sniffed it cautiously and drew back. The other canine was either fearless, or short sighted, and before I could stop her she'd slipped in. I had no idea how deep the water was. My heart missed a beat but I reached forward and caught her by her collar. Then I put my other hand under her bottom and lifted her out. I was rewarded for this feat of bravery by a small *"drookit"* dog happily shaking herself all over me. Heaving a sigh of relief, we retraced our steps and were soon back in the sunshine. By the time we got back to Wallace Place the small dog was completely dry. She had obviously learned her lesson for she never ventured near the well on any other occasion that she came for a walk with us.

I felt quite content exploring the area, but I did miss our friends, colleagues and family in and around Dundee. Luckily, my school friend Liz and her husband Geoff came up on the train to visit. They were now living in Edinburgh, where she worked as a nursery teacher and he as a hospital doctor. I remember awaiting the long blue British Rail train in the draughty Inverness station terminus and being overjoyed to see these two familiar faces – Liz with her beautiful long blond hair and Geoff with his trendy horn rimmed specs and dark wavy curls. It was great to see them again to catch up on all of their news and we'd a wonderful few days going on walks and visits to the pub before they headed back to the Windy City.

Because we now lived closer to her, Aunt Margaret came to visit us several times in her VW camper van. She would take an outing from rural Ullapool to stock up on supermarket goods and kitchenware in the big smoke of Inverness for her Bed and Breakfast guests. There wasn't a wide range of shops where she lived, so she relished these sojourns and the chance to buy some practical shoes and utilitarian outfits, such as pinafore and aprons, that she considered essential for a B&B proprietor. It was so lovely to see her rosy face and hug her rotund figure and we promised to spend a few days with her in Ullapool during Ron's October school holiday.

My New job – Teaching Maths!

One day Ron's Head teacher at Millburn Academy, William Weatherspoon, said to him: *"So your wife's a teacher Mr Wynton. Well you tell her to come into school. One of the teachers is retiring and we need a replacement."* Maths was never my strong point, but all of a sudden I was offered a job teaching this dreaded subject to children who were struggling with it. At least I had had something in common with them.

I was delighted to be offered a job and soon after I met Mr Weatherspoon and thus began my new career in the Remedial Department teaching secondary school Maths. I shared the only available classroom with Audrey Kemp, the other Remedial Teacher, who taught English. We divided this classroom with screens and, since the groups of children were small, it worked well.

Audrey's husband Charles worked in the Technical Department with Ron. Both were in their 40s and had formerly lived in London. Over the years they had spent many caravan holidays in the Highlands. They decided to move north because they enjoyed the slower pace of life, the scenery and, above all, the friendliness of the people. I remember being shocked when Audrey told me she did not know her neighbours in London.

After they sold their house, they bought a plot of land from the farmer at Dalchriechart, where they parked their caravan, and then they built a Norwegian timber house, complete with a saater (grass roof). Audrey had taught French in a large inner-city secondary school, but said that it seemed pointless teaching a foreign language when the children couldn't really communicate satisfactorily in English. Along with the other women teachers she had long abandoned wearing skirts or dresses and instead taken to wearing trousers. This was to prevent some of the lads peering up at their stockings, suspenders, petticoats and knickers while they were ascending the stairs.

Although the school was much larger than I was used to, I thoroughly enjoyed being part of it. The small groups I taught comprised mainly boys and, luckily, they were fairly easily managed. I worked very hard and occasionally managed to teach basic arithmetic, though often a great deal of time was spent talking and trying to help them with various other difficulties, such as problems with family relationships that had absolutely nothing to do with school.

Thankfully there was no playground duty to do during intervals since the janitors undertook this. And there were several choices of venue to go to for the break. Sometimes Audrey and I would join other staff members in the staff base of the art department where the Head of

Department Walter Cumming would entertain us with lots of jokes and anecdotes.

At other times I'd go down to the technical department where I'd find myself a seat in the untidy overcrowded staff base and enjoy the banter. There was always something or other going on and the Head of Department Al Gunn told stories that were priceless. Colin Baillie, who was a PE teacher and one of the Assistant Rectors often visited too. *"You should have been at the Board of Studies meeting yesterday Al,"* he said. *"Why,"* asked Al innocently, *"What happened?"* Everyone fell about laughing. Al looked around in wonderment. Of course he'd forgotten he was meant to attend the board meeting and after school had returned home to take his dog for a walk.

Several years later when Al retired, at Christmas time, the customary dinner was held in the Craigmonie Hotel. There were the usual speeches, which Ron videoed, and the presentation was greeted by uproarious laughter when Stuart Mackay, one of the technical teachers walked in with the aid of a Zimmer frame decorated with tinsel and flashing lights. Al was delighted with this mobility aid, although he was still extremely fit and active.

Sometimes I'd go down to the large staffroom on the ground floor where the hums of conversation from various groups of people abounded. Underneath one of the windows was a large leather settee on which three female members of staff generally sat. Interestingly they all became pregnant around the same time and after that men generally occupied the settee.

House Hunting

We stayed at Wallace Place for all of 14 weeks and during that time viewed countless properties in Inverness, the Black Isle and Drumnadrochit. There was the neat little bungalow at the end of Culduthel Road in Inverness, which would have been a stone's throw from the IRA and close to the picturesque Loch Ness. We visited it twice before deciding that we'd prefer to live out of town. We quickly discovered that selling agents tend to gild the lily somewhat in their property adverts. One Saturday we set off to view two houses on the Black Isle and one in North Kessock, all of them unoccupied. None of them proved suitable: one boasted a utility room, which turned out to be a tap under the stairway; another advertised a breakfast room that was actually a tiny rickety extension; and the last specified three bedrooms when there were only two – the third turned out to be a large walk-in cupboard!

After a great deal of searching we went to view a cottage in Drumnadrochit. Westbury is the first house on the Achtemarack Road. Achtemarack means the place of the shamrock. The house stands near the bottom of the steep hill that leads to the farmland at Easter and Wester Achtemarack. Its walls were and still are white. Mrs Cameron, who owned it, had recently been widowed and wanted to move back to Leigh in

Wiltshire to be with her family. I think that the original name of the house was Calituinn (Gaelic for hazelnut) and when they bought it the Camerons changed the name to Westbury after the place called Westbury in Wiltshire. Mr Cameron had enjoyed working in the large garden where he grew lots of flowers, fruit and vegetables. But Mrs Cameron felt unable to continue to maintain these grounds.

Westbury was a typical Highland cottage, two up and two down and with rambling red roses growing up the wall. A small storm porch with red painted timber supports sheltered the front door, the eaves and fascia boards were also red, the windows were small and there was no back door. There was a small hall with doors to the left and right. The door to the left led into the parlour, while the one to the right led to the living room. This living room had another door that led into a small scullery with a tiny window. Upstairs and off the landing were three doors, two of which led to bedrooms facing the front and the last led into a small bathroom facing the rear. The landing area between the bedrooms had been partitioned to make a long cupboard with a door at the left hand side and a small window in the middle. At first glance I thought that if the partition was removed it would make a lovely open area. But I decided that if we made an offer for the cottage this would not be an option since it would be really useful to keep it as a storage cupboard.

Although the cottage needed lots of renovation we both felt that we'd be happy and settled there. We really hoped to have some children of our own and felt that this would be the perfect environment in which to raise them. We offered the asking price – £8,300 – and soon enough it was ours and we came to live at Westbury. Not long afterwards, I found I was expecting a baby – and I had not even sat on that settee at Millburn Academy!

Putting down Roots at Westbury

Schiehallion

Schiehallion is a Scottish Munro in Perthshire; you'll often see it on picture postcards. I well remember seeing that magnificent mountain while canoeing on Loch Tummel. I was in second year at Dundee College of education and on an Easter trip to Bonskeid House near Killiecrankie. Fast forward ten years and this mountain was all I could think of after Ron and I and our removal men had arrived at our new home in Glenurquhart – Westbury – and unpacked all our belongings. By the end of our first day in our new abode, the living room was piled so high with boxes it seemed to resemble a cardboard copy of Schiehallion.

I had not been sad that morning when we left our temporary home in 14 Wallace Place, Inverness, after just 14 weeks there. Actually I was relieved as the removal van left and I closed the door for the last time. I didn't look back once as we drove the 20 mile scenic journey along the banks of Loch Ness, admiring the orange bracken and autumnal leaves: it was magical. All too soon we drove past the village of Drumnadrochit and into Glenurquhart and drew up at our cottage with its pillar box red door and window frames and matching red roses climbing the front wall. The view over the stone wall at the end of the garden of the afforested hills in front was spectacular: it seemed like a perfect rural retreat.

The removal van was already parked in the wide lay-by opposite when we arrived. The next few hours passed quickly as the two removal men and Ron carried our furniture and boxes upon boxes through the front door. When the van eventually left we sank gratefully onto two of our chairs. The autumn daylight was fading fast. That was when the enormity of the task of unpacking and modernising this historic cottage dawned on us. When much later two very tired people flopped into bed, I was very thankful for the small mat that Ron had put on the bare floorboards at my side, just in case my exhausted personage fell out in the night.

New Neighbours

Unlike my friend Audrey Kemp, who had not known any of her neighbours in London, we didn't have to even try to meet ours. Highlanders are naturally friendly folk and so they came to us.

"Hello, anyone home?" called a voice the day after we had moved in. I went to the door leaving Ron still finishing the long list of essential work we needed to do. In the hall stood a man and woman in their 50s, both of whom were smiling widely. *"Hello I'm Cathy,"* said the woman as I shook her outstretched hand. *"And this is my husband Jackie."* Jackie looked around and with a twinkle in his eye said: *"It'll be grand to have a young family living here!"* *"I wonder how he knows,"* I thought. I'd just had the results of my pregnancy test and they confirmed that I was going to have a baby the following summer. I just smiled and said nothing because at that point we hadn't told anyone because it was very early days!

Jackie and Cathy were tenant farmers who lived some two miles away at the very top of the winding single-track road, across a burn and over a cattle grid. Both were originally from Sutherland and had lovely lilting voices. They stayed in one of the two whitewashed stone houses while Mr and Mrs Michael, the owners of the farm, lived in the other. There, Jackie tended to a herd of cows, who were all given Christian names, and a flock of sheep as well as some truly free range hens.

At the time I did not realise that this was the beginning of the first of many reciprocal visits and a long and lasting friendship, with countless cups of tea and home-baked pancakes and scones to be consumed together over the years as we went through the ups and downs of our lives together.

Soon afterwards, I was pegging some washing out on the line when a plump, softly spoken elderly lady passed by the garden wall. *"Welcome to the Glen,"* she announced. *"I'm Mairi Mackenzie and I live in the cottage just behind your back garden. Come in and see me anytime."*

Mairi was one of life's eccentrics. She would regularly walk the three miles to the village, usually near the middle of the road, swinging her shopping bag and paying no heed to any traffic in either direction. She was easily recognisable in her Trilby hat, flowing coat and stripey stockings. She had been brought up in the Free Presbyterian faith and continued to be a devout worshipper in the local church. Yet she enjoyed reading the weekly publications of The Jewish Chronicle newspaper and would buy a copy any time that she was in Inverness. After we went to live at Westbury, Ron would regularly bring one home to her. She had visited Israel on several occasions and I recall her telling me that, on one occasion, she took a quantity of hard-boiled eggs there in her suitcase, although I have no idea why.

On our first meeting, she told me that her sister Peggy lived beside the village green in Drumnadrochit and offered Bed and Breakfast. The family owned Dalreoch, another cottage that they rented out during the summer months, further up the road towards Achtemarack. Over the coming months and years we got to know Mairi and Peggy well, often checking on Mairi after she developed dementia and became forgetful, even taking to starting fires in the bracken a couple of times.

A Pregnancy Pal

As I reach my third month of pregnancy I have to attend the ante-natal clinic at Raigmore Hospital in Inverness. I am sitting in the waiting room and, as I look up from my magazine, I catch the eye of a slightly larger-tummied lady sitting nearby. We both smile simultaneously and are soon chatting nineteen to the dozen. She's called Denise and lives nearby in Drumnadrochit. She works as a radiographer at the hospital in Dingwall and her first baby's due towards the end of April. We exchange addresses and phone numbers then she's called into her appointment. Soon afterwards my name is called and by the time I come out Denise has already left. I return home feeling really pleased to have met someone from the village who is having a baby too and we soon become firm friends.

Chapter 7: Two Christenings, Two Funerals

There are some conversations in life you never forget. The words resound in your mind as if you just heard them for the first time. I remember such a conversation with my Dad soon after my Stepmother Margaret Ferguson died. We talked about my Dad's biggest regret in his life, that he was not with my Mum when she died. She had been unconscious in hospital and he had been persuaded by his Aunt Susan to go home and rest. As I tried to reassure him, he told me: *"Margaret, I lost you when your Mum died."*

How tough it was for my Dad, not just losing my Mum, but his two-year-old daughter as well. Although I always saw him regularly even when I lived with other members of the family or family friends over the years, the happy family he had hoped to have with his beloved Annie, my Mum, was thwarted so soon and so tragically. After that he somehow managed to get on with his life and find a level of contentment, but I only wish I could have had more conversations like this, to really know how he felt and how he managed.

Linsey Ann Wynton

My first child Linsey was very well behaved, at least during the time she was inside me. Apart from her having to be turned a couple of times at the antenatal clinic, I enjoyed excellent health. I was told that if my baby didn't make an appearance by 10 days after the due date then I would be admitted to hospital. Linsey appeared quite cosy and comfortable in situ, but certainly needed a wee bit of prompting in order to make her entry into the world.

As arranged, Ron took me to Raigmore Hospital and stayed until I was booked in. I quickly made friends with a lady called Anne who was in the room next door and whose baby was also due anytime. As we chatted we could hear a great variety of noises from some of the other women who were in various stages of labour. Anne and I looked at each other and said simultaneously, *"What have we let ourselves in for?"* At this late stage there was definitely no turning back. I naively told myself: *"If it was so bad then women wouldn't have babies."*

Next day after a thorough examination I was hooked up to a machine that monitored Linsey's heartbeat and another that injected a drug that was intended to make my muscles contract. Nothing happened for ages and then when it did it was very intermittent. Ron left Honey in the car when he came to visit, but didn't stay too long because the weather was quite hot and he didn't want Honey to overheat. Eventually the doctor said that they were going to take me to theatre because Linsey was showing signs of distress. The last three things I remember are Mr Jennings, the anaesthetist explaining what he was going to do, swallowing the tube so that the contents of my stomach could be removed and then hearing a voice calling from a long, long way away, *"Mrs Wynton you've got a big girl!"* I considered this and thought: *"That must be someone else."*

And I went back to sleep. Ron's attempts to waken me also failed. Just before midnight Linsey Ann Wynton made her entry into the world and was wrapped up and snuggled in a cot by the midwives. Meanwhile, I spent the night asleep in a nearby ward enjoying the last full night's sleep I'd have for a few months. Luckily the midwives gave Linsey a bottle of milk.

Next morning when I woke it took me quite a while to focus because I felt so spaced out after all the medication, which still seemed to be in my system. I propped myself up and had just swung my legs over the side of the bed when two nurses appeared. *"Where do you think you're going?"* they said. I recalled the events of the night before and that I had had a little girl. *"Where's my baby? Please can I see her?"* The nurses smiled and said that they'd fetch her right away. Shortly afterwards the door opened and a sleeping Linsey in a hospital bassinet was wheeled into the room. She was gently lifted out and placed in my arms. I looked down proudly on this beautiful baby girl who was sleeping so soundly, hugged her tightly and sincerely thanked God for her safe delivery.

An ecstatic Ron visited later. He told me that on the way into hospital he had given a lift to two hitch hikers, as we often did in those days, and told them all about Linsey. He'd just gone to take Honey for a walk when my Aunt Margaret came in carrying an enormous bouquet of flowers. It was so kind of her to have come all of the way from Ullapool, but I suppose I never really realised at the time just how much Aunt Margaret was like a Mum to me. We chatted for ages while Linsey slept.

It was late afternoon when my Dad and Margaret visited. They'd arranged their holiday assuming that Linsey would be born by her due date and we'd be back home. By the time Ron phoned to tell them about their new grand-daughter, they'd already left for Inverness. My Dad was absolutely delighted, Margaret was annoyed that Ron hadn't phoned earlier, although he hadn't wanted to wake them by calling in the middle of the night. She also seemed put out when she found out that we were to stay in hospital for the next ten days. But she had not had children of her own, so probably did not really understand that that was the custom after a Caesarian section.

When she asked, and was told Linsey's names, she seemed really taken aback. She obviously didn't approve of our choice of names. We had chosen Linsey because we both liked it. One of the boys in my class had had a sister named Lindsay and that's when I had first heard it used as a Christian name. And there was no question for me that I wouldn't name her anything other than Ann after my Mum. But Margaret could never have understood that longing that I had for my Mum and that love even though, sadly, I scarcely remember her. When I first held Linsey in my arms I really understood what it meant to be a Mum and how tragic it was that I no longer had *my* Mum. Only then could I feel how much my Mum must have loved me.

After Margaret and my Dad left, I felt very deflated. The wonderful euphoria that I experienced simply evaporated and I shed quite a few tears. It felt like we would never see eye to eye – the situation was impossible. She could never love me like a mother and because of this I could not respond in the way she wanted. When Ron found out what had happened, he wanted to go and speak to them but I persuaded him not to since I saw little point in making the situation any worse.

They visited a few times the following week before returning home – on one occasion Margaret remarked that I looked like an old lady on account of the fact that I was unable to stand upright. Although I would have liked to see my Dad, we didn't see them again until the Christmas holiday.

"You're going to have three units of blood Mrs Wynton and after that you'll feel great," the nurse informed me a few days later. Apparently I had lost a considerable amount during Linsey's birth and so needed a transfusion. She was quite right because after this had been done I felt absolutely wonderful.

During our time in hospital I spent time with other new Mums exchanging stories as well as tips on childcare. The majority of women preferred to bottle feed their babies, the justification for this was that they'd know exactly the amount they were taking. I guess that I was in a minority since I opted to breast feed Linsey and, from the outset, the pair of us managed credibly well. It was a lovely unforgettable experience, much better for both of us and no thought given to having to sterilise bottles and make up the formula milk.

My Aunt Margaret visited again as did her friend Ethel who had recently moved from Lindores in Fife to Croy. Although I'm unsure as to where and how they met, I do recall that Ethel had been a friend of Aunt Margaret for many years. She was small, had lovely white hair and a kindly face and manner. She was also the owner of two Papillon dogs called Tosca and Pepe.

One morning a nurse announced: *"Now Mrs Wynton, I'm going to take out some of your stitches!"* My body froze and my left hand felt under my nightie for the strip of plaster that covered these. *"I'll run you a bath and you can have a lovely soak then I'll take each alternate one out!"* I did as I was told and gingerly stepped into the warm water. After about five minutes she returned armed with a pair of sharp scissors. *"I can't bear to look,"* I thought to myself, as she gently peeled back the plaster to reveal seven neat bright blue stitches. I steeled myself but I needn't have worried because in no time at all she'd snipped the 2nd 4th and 6th *"I'll do the others tomorrow,"* she said as she closed the door leaving me to enjoy my bath.

All of the new Mums were shown how to bath, feed and change their babies. The first time that I bathed Linsey I was rather nervous because her little head was so wobbly. But I managed quite well. I found that feeding and changing were a bit easier in comparison. The hospital nappies were paper triangles – a disposable version of the Terry Towelling ones that I had bought to use at home.

During the time that we were in hospital Ron fitted our new kitchen. The nurses used to come and give me daily reports of the progress he'd made. By the time Linsey and I arrived home most of it was in place. I loved the gleaming mustard coloured units and the breakfast bar that ran alongside the dining table. And the view out over the afforested hills to the south was always breathtaking. Before you have children you never realise how much time you will spend in the kitchen and I was really blessed that mine was so cheerful.

The Four of us, and More

Back at Westbury I did my very best to establish a routine, but Linsey had other ideas and I learned very quickly how to do lots of things one handed while holding her in my other arm. She very obviously enjoyed the close contact, feeling my heartbeat and being held securely. So I bought a baby sling, which certainly made things easier. Often she'd fall asleep but as soon as I laid her down in either her pram or cot she'd waken and start to cry, so we went for a lot of long walks. I walked the two miles up the hill to Cathy's, the three miles down to Drumnadrochit to Denise's, or along the road and down to the River Enrick. Often in the afternoon I'd take her upstairs to bed and we would both have a nap. We'd lie down on top of the bed and snuggle up together and when Ron came home from school he'd find us there still fast asleep. Honey would usually join us, curling up on the sheepskin rug. She was not in the least jealous of this newcomer and never regarded her as a usurper. She often lay down beside her and would walk close by the pram or me when I took Linsey out in the sling.

In August, Ron's parents came to meet their third grand-daughter. They stayed at Peggy's for Bed and Breakfast while Ron's sister Moira and her husband Douglas and their girls stayed in a caravan on the banks of Loch Ness. It was lovely to be part of an extended family.

However, it soon became clear from talking to both the GP and the health visitor that Linsey had colic. She was most comfortable of all over my shoulder when her tummy was sore. When she wakened during the night Ron would regularly push her back and forward in her pram beside our bed. The rocking motion certainly helped soothe her. Her delicate skin was extremely sensitive and I was advised to leave her nappy off in order to let the air onto her skin. Although I was breastfeeding her, on reflection she might have been allergic to the cow's milk I was drinking. But no one seemed really aware of this possibility at the time. But, as any parent who has been through colic knows, it is exhausting.

Most Wednesdays Linsey, Honey and I would go to Inverness with Ron when he went to work so that I could do some shopping and visit Aunt Margaret's friend Ethel. At that time Boots the chemist was on the corner of the High Street and Academy Street. Since there were some steps up to the entrance and narrow aisles inside, I always left Linsey outside in the buggy with Honey guarding her.

160

One particular day I bought all the things that I needed and left the shop, heading off down the street. I must have walked about 500 metres and, when I got to Chisholm's the Kiltmaker, I suddenly realised that I'd left both Linsey and Honey outside Boots! With pounding heart I raced back to the shop imagining all manner of dreadful outcomes. As I drew nearer a wave of relief swept over me when I saw that they were both where I'd left them. As I hugged Linsey I fancied that she glared at me as if to say: *"How could you have abandoned me?"* Whereas when I patted Honey, she simply stood up and shook herself as if to say: *"Where are we off to now?"*

We'd thought it best to postpone Linsey's christening until the colic attacks subsided and so, on a cold crisp Sunday in November when she was just over three months old, she was christened at Kilmore Church in Drumnadrochit. She wore Aunt Margaret's beautiful Victorian full-length lace christening dress. Although she snuggled into my musquash fur coat, she cried intermittently during the ceremony. Unfortunately neither Ron's parents nor my Dad and Margaret felt able to travel because of the onset of winter. However my Aunt Margaret, Mairi and Jackie and Cathy came to the service and we had a celebratory lunch at our house afterwards.

Not long afterwards I developed mastitis and was advised by the doctor to stop breastfeeding and give Linsey bottles of milk. I was given tablets to stop the milk production and antibiotics to cure the infection. Had I known what I know today, that you can shove a Savoy cabbage leaf down your bra and feed through it, I would have continued to breast feed. Then I would not have suffered the guilt from having to stop, as well as the discomfort and violent sickness that the medication had on me. Denise had also developed mastitis and suffered exactly the same symptoms as I did.

My old school friend Liz gave birth to her first baby, the week before Christmas. She and Geoff were now living in Edinburgh. So when we went to stay with my Dad and Margaret for Christmas we visited them in hospital. We were invited for tea at Liz's parents house where Linsey, who had been a milkaholic till this point, had her first taste of fish. She loved it.

By this time Linsey's colic had gone, but she had developed a nasty nappy rash, which made her poor wee bottom very red and sore. I used to leave her nappy off for as long as I could in order for the fresh air to do its work. At this time the skin on her wee face appeared red and angry and the doctor diagnosed eczema. Since Ron, his sister Moira and their Mum had hay fever, it wasn't surprising that Linsey developed eczema because both are related.

Linsey sat unsupported at six months and began tottering around by the time of her first birthday. Ever the curious and adventurous child, Linsey enjoyed exploring, playing with the pots and spoons from the kitchen cupboard as well as her toys. When at 15 months, she was able to walk independently, Ron made a strong wooden gate and fitted fixings so that it could be used at both the top and bottom of the stairs. This worked well until one Saturday when I was in the kitchen preparing lunch I heard her screaming. Rushing through to the hall I saw Linsey lying in a crumpled heap on the second step sobbing and saying, *"sore arm!"* She'd obviously decided to climb over the gate but unfortunately lost her footing and catapulted over it.

After a phone call to our GP, Dr Sutherland, we were advised to take her to the A&E department at Raigmore Hospital where an X-ray confirmed that she'd a greenstick fracture in her arm. This was duly plastered and supported in a sling. We were given a return appointment for three weeks. I couldn't believe my eyes a few days later when Linsey managed to extricate her arm from the plaster. This happened on several occasions despite my best efforts and I felt very relieved when it was removed, X-rayed and declared mended.

Just before Linsey's first birthday, my friend Karen and her golden retriever Shane came to stay with us and we spent a lovely week together reminiscing over the old times as primary school teachers. By then I was used to roaming around in jeans and hand-knitted jumpers. Meanwhile Karen, who as yet had no children and was very much the city girl, brought an amazing selection of the latest fashions with her and never went out without her handbag and lipstick – even if we were just having a walk through the surrounding countryside. Happy days.

Extra Work

During our first few years at Westbury and to augment our income, Ron taught woodwork at two evening classes – one in the local secondary school and the other in Inverness College. He thoroughly enjoyed doing this and although he came home for tea, I often felt quite lonely despite thoroughly enjoying being a Mum. Just before Linsey's first birthday, I spotted an advert in the local paper for an evening job as a housemother two evenings a week at a children's home in Inverness. Ron encouraged me to apply and said that he would be delighted to look after Linsey and put her to bed. I think the job appealed to me, not just because I was a Mum myself, but because I knew how tough it was growing up without a Mum. I had a successful interview and shortly after that went to work at Scotscraig children's home in Southside Road Inverness.

During my time there were about 12 children whose ages ranged between two and 12 years and there were several members of one family. Staff comprised a matron and two other housemothers, all of whom had worked there for a considerable time. All exuded great warmth and provided much needed security to the children, all of whom had troubled backgrounds. Our tasks were to do the things that mothers do for their children – bathing, giving supper, reading stories and settling in bed. I quickly learned the children's names, the procedures and protocols and thoroughly enjoyed the seven months that I spent there before I left to have my second baby. Although I felt quite sad to leave I kept thinking how lucky Linsey and the unborn baby were to have a loving settled environment in which to grow and develop. When I left I was presented with a beautiful pair of cosy sheepskin slippers that kept my feet warm for quite a number of years afterwards.

Andrew Ronald Wynton

It's Monday evening at the Women's Institute group and tonight a member of the Cairngorm Mountain Rescue Team has been invited to talk to us about his job and the sorts of accidents he deals with, which he illustrates with slides. These are extremely graphic. One shows the body of a man who has fallen several hundred feet. Every bone in his poor body is broken! Denise and I look at one another, both of us wishing that we'd stayed at home, but neither of us feels able to interrupt by leaving. I begin to feel slight twinges.

Afterwards we have some tea and cake. The twinges continue and I tell Denise that I ought to go. Of course she announces to everyone that I'll probably be off to Raigmore very soon afterwards.

After driving home, I phone up the hospital and I am advised to come in. Ron calls Mairi to ask if she'll mind the sleeping Linsey until he gets back. She soon arrives in a great fluster, her coat flapping and her legs encased in the familiar stripey stockings.

Twenty-five minutes later we arrive at the hospital and I'm checked in. I'm hooked up to monitors and have a needle inserted to help speed things up because the contractions kept stopping and starting. Soon afterwards a nurse asks if I'd like a cup of tea and when I reach for the cup the needle comes out of my arm. The colour drains from Ron's face and he has to sit down. I advise him to go home so that Mairi can go to bed. After he leaves, the needle is re-inserted, I drink my tea and fall asleep.

During the morning I am examined and monitored by different staff and I'm told that things should happen in the next few hours. Ron phones several times – Linsey has thrown some jelly at him. He wants to know how to make custard. I sleep fitfully and by late afternoon things do begin to happen, but not quickly enough for me. I distinctly remember asking one of the midwives if I can just go back to sleep and have my baby the next day. She laughs and tells me that it won't be much longer.

Very early one spring morning Andrew is born. As I cradle this precious wee bundle I ask one of the nurses if she'll phone home to tell Ron and she does. I am wheeled along to a two-bedded room and gently laid into a pre-warmed bed – sheer bliss. Andrew is taken off to the nursery for the night so that I can sleep soundly.

Initially Andrew was a very sleepy baby and needed quite a lot of prompting to feed. By the third day his skin had a definite yellow tinge. Jaundice was diagnosed and he was taken to the Special Care Baby Unit (SCBU) so that he could lie under the special lamp. I was worried, having lost my own baby brother who died after just a day. However I was reassured by the medical staff that jaundice was quite common and fairly easily treated. I remember I had to walk for what seemed miles when it was time for his feed. If I was even a minute or two late, Sister Falconer, who was in charge of the unit, would fix me with a fierce stare. We spent the next six days in hospital till the jaundice cleared.

I remember Denise visiting and bringing me a mouth wateringly delicious cream cake. It was so good to see her and celebrate as baby Andrew was born on her birthday.

It snowed hard the day that we went home. Our neighbour Cathy was looking after Linsey and had already become a surrogate Aunty to her, showering her with affection. As her husband Jackie was collecting something from town, he and Ron came to pick up Andrew and me and take us home. It was so good to be out in the fresh air, even though it was cold. Thirty minutes later we were climbing up the hill to Achtemarack. When she heard the car, Cathy came running out with Linsey, who was delighted to see me. Initially she paid scant attention to her new brother.

The Five of us

By the time that Andrew was born the renovation of the cottage was complete. What was really satisfying was that Ron had done a great deal of it himself. The old red brick fireplace in the living room had been faced with natural stones that we often collected when we went out in the car. My particular favourite was the lovely green Polmailly serpentine that was found nearby. A local man had shown Ron just how to piece these stones together for best effect and he had also built an open fronted log and coal box alongside. The top was made of thick glass and though it might have

164

seemed foolhardy to use that material, none of our children ever damaged it. The mantelpiece was made from an old painter's baton that Ron brought home from school after putting it through the planer machine in the Technical Department. He was an up-cycler long before the term was invented.

In early May my Dad and Margaret came to stay and meet their new grandson. Although it was really good to see them both and they did their best to help, I was exhausted with two young children and being up in the night breast-feeding. So I was in no position to be the best hostess. Of course, Margaret had never had her own children, so did not really understand the level of exhaustion new Mums go through and the never-ending amount of tasks you have to complete just to get through each day. At the time Ron was also looking after the house that was rented to Gerry and Eileen McCarron and which was just up the road from Mairi, while they were on holiday.

One morning after breakfast while Linsey and he went up to check, my Dad and Margaret packed all of their things and told me that they were going home because they hadn't felt welcome. They spent a few minutes looking at baby Andrew as he slept peacefully in his pram in the living room then drove off without waiting for Linsey and Ron to return. I felt absolutely dreadful and was still standing frozen to the spot in my tartan dressing gown when Ron and Linsey came bouncing in and singing nursery rhymes. I did not realise then, that we would never see Margaret again.

Later that same month Liz and Geoff and their wee son came to Drumnadrochit for a holiday. They stayed with Jackie and Cathy and spent the days with us. Every evening they'd put him to bed at Achtemarack Farm. Once he was asleep, they'd return because Cathy would listen out for him. She was so happy to do this because she absolutely adored children of all ages. She had a son of her own and often looked after the children of family friends in the school holidays.

I still felt very raw as a result of my Dad and Margaret's sudden departure. Liz was a great listener and her unending patience helped me enormously. She had also known me for such a long time and had been through all the trials and tribulations of my troubled relationship with my Stepmother with me. As the weeks and months passed, the heartache eased a little. I made contact several times by both letter and telephone with little response and eventually we had weekly catch ups.

Andrew was christened at Kilmichael Church that summer. Ron's parents weren't able to come and of course I knew that Margaret and my Dad wouldn't make the journey. Aunt Margaret, Mairi and Jackie and Cathy came to the church. Aunt Margaret had bought Linsey a lovely multi-coloured dress with a frill around the bottom. The frill was a bit too long, so I unpicked it and put it in my sewing box to re-stitch on when she grew taller. As Reverend John Campbell took Andrew from Ron to baptize him, Linsey, who by now dearly loved her brother, anxiously called out:

165

"Get him back Daddy, get him back!" Everyone in church laughed heartily and we had a lovely day.

Terrible News

My Dad and I usually had a 'catch up each other' either in the evening or at the weekend, but this particular Tuesday he phoned during the day. I was so pleased to hear his voice. But before I was able to ask him how he was, he told me that Margaret had died earlier that morning! I could hardly believe this shocking news and listened intently while he told me exactly what had happened.

Margaret had woken through the night feeling unwell. My Dad wanted to phone the doctor but she refused to allow this. She did not realise she was having a heart attack. By 8am she was in such discomfort that he did phone, an ambulance arrived and though she insisted on walking out to it she was told, *"No my dear, you will not!"* During the 3-mile journey to hospital she passed away and was pronounced dead on arrival. *"I just kissed her and left,"* Dad told me. *"This is the second time this has happened to me."*

I felt dreadful because this was indeed the second time that he'd been widowed. I had a difficult relationship with Margaret that I have never really got over. I believe she was jealous of me because I reminded her of my Mum and she resented that she had not been my Dad's first wife and perhaps had a family with him.

Despite this, I firmly believe she had made him happy and secure and I knew that he would be so lost without her. She had so much vitality and had been a great companion for him. He was a gentle, unassuming man who lived his life quietly and, though he had a tight knit circle of friends, he was quite happy to either potter by himself in the garden or enjoy a good book. On the other hand Margaret enjoyed being at the heart of things and when she retired she ran the local Sunshine Club, was the president of the Women's Institute and the Women's Guild. She cleaned and tidied the house and did the cooking while my Dad, like his father before him, kept a beautiful garden. I knew instinctively that his heart was broken and that nothing that I could say or do could possibly fill that void.

I phoned Ron at school then packed two suitcases. When he arrived home from school, I telephoned my Dad and told him that we'd come down the following day. We packed everything into the car and set off. Linsey was 26 months and had just started sleeping in a bed and Andrew was only 5 months old and would have to just sleep in his pram/carrycot at my Dad's house.

We arrived to find that my Dad's friend Peter Torley was staying with him. He was also a widower. Although this was beneficial during the first few days, I often wished that he'd return to his own house for some of the time, as I desperately wanted to have some time with my Dad to myself. However, Linsey and baby Andrew enjoyed the undivided attention of two doting men and certainly cheered my Dad up as much as was possible. Honey had lots of new and interesting places to explore. Although, one evening, my Dad and Peter, who were going to take her for a walk, set off without her. Luckily when they returned a few minutes later they found her still sitting by the coat rack, where they'd told her to stay.

Kirkcaldy crematorium was packed on the day of Margaret's funeral. She was a very popular and well remembered woman. The Sunshine Club hired a single decker bus, former employees, colleagues, business associates from her shops as well as her friends and family attended. The wake was held in the Dunnikier Hotel in Kirkcaldy and her ashes were to be buried in Beath Cemetery in the family plot. Ron's parents looked after Linsey and Andrew at their home in Dundee on the day of the funeral and Ron brought them back to Crossgates later that evening.

Margaret's ashes were interred a few days later and in the same grave as her parents and Ben and John her two brothers. My poor Dad asked me if he looked all right as I tied his tie and adjusted his collar. A wave of anguish swept over me as I recalled the family funerals he'd attended – how his Mum had passed away at the young age of 48, his only sister and oldest brother while in their teens and his young wife and baby son. And now Margaret, his second wife, whom he loved and had grown to depend on.

When we arrived at the cemetery, Ron took Linsey and Andrew off for a walk. Margaret's ashes were brought in a small urn and my Dad looked aghast. *"How can that be all that's left?"* he sobbed. I had no answer because I too was shocked never having either seen or considered this kind of interment before. I don't think that he ever recovered from that experience.

Linsey, Andrew and I stayed with my Dad for the next six weeks. Ron drove down on Friday after school and returned every Sunday evening. Peter was a constant companion to my Dad. The only time he left the house was when he went to cut people's hair – he was a barber and in his retirement cut people's hair at home. He thought highly of Ron and on several occasions remarked that he was *"a great Dad."*

During the time we spent at Crossgates, I cleaned the house and cooked and froze a lot of meals for my Dad. I don't remember there being any ready meals in those days. Dad's penchant was certainly neither of these activities. He wouldn't allow me to sort out any of Margaret's clothes, and she had many, although he did offer me her musquash coat – an offer I refused. We had a bit of quality time together but not as much as I'd have liked because Peter always seemed to be around, particularly in the evenings when Linsey and Andrew had gone to bed. I will *always* treasure the conversation that I had with him about my Mum.

One night after I'd put them to bed, and Peter had gone out to do some haircuts, we sat and talked for absolutely ages. My Dad told me about Margaret's death, and added that this was the second time that this had happened to him. He also told me that it had been discovered at her autopsy that she was also in the early stages of cancer.

He went on to tell me his biggest regret in life: *"I wasn't with your Mum when she died."* She was unconscious at the end and his Aunt Susan, his Dad's sister, had persuaded him to go back to her house to rest. All that I could say to him was: *"But Dad she was unconscious and wouldn't have known that you were there. Please don't blame yourself!"* He then said: *"Margaret, I lost you when your Mum died. I should have married Margaret Ferguson earlier."* The inference was that we would all have had a home together sooner, rather than me living with various extended family members and friends until my Dad remarried seven and a half years later.

Our peace was shattered soon after when Peter returned and I never had another chance to talk about my Mum after that, because my Dad died exactly five months after Margaret's death. I treasure that last profound conversation with every fibre of my being.

At the beginning of November we decided that we ought to return home. Ron was very lonely and missing us very much. It must have been pretty miserable going home to an empty house. I felt very torn too, for though I'd tried very hard several times to persuade my Dad to come to live with us, he stubbornly resisted. Now that I am older I can well understand why. My Dad would have found it very difficult to uproot himself from the life to which he'd grown accustomed. He said that he'd possibly come for Christmas and New Year but *"would see"*. It was extremely sad when we left though I tried hard to keep my emotions in check. My last abiding memory is of him standing at the gate smiling and waving vigorously until we rounded the corner of the road.

As it was, that winter was one of the worst that I'd known. The snow came early and with it ice and gales. Snowfalls were frequent and helicopters had to rescue the passengers from the derailed Inverness to Wick train. Motorists were trapped in their cars and climbers were stranded on the mountains. Schools were closed and the weight of snow on the telephone and electricity lines brought them down. We had no telephone for a week and no power for four days. Thankfully we had an open fire, a gas camping stove, a Tilly lamp and a variety of candles. Because the weather was so severe, we all decided that it was better to stay at home over Christmas and visit my Dad once there was an improvement in the weather. We phoned each other twice a week and I'd write letters too – to me letters are important as they can be read over and over again. In January my Dad exchanged his denim blue Wolseley car for a beautiful orange coloured Fiat Mirafiori. I was delighted and thought that he'd definitely opened up a new chapter in his life. He thoroughly enjoyed it till he got a big fright when he skidded on black ice while on the back road to Kelty. Luckily he and the car were fine and otherwise all seemed well.

When he phoned us on a frosty Sunday night in February he said that he was feeling very cold. Ron suggested that he turn up the central heating and warm his bed with the electric blanket. We spoke for a very long time about Linsey and Andrew, Ron, his car and the weather.

Worse News

At 1.30pm the following day I had a phone call from Nancy, Margaret's sister. She told me to sit down, which I did, then she told me that my Dad had passed away earlier that day. He'd gone out for his customary walk to buy his paper, felt unwell and had been holding onto some railings for support when his neighbours' (Anne and Archie Allan) son-in-law passed by, stopped and took him home to his mother-in-law's house. Anne had helped my Dad into bed and called the doctor. His last words to her were: *"You're very good to me."* She'd left him sleeping and by the time that the doctor had called my Dad had left this world for the next. He was only 67 years old.

I was completely shocked, but with two small children, I had to focus. I must have gone into overdrive and phoned Ron at school. He came home, calling in at the doctor's surgery on the way to ask if he'd take some tranquilisers for me. Dr Sutherland said that he thought that I'd be fine but to wait till he got home. By the time that Ron arrived back, I had packed up our things, including the cot for Andrew, who could not longer sleep in the pram carrycot at night. I phoned my Aunt Margaret, Ron's parents and my Dad's neighbours. We set off after tea and by the time we climbed Drumossie Brae it was snowing hard. The ploughs were hard at work and we reached the snow gates at Dalwhinnie just before they were closed. Ours was the last car allowed through.

As we made our way down the A9 the fuel light came on. We knew that we had enough to reach Dunkeld some twenty miles south. Unfortunately the petrol station was closed and in desperation we called at the police station. We got some fuel from there and were able to reach Perth where we filled up.

We spent the night with Ron's parents and then left next morning for Crossgates where we went to the neighbours' house to thank them for both their friendship and kindness to my Dad and Margaret and also to collect the key.

Going into the house was extremely surreal and I experienced a plethora of emotions. I can still see my Dad's glasses on the coffee table and his dark blue jacket hung neatly over the chair. His presence was everywhere and many, many times I imagined him coming in through the door. It was a very long time afterwards that the finality of it dawned on me. In some respects he had had his wish. He was not afraid of Death, rather he was afraid of becoming old, frail and demented like his father.

Ron went alone to arrange the funeral with the undertaker. He was asked if he wanted to see my Dad before the coffin lid was secured. *"No,"* he said: *"We have our own memories."* The decision to have him cremated was easily made because I had no desire to upset anyone by laying him to rest beside my Mum. I resolutely resisted Nancy's wish to have his ashes interred with those of Margaret's, choosing instead to have them scattered in the garden of the crematorium and have his name inscribed in the Book of Remembrance. A few years later I visited the crematorium on the date of his death to view his name. The diarised page for each date is turned daily so that friends and relatives can look – rather like being able to visit the grave of a friend or family member.

I don't remember much about his funeral because I was too upset. Only five months earlier I had sat with my Dad in the car following the hearse that carried Margaret's coffin. I had held one of his hands very tightly, while his other was grasped by Nancy. During Margaret's service I found it very hard to cry but this time the tears coursed relentlessly down my cheeks. At the age of thirty-one I was an orphan and despite having a loving husband and two wonderful children I experienced an enormous feeling of emptiness.

Afterwards we went to Dundee to collect Linsey and Andrew from Ron's parents. I would stay with the children in Crossgates while Ron had to return to Drumnadrochit. I spent the next few weeks in Fife contacting the family lawyer, writing to people who hadn't been at the funeral, sorting out clothes and furniture and getting the house ready for sale. It was no easy matter with two youngsters, but I managed with the help of Ron's parents and my Aunt Margaret.

Aunt Margaret had not been able to come to the funeral because of the weather and came down a few weeks later to help me sort out his belongings. She stayed with her old friend Pearl in Aberdour and helped me by moving some of the things that I wanted to keep to Dundee where Ron's parents stored them in their loft. One Sunday evening Liz and Geoff came by on their way home after a visit to her parents. I did so appreciate their visit because I'd just put Linsey and Andrew to bed, Ron had left for home and I was feeling very sad. Liz, who was expecting her second baby in May, was positively blooming and this fairly cheered me up.

I gave many of the house contents to friends, neighbours and relatives. Nancy got her family things and I gave her Margaret's fur coat, her watch, engagement ring, wedding and eternity rings. Nancy liked jewellery and I thought that these rings deserved to be worn, rather than being kept in their boxes. I felt, that, as her sister, she should have them – I already had my Mum's rings from just before I was married and these were all that I really wanted. I wear my Mum's wedding ring all of the time and that way I feel that she's always with me. I didn't have the same attachment to Margaret's rings, even though they were worth a lot more money than my Mum's were.

Being Parentless

Since I was my Dad's only child everything he had was left to me, including his bright orange Fiat Mirafiori. It was a very daunting prospect to inherit a considerable sum of money and property and what to do next was the question. The house in Crossgates was quickly sold. Ron found a loophole in the inheritance laws and we found a lawyer who organised a Deed of Family Arrangement whereby we were able to recoup half of the estate duty that would otherwise have had to be paid to the Treasury.

We seriously considered building a larger house but since there were few sites nearby, and those that were available were both overpriced and had little outlook, we decided to extend Westbury. Ron sourced an architect, Hector McDonald, who drew plans for a rear extension that would preserve the original appearance of the cottage. Since the back garden was on an upward slope and the drive was behind the house, the extension was to be built into the back garden, thus bridging the drive. It comprised an upstairs living room, two bedrooms and a bigger bathroom, long corridor and store cupboard. At ground level, at the back of the drive, a storeroom with a log and coal store was to be built. Our original bathroom was to be made into a linen cupboard and a small window was to be inserted in the gable wall of the kitchen/dining room.

It took several months to plan, organise and complete the work. There were many occasions when I bitterly regretted even starting. It was so different from when Ron and I had been renovating Westbury without young children. Linsey had developed into an outgoing and confident little girl who loved finding out about everything in her world. She loved animals and insects including spiders and enjoyed books, jigsaws and drawing. Every night she would sleep with about seven soft toy animals including her owl and her bear. She would even take them on holiday to Granny Wynton's and Granny's friends would ask if there was room for Linsey in the bed.

On the other hand Andrew was a quiet, cuddly wee lad who thoroughly enjoyed books and stories, his variety of vehicles, constructing Lego models and riding around the garden in his yellow AA pick up truck and trailer. He was very interested in how things worked so keenly watched his Dad at work, learning the names and uses of the tools. Over time he became Ron's apprentice by holding, passing and eventually helping to use the tools that were needed.

During the next few weeks' work on the extension began, and so I took Linsey and Andrew to stay with Ron's Mum while Ron's Dad was in hospital after circulatory problems. One afternoon we went to Camperdown Park where Linsey and Andrew played in the park and visited the small zoo that housed Hercules the bear, flamingoes and an assortment of small mammals including stoats and ferrets. Andrew was really fascinated by the ferrets, but before I could stop him, he poked one of his fingers through the cage. The ferret soundly nipped it. Andrew cried out in pain as he withdrew his finger and howled even louder as he noticed that the rodent had left one of its teeth embedded in it! There followed a visit to A&E where the offending tooth was removed!

In the autumn of 1978 Liz's baby daughter was christened in the church at Duddingston. I was delighted to be invited to be her Godmother. We decided to combine this with a family holiday in the nearby town of Gullane. Linsey came with me to church while Ron took Andrew to see the ducks and swans on Duddingston Loch. Now that we were both mothers of small children Liz and I wrote weekly letters to each other and phoned when we could: there was neither texting nor facebook in those days. The following year Geoff applied to work abroad for six months. It was a wonderful opportunity for the four of them to live in another country and experience such a different culture and we still managed to write letters, though not quite so often.

By the spring of 1979 the extension was at last complete – from the shagpile carpet and velvet drapes in our upstairs living room to the peach bathroom suite and bidet, it seemed like we had created our dream home.

WESTBURY RENOVATED

Chapter 8: A Very Special Daughter

The starter dropped the flag and they were off. The Shetland Pony Grand National had begun. My ten-year old daughter Linsey was taking part on Pigeon, an adorable black Shetland, who was rather fonder of eating than competing. They cleared two jumps before Pigeon stopped. *"Walk on,"* urged |. *"Walk on Pigeon."* The small equine had other ideas though as she nibbled some of the vegetation on the 3rd jump. *"Mmmm that's rather tasty,"* she thought as she slowly munched her way through more of it, paying no heed to Linsey's increasingly desperate entreaties to move.

And that was the end of Pigeon's Shetland Grand National. After the other jockeys had completed 2 circuits, of the course, the winners were presented with rosettes from the then Right Honourable Malcolm Rifkind MP. Of course Pigeon won nothing but she didn't care. So when Lord Burton, a local landowner, who was accompanying Malcolm Rifkind, remonstrated and wagged his finger at her, Pigeon simply turned her back on him nearly knocking him off his feet. This came much to the amusement of Mr Rifkind.

Eilidh Susan Margaret Wynton

At the beginning of December 1978 I found out that I was going to have a third baby. At that time I was delighted. Had I known the journey that was in store for me, my baby-to-be and the rest of the family, I would have felt entirely differently.

Ron and I had always hoped to have three children. And after my Dad died, I wished for another child even more to fill that void left by him and by a lifetime of never having my Mum around. I had been an only child. Ron was part of a family of four siblings and it always seemed that they had had such fun together, though I appreciate that the three boys drove their big sister Moira round the bend on many occasions.

The pregnancy itself gave no one any cause for concern and I carried on much as I had done during the two previous occasions. With two other children under four, there was not much time for resting. I kept telling myself that childbirth was a natural function and we all looked forward to mid-June when this baby was due to be born.

On the last Monday morning of March 1979 – the date is indelibly stamped on my memory – Linsey and Andrew had just finished breakfast when there was a knock on the back door. Just as I went to answer it, I felt a trickle run down my leg. My initial thought was that I was bleeding. Immediately afterwards I visited the loo where I discovered that I was leaking fluid rather than blood.

When our GP called later that morning in response to my frantic phone call, he told me that the membrane containing the baby had a tear in it and it was from there that the liquid was leaking. His medication was straightforward enough; antibiotic tablets to guard against infection and rest. Perhaps the tear would mend itself and the baby would be born on time. It was possible, so rest I did. By the next day Ron had managed to contact a local lass, who looked after Linsey and Andrew until he returned from work and so the next few days were spent in bed hoping that the tear would heal.

Unfortunately it did not heal and by Friday of that week, I had developed a high temperature and felt very ill. When the doctor arrived he found my temperature was dangerously high – over 104 Fahrenheit (40 Celsius). He told me that I'd have to go to hospital to have the baby and warned us that there would be little chance of its survival. He said it would be best to try again, as there would be little likelihood of this situation recurring.

I must have appeared as some strange apparition as I got myself ready for hospital. Thick welly socks under my slippers, a sheepskin coat over my nightie, while hat, gloves and scarf completed the ensemble. My recollections before leaving were of our friends Cathy and Jackie arriving to look after the children – Cathy was in floods of tears and I remember Andrew sitting up in bed saying: *"Goodnight Mummy."* I ruffled his curls, so reminiscent of his Dad's, and hugged him. Linsey was already fast asleep so I just dropped a kiss on her cheek.

Ron and I shared our hopes and fears during that 25 minute drive to the hospital where, after a cursory examination, I was given more penicillin and an injection of something that enabled me to sink into welcome oblivion, but not before I heard one of the nurses say that I ought to have already been in hospital. I really wish that I hadn't heard that comment because it planted the initial seeds of doubt in my mind; I lay thinking about it until I finally fell into a fitful sleep.

Next morning after being thoroughly examined by the doctor, I was told that the baby would have to be induced. Before this was instigated, I was scanned, presumably to give them guidance as to the size of the baby. But at no point was my baby's heart rate monitored. I expect this is because they thought there was little hope of survival.

The labour was over very quickly, its duration being about three and a half hours. The degree of labour pain was similar to that experienced at the births of Linsey and Andrew, but the actual delivery itself was so effortless due to the baby's size: two pushes and she was there. Suffice to say, and despite the circumstances, the experience left me with happy memories of childbirth, as on this occasion there was neither a Caesarian section nor a forceps delivery. This tiny baby cried immediately and was rushed off to the Special Care Baby Unit (SCBU) where she was put in an incubator on an apnoeic alarm mattress (a mattress that monitors breathing). I relaxed thinking that because she'd cried, all was well.

Ron had been told by one of the doctors to: *"Think of this as an abortion, but we'll do what we can."* Survival had not been expected. She was viable and no more: 28 weeks gestation or 12 weeks premature. Eilidh was born when John Corrie's abortion bill was being read in Parliament. On the previous Monday, I'd been listening to a play set in

174

America where lawyers were thrashing out as to when it was thought that a foetus was viable and when it was not. On reflection that programme was a portent, an omen of things to come.

We cannot praise the Baby Unit enough for the love, care and attention that Eilidh was given during those first few months of her life. At birth she weighed only one kilogramme – the equivalent of a bag of sugar. During the first week all went reasonably well: she managed to cope apart from a few apnoeic attacks (absence of breathing). She seemed to be proving everyone wrong.

However, on the eighth day, she became quite ill: the previous infrequent apnoeic attacks now became more frequent, her colour was grey and she seemed to be giving up her struggle for survival. I'd been allowed home after three days as my infection had been cured and there were others at home who were dependent on me. I always phoned first thing in the morning and last thing at night. When I telephoned that Sunday morning, I was told that her condition was *"giving cause for concern"* so, after leaving Linsey and Andrew with Cathy, Ron and I rushed off to the hospital where we spent a harrowing time. How long? I've no idea. We were advised to have her baptised and we did: Arthur Fraser, the hospital chaplain, conducted the ceremony.

Unlike her sister and brother, Eilidh wore no christening robe, only a hospital disposable nappy and the short service was punctuated by the steady clicks from the apnoeic mattress on which she lay. These sounds reminded me of the metronome that Miss Calder, my music teacher kept on top of her piano. She firmly believed that it was a great way to improve the natural timing of her pupils.

Eilidh's baptismal water was contained in a cut glass ashtray and Arthur Fraser, along with us, wore a sterile gown. I remember thinking: *"I hope he has washed his hands."* As he said her name, she opened her eyes and looked at him. On reflection, I think that this was the turning point for Eilidh.

Over the next two or three weeks Eilidh's life hung in the balance. Always she managed to cheat Death. She used practically every piece of equipment that that department had. Her tiny body was barely visible because of the probes, tubes, and catheters. She rewarded the staffs' efforts to keep her alive by doing just that. One doctor had apparently banged on her incubator saying: *"You've got to make it Eilidh!"* And she did. Once she'd recovered from the infections that had beset her from the start, the road to recovery was straightforward. After six weeks she was out of the incubator and then, instead of being tube fed, she had a bottle. It had never occurred to me to try to express milk and no one had suggested that I could. By the time that I considered this possibility it was too late as my milk supply had dried up. I found myself feeling positively guilty and utterly stupid as breast milk would have been particularly beneficial to her.

While Eilidh was in hospital, Ron and I were due to attend a wedding. My friend Sheila, with whom I'd taught at Powrie Primary, and her husband Alastair had invited me to their younger son's wedding. I had not been sure if we'd be able to go, but Cathy readily offered to look after Linsey and Andrew. The reception was to be in the luxurious Banff Springs Hotel that has some beautiful views out to sea. I had bought myself a lovely green print maternity dress in soft silky material and a pair of green leather shoes with a low heel.

Of course I was no longer pregnant. I sighed and looked wistfully at my new dress as I took it out of the wardrobe. The fabric felt soft as I ran my fingers over it. I slipped it over my head then stood in front of the mirror. Although it was a maternity dress it still looked very stylish so I decided that I'd wear it as planned.

We had a wonderful time at the wedding. I'd had this idea that I'd like to watch a late film and then have a lie in the next day, though by the time the reception finished bed beckoned as sleep overtook us. Next morning after breakfast we had a leisurely return journey. We'd arranged to meet Jackie and Cathy with Linsey and Andrew at the hospital so they could all visit Eilidh for the first time.

It was so lovely to see our two wee ones who hugged us so tightly. Then we went into SCBU and met Sister Falconer. She gave us all the white disposable hospital gowns necessary for wearing over outdoor clothes as a guard against infection. Then she took us into the nursery. I remember helping Linsey into her white gown with her long hair in 2 bunches that curled at the bottom. She held my hand tightly, her eyes open in wonderment as she saw her new sister for the very first time. Ron held wee Andrew in his arms so that he could see her too. *"She's so small"* he said. Jackie and Cathy were lost for words. I remember Cathy with tears pouring down her cheeks. When she finally found her tongue her words were, *"It's a miracle!"*

Eventually the magical day when I was allowed to feed Eilidh myself arrived. Sister Falconer, of whom I'd been so apprehensive when Andrew spent two days under her care, was both supportive and attentive. *"Come and see this,"* she said. As I looked into the cot I saw that my Eilidh had found her thumb, which she was sucking contentedly. *"Clever girl,"* I thought as I gently lifted her out and cradled her in my arms. The contact seemed strange after so long. It had been so impersonal, though fascinating to watch her grow in the incubator instead of inside me, but as I held her I was filled with a warmth that radiated into every part of my being. I felt that my heart would burst with joy as I cuddled her tiny wee body close to me. Two days later, weighing five and a half pounds and on the 21st June, the day on which she should have been born, we took her home.

The parting from SCBU was very emotional. Eilidh had spent so long there that she was almost a fully-fledged member. We were so very, very grateful for everything that had been done for her. We left gifts of money for each nurse and at the paediatrician's suggestion bought an apnoeic mattress; Eilidh had benefited so much from the one she'd used and he told us that another one would be a great asset. Armed with some small bottles of milk and her medicine, folic acid pills neatly and conveniently halved, we left for home.

The Six of us

Eilidh was a very contented baby and seemed to do things by the book. We had a surfeit of miscellaneous baby clothes all in pristine condition. Since Linsey weighed almost 9lbs at birth, many of the clothes that she'd been given as presents had never been worn. The same applied to Andrew, who despite weighing only 6lbs 2ozs, was a much longer and slimmer baby than she'd been. Their first size baby clothes would not fit Eilidh for weeks to come. Doll's clothes were more appropriate since Eilidh resembled a dainty little doll. And until she grew a bit, putting on a nappy was a Herculean task. There seemed to be hardly any baby and lots of nappy.

All the children

Eilidh slept in our bedroom for several months. Like all premature babies she had an extensive vocabulary of very special sounds, quite unlike full term babies. One morning, not long after we brought her home, Andrew wandered through. Hearing Eilidh's repertoire of sounds, but not noticing her in her cot, he asked: *"Is that a seagull?"* Presumably he had forgotten about his new baby sister.

At the beginning of September 1979 we held a special service of thanksgiving for Eilidh in Kilmichael Church. Ron's parents had come to visit but were unable to attend the service because his Dad had developed phlebitis the day before and was advised by the doctor to stay in bed. Ron's Mum dressed Eilidh in my Aunt Margaret's beautiful christening gown. She looked every bit as lovely, as her older sister and brother had done when they were christened.

John Campbell, who had baptised both Linsey and Andrew had since retired leaving the charge vacant. Since Eilidh had already been baptised in hospital this part of the ceremony could not be repeated. Our interim moderator, Fergus Robertson, took the service, which was unforgettable, and Reverend Arthur Fraser, who had christened her in hospital, said the first prayer. Eilidh looked beautiful as Fergus carried her around the church, thus introducing her to the congregation. After the service I remarked that it would have been wonderful to have recorded it and was told that this could have happened had I asked. Once more I felt just like I had done when I'd not thought to breastfeed Eilidh. At least I have my memories. We all returned home with my Aunt Margaret and Jackie and Cathy where we spent a happy afternoon with Ron's Mum and Dad.

Between June and October, Eilidh and I attended several paediatric clinics where her progress was recorded. At no time did the thought ever occur to me that she might have suffered brain damage, especially as she had cried spontaneously at birth. I suppose that this possibility ought to have crossed my mind, but it had not been raised by any of the doctors or nurses and my main thought had always been for her survival. When survive she did, my mind was at rest.

From the outset I tended to be over anxious about Eilidh's eyesight, as oxygen in the incubators can damage premature babies' eyes. But somewhat later than the customary six weeks she rewarded my friend Denise with a beautiful smile. Now all of my worries seemed over. She could hear, see and responded well to everyone… at least that was what I thought.

During the first few days of November she did not seem to be her usual contented self and positively screamed when I lifted her up. After removing her clothing, I discovered a huge lump, the size of a golf ball, at the base of her right front rib cage. Our GP was baffled and immediately sent us to hospital where she was admitted and later diagnosed as having osteomyelitis – a condition that normally affects the long bones in the legs. That night Dr Watmough, who had banged relentlessly on her incubator when she was so tiny, telephoned to explain exactly what was going to be done to her. I really appreciated this as I felt terrible having had to leave her. The lump was duly lanced and drained and Eilidh spent the next ten days in hospital. On the advice of the staff, I did not visit her often since she would cry uncontrollably as I was leaving. However, the doctors took advantage of this period to assess her vision and hearing.

Over the next few months we visited the Ear, Nose and Throat consultant who performed all manner of aural tests on Eilidh till he was satisfied that there was nothing amiss. Eilidh's hearing is very acute. An illustration of this, albeit some time later, springs to mind. Our health visitor, while carrying out an aural test was rattling all manner of objects, each one of which made a different sound, in an effort to encourage Eilidh to look in the direction of where the sound had come from. Without as much as a backward glance, Eilidh said quite distinctly and much to my acute embarrassment: *"I don't think that's very funny!"* It was just as well that the health visitor and I knew each other very well.

Ron made Eilidh's little chair

Raindrops Keep Fallin'

At the beginning of January 1980, Ron's Dad was admitted to hospital. He'd been ill for quite some time and, during December of the previous year, his condition had gradually deteriorated. Ron drove to Dundee on New Year's Day and during visiting time the following day his Dad slipped away. Ron stayed to help his Mum with the funeral arrangements and the service before coming home.

At this time I began to wonder if there was something wrong with Eilidh since she didn't seem to be reaching the prescribed milestones, even allowing for the fact that she was so very premature. I was told, *"don't worry"* and *"everything will be fine."* But when I noticed her clenched stiff right hand, I knew for sure that something was wrong. In May, two months after her first birthday, Eilidh was diagnosed with cerebral palsy, a condition that had been brought about by a combination of factors, her prematurity, her frequent apnoeic attacks and a bleed into her brain – the equivalent of a stroke. This had happened soon after she was born, but no one had said much about it at the time.

During the days that followed I suffered from many varied emotions, the main one being guilt. Had I been careful enough during my pregnancy? I had always thought pregnancy was a normal state and not an illness. I'd had two perfectly normal pregnancies and no miscarriages. My life had followed the same pattern as before: housework, gardening, playing with Linsey and Andrew and taking them for long walks with Honey. The guilt used to gather into a tight ball and usually at night while I was in bed, where I had time to think and unwind and when there were no little voices clamouring for stories, cuddles or drinks. Ron tried to allay my fears, but in vain. Finally in desperation I poured out all of my anxieties to the GP who assured me that it was *not* my fault.

Nevertheless, it did happen and I will wonder to the end of my life if indeed I was responsible for Eilidh's premature birth. Should I have lifted and carried Andrew so much? Should I have barrowed logs from the lay-by opposite our house where Ron cut them, to the log store. I did much the same during my other two pregnancies; more in fact, since at those times we were still renovating the cottage. I wondered if I'd had the chance to put my feet up and rest a bit more, would the outcome have been the same? Perhaps we all look for something or someone to blame. *"Why?"* I used to cry in anguish: *"Why me?"* Always the reply would return like an echo… *"Why not you?"* Much later I thought: *"Why Eilidh?"*

People can claim to understand the situation that occurs in a family where there is a child with special needs, but no one except another parent in a similar situation can possibly empathise. As I was about to find out, the disability affects the whole family in nearly every aspect of life.

Cerebral palsy covers a wide range of disabilities, including paralysis of the muscles, inability to co-ordinate movements and the occurrence of involuntary movements. It affects two people in every 1,000. Most cases are from birth injuries, either from instrumental or obstructed delivery or from lack of oxygen during birth. Other causes can include developmental defects of the brain, maternal infection during pregnancy, rheumatic heart disease and jaundice in the first few days of life. In its mildest form cerebral palsy results in a clumsy child while in its most severe form it results in a child with serious disability. Some children are floppy. Some are stiff. Some have just one side affected either above or below the waist or both, whereas in other cases all four limbs are affected. In addition, some have speech, visual or aural problems, while others have a combination of all these disabilities.

      Eilidh was diagnosed as having asymmetrical spastic cerebral palsy – bilateral hemiplegia type with ataxia and athetoid features. This means that all of her limbs are affected and sometimes stiff. Her right arm is much weaker than her left and, as she grew, sometimes her legs would buckle when she was standing or walking with support.

Asymmetric – difference in either side of her body
Spastic – stiff
Bilateral diplegia – mainly affects the legs
Ataxia – lack of voluntary co-ordination of muscle movements
Athetosis – involuntary movements

      It is incredibly difficult for able-bodied people to appreciate the movements that we make without really planning them. We would all do well to consider just exactly what we take for granted each day without giving it much thought; walking, our personal care, eating and drinking unaided, to name but a few. Although a person with cerebral palsy often knows what he or she wants to do, it is not always possible because the message is not being transmitted from the brain to the appropriate part of the body as these particular pathways have been damaged.

      At that time I didn't realise that the brain's plasticity meant that other routes could sometimes be found and the central nervous system encouraged to re structure itself. While I cannot recall an example of anyone to whom this has happened, I remember reading an article about this. What super human beings we would be if we all used all of our brain all of the time.

      Shortly after diagnosis both physio and occupational therapy were arranged for Eilidh at Raigmore Hospital. Here I was to begin the familiar round of clinics that every parent of a disabled child knows only too well. Every Monday we would make the 17 mile journey from Glenurquhart to Inverness in the orange Fiat Mirafiori I had inherited from my Dad. It wasn't the idyllic life I had hoped for after he passed away. I had not anticipated any of this and did not know any other parents of disabled children. I would try to be happy and cheerful, chatting to Eilidh and listening to the cassettes I kept in the car to try to keep things buoyant. The soundtrack I most vividly remember for these journeys was B J Thomas singing Raindrops Keep Fallin' on my Head.

At that time both physiotherapy and occupational therapy sessions took place in their respective departments within the main hospital. During the first of the physiotherapy sessions Eilidh was extremely keen and cooperative. On the second occasion, however, she was put onto a large Bobath ball, which is like an enormous gym ball. (Bobath is an approach to neurological rehabilitation that seeks to improve motor control in different environments, thus improving function. In the main it is carried out by physiotherapists, and sometimes by occupational therapists and speech and language therapists.)

Eilidh screamed and cried in terror and ever after that she sobbed inconsolably at these strangers in white coats. Occupational therapy fared no better. In fact, it was often worse since we visited the physio department first. Perhaps the cause of all of the unhappiness was the ball, or it may have been that, at long last, Eilidh realised that people were trying to encourage or coerce her into doing things that she didn't want to co-operate with, for her own reasons. This was a very difficult period in my life, because I wanted to do the best I could for her, yet I felt that everyone's efforts were being both thwarted and wasted, because she was so uncooperative and stubborn.

As a baby of several months I'd always put Eilidh on her tummy in an effort to encourage her to roll, but she hated this, much preferring to lie in a supine position. Undaunted, I persevered as long as my ears could stand the screams. When I felt that we'd both had enough, I would transfer her to her bouncer. This was useful when she was small because it allowed me to take her from room to room. When she moved, the bouncer rocked. I'd used this with my other children. Linsey positively hated the sight of it, but Eilidh, like Andrew, loved being in it.

One day after I put Eilidh on her tummy, she rolled over. I couldn't believe it. I repeated the action, while she in turn repeated hers. After that she tolerated lying over a wedge and thus was able to use both of her hands. Her weaker right hand was, and still is, used for holding objects, while she gradually developed almost full use of her left hand. She also learned to commando crawl: the way soldiers move on their fronts.

It was a huge relief when Anne Chambers, a new physiotherapist, took over and combined home visits with hospital ones. During this time physiotherapy sessions took place in the old ward 17 at Raigmore Hospital, the part of the hospital that had been constructed in 1941 as a Medical Emergency Hospital. This section of the hospital had a total of 666 beds and comprised 16 single storey blocks and one isolation block, all built of bricks. Although there was a recognised need for a Child Development Centre this was not built until many years later.

Matters improved slightly with Anne's help, though in truth some sessions were a complete disaster. By this time Linsey had started school, but Andrew hadn't. He really enjoyed Anne's visits and would bring his jigsaws and Lego constructions for her to admire. Often he would go to Cathy's house when I took Eilidh to the hospital sessions. I was very grateful for this because it meant that I could give my full attention to the particular exercises that Anne was doing with Eilidh as I always carried these on with Eilidh at home. Life was exhausting. So Jack MacDonald, the paediatrician, suggested that Eilidh went into hospital for a week in order to give me some respite and, very reluctantly, I agreed. Somehow I felt that I was being selfish and shelving my responsibility, but in January 1981, Eilidh went off for a week when a bed became vacant and I was asked not to visit. So my only contact was by phone. I did not enjoy the "break" as was intended. Apart from feeling guilty, an acquaintance with family problems arrived and asked to stay for a few nights. These stretched to a week after which he departed – one set of worries exchanged for another.

I will never forget my little Eilidh when I went to bring her home. It was mid-afternoon and she lay in a small hospital cot. When I called her name she looked very bewildered. She also had a streaming cold. *"Oh my God,"* I said aloud: *"What have I done to you?"* I put my arms around her and cuddled her tightly, then dressed her and took her home resolving never ever to do this to her again.

A Surrogate Grandmother

As the spring came I used to take the children for walks down in the nearby village of Lewiston, which adjoined Drumnadrochit.

There was a lovely Icelandic pony called Trigger who lived in the field at the top of the village and we'd stop there to pat him and feed him either a carrot or apple. At that time there was little traffic and the road was reasonably level. Linsey took her doll and pram, Andrew rode on a small blue push-along milk float, while Eilidh travelled in her buggy. One day in the summer of 1980 I noticed two elderly ladies standing outside talking in the sunshine. I recognised the smaller of the two from church. Her name was Mrs Margaret Swan. We all stopped and chatted for quite some time and I discovered that she had recently become a widow. From that day there began a friendship that lasted until her death 26 years later at the amazing age of 106 years and 9 months.

Mrs Swan became not only a very close friend, but also a surrogate Granny to Linsey, Andrew and Eilidh. She was a keen member of both the church guild and the WI. Ron had got to know her and her late husband Jack quite well from the local bridge club and also from their enrollment in his woodwork class.

Although Mrs Swan was quite small and portly, she was remarkably fit and regularly had guests for bed and breakfast. She continued to do this from time to time after Jack's death because she enjoyed the company of others. She had the most beautiful Copper Plate writing and often wrote in fountain pen. I still have some of her calendars with beautiful photographs of Highland scenery and her wonderfully stylish handwriting.

I would regularly take her to Inverness and leave her to go shopping while I took Eilidh to her hospital appointments. On the odd occasions when Ron and I actually got time to go out in the evening for dinner with friends or the occasional birthday party or social gathering, she'd come up and babysit. Once we were well away Andrew and Linsey would often sneak out of bed. *"Please tell us stories about the old days Mrs Swan,"* they'd ask and she'd tell them lots before saying: *"Now off you go before your Mum and Dad get back because if you're still up then I'll get into trouble."*

We all marvelled at Mrs Swan's acceptance of change for she must have lived through so much: two world wars, the dawn of the inside toilet and the widespread availability of running water and electricity and, eventually, the computer. I'll never forget the day, quite a few years after we had first met, when she sat in front of our Commodore computer and used the keyboard. In her working life she'd worked in an office where she'd been a typist and bookkeeper. Ron set everything up for her and, as she started to type, a smile spread slowly across her face. *"This is absolutely wonderful,"* she said, *"and a big improvement on my old typewriter."*

I came to discover this fourth significant Margaret in my life had lost two babies. She discovered that it was because her husband's blood group was incompatible with hers. These days the babies born to women in her circumstances are given a blood transfusion. This was why Mrs Swan loved our children so much and to me, as well as my dear Aunt Margaret, she became a second surrogate Mum, always so supportive and kind and filling the aching voids I had with care and warmth. She never judged and always empathised.

School Days for my Children

Before the children started school I used to take them to two local playgroups. One was in Drumnadrochit and was run by Christine

McCallum, a lively and warm Mum who had two older children. My main memories of it were Linsey being terrified after they read the Grimm's fairy tale about the Musicians of Bremen, a group of runaway farm animals who savagely scare a group of robbers. The other was when she made herself a meal out of Plasticine and ate some of it.

There was also another local playgroup in the old school at Corrimony. Usually I stayed with the children but on one occasion I dropped Linsey off and took Andrew and Eilidh home because Andrew was under the weather. When I returned to collect her, she was being piled into the back of a Mini driven by one of the Mums with about ten other children. After that I stayed to keep an eye, but on one occasion when I was playing with Eilidh, Andrew climbed up a book-case and it fell down on him. Luckily he was not seriously injured, just a bit bruised.

Just after her fifth birthday, Linsey started school at Balnain Primary: a two teacher school. It was a three mile journey and another parent from school, Mrs Will, drove the so-called *"school car"* transporting her children and three girls who lived up the road who were named Susan, Carol and Iona McKenzie. This was Mrs Will's own car, but she received a transport subsidy from the local council.

Linsey's teacher was Rosemary Forbes. This plump lady with black hair and 1980s round framed glasses was quite warm. I remember taking Linsey to visit before she started school and Miss Forbes picking her up and turning her upside down – because I'd dressed Linsey in a Mr Men jumper with Mr Topsy Turvy on the front.

Linsey settled into school and as far as I know she was very happy. From an early age she had always loved a wide variety of books and stories, particularly those about Topsy and Tim, the Mr Men books and Noddy stories. She quickly learned to read. She loved drawing, painting, modelling and proudly brought home some of these creations to display on the walls of the kitchen and her bedroom. Cathy never ceased to be amazed by her extensive vocabulary, which included words like *"arachnids"*! Linsey stayed for school dinners and proudly recited the grace that she'd learned to say before her meal: *"For Health and strength and daily bread we give thee thanks oh God,"* translated into Linsey-speak became, *"For heaven's Death and daily bread we give thee thanks oh God."*

Linsey really liked the white-haired Miss MacLeod, the ageing Headteacher, who kept some interesting things on the shelves in her classroom. One of these was a jar containing a pickled adder. Though Linsey loved animals, she did not care for this reptile, even though it was dead.

The highlights of Linsey's early school life were the show and tell table and playing games such as British Bulldog and What's the Time Mr Wolf? in the playground. Then there was the day that a Capercaille came to call. This majestic wild bird, that could be compared to a jet black turkey, suddenly appeared in the school playground and stayed there for quite some time. Much to the children's excitement, this amazing creature was the subject of an article in the local newspaper.

During Linsey's first year at school, I tried very hard to keep Andrew happy and busy as well as continue to do Eilidh's exercises. Anne, the physiotherapist, continued to visit fortnightly. Often we'd visit Denise and her younger daughter Jenny and sometimes she and Jenny would visit us. We'd often walk up the hill and over the bridge that spanned the wee burn, past the cows and sheep that grazed at the side of the road to Cathy's farm. The cows and bull all had names: there was a Linsey, an Andrew and an Eilidh. Cathy used to cry when any of them went off to either the market or the abattoir. She also cried later when they returned and she put the cuts of meat from them into bags for the freezer.

The children loved helping her to gather the eggs from their properly free-range chickens. At lunch-times we'd enjoy a steaming bowl of soup, girdle scones, oatcakes, pancakes and chocolate crispy cakes. Jackie was very fond of all of the children and, after lunch, Andrew would often sit on his knee. One day when he happened to put his hands around the back of Jackie's head he felt what he thought was a lump. *"What's that lump on the back of your head Uncle Jackie?"* asked the curious youngster. *"That's the knot in the string that holds my false teeth in place,"* answered Jackie and Andrew believed him for quite some time afterwards. Cathy always told the children that the reason Jackie had false teeth was that he was so fond of sweets. Chocolates were a particular favourite and I remember the time he ate a whole box of Matchmakers we'd given him at one sitting. After that we always gave any chocolates to Cathy first of all.

In January 1981, Jack MacDonald, Eilidh's paediatrician, suggested that I make a request for Andrew to attend school part-time for there were very few nurseries then. He was a very bright little boy who had clearly outgrown playgroup. Jack felt that he would greatly benefit from the experience, rather than coming regularly to hospital with Eilidh and me as we attended the physiotherapy and occupational therapy clinics. We also had to attend regular eye clinics and paediatric clinics. As any small child who has spent much time in hospital in the 1980s will know, the highlight of such visits was visiting the WRVS café and getting a sausage roll, a Scotch pie or a floury bread roll smothered in butter with a Kraft cheese slice in it. Luckily there was usually a Tunnock's teacake afterwards.

I felt that if Andrew was happily settled in school, then he would be having more attention there than he was getting at home. I often felt extremely guilty about the amount of time that I felt I needed to spend with Eilidh both at hospital appointments, doing her exercises and taking her to the toilet. The criterion for admission to school was that a child had to have his or her 5th birthday by the 28th February. Andrew's April birthday meant that he missed the cut off date by five weeks.

However, Ron and I wrote a request for early entry and submitted it to the Highland Council. Unfortunately, this was turned down, even though I had various letters to substantiate the claim from the paediatrician and the school. We were given the right of appeal, but on the day on which the appeal was due to be heard, the appeals procedure was abolished. Ron and I, feeling that justice had not been done, contacted the

Ombudsman for help. After a lengthy legal enquiry lasting nine months he found in our favour. Andrew was allowed to attend school for the mornings from January 1982. Then when he became five in April he was allowed to attend full-time.

Not long afterwards I decided to try to enrol Eilidh in a playgroup in Inverness and thus combine the session with a supermarket shopping trip and a little bit of time to myself. By this time Eilidh was three years old. Though not able to walk, she could use her hands to feed herself finger food. She used a buggy to get out and about and could walk if someone supported her under her arms.

She had also been diagnosed as long-sighted. She was given a pair of those classic 1980s NHS pink spectacles. Ron is also long-sighted and had NHS specs as a youngster too and he broke them on several occasions. Eilidh managed to do this on one occasion too – the day she had got a new pair. Luckily she always had a spare pair. She had a squint and particularly hated having to wear an eye patch over her left eye. Initially we would all wear an eye patch to try to entice her. In the end she got a second pair of glasses and the left frame was always covered with the eye patch.

Finding a playgroup willing to take her proved a much more difficult task than I had envisaged. The first private nursery I approached turned us down. This was not because they were trying to reject Eilidh, but rather it was felt that it would be a much greater responsibility than having an able-bodied child. Though I didn't agree, I didn't feel up to arguing either. What would be the point in going somewhere she was not welcomed?

Then, as if in answer to a prayer, Dr Roche, the school medical officer, called to see us shortly afterwards. She arranged a place for Eilidh at the Playbox Playgoup which was held in the Salvation Army premises. This excellent group was organised by Morag Wheatley, wife of the then Provost of Inverness Cathedral. Eilidh quickly settled in and each Wednesday was eagerly looked forward to by both of us. I felt as if a huge weight had been lifted from my shoulders. It is hard enough looking after young children but, with a disabled child, it is a constant worry and I just felt so overwhelmed at times by the sheer amount of hard work that was demanded of me.

At playgroup she was encouraged to play in the sand, water and roll the play dough, as well as learn a variety of nursery rhymes and action songs. She was particularly fond of a blue teddy bear that played, *"Merrily we roll along",* when the key on its back was turned. Mrs Wheatley quickly realised this and at the end of the year gave it to Eilidh to keep. She actually still has this beloved bear in her bedroom. Mrs Wheatley was so kind she actually took Eilidh to her house in Ardross Street one time and Eilidh helped make some fairy cakes. When I collected her she was just delighted. Mrs Wheatley was one of those lovely warm people who selflessly go that extra mile. She was a saving grace for me.

The following year Eilidh got a place at Dalneigh Nursery in Dalneigh Primary in Inverness. It was a lovely little class with a teacher, Celia Graham, a nursery nurse and two nursery nurse students. She was the only child there who had a disability, but she soon settled well and attended three weekly afternoon sessions. The other children were very kind to her. This gave her a brilliant introduction to school. There was a great variety of activities and each afternoon a small group of children would make a snack to be eaten by everyone at break-time. At last I felt I was getting a little bit of my life back. I had a little bit of space to think and to bake or make marmalade or just go to get my hair cut without an entourage of children.

Eilidh's Progress

Though Eilidh was not at this point sitting up independently, there was no doubt that her balance was steadily improving. She was desperate to walk. She would repeatedly say: *"I want to walk."* Unfortunately her legs kept scissoring – the right would cross in front of the left and therefore get locked and I was powerless to prevent this happening. In April 1982, and just after Eilidh's third birthday, it was considered prudent by the medical staff at Raigmore Hospital to send her to Edinburgh in order to have an assessment done. Ron and I were keen for any further advice and support.

We aranged for Ron's Mum to look after Linsey and Andrew at her home in Dundee and we spent four days in Edinburgh in our grey Mercedes motor home that we had recently bought. Our first consultation was with Mr Keith Brown, a consultant paediatrician, who held a clinic for children with cerebral palsy, then with Mr George Fulford, an orthopaedic consultant. After these preliminary interviews we went to Astley Ainslie Hospital where Eilidh was assessed by speech therapists, occupational therapists, physiotherapists, orthoptists and other doctors. Her pelvis was X-rayed to ensure that everything was in place and not liable to dislocate. A scan and EEG (electroencephalogram) were requested. This was to try to discover if her brain damage was liable to progress. Unfortunately neither the scan nor EEG could be done because of staff illness, so we were asked to return at a later date. We were very grateful for both the advice given and the interest shown. By this time Eilidh had grown too big for her buggy and so we were given a Major Buggy, which was a larger version of an ordinary buggy generally issued to children who were unable to walk.

During this assessment we visited Liz and Geoff and their children a few times. Despite the uncertainty regarding Eilidh, we enjoyed the company of old friends and it was a happy time: little did we know, but it was the calm before the storm. Some months afterwards Liz phoned with the devastating news that she had breast cancer. I think it was the first time that I thought of our collective mortality. Although Death is a common bond that I associated with people of my Dad and my Grandpa's generation, none of my contemporaries had died. My Mum was the only person in my life who had died in her 30s. Liz's cancer evoked upsetting memories of what I had been told about my Mum and how heart breaking her story was.

Liz had the necessary treatment and we all fervently prayed for her full recovery. She and I phoned each other regularly and exchanged weekly letters. She spoke quite frankly and at length about the situation, the sheer helplessness she felt, the fear of the unknown, the great anxieties about her children and how supportive Geoff was.

During this time my focus was very much on Eilidh's well-being and progress. Linsey and Andrew were making good progress at school, learning to read and write. Ron would read books to them every night – their favourites were Bod, The Teddy Bear Coalman and Richard Scarry's stories of Pierre the Paris Policeman and Schtoompah the Austrian musician. This last one was a particular favourite of mine too. The main character threw all his possessions into a cupboard and when he dug out his tuba to play at a concert, scores of household items were blown out into the concert hall.

At the weekends Ron would often take Linsey and Andrew out exploring. Once they went on a hill walk and discovered amethysts in a rock. At Christmas time they would go into the forest and "take" a Christmas tree and we would all decorate it together with a combination of decorations panning the last decade, from little angels and stars they had made at home and at school. I would often stay at home and entertain Eilidh and tidy up and cook.

Linsey was very independent and spent a lot of her time drawing and paid great attention to detail, always including shoelaces and eyelashes in her depictions of people. She also loved animals. As a youngster she had had a goldfish called Frank. Little did she know that Frank had died and been replaced by another Frank.

For her fifth birthday she got a pet rabbit, which she named Sooty. She adored him. Sadly a few months later our neighbour's horned sheep broke into our garden and unhinged Sooty's run from his cage. Linsey was very distressed as we frantically searched for him without success. Poor Linsey had to go off to school worrying about his whereabouts. Some time later I heard a scream and Andrew, who'd been playing in the front garden, ran in to the house crying hysterically: *"Sooty's dead, Sooty's dead!"* I followed him and sure enough poor Sooty was under the hedge: a pine marten had killed Linsey's beloved black rabbit with a bite to the neck. I dreaded telling her the awful news when she returned from school: she was absolutely distraught.

Andrew was happy wee lad and, although very sociable, was content to amuse himself. He continued to love Lego. We bought him a Lego book with instructions of how to make a variety of models and he built countless creations including a telephone, a detonator and a windmill. He even joined the Lego Club and had his photograph in their magazine showing off his model telephone. He also enjoyed doing jigsaws, reading books and learning to use Ron's tools any time his Dad was making or mending anything. Like many boys, he was intrigued by guns. I bitterly disapproved. One time Mrs Swan, who was going to visit her sister in Dundee, took Andrew with her. Ron's Mum met them at the station and Andrew spent a lovely week before returning on the train with her. When Ron met them at Inverness Station Andrew was brandishing a plastic rifle that fired table tennis balls. I hit the roof.

Eilidh's Equipment

Anytime that Eilidh needed anything in the way of equipment, Ron would make it. He has always had a great talent for his woodwork creations, making an assortment of useful equipment for her or other friends and family who needed it. He loved to potter in his garage and was always whistling as he worked, often with a cigarette hanging half out of his mouth. If I had a penny for every time he whistled John Denver's Annie's Song, I would be very rich.

The first piece of equipment Ron designed and made for Eilidh was a prone board – or solid standing frame. He made this when she was about 20 months old. This enabled her to stand upright at the dining table with a selection of toys. It had Velcro straps to keep her trunk, pelvis and legs secure. It was truly wonderful to see her standing confidently in an upright position since an able-bodied child would have been doing this independently by this time.

He also made a small three-cornered chair and matching kidney shaped table with a lip around the edge to prevent her toys rolling off onto the floor. Numerous toys were also made for her to ensure that she had opportunities to use both hands. When she outgrew anything it was always passed on to the hospital, so that any other child with additional needs who did not have a parent with the talents to make special equipment, could use it.

When Eilidh outgrew her prone board, Anne the physiotherapist arranged for her to have a standing frame from the hospital. Both of these pieces of equipment allowed Eilidh to stand at the sand box, the sink or a table where she would spend many happy hours busily engaged in activities that able-bodied children take for granted. Sand castles, mud pies, sand wheels, water play of all kinds and playing with pastry leftovers with cutters provided enormous pleasure. Besides I knew that she was safe and at last I could leave her in the room for short intervals.

We were thrilled later that year when Eilidh sat up independently. This happened on the grass at the car park in Camperdown Park in Dundee on a visit with Granny Wynton. She didn't do it again till much later, but the mere fact that this had happened gave me tremendous hope. Once she had sat up on her own for the second time, a few months later, she did so more frequently, becoming more proficient each time.

Shortly after that Eilidh graduated from commando crawling to conventional crawling. I was delighted because it meant that she could move independently from room to room. However, once she found something with which she wanted to play she tended to sit in a W (her hips on the floor and her legs splayed on each side in a W shape). She did this rather than sitting on her heels. While this W shape provided her with a stable base, it was quite detrimental to her hips as Anne, the physiotherapist, explained when she saw her doing this. That said, it was easier said than done trying to prevent Eilidh from doing this for, once I'd sorted her legs, she quickly reverted to her W position. If I put her in a long sitting position, with her legs stretched in front then she couldn't access her toys so easily. It was so very difficult.

Later on that year Eilidh and I returned to Edinburgh so that she could have the scan and EEG. We stayed overnight in the tonsils ward of The Sick Children's Hospital where I'd been a patient some 32 years previously. I'm certain that Eilidh's bed was in the exact place mine had been. How I wished that her thick wavy hair had been very short since the glue with which the tiny contacts were attached to her head was almost impossible to remove. Both tests showed that all was well and that no further damage had occurred.

All Going Swimmingly

Water is a tremendous medium for physically disabled children since they can often do so much more in the swimming pool than on land. Once Linsey started school, I would take Andrew and Eilidh to the swimming pool in Inverness every Wednesday when there was a session for families of children with special needs. It was during these sessions that Andrew became confident in the water initially to swim with armbands and then without. Luckily a volunteer would swim with him while I could focus on Eilidh, who was terrified.

She took an instant aversion to the water and tended to herald each session with wails and screams. Despite this, I persevered, more for Andrew's sake than hers. It seemed a great waste of time getting two youngsters ready for the pool, only to find that the younger of them would only tolerate five minutes. But gradually her confidence grew as her fear diminished and she began to enjoy herself. After that I spent time with Andrew while a volunteer would take Eilidh.

Before we left the house, we always put on our swimsuits in order to save time at the pool. One day I forgot to put Andrew's underpants in the bag and he had to wear my floral ones on the way home. Linsey cracked up at bedtime when she saw him getting undressed and into his pyjamas. Linsey also would come to the swimming pool with us in the holidays. On one occasion, I absent-mindedly left her swimming float and Andrew's on the roof of the car and drove off. *"Stop mum!"* they chorused. I did and managed to retrieve them undamaged.

Sometimes after school we'd all go to the pool in Dingwall and later both Linsey and Andrew joined the swimming club there and Ron would take them. By this time I had swapped my orange Fiat Mirafiore for a beige Subaru. One winter's night Linsey and Ron headed off to the pool in

Dingwall in the Subaru; Andrew had an ear infection so stayed at home. It was very frosty, so Ron took great care on the road. But as he came round the bend beside a small burn he hit a patch of black ice and despite his best efforts to correct the skid the car hit an embankment. *"We're going to go over Linsey,"* he said, *"So don't worry."*

Luckily the law about wearing front seatbelts had recently been passed because the car rolled over onto its roof and Ron's assuring gambit to Linsey was: *We're going to get out like the Dukes of Hazzard."* At the time our kids were avid watchers of the Dukes of Hazzard and dreamed of being allowed to get out of the car through the open windows. Linsey was a bit confused being upside down and looked at Ron and asked: *"How are we going to get to the swimming now?"* Ron hugged her, told her they wouldn't be able to go swimming and they would go home to see Mum. So she then, knowing it was my car, asked: *"What will Mum say?"* Her Dad told her not to worry, saying: *"Mum will be very pleased to see us and we'll get a lift home."* They stood by the side of the road and Ron waved down a car. The occupants were two school photographers who brought Linsey home and then dropped Ron off at the local garage. The car was a write off.

Linsey and Andrew, though sworn enemies at times, loved Eilidh and when they were little neither ever gave the impression of being either jealous or resentful. Ron and I strove to give them as much of our attention as was humanly possible and we tried to participate in as great a variety of activities that we could as a complete family. We enjoyed using our motor home for family holidays, visiting Aunt Margaret in Ullapool and days out. I can still see Ron at the wheel in his lumberjack shirt, with a packet of Benson and Hedges glistening from the top of his breast pocket, heading along the A835 and the A9 and listening to tapes of the Spinners singing Dirty Old Town and Johnny Cash bellowing out A Boy Named Sue.

The inside of this Irish plated mobile holiday cottage was very well designed and could sleep the six of us (Honey included) quite comfortably. There was a gas fire, a full size cooker, a toilet and shower and there was a ladder on the back so that extra luggage could be put onto the roof. In time we bought a trailer so that we could take our bikes with us.

Ron's Mum had a neighbour with two children who had outgrown their bikes and we decided to buy them from her. She very kindly kept them for us until we went to Dundee for Ron's brother Graham's wedding to Jennifer. Linsey's was just the right size, but Andrew needed wooden blocks on the pedals because his legs weren't quite long enough to reach them. They both had the golden opportunity to practise and develop their cycling skills that week. We stayed at Monifieth with his younger brother Martin and his wife Irene and parked our motor home in their driveway, alongside Martin's BT work van and his collection of bangers that he did up in his spare time. Nearby was an open space surrounded by a cycle track and over the next few days the wobbling quickly waned. By the time we went home, Linsey and Andrew could cycle quite confidently.

Not to be outdone, Eilidh had a small trike provided by the hospital. When we went to my Aunt Margaret's in Ullapool for our summer holiday, Ron secured her trike on a small trailer, which he towed with his bike. This allowed Eilidh to feel like she was cycling too. We'd often try to see how far we could cycle up the steep hill on the North Road and invariably I'd be first to dismount from my green fold up shopper bike. Sometimes Linsey and Andrew would make it all the way up the hill and love whizzing down afterwards. Ron towing Eilidh, would cycle cheerfully past me. *"How can he possibly do that?"* I'd say to myself. *"He smokes and I don't."*

Most Sunday evenings Ron would take Linsey and Andrew to the ice rink, sometimes with Lorna and Paul who were a couple of their friends. It didn't take them long to learn to keep their balance and after a few sessions they managed to glide round the ice without constantly falling. Andrew perfected his skills one evening when he and Ron went by themselves because Linsey was unwell, probably with tonsillitis, which she seemed to get several times each winter. This gave Andrew the ideal opportunity to practise and each time he fell over he increased both the distance that he skated and his determination to master it. The knees of his trousers were wet, as were his gloves and his fingers were tingling with the cold, but finally he was able to skate slowly round the rink. And as his confidence grew he was able to travel faster. By the end of the night both he and his Dad were happily skating round to the music. As they clomped towards the changing room a lady approached Andrew and handing him a chocolate bar said: *"Here's a prize son. I've been watching you for some time and you've done very well indeed."* Andrew was delighted and brought his prize home to show me.

During a severe winter Loch Meikle, which was quite near Balnain Primary School, would freeze over and one year Ron noticed the ice was thick enough to skate on. The trees were beautifully decorated with ribbons of ice and the birds chirruped sweetly. Ron even skated across the loch with Eilidh on his shoulders. It was an amazing experience, although I preferred to stay on dry land.

Since we had a piano I thought that it would be a good idea for Linsey to learn to play. We found a piano teacher called Mrs Janney who lived in an amazing, rambling house in Glenurquhart with her composer husband Rodney. Mrs Janney played the violin as well as the piano while Rodney played the oboe and made oboe reeds. It was always freezing and you had to wear warm clothes inside, even in the summer time. They had about four pianos, including a grand piano and a harpsichord. Each week, Ron would take Linsey along with her brown music bag, in his little red Mini van. She passed grade 1 and 2 although she later admitted she found it more interesting having a nose around the Janney's home than learning to play the piano, which she later told me she did just to please me. I think she preferred going to Brownies and working towards badges such as the cook, the artist and the writer.

Walking by Horse

Borlum Farm, a local stable, offered Riding for the Disabled to children who were unable to walk so that they could experience the sensation of walking on a horse. So when Linsey was seven, Andrew five and Eilidh three they all began riding lessons. Linsey loved it and became a proficient equestrian, taking part in gymkhanas and jumping competitions and winning lots of rosettes.

To begin with Eilidh sat in a basket saddle – this was simply a small chair made out of the basket twigs that you'd get on a laundry basket. It was fitted onto a saddle with safety straps. First of all she simply sat in it while the pony remained stationary, then she went for short walks. Progress was halted temporarily when the pony sneezed and shook his head. As with the physiotherapist's Bobath ball and the swimming pool, she howled. However, I did not always take her off immediately and this tactic finally paid off when she realised that there was nothing to be afraid of.

The following autumn we were lucky enough to be loaned Pigeon, a Shetland pony who belonged to Mrs Dennison from Inverness and was stabled at Borlum. It was felt by the staff from Riding for the Disabled that if we had a pony on hand Eilidh could get maximum benefit. Although we had no field, our neighbour, who owned an adjacent property with land, came to the rescue and allowed us to let Pigeon graze in one of her fields. And so Pigeon came to stay.

It was largely Linsey who looked after Pigeon. She knew that, in return for this, she could have as many pony rides as she wanted. Pigeon was a black smooth-coated Shetland pony, who was very affectionate and quiet by nature. Her kindly expression endeared her to us all and she would nuzzle us at every opportunity. Ron built her a little shelter and carpeted the floor with wood shavings from the school workshop. Outside Pigeon had her water trough.

Eilidh's confidence grew as she soon graduated from walking to trotting and using an ordinary saddle with one of us supporting her. I can truthfully say that Pigeon was very happy for the two years that she stayed with us. As the golden days of autumn turned to winter so Pigeon grew a thick, cosy, dark brown winter coat that I was assured would keep out the winter chills.

The field was a stone's throw from our house and conveniently beside a burn. This water on tap meant that Linsey could fill up the water trough by herself. When there was no further growth in the field, Pigeon was fed on hay. Every morning before school, Linsey and Andrew would go down to tie up a hay net and break the ice in her water if it was frozen over. Pigeon's head with its white moon-shaped crest was always over the gate waiting and a welcoming whinney always rang out when she saw the children. When snow covered the ground, Pigeon's hooves resembled hairy après-ski boots.

The worst weather for horses is a combination of wind and driving rain, then cold can really set in. Pigeon was safe in her shelter and she often got extra hay to keep her in-built central heating system going.

As winter turned to spring, Pigeon began to lose her thick coat. Then we discovered that she suffered from sweet itch, a skin condition that made her itch, scratch and consequently have bare patches on her mane and tail. The vet prescribed thick white fluid and advised stabling her for part of the day. This was not easy.

The children had many happy treks with Pigeon and the culmination of this was when Linsey rode her in two Shetland pony Grand Nationals at the Moy Game Fair. This race of Thelwell ponies involved riding twice around the arena and negotiating the small jumps that were stationed at regular intervals. On the first occasion Pigeon started off well, but then decided to stop in order to eat the vegetation that made up the jumps. No amount of coercing, wheedling or poking in the ribs would convince her to move and afterwards Lord Burton and the MP Malcolm Rifkind, who were presenting the medals, came over to talk to her. While Malcolm Rifkind talked to Linsey, Lord Burton remonstrated with Pigeon who by this time had had enough and backed into him almost knocking him off his feet. Malcolm Rifkind spluttered into his hanky.

The following year Pigeon managed to complete the two circuits. This was bittersweet for Linsey because Mrs Dennison had told us that she wanted to pass Pigeon on to her grandchildren. This would be the last time Linsey would see her best friend as Mrs Dennison's grandchildren lived in Devon. She truly loved this adorable pony and would have gone to any lengths for her. Robin Pape, the farrier who used to shoe Pigeon, once remarked: *"Linsey would crawl over broken glass for that horse."* At the time it did not occur to us to offer to buy Pigeon because it seemed that Mrs Dennison had made up her mind.

Losing Honey

Before Pigeon's departure, we also lost dear old Honey. By the autumn of 1984 our delightful chocolate brown Labrador had almost reached the ripe old age of 15. On autumn and winter nights she'd stretch full length in front of the fire, snoring her head off. Still she would always eat the table scraps and lick up any spillages that the children made. Human beings' emotions are many and complicated, but Honey was completely happy if fed, exercised, sheltered and loved. One of the nicest bonuses for me was coming home to a tremendous welcome if I'd gone out. She'd sense sadness and push her cold wet nose towards me, or simply come and lay her head on my lap. She was such a wonderful member of the family.

Like most people, animals grow old too. She'd been an incredibly healthy dog all of her life, but towards the end her back legs began to fail her from time to time and occasionally she would lose bowel control. One of the valves in her heart also began to fail. Our friend Peter Grant, the vet, discussed everything with us and left us to decide what we wanted to do. A few weeks later he called round concerning another matter and we discussed everything again. Peter told us that he could: *"Keep her going for another six months, but she wouldn't thank us."* As a consequence we asked him to euthanase her there and then.

Honey had had a wonderful day and was very happy, she'd even managed to twirl on all legs and, best of all, none of us knew that it was going to be her last day, least of all Peter. The children were in the upstairs living room watching television before they went to bed. Ron and I went into the kitchen with Honey. She sat obediently, as ever looking straight up at Peter as he administered the injection. It was as if she knew what was going to happen and it was over and done with both quickly and painlessly. Peter and Ron put her in her basket and later Linsey and Ron wrapped her in a blanket and buried her in the garden. Linsey was really distressed and could not believe Honey was dead and that she had not been able to say goodbye. She did not want to let go of Honey as she sat beside her still warm body in her basket. She kept wondering if Honey would wake up. We all shed tears as we mourned the passing of a faithful friend. Andrew made a cross to mark her grave and a few days afterwards he and Ron made a little headstone for her out of Polmaily serpentine and engraved her name upon it.

The Three Ts

After Pigeon was driven off to Devon in a horsebox, we immediately investigated the possibility of buying a pony for Linsey. Val Piggot, who'd taught Linsey to ride, took her to see Tara, a striking albino Welsh/ Arab pony with bright blue eyes, white hair and pink skin. Tara had been bought for a farmer's daughter who hadn't really enjoyed riding. For Linsey, Tara was a huge challenge and very different to Pigeon.

To say that Tara was rather frisky and high-spirited was an understatement. For the six months before she came to live with us she'd been grazing peacefully in a field in the company of Maisie, an aged white Shetland pony. She'd been allowed to do her own thing and she was a far different creature from the canny, dependable, faithful Pigeon. Despite having a replacement pony, Linsey still grieved over the loss of Pigeon. Her reasoning was excellent. One time I said to her: *"You never cried this much for Honey the way you do over Pigeon",* she replied, "but *Mum Honey's dead and can't come back, but Pigeon isn't."*

Experienced rider though she was, Linsey could not go out on Tara unless either Ron or I went with her. Val came round every week to give Linsey a lesson and a girl who worked in the local hotel used to exercise Tara regularly. Gradually Tara calmed, though not before she managed to escape from the field on a couple of occasions. The second time this happened she was found along the main road by our friends Val and Stuart Wilson, heading for a field where two horses lived. As it was in the middle of the day, they went to school and collected Linsey who escorted Tara back to her field – she had refused to go with anyone else and kicked out.

The Wilsons lived in Almondbury in Yorkshire and had rented Mairi's cottage for the holidays while she stayed in the little nearby chalet that had previously belonged to her late brother. Their son Andrew and daughter Sarah were about the same age as Linsey and Andrew and so had quickly made friends with them: Sarah like Linsey was mad about horses. The family really loved Scotland and thoroughly enjoyed spending their summer holidays here each year. They always visited us and Andrew and Sarah would stay over with us for a few days.

I suspect that Tara simply wanted company. Most horses, like most people, are gregarious. Pigeon had obviously been an exception to the rule, being content to be on her own. Tara was just too big for both Andrew and Eilidh, so we decided to advertise for a Shetland pony to keep her company. The response was amazing and after viewing all of the horses we finally chose Tina, a shaggy dark brown little Shetland owned by Anne Tidmarsh, who'd previously used her as a driving pony. Tina's arrival proved to be a great hit with Tara and the pair immediately became inseparable.

Some time later we bought Toyah, an Icelandic pony and very aptly named since her thick red mane and punk like forelock resembled the tresses of the singer Toyah Wilcox. We bought her because she was a good steady pony and very suitable for trekking. We felt that Linsey and Andrew could use Toyah for treks until Tara was thoroughly schooled and then they could both go out on their own. Toyah was a very solitary and shy horse. Like Pigeon had been, she was perfectly happy to graze by herself. She had been shipped over with a herd of Icelandic ponies from Iceland. The men who had brought the ponies over had treated them badly and they had not been fed properly on the journey. As a result Toyah had developed a real aversion to men and would generally turn her back on Ron.

School at Last for Eilidh

After spending a year at Dalneigh Nursery, we enrolled Eilidh at Glenurquhart Primary School. I had moved Linsey and Andrew there at the end of the summer term of 1983. They were already happily settled there and, since Eilidh required support, a Record of Needs had to be drawn up, detailing how her educational needs would be met. Eilidh was also given a wheelchair to use in school, although we tended to use her major buggy to go out and about as it was lighter to push and to lift in and out of the back of the car.

An auxiliary also had to be found to ensure Eilidh's needs were met in school. I was overjoyed that the person appointed was Mrs Christine McCallum who used to run the local playgroup and who had two children of her own. She had known Eilidh practically all of her life. The two of them became firm friends very quickly and an excellent rapport was established. Eilidh's first teacher was Miss Carmelita Fraser who was very experienced and sympathetic towards Eilidh's needs. Both she and Christine combined excellently to get the best from Eilidh.

The school was small and just had four teachers for the 72 pupils on the roll. The Headteacher, Miss Miller, was somewhat apprehensive about having a disabled child. That said, Eilidh soon wove her magical influence on staff and pupils alike and previously held fears were quickly dispelled. There were 15 pupils in Eilidh's class – a composite Primary 1 and Primary 2. I was heartened that one very boisterous boy, whom I was used to seeing running about and horsing around with his brothers, was actually so kind and welcoming to Eilidh. I also remember a boy who actually lived in a caravan with his Mum giving her a gift of a Postman Pat floor mat, while yet another lad gave her a record of Postman Pat songs – Eilidh loved Postman Pat.

Anne, the physiotherapist, visited the school weekly to do exercises with Eilidh, advise Christine and monitor progress. During the holidays she visited Eilidh at home. Initially Eilidh attended school for mornings only and on just her second half day she awoke with a very spotty face. The doctor confirmed my diagnosis of chickenpox and so she missed the next two weeks of school. The spots were everywhere. One morning we attempted to count them. But after several fruitless attempts we gave up because there were so many. She had more spots than I'd ever seen in my life and was covered from head to toe – scalp, eyelids, nostrils, insides of both mouth and ears, under her arms, between her fingers and on her toes and her trunk, legs and bottom. Though Eilidh didn't scratch much, she has still got some pock-marks.

Linsey contracted chicken pox a few days later and also had many spots, though Eilidh's definitely outnumbered hers. When Andrew's turn came he had only a very few. It made a pleasant change for them to have this childhood illness during term time since holidays had usually been specially reserved for acquiring infections. During the previous Christmas all three had mumps, both Eilidh and Linsey having really swollen faces while Andrew emerged relatively unscathed. I now wonder if this was because he was the one who had been breastfed for the longer time.

Cataloguing these childhood ailments proved no mean task and I discovered, after one recent count, that they'd quite literally had everything from German measles to Scarlatina. Linsey and Andrew also had whooping cough. Although it is a wretched infection and sometimes leaves the sufferer susceptible to chest problems, we had decided not to have them inoculated as there had been so much adverse publicity with regard to brain damage. I later asked about getting Eilidh inoculated as I didn't want her to experience the awful symptoms Linsey and Andrew had had. But because of her prematurity, she was unable to have this inoculation as we were told there could be a risk of further brain damage.

When she returned to school Eilidh thoroughly enjoyed number work, particularly counting. Christine would often enjoy a quiet chuckle when Miss Fraser would ask someone a question such as: *"Do you mean to say that you don't know what 4 + 3 is?"* A gruff wee voice would pipe up: *"It's 7 Miss Fraser."* Music was also thoroughly enjoyed. Eilidh has an extremely tuneful voice and an excellent sense of rhythm. Glenurquhart Primary was fortunate enough to have Sheila Bruce, a peripatetic music teacher, who exuded such enthusiasm that all of the children gave of their best. There were recorder lessons provided for those who were keen and there was also a little percussion band.

Eilidh learned the alphabet and sounds. She has always loved books and though she regularly brought one home with her, she found reading independently very difficult. In time she became very confident in recognising social signs. Eilidh made many friends at school and though naturally shy, over time she has become increasingly friendly, self-assured and confident.

When Eilidh started attending school for the whole day, I used to take her home most lunch-times. I would then take her back afterwards as it was felt the whole school day would be tiring for her. We'd also go to Mrs Swan's house for lunch sometimes. And after a while Christine kindly offered to take her home once a week to her house, which was nearby. By the time Eilidh got to Primary 2, she was able to stay for a packed lunch.

At school, Eilidh walked somewhat erratically with a wheeled walking aid called a rollator. The corridors were beautifully wide and there were no awkward steps. Because of everyone's hard work, Eilidh's balance continued to improve and we were amply rewarded when she could sit unsupported on a little stool.

Not a Bowl of Cherries

My best friend Liz had been in remission for a couple of years. But she wrote me a letter after having been to the clinic for a routine check up. Her cancer had returned. Not only this, but this time it was terminal. Liz as ever was philosophical and wrote: *"Well my dear, life's not a bowl of cherries!"*

During the Easter holiday of 1985, Geoff drove her and the children up to spend a holiday with us. They referred to the car, a Renault 4, as *"the brown jobbie".* We had a lovely time and I remember the sunny Saturday when Ron and Geoff took the children out on the bikes while Liz and I relaxed outside. I vividly remember her telling me about the cost of the very expensive drugs that she'd been prescribed and also sharing her anxieties as to how Geoff was going to manage when she was no longer there. A few short weeks later she was in St Columba's Hospice in Edinburgh.

Ron and I went to Edinburgh in the motor home to visit her there several times. We were so lucky that Granny Wynton and Cathy and Jackie were able to look after the children. We also went to see Geoff at home. He hoped that Liz would be able to return home once they'd stabilised the nausea that beset her. He told us that when he took the children to visit, their daughter would always wear her nurse's uniform so that she could try to make her Mum better. The thought of her doing this still makes me cry all these years later.

By this time Liz had discarded her wig as her blonde hair, once so long and thick, had started to grow in again. She reminded me very much of the actress Mia Farrow with her pale skin and boyish crop of hair framing her elfin face. We chatted about our respective children, her Mum and Dad and the hospice, which was a haven of tranquility and peace. Liz's bed had a cosy sheepskin for her to lie on, the food was appetising and nursing staff were on hand at all times.

I felt that under these circumstances she was in a place where staff helped terminally ill people allay both their fears and make their passing as peaceful and painless as possible. I knew when I left after the last visit and paused once more to wave through the glass window of the door, that I wouldn't ever see her again. I felt absolutely drained when I left and wept uncontrollably once we returned to the motor home.

I believe that her spirit is still around and to me she's still my very best friend. She died in the summer of 1985 at the young age of 38. It was particularly heartbreaking for me because she was only two years older than my own Mum when she died. It was the first day of our holiday at Aunt Margaret's in Ullapool when Geoff phoned. Whenever I heard his voice I knew instinctively that Liz had died. He told me that it had taken her a long time to settle to sleep. For some strange reason, I already knew this, because the previous night I had been thinking about her as I usually did and it had also taken me a long time to fall asleep. We talked about the children, Liz's parents and the funeral arrangements. Ron drove Linsey, Eilidh and me to her funeral in Duddingston Church, where just a few years earlier both children had been christened. Andrew stayed with Aunt Margaret because he still suffered from car-sickness, particularly on long journeys. On this occasion it would not have been fair to him and I knew that Aunt Margaret and he would have a lovely time together.

The church was filled with her many friends and family and I remember her wee girl, only seven, with her wavy blonde hair sitting with her Dad and her big brother. She wore a blue spotty dress, the sort of outfit she should have been wearing to a party. I remember singing All Things Bright and Beautiful and I remember the elderly minister, who was a locum. He was a kindly man, although painstakingly slow. As I sat there looking at Liz's coffin with the beautiful flowers on it, I half expected Liz to push open the lid indignantly saying: *"Just get on with it, will you."*

As I watched Geoff and his precious children, I thought about my own Dad and the overwhelming grief he must have felt when my Mum passed away and he was left with me only 27 months old. I wondered how Geoff would manage with the daunting responsibility that lay ahead of raising two youngsters with no Mum. Since then I have thought about Liz every day. It has undoubtedly been tough for Geoff and their children, but they have done ever so well. I know she would have been so very proud of her children and the grandchildren they now have, whom she never got to meet.

Chapter 9: Pastures New – at Home and in Hungary

It was Saturday evening and I was preparing a family favourite for dinner: fish in ruskoline. I turned on Radio Scotland and to my delight I heard the Doric tones of Robbie Shepherd, the presenter of Take the Floor, announcing the reel The Duke of Perth. I waited for the chord that heralded the start of the dance and did some pas-de-basque steps followed by a few skip change ones. It was then that I spotted the eggs. *"I wonder if I could juggle with 2 of these while doing a pas-de-basque,"* I thought, picking them up. Our chocolate brown Labrador, Honey, looked up expectantly: like all Labradors she enjoyed her food and never missed an opportunity for a tit bit. I started off slowly, then speeded up. All was going well until I thought that I'd be a bit more ambitious and pass one of the eggs under my leg and into the air. Suddenly there was a crash. Not surprisingly, the egg had hit the floor and the shell had broken. Yellow yoke mixed with the clear albumen was now on the beige floor tiles. I thought I had better get the floor cloth, but before I could, Honey sprang to the rescue. Never one to miss an opportunity, before I had time to say *"Help my kilt"*, the egg and its shell had vanished into her tummy.

Walking Abroad

In July 1985 I read a newspaper article that was to turn our lives upside down. It appeared in the teachers' newspaper, the Times Educational Supplement, and was written by Howard Sharron. It described Conductive Education, a method of teaching children with motor disorders that was carried out in Budapest at the Peto Andras Intezete. It described the holistic approach that Dr Peto had found effective in helping those children with Spina Bifida and Cerebral Palsy to improve their mobility. The institute's curriculum was based around programmes of exercises that were carried out using simple wooden equipment. This included slatted plinths, ladder-back chairs and small stools that were easy for hands to grip. As they took part in this intensive exercise regime children sang traditional songs and rhymes at the tops of their voices.

I read and re-read the article. My disabled daughter Eilidh was now six, and I assumed that she was having all of the support she needed. No one had ever mentioned this method and so I thought no more about it. However, a few months later The Observer newspaper published another article by Howard Sharron and a few weeks later the BBC screened a documentary entitled Standing up for Joe, which told the story of a young English boy with Cerebral Palsy and his parents' efforts to aid him to walk.

Joe was quadraplegic, meaning his arms and legs were all affected. His parents Lise and Mike Horseley had emigrated to Hungary so that Joe could attend the Peto Intezete. This evocative documentary showed him and other children and their parents learning techniques to enable the children to move as independently as possible.

I watched the film with Ron and Linsey. It had the most tremendous impact on me, more than I had ever experienced in anything I had seen, so I wrote to the BBC for an information pack and I also wrote to Dr Maria Hari, the Director of the Intezete, asking if Eilidh could be assessed. I also ordered a copy of the book entitled Conductive Education written by Andrew Sutton, a research fellow in the Department of Psychology and an associate for Russian and East European Studies at Birmingham University and Phillipa Cottam, a lecturer in Language Pathology and Therapeutics in the Department of Linguistics at Sheffield University. The book explained in great detail the philosophy of Conductive Education and the philosophy of the Peto Intezete staff, known as conductors, who used simple repetitive programmes of exercises throughout the day to help the children maximise their mobility. There is no cure for motor disorder and Conductive Education never claimed to be able to do this.

When I told Anne, the physiotherapist, what I'd done and asked if she'd ever heard of Conductive Education she told me that she'd visited a school in England which practised these principles and that she hadn't been impressed. She felt that the methods used were very repetitive and said: *"Eilidh's too bright for that."* At the time there was only one such school in the UK. It was not widely known about and there was later a debate about whether it was using the true principles of Conductive Education or simply cherry picking elements that staff felt were most relevant.

Despite this, I really wanted to go to Budapest to see for myself, as a Mum who just wanted the best for her child. I had no idea of the effect that this would have on all of our lives.

Back in November 1984 I had attended a regular combined clinic where Eilidh was assessed by a string of experts – a physiotherapist, a paediatrician, an orthopaedic consultant and an occupational therapist. Eilidh's legs often crossed like scissors and, because of her spasticity, she was unable to unlock them. This caused her muscles to tighten and pull on her left hip socket, causing it to sublax (come out of joint) at times. It was at the combined clinic that it was decided that she should have surgery, namely an adductor tenotomy (division of a tendon) and obturator neurectomy (trimming of the nerve), which would help to prevent this. An incision was to be made at the top of the inside of her left leg and some nerve trimmed in order to release the tendon. Because of the length of the waiting list the operation was not scheduled until May 1986.

Moving from Westbury

Around this time we decided to move home from Westbury. It was not that we did not love this house in Glenurquhart – we did. But we felt it was no longer suitable for the needs of our family, Eilidh in particular. We decided to buy or look to build a bungalow so Eilidh would not have to go up and down the stairs to the bathroom and her bedroom. We also wanted some land of our own for our three ponies to graze on. Plus Linsey and Andrew were due to start secondary school soon and there was talk of the local secondary closing and the alternative, though a great school, was a 30 minute bus journey away in Inverness.

We spent many weekends viewing properties around the outskirts of Inverness, Beauly and the Black Isle, before we made an offer on a bungalow with 15 acres of fields and woodland. It was named Fieldhead and was near Fortrose on the Black Isle, not a stone's throw from where our Shetland pony Tina had come from. It was not nearly such a nice house as Westbury, but it had gorgeous surroundings and was close to a great secondary school, Fortrose Academy. Although it only had three bedrooms, we decided that we could extend the house and be eligible for a home improvement grant because of Eilidh's needs. Our offer of £52,000 was accepted in November 1985 and for a short time we were the owners of two homes, three horses and, of course, no money.

We remained at Westbury, hoping to find a buyer. Although it seemed to me the loveliest house in the world, it took seven months to sell. Finally a couple with a teenage son from Edinburgh bought it. Our children were very sad to leave since it was the only home that they'd known, but we hoped that they'd learn to love Fieldhead in the same way and that they would carry their memories of Westbury with them of all the fun they had had there – especially in the garden. Linsey wrote a little note asking to please look after her bedroom and she was relieved when Mrs Wilson, the new owner, wrote to us to say their Jack Russell terrier would sit on her old windowsill.

We had decided to move at the end of May so that the children could make friends at their new school ahead of the summer holidays. However, with Eilidh's operation planned for May 1st, things were going to be a little tricky. I naively thought that after a few days she'd be home and back at school.

"Don't Cut my Legs off!"

Eilidh left Glenurquhart Primary on 30th April. When I went to collect her after school, thoughtful Christine had been reading a book to her called Going into Hospital. We said our goodbyes, not realising that that would be her last day there.

Ron's Mum had arranged to come up and look after Linsey and Andrew while I stayed with Eilidh in hospital. Eilidh slept soundly that night and she was first on the list for her operation in the morning. Her face crumpled and she began to cry as she heard the rumble of the trolley making its way to the ward. She was swiftly and carefully lifted on and very soon we were in the small room where the anaesthetic was administered. I looked like nothing on earth as I donned gown, hat and shoes. Once she was asleep I went for a much needed walk in the fresh air. I had no idea what was in store for me on my return.

When Eilidh returned to the ward, I was totally unprepared for the sight that met my eyes. Little Eilidh's legs were both plastered and were splayed apart. A stick measuring 38 inches (just under 1 metre) was attached between her plastered ankles, to keep them wide apart. Further up was another shorter stick. I was told these broomsticks were also for holding when lifting her to transport her or take her to the loo. I was aghast. It was such a relief that my friend Denise, who was working that day in the radiography department, came in to see Eilidh and gave her a Get Well card. Eilidh held it tightly for ages. Both of us were devastated. In fact, Eilidh was so shocked that she could only whisper for quite a long time afterwards.

No one had told either of us that her legs would be splinted and I hadn't asked or thought. But on reflection I suppose common sense ought to have told me that this would be the outcome. After all what would have been the point of doing such an operation and not stretching out her legs.

I stayed with Eilidh in hospital and it was very claustrophobic. After a few days we got home. The splints were to be kept on for two or three weeks. I worried as to how I was going to manage. In the end I did, though it wasn't easy. Luckily Granny Wynton stayed for an extra few days while I got into a routine and thank goodness I did not have a job. I have no idea how that could be possible for a parent of a young child with a severe physical disability. Eilidh was a very good little girl, especially at home in a familiar environment. She was not especially demanding either during the day or night. I was really proud of her, but just felt so heartbroken that she had to go through all this.

She would sit in my old nursing chair, which had belonged to Aunt Margaret's Mum when she was nursing her. It was a big comfy chair that kept little Eilidh upright and secure. She could either sit or lie on the settee and watch TV and videos. During that time I was singing the theme tune to Postman Pat in my head – Eilidh must have seen every episode countless times. Ron and I moved her bed into our room, lest she should wake during the night. When the weather was fine I took her out in her wheelchair, having first removed the sides to accommodate her splayed legs.

During this period of convalescence, I received a letter from Dr Hari the Director of the Peto Intezete in Hungary. She told me that Eilidh could come for two weeks from 26th August. When I told Anne, the physiotherapist, she was non-committal. At least she was very pleased with Eilidh's post-operation progress and said we'd work hard once the plasters came off. I booked flights and accommodation through a travel agency, which specialised in organising such packages.

"Well young lady, your plasters can come off now." said the doctor three weeks after Eilidh's operation. It was with great relief that we went to the plaster room, where a kindly nurse met us. I lifted Eilidh onto the bed, made her comfortable and told her not to worry. The nurse returned with an electric cutter and explained what she was going to do. At the sight of the blade Eilidh froze and said: *"Please don't cut my legs off."* We

reassured Eilidh and chatted to her while the nurse cut through the plasters and then washed her legs with warm water and rubbed some cream into the skin.

Afterwards I took her home and made her comfortable on the settee. Having had her legs stretched for almost three weeks, it was initially quite painful for her to close them. So for several nights we put a pillow between them, so making her as comfortable as possible. Eilidh was a right little soldier. She seldom complained.

Because of her incapacity she was unable to return to Glenurquhart Primary (although one afternoon I took her for a visit) and stayed at home until we moved to the Black Isle at the end of May. We read stories, sang songs and she watched Postman Pat and Pingu videos. By this time she was becoming proficient at snipping with scissors and with some help would make a good attempt at cutting out coloured strips of paper, which I curled to make pictures. She also liked to cut out photos from magazines – the Index catalogue was a particular favourite.

As she recovered from the surgery I noticed her legs did not scissor quite so much and her alignment was better. Beforehand she had had a slightly windswept form with her left hip being pulled in. The key to preventing this recurring as she grew seemed to me to be keeping up with the exercises prescribed by Anne, her physiotherapist.

At this time Ron and I had, quite by chance, met the educational psychologist who asked us how we'd feel about Eilidh attending the Special Unit at Cauldeen Primary in Inverness. This was a classroom that had six places for children with additional needs. The teacher was Maggie Shearer and the classroom assistant was Janet Holmes. We both visited and felt that it would meet Eilidh's needs very well, despite the daily journeys (it was 15 miles each way from our new home). So we returned later with Eilidh who was absolutely delighted to have the chance to be at school with other children like her. She was offered a place for the following school year and arrangements were made for her to spend the last few weeks of term at Avoch Primary after we moved to Fortrose at the end of May.

The Angel Delight and Ruskoline Years

The first residents at our new home were our three ponies. I remember being surrounded by twice as many boxes as there were when Ron and I first moved to Westbury, 12 years before in 1974. Then the phone rang. Linsey got it and to our relief it was Anne Tidmarsh, who had sold Tina to us. She had kindly transported the three ponies over that morning. She'd said: *"Tell your Mum that the horses are enjoying the grass in the field."* A wave of relief engulfed me that they had settled in straight away with the simple appeal of the boundless supply of grass.

By the time that Ron got home from school, we were ready to leave for the new house. We'd said our goodbyes to Mairi, Jackie, Cathy, Mrs Swan, Christine McCallum and Denise. Linsey and Andrew had also said goodbye to their school friends. We'd packed our sleeping bags and food for the next day into the car. Ron would be the last member of the family to leave our house. He'd stay one last night and leave with the pantechnicon the next day. Linsey and Andrew went from room to room saying their goodbyes to the only home they'd known while Eilidh and I went out to the garden to say goodbye to Honey in her grave. I hadn't imagined it would be so hard to leave our lovely house. Though I tried hard, I couldn't stop the tears from pricking my eyes. I suppose I was also saying goodbye to all my hopes and dreams, all the work that Ron and I had put into the stone crafted fireplace, the beautiful garden and fruit cage and having to make a change so we could best accommodate Eilidh's disability.

It was around 6.30pm on Thursday 30th May we moved out. Linsey and Andrew waved to the house till we got to the bottom of the hill and could no longer see it.

Though the children were extremely sad to leave Westbury, they gradually grew to settle and enjoy their new home. At that time the panoramic view from the living room window was breathtaking. We could see not only round the east coast for many miles, but also watch the oil rigs being built at McDermott's Fabrication Yard in Ardersier. When darkness fell, this yard looked like fairyland because the twinkle and sparkle of the many lights was reflected in the water.

Our house nestles in a sheltered hollow and there are around four acres of woodland behind it. Wildlife is prolific. Deer regularly graze, foxes, pine martins visit occasionally and on several occasions a red squirrel has been sighted, while the sound of woodpeckers echoes through the woods.

When we'd bought the house we knew that we'd need to extend because it was smaller than Westbury. Since the walls were made of concrete panels, we wanted to build an additional brick wall to further insulate them for the winter time. The existing accommodation was a lounge, kitchen, bathroom, toilet and three bedrooms. As the ground on the kitchen side sloped downhill, we felt that that would be the best area to extend. Our architect drew up plans to excavate and build a retaining wall. Along that gable we decided to build on a dining room and en suite bedroom for Eilidh with a balcony and French doors in both rooms. In the basement below there would be a garage, storeroom, utility room and carport.

We found a local builder who was willing to tackle the project. We also secured a home improvement grant for a wet room with a shower for Eilidh where she could use a shower chair. This also included a low level toilet. The plans were finalised and the work scheduled to begin on October 21st.

That first summer at Fieldhead passed lazily by. Linsey and Andrew were able to be quite independent – they rode the horses and bikes to the beach, the forest and the enchanting Fairy Glen. They also made new friends, including two girls who also had ponies. Eilidh went out on her wee bike or in her buggy, or on my back and we also did her programme of exercises.

I missed my old kitchen with its stunning view of the forest. But I got used to the new one and enjoyed making my firm favourites: lemon marmalade and chocolate fancies, which were little sweets with a walnut on top. I well remember listening to Robbie Shepherd's Take the Floor programme on Radio Scotland on Saturday evenings while frying fish dipped in eggs and Ruskoline. I would actually dance round the kitchen as the ceilidh band played the musical accompaniments to the Gay Gordons and Strip the Willow and I would try to juggle eggs under my legs. Only once did I break one and that was at Westbury: Honey cleared up the mess. We always had pudding after dinner back then. At the height of the 1980s popular favourites in our household were Vienetta ice-cream, flan with fruit jelly and spray cream, or Angel Delight with tinned peaches or apricots.

The autumn term at school began on Tuesday 19th August, which meant Eilidh only had four days before we went to Budapest. I remember her new teacher, Maggie Shearer, phoning to tell me that Donald Menzies, who drove the taxi, was just like a Grandpa to her. After the first day she settled down very well considering all of the disruptions and traumas of the past three and a half months. I doubt if Eilidh fully realised just where we were going and why.

As the time for departure drew closer, I was filled with trepidation and felt very emotional about leaving Ron, Linsey and Andrew. Two weeks seemed a very long time: the longest time we would have been away from each other. Just what was I going to do and how was I going to cope in a foreign country with a devilishly difficult language? I'd been so very single-minded regarding this, so I'd never fully considered either of these aspects. I only knew that I wanted to go to see the Peto Intezete for myself.

Ron's Mum came to look after everybody while we were away. Her visits were very much appreciated and I felt relieved knowing that she would look after Linsey, Andrew and Ron. I'd only been away for a few days at a time, when each child was born, when Liz was ill and for Eilidh's various hospital admissions in Inverness and Edinburgh. I'd also once spent a weekend myself with Aunt Margaret. And on another occasion my friend Mrs Swan took Andrew to Dundee when she was visiting her sister and he spent a lovely week there with Ron's Mum who took him on lots of adventures.

It took a monumental effort to stop myself from breaking down. Taking a deep breath I hugged them and promised that I'd bring back Hungarian souvenirs for them. Ron took us to Dundee the day before and we spent the night staying with his sister Moira and her husband Douglas because we were flying from Edinburgh, an hour's drive away. As we waited to check in I said: *"I really don't want to go. I've changed my mind."* Ron did his best to reassure me: *"You'll be fine. Now have you got everything?"* I nodded and he hugged both of us tightly. Eilidh waved cheerily but I didn't look back as we made our way through the departure gate because I knew I would cry as I saw his big green bespectacled eyes through the glass.

A Leap of Faith

Eilidh was one of the first Scottish children to attend the Peto Intezete. (Institute) It was such a daunting experience flying behind the Iron Curtain with my little girl and her wheelchair, hoping she might come back able to walk perhaps with sticks eventually. No one knew at the time but Communism was on its last legs. Boris Gorbachev was the reformist Russian Prime Minister and his glasnost and perestroika regime would soon seed to the rest of Eastern Europe.

It was a beautiful morning when Eilidh and I flew to Budapest. From the air the clouds resembled the polar ice cap. Unfortunately I did not enjoy the flight from Edinburgh to Heathrow as I was so anxious. Eilidh was quite unconcerned. I suppose she put her trust in me and took it for granted that all would be well. *"Mum will we see God?"* she asked at Heathrow. I hoped at this point in time that we wouldn't! So I replied: *"He'll be taking good care of us."* Then a porter with a wheelchair took us from one terminal to the other. Thankfully the suitcases did not have to be collected and were checked straight through to Budapest.

When our flight was called, I found to my delight that there were another two British families travelling to Budapest to the Peto Institute. They were Chris Buckley and her son Andrew and Frank Clarke and his son Sebastian. Both Chris and Frank had been there several times previously. Fortunately they were friendly and this went some way in allaying my fears. Unfortunately our seats were by the aircraft wing, not near either of them so I couldn't pick their brains during the flight. While Eilidh had some fruit juice, I decided a glass of red wine was called for. After our meal of bread, salami, yogurt and a chocolate bar, Eilidh fell asleep. I remained apprehensive about what lay ahead and these thoughts were exacerbated when I looked out of the small window. My eyes were continually drawn to the rivets on the wing of the old Aleutian Russian jet aeroplane.

On arrival, a man with a wheelchair met us and took us to collect our suitcases. I changed some money and went to look for the taxi driver to take us to our flat. As I scanned the people I noticed a young man holding a callboard bearing the name Mr Wynton. He apologised for his mistake and we laughed. It was great to hear an English speaking voice. The man was called Andrasi Gyula (Julius Andrews – the Hungarian custom is to write the surname before the Christian name). I did not realise then, but he was to become a very good friend to us over the next two years, when we'd visit the Intezete five times.

Gyula took us out to his taxi and we set off at great speed for the flat in Varosmajor, meaning "very central". *"All of the cars are driving on the wrong side of the road,"* commented observant Eilidh. The journey was very interesting, though, if I'd thought that the standard of driving in

Britain was bad, it was much worse in Budapest. Tail gating was the way. The only cars on the road seemed to be Ladas, Skodas, Wartburgs and Trabants. These were driven along with bicycles, buses, trolley buses and trams within inches of each other. At regular intervals there would be a squeal of brakes and the burning smell of rubber on the ground would assail our nostrils.

In 1986 Hungary was still in the Eastern bloc of communist countries. Historically Budapest was a beautiful city boasting ornate historic architecture on a par with that of Rome or Florence. But it was also full of grey concrete tower blocks. At last we reached the flat. I was unperturbed by the concrete exterior, but inside it was ghastly! I had initially failed to notice this since Gyula was explaining various things to me and the landlady was also talking in Hungarian.

Gyula said that he'd come back for us on 6th September. Once he'd gone I had a good look round. Only then did the full horror of our surroundings finally dawn on me. The "suite", as it had been described, being on the ground floor had bars on the windows, supposedly to deter burglars, though what any burglar or saboteur could possibly hope to gain by infiltrating such a den completely baffled me. I told Eilidh we would unpack her things and then have a little walk in the park nearby. I'd brought some juice, tea, coffee, fruit and biscuits and since neither of us was particularly hungry, we made do with a wee snack before collapsing into bed.

I awoke several times during the night, disturbed by noises that I didn't normally hear at home in the countryside. The room reminded me of a prison cell because of the bars on the window and the two locks and chain on the door. There was a tiny kitchen and a bathroom with a separate toilet off the hallway. It was basically a bedsit. Eilidh had the bed and I slept on the settee.

The following morning after breakfast, Eilidh and I set off for the Intezete to discover where it was in relation to the flat. The taxi rank was but a stone's throw away and beside the underground. However, I had inadvertently forgotten to bring my letter from Dr Hari with the Intezete address in Hungarian. None of the taxi drivers knew where I wanted to go. Eventually, and very close to tears, we went to the bus station where we were lucky enough to find a lady who spoke English. She wrote down the address for me in Hungarian and I gratefully thanked her, setting off once more and this time with a light heart. It took me three attempts to get a taxi driver who would take us. Each time I tried to hail one, the cars would stop, see the wheelchair, then drive away.

The Peto Intezete

Eventually we found a taxi driver prepared to take us on what turned out to be a very short journey. It was only about half a mile from the flat. Within minutes he drew up outside a large, grey, modern, five-storied building that I later discovered had been opened the previous year in place of the Intezete's smaller predecessor. The institute was also a training college for the conductors of Conductive Education, who combined practical skills and theory throughout the rigorous four-year course.

I later found out that at that time those Hungarian children with medical conditions such as deafness, visual problems, learning difficulties, physical impairments, including those children who could not walk, were educated in residential special schools according to their need. It was thought that children with similar difficulties would develop faster under special and more beneficial conditions and therefore the children in mainstream would be a more homogenous group.

I put Eilidh in her wheelchair and looked for the door into the Intezete. I gasped as I looked in disbelief at the long flight of stone steps up to the entrance and braced myself in readiness to bump Eilidh up. *"It would have been easier if you'd brought my buggy Mum,"* said Eilidh. *"Oh well let's count them then,"* I said. There were 37 in total. Inside while we waited, we watched children practising walking. One young man in particular caught my eye. He was practising walking up and down stairs. His steps were painfully slow, but he was independent. Tears pricked my eyes as I watched. Later I spoke with a conductor, who explained that I was to return at 10am the following day in order to see the director Dr Hari and she would then work with Eilidh for two hours each day. Waves of relief and hope rose in me as we left.

A Hidden Gem

In order to go sightseeing in Budapest during communist times, we had to register with the police – or the Rendorseg. I later found out, after taking a photograph of a Lada police car, that this was forbidden.

My first impressions of Budapest were that it was big, bustling and teeming with both traffic and pedestrians. But I was soon to realise just how magnificent this hidden gem was. It was not the tourist destination it is today during the dark decades of communism. Yet there is an old 16th century Italian adage, according to which there are three pearls in the world: Venice on the water, Florence on the plain and Buda on the mountain. According to the Hungarian author Gyorgy Szaraz, this is *"in all probability still true"*.

Budapest certainly is a most beautiful city which is made up of three towns: Pest on the plain and on the left bank of the River Danube; Buda with its beautiful hills on the right bank; and, to the north, is Obuda where houses are built around ancient Roman and medieval ruins. During my many visits there I loved visiting the 14th century St Matthias Cathedral, with its red and yellow tiled roof with a pattern that resembled a Turkish rug. It is situated near the 13th century Buda Castle and the neo-Gothic Fisherman's Bastion, a hilltop structure with seven towers representing the seven tribes who settled in the city more than 1,000 years ago. Among the Bastion's nooks and crannies you'd often encounter young musicians dressed up in medieval clothing. It came as no surprise to me that this area became a World Heritage site in 1987.

I enjoyed crossing the many bridges that spanned the River Danube. My favourite was the 19th century chain bridge, the first bridge built across the city, overseen by a Scottish engineer Adam Clark. Two statutes of lions, without tongues, guard each side. On the Pest side of the river I loved the immense and stunning white Gothic Parliament building with its deep red Renaissance dome. I also enjoyed walking up Gellert Hill and later discovered it was named after St Gerard, an 11th century bishop who was made a martyr and rolled to his death in a barrel.

I soon found out that Budapest's public transport system was second to none. Blue public buses, red trolley buses, yellow trams, blue trains and the yellow underground, together with the river traffic, whizz along packed to the nines. Our favourite mode of transport was the tram. These vehicles were generally never held up. During peak periods, most would appear at one or two minute intervals. It is up to the passenger to either buy a monthly pass or separate tickets to punch as you board. Inspectors hopped on and off and imposed on the spot fines on those travelling "free".

Starting School, Hungarian Style

On our second day at the Peto Intezete, we decided to walk to school and gave ourselves 45 minutes to do this. It was pretty strenuous work pushing Eilidh's wheelchair up the hilly Varosmajor from one end to the other, then up the much steeper Kutvolgyi Utca. I reasoned it would be more pleasant going home! Little did I appreciate at the time that I was to make the journey up Kutvolgyi Utca many, many times more on foot, by car, taxi or bus, sometimes with the wheelchair, sometimes with the buggy and sometimes with Eilidh on my back.

Reflecting on this, I realise the true meaning of the saying *"ignorance is bliss"*. On the previous day I'd been told that I'd be seen at 10am, but after waiting for quite some time I decided to go in search of the director, Dr Hari, myself. Abandoning the wheelchair, I hoisted Eilidh onto my back and asked directions. A few minutes later I knocked on Dr Hari's green door, and after what seemed an eternity, it opened revealing a group of people, one of whom I instantly recognised from the documentary as Dr Hari. Clearing my throat I said as calmly and clearly as my shaky voice would permit: *"Good morning Dr Hari. I'm Maggie Wynton from Fortrose in Scotland, and I've brought my daughter Eilidh for assessment."* Turning to the others, Dr Hari asked me to wait outside for a few minutes.

Presently two conductors – Agnes and Eva – asked us to accompany them. I was to get to know them well. Armed with dictionaries and a copy of the letter I'd written, Eilidh and I followed them to a small room where I answered questions and Eilidh performed some tasks. Mid-way though this Dr Hari came in and spoke to us. Finally I was told that we could go up to the 5th floor where the assessment group was. We'd entered by the Ambulancia entrance that housed the mother and baby group and the groups for adults with Parkinson's Disease.

Agnes took us upstairs to a large bright room with yellow doors and talked to the conductors. The first person I saw in the group was Chris Buckley, whom I'd met at the airport, and very glad I was. By this time, the morning session was over and soon the lunch trolleys arrived offering thick vegetable or ham soup followed by stews or goulashes, made with pork or bacon. There was yogurt for dessert. At last Eilidh's programme had begun in earnest.

While Eilidh rested after lunch with the other children, I surveyed the environment that was to be our place of work for the next two weeks. The equipment contrasted sharply with that of the child development unit in our local hospital. The wooden furniture was very basic. Key items included slatted plinths to enable the children to hold easily whilst exercising and small chairs some with arms and some with a central pommel to keep legs apart. There were also tall ladder-back chairs that children could hold onto when standing, pushing and walking and also for performing hand exercises – all so simple, basic, elementary and necessary.

Initially Eilidh found the plinth programme very difficult. I have a photograph of a multi-purpose slatted table. It is used for exercising, sleeping and as a table for handcrafts and meals. The slats are terrific for grasping while sitting, standing or sidestepping. To begin with the children sat at one end of the plinths on small chairs and did breathing exercises under the guidance of the conductors. These included inhaling while lifting a stick as high as possible with both hands then making various musical sounds in unison. After these exercises had been done to the conductors' satisfaction, the children stood grasping the plinth and singing a Hungarian song. After this, some, with help, hoisted themselves onto the plinth and performed a series of rigorous exercises, such as rolling and kneeling. All of these movements were performed to the accompaniment of music or poetry and led by the conductor. It didn't take us long to learn the tunes at least. The words, well we did our best.

Music plays a tremendous part in Hungarian education and this is largely due to the influence of the

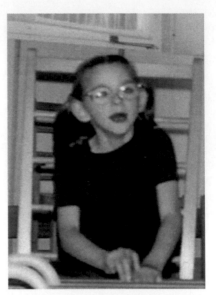

Eilidh seated on ladder back chair at the plinth.

composer Zoltan Kodaly. At this time when both parents were expected to work in this communist state, 98% of Hungarian children attended nursery school from the age of three. During that year the children learned eighteen songs. Each year that number was doubled. So, by the age of six, their repertoire would consist of 72 songs. All of the Hungarian mothers in our group sang lustily. All Hungarian children were taught to sight read, to recognize time signatures, beat rhythms and recognise the sounds made by various instruments.

At that time the Peto Andras Intezete had a choir of children aged between four and nine of varying disability. I wasn't privileged to hear this choir, but when I read the book Conductive Education by Andrew Sutton and Phillippa Cottam they say: *"These frail little beings stood up, however best they could, some with sticks, some without and some with the help of a conductor. Perhaps it was the fact that they looked so vulnerable, some visibly tottering that the strength and the tunefulness of their voices came as something of a shock. Their singing would have been the envy of any children's choir and so typical of the Intezete's philosophy. Not only do they help improve mobility of children with motor disorders but also encourage them to sing out and be happy regarding their achievements."*

Over time I was shown how to handle Eilidh in order to achieve the best results. It seemed such a logical system involving no gadgetry just simply regularly inculcating small, incremental movements till the desired result was achieved. As for Eilidh she did not like these programmes; she cried, she sobbed, she entreated, she refused and as for me, I experienced such a plethora of emotional traumas that I often asked myself: *"Is it worth it?"* The answer was always the same, *"Yes it is!"* I often thought that if we could put all of the children at the Intezete into a melting pot, the outcome might have been able-bodied boys and girls.

The Class of 1986

Our group, besides Eilidh and me, comprised of several English speaking families: Chris and Andrew Buckley, Tom Hanley and his son Darren, an American paediatrician called Bea Banarjee and her daughter Mana as well as Lise and Mike Horseley and their son Joe, who had been the subject of the BBC documentary. Chris and Tom were particularly kind and helpful to us. There was also a handful of Hungarian Mums and their children who lived outside Budapest. Because they were unable to travel every other day, they came for a month at a time and then went home to practise what they'd learned.

Since we had travelled on a Sunday I was unsure whether the shops would be open, so had brought tea, coffee, powdered milk, cereal and some biscuits. I soon discovered that ABC was a logo for a supermarket where I could buy the basics. There was very limited choice during communist times in comparison to the supermarkets here. I guess I could compare the ABC contents to those of Lidl and Aldi when they first came to Scotland.

School started at 8.30am and finished at 4.30pm. The children ate breakfast and lunch at school, though Eilidh always had cereal at home. After the children had eaten, it was the turn of the parents and conductors. At breakfast there was always a selection of ham, salami and cheeses to put on the fresh bread. Since the midday meal was quite substantial, such as a filling soup or goulash, I did not bother to cook an evening meal and usually made do with bread, cheese, jam, biscuits and fruit in the evening. I soon discovered that Tom and his son Darren lived round the corner. We often walked home together, discussing any progress that the children had made that day.

Lessons Learned

On our first visit to the Intezete I naively bumped Eilidh's wheelchair up the 37 steps up to the front door of the Intezete. By the end of the two week assessment period I realised two things, the first being that her Major buggy would have been far more manageable and the second that there was a ground floor entrance right beside the lift. I resolved that if Eilidh was asked back I wouldn't take the wheelchair, since it was a liability in more ways than one. It was too much of an encumbrance to use on public transport, plus I'd also forgotten to bring the bicycle pump for the tyres.

Eilidh's wheelchair seemed to be something of a curiosity. As we went about, people's eyes would fix upon it. At first I was very angry, feeling fiercely protective towards Eilidh and even going as far as to pull a face once in response to several hard stares. However, I began to realise that it was because a wheelchair was rarely seen that we were a subject that merited the curious glances and stares. I think that at that time the majority of disabled adults lived separately from their families in

215

residential care, in much the same way as we used to treat people with disabilities. During that first visit I believe I only ever saw three wheelchairs – the occupant of one of them used to regularly sit outside his apartment on Krisztina Korut. It seemed to me that he'd been "put out for an airing".

Despite this, I was used to people at home staring at Eilidh too. Besides those Hungarians who stared, there were many kind folk. Each time we went shopping Eilidh was given some memento by a generous shopkeeper: a terracotta piggy bank, a wooden painted egg, a small plaque to name but a few.

The two week assessment didn't give us the opportunity to see much of the city. Darkness fell earlier than at home. After dinner we would sometimes go for a walk locally. A favourite hang-out for us was just sitting by the Deli railway station watching the busy city bathed in electric light. Eilidh was absolutely fascinated by this while I spent the time thinking about how much I missed Linsey, Andrew and Ron. At that time it was perfectly safe for women to walk after dark without fear of being either attacked or mugged. Graffitti was not very much in evidence either. Perhaps the penalties were a good deal more severe in this communist system than at home in Britain.

The Hungarian Peace Council staged a musical festival during the weekend of August 30th and 31st, the venue being the impressive Vorosmarty Ter. It was a large cobbled square surrounded by shops and cafes, including the beautiful Gerbaud Café that served wonderful cakes and pastries. There were always lots of people there and it had an uplifting atmosphere. Eilidh and I strolled along Vaci Utca following the music. Lots of groups who played haunting South American music on pan pipes, traditional Hungarian music on accordions and fiddles and modern music from the charts on guitars and drums. There were also hundreds of spectators – even the TV cameras filmed it. I signed the beautiful peace book on behalf of Eilidh and myself. I felt very honoured to be part of it.

By the end of the two-week assessment, Eilidh had settled. The day before we were due to return home I was interviewed by Eva and Agnes, the two conductors we'd seen at the initial assessment. They spoke to me at length as to what exercises to practise and the goals to strive for. They asked if I could return for a month in January, a request to which I readily agreed. I resolved to ask if these exercises could be carried out as far as possible at school.

Of the four English-speaking children in the group, Eilidh was the only one who'd been there for a short time. Andrew Buckley was on his third visit, Darren was there for a year and Joe Horsley, whose story was documented on television, was going to be there for the foreseeable future. I felt that I was leaving just as I was getting to know everyone, but my heart was lighter as I left and I felt confident that the staff at Eilidh's school in Inverness would help. I also knew that Ron would quickly make Eilidh the ladder-back chair that was an essential part of the equipment.

On our last day we were given a lovely toy caterpillar that the conductors had made. Its head was made from a table tennis ball, while its body was made from circles of felt threaded onto a piece of string. A piece of ribbon in Hungarian national colours was tied round its neck. Eilidh also got two Hungarian books from two of the Mums, so she gave them two Mr Men books in exchange. I was totally overwhelmed by these kind gestures.

Home and Hiccups

We travelled back to London with Darren's mum Cath and his younger sister Siobhan, who had come out to visit him and his Dad Tom. They were returning so that Siobhan could start school. We talked about Darren's progress, how happy he was and how pleased he'd been to see his Mum and sister. That Saturday was particularly eventful. Firstly, Cath was initially not going to be allowed to travel back without Darren: his name was on her visa, but he was not with her. Eventually the red tape was sorted. Secondly, we boarded the plane only to be told, minutes from take off, that there was some "technical difficulty". An hour and half later we were on our way. My heart skipped as we taxied down the runway and as I relaxed I kept thinking about just how much I was looking forward to seeing Linsey, Andrew and Ron again.

"Dad will be there to meet us," I told Eilidh as we waited for our luggage. But Ron was nowhere to be seen. *"Where is Dad?"* asked Eilidh. I phoned and spoke to a very surprised and apologetic Ron. *"I'll come right away,"* he said. It was wonderful to see him and we all hugged each other tightly. He told me that because we had left on a Sunday he thought we were coming back on a Sunday. He said: *"Linsey was going to decorate the house and garden with streamers and banners to welcome you home."* This made my heart want to burst with joy.

Then he told us that there was an article about Eilidh and me in the local Highland News and a generous cheque that some local people had donated. At this I started to cry because I'd never asked for any financial help, though I knew that some families did. I sobbed at the thought of those kind people who wanted to help my daughter. This money would go to pay Eilidh's school fees. Although Hungarian children did not have to pay under the communist system to attend the Peto Institute, foreign children did.

Half an hour later we were at home, all hugging each other and talking at once. During the rest of that day my Linsey kept hugging me spontaneously and my Andrew kept looking at me and smiling. They told me later that they were so glad that Eilidh and I were home. *"We prefer your cooking Mum,"* Andrew said, *"You know one day Granny Wynton served boiled lettuce with our tea and it was REVOLTING!"* I tactfully explained that Granny had lived through the war when food was rationed and seldom wasted. Granny's maxim, like many elderly people of that time, was: *"Waste not, want not!"*

The following Monday Eilidh returned to the special unit at Cauldeen Primary somewhat tearfully. A meeting was arranged so that I could update her teacher about what Eilidh had been doing at the Peto Intezete. Unfortunately and understandably during the days that followed her little heart appeared to be breaking when going to school. She wouldn't settle in her bed in the room next to ours and eventually I'd to put her in Andrew's room each night so that she wouldn't be lonely. Recriminations seemed to pile on top of me until I felt utterly stifled and emotionally drained. In addition to these problems Eilidh's school bag always seemed to be full of wet washing. It appeared that we'd taken one step forward and three back. I thought that perhaps I shouldn't return to Hungary.

However, as the autumn wore on she became more settled and happy and we worked on the various programmes of exercises done in Budapest. Through practice she became proficient at clasping her hands together. While seated with me pressing down on her knees, she'd clasp her hands, stretch her arms forward as far as she could and stand up. She also practised walking with the ladder-back chair on the ski like runners that Ron had made for her.

My anxieties regarding Eilidh's well-being subsided only to be replaced by another set, namely the start date for the extension to our house. As well as being the date of my late Dad's and late best friend Liz's birthday, October 21st is the anniversary of the Battle of Trafalgar, and what a battle it was to be. I naively hoped that everything would go smoothly. On top of this, Andrew spent three days in hospital after minor surgery and spent his convalescence watching the digger at work.

The work began on the agreed date, though various factors prevented it being completed on time, not least being the fact that autumn was drawing to a close and the weather could be so unpredictable. I guess it must be easier to build a completely new house rather than to extend an existing one. By the end of November and in between gales, hail, rain, sleet sunshine and snow, the excavations had been dug, foundations laid and the ground floor shell completed. To further complicate matters, the oil-fired Rayburn began to leak and we realised that this was going to be a BIG repair!

Before we had left Hungary Agnes, the conductor, had assured me that we'd get a letter giving us a date to return. However, since nothing was forthcoming I determined to try to postpone the visit until the spring and Eilidh's schoolteacher agreed that this would be best.

At the beginning of December I had a phone call from the shop steward at McDermott's oil fabrication yard telling me that his committee were considering funding Eilidh's next trip to Budapest. I was overwhelmed by this kind gesture and decided to telephone the Intezete to ask about the return date. Having amazed myself by, not only getting through, but also speaking to Agnes, she floored me by asking: *"Is January 6th or 7th would be good for you?"* *"Oh yes,"* I replied throwing caution to the wind. It was only when I replaced the receiver that I considered exactly what I had to do: visas, tickets and it was the festive season and we would be going for a whole MONTH.

A holiday can be a magical experience, and the week before Christmas 1986, Eilidh had the opportunity to visit Glasgow, courtesy of the Variety Club of Great Britain together with her classmates. Many children with additional needs travelled from all parts of Scotland converging on Glasgow, where they were treated to a veritable bean feast of entertainment for three days. At lunchtime on Monday they set off by train from Inverness. Their first stop was to see Glasgow's Christmas lights. The following day was packed with all sorts of activities, a carol service, a party and the circus. They travelled home somewhat shattered on the Wednesday. Eilidh was only seven but was excited to go away for the first time that she could recall without me. (She couldn't remember the three occasions she'd spent in hospital as a baby and toddler.) The house seemed very different without her.

When Ron met her from the train, she was covered from head to toe in a measles rash; the spots had manifested themselves on the return journey. When she arrived home she hugged me and held out a string of small purple beads that she had bought with her spending money.

She was a very good patient. The doctor gave her some antibiotics as a precaution and she slept herself better. The rash took about a week to disappear and soon she looked her old self again. During the spotty period, two men from McDermott's yard visited us and gave us a cheque for £900 from the workforce charity fund towards our next trip to the Intezete. Any employee who wished could contribute 50p per week and over the years thousands of pounds were collected. This was distributed to various charities and also to local hospitals to help with the cost of buying special equipment. It was incredibly touching that they wanted to help Eilidh in this way.

Because of measles, Eilidh couldn't return to school before the Christmas holidays. The two-week period was extremely traumatic and I shudder each time I think about it. Ron went to school to explain about Eilidh returning to Budapest because I couldn't face telling her teacher. Only two days before she'd told me how well Eilidh had settled and how relieved she was that I intended postponing the visit till spring. *"Do what you think is best for Eilidh and we'll cope whatever,"* came her reply.

Christmas 1986 will remain emblazoned on my mind forever. The extension had long been abandoned because of abysmal weather conditions and the torrential rain, combined with the excavated clay had formed a terracotta morass. Our Rayburn gave up the ghost and the ponies seemed miserable. Tara had a blanket, but neither Toyah, our Icelandic pony, nor Tina, our Shetland pony, did as they'd grown thick winter coats. I was in a cold sweat lest the tickets, passport and visa would not arrive on time.

To my great relief, our travel documents arrived on Hogmany and I nearly wept when the postman dropped them through the letterbox. The consequences of passports, visas, etc being delayed seemed too horrific to contemplate with less than a week before our departure.

Since we had booked to travel on Tuesday 6th January, it meant that Eilidh could attend school on the Monday. She went very happily and for that I was very thankful. Ron's Mum was coming to look after everyone on the Tuesday and so I'd arranged for Linsey and Andrew to spend the night at a friend's house because we'd have to leave for the airport very early in the morning. Into the middle of this mêlée came Isabel Fraser and the TV crew to interview us. This was because Eilidh was one of the first children from Scotland to go to the Peto Institute and interest in Conductive Education was growing – it seemed such a revolutionary strategy.

Earlier that day the crew had been filming in the mountains. After setting up all of their equipment, the cameraman found that condensation from the earlier filming in the mountains prevented him from viewing what he should have seen. Everyone was quite disappointed and so it was with heavy hearts that Linsey, Andrew and I said our goodbyes – Ron took them to our friends for the night, while I put Eilidh to bed. She always slept well no matter what.

We finished what packing remained, put the cases in the hall and went off to bed. The morning flight to Heathrow was at 6.50am and that meant we'd have to leave by 5.45am. Eilidh was full of beans, just desperate to set out on an adventure, whilst I was full of trepidation. What on earth were Hungarian winters like? Why should anyone forego the "pleasure" of a winter on the Black Isle for the rigours of an Eastern European one? The answer was Conductive Education.

Winter in Budapest

The winter at the start of 1987 was apparently one of the worst for many years in Budapest, although when the plane landed there was only a slight covering of snow. Again we were met by Gyula. He took us first to register with the police, second to buy bus tickets and third to our home in

220

Zugligeti – up by the ski lift. What a difference from the previous flat. It was beautiful. We had a large bedroom and balcony, a bathroom with washing machine and spin drier, a neat kitchen and a comfortable split level living room with a veranda. I was thrilled. Unfortunately there was no lift and there were a fair few steps up to the house from the road, but I didn't mind. We were opposite the terminus of the 158 bus that stopped at the foot of Kutvolgyi Utca, which was perfect for the Intezete.

The next morning Eilidh and I set off on the 158 to school. It was if we'd never been away. There were several familiar faces, including those of the conductors, and a few new ones. We found ourselves sitting beside Darren Handley whom we had met on our last visit, and Nicky, a wee lad from Western Australia.

Also in our group was Cherry Sheppard from Oxford with her son Mark, Lise and Mike Horseley and their son Joe and a few Hungarian Mums and children. Eilidh quickly settled and very soon established a terrific rapport with Darren.

We decided to take the bus to school each morning and have a taxi at night. This worked very well for the first few days. However, by Friday afternoon, the weather worsened and light fluffy snowflakes fell from the heavy grey skies. We arrived home safely, turned up the heating and drew the curtains to shut out the night.

We woke to a white world and the sound of children's voices. Outside people were sledging, skiing, snowballing and enjoying themselves. There was not as much traffic as usual and such as there was skidded and slithered about. Donning coats, hats and gloves we ventured forth in the direction of the Etelmiszer – the corner shop. It was very difficult negotiating the rutted snow with Eilidh's Major buggy, but we managed unscathed. Having purchased the few necessary items we headed back. Once we made it upstairs with Eilidh, the Major buggy and the shopping I collapsed gratefully into a chair. The rest of the weekend was spent indoors in the warmth – exercising and entertaining Eilidh. She helped me to cook, we played snap, sang, drew pictures, wrote postcards and gathered strength for the coming week.

The following Monday we waited hopefully at the bus stop together with a crowd of school children. Understandably the bus was late and, when it appeared, a cheer went up. The road was treacherous and it was nothing short of a miracle that we arrived at the Intezete at all. Transport was very erratic and throughout the morning parents arrived late with their children. By lunch-time it had started to snow again and so Tom, Lise and I thought it prudent to stay overnight. We decided to go home for overnight bags. By sheer luck I hailed a taxi at the foot of the road, arrived home, collected my bag and walked back.

The weather, though severe, was invigorating. It was unlike the damp Scottish cold that can be both raw and penetrating. I found that with my thick Guernsey jumper and wax coat I was fine, though I was careful to cover both my head and hands, having been warned of the dangers of frostbite from Tom. On my return journey, I passed many lovely houses.

The sky was pale blue and the few snowflakes that fell resembled those as illustrated in children's books. I watched fascinated as these tiny stars landed on my dark green jacket. Half an hour later I was back at school.

Eilidh and I spent both Monday and Tuesday night at school. Although it was hot and claustrophobic, we felt safer doing that than trying to get home. The traffic was running more smoothly, but since the pavements were still virtually impassable for prams, buggies or wheelchairs, I decided to carry Eilidh piggy-back style because she could now clasp her hands around my neck and hold on. The days passed slowly. Eilidh worked very hard and several times I was asked to *"go away"* by the conductors. She delighted both Eva and Agnes by being able to stand with her hands clasped and arms out-stretched for balance virtually unaided!

One Sunday night as I was getting into bed, I felt a sharp pain under my ribs. I'd experienced this before and been told that it was likely to be an irritation of the oesophagus. Usually it passed, but this time it didn't. The night passed both slowly and painfully. So in the morning, after leaving Eilidh in class, I went to the doctor who gave me some painkillers. I resolved to have this investigated again when I returned home.

One Saturday a trip to the circus was arranged for the children. It was unexpected, enjoyable and very hot. In fact, many of the children in our party ended up spectating clad only in vests and pants. Usually Saturday lunchtimes were spent at the British Embassy where we would meet between 12.30pm and 2.30pm. A buffet lunch was served and videos were provided for those children who wanted to watch them. On January 17th Joe celebrated his 6th birthday and Lise and Mike came in with a birthday cake. I'll never forget his wee face as he watched the glow from the lighted candles, listened to the children singing and then tried to blow. Lise told me that he'd been thoroughly miserable the year before. What a difference a year can make.

For quite some time, various conductors had been sewing during odd moments and refused to tell us what they were doing. During the last week of our stay it turned out that there was a fancy dress party. The children were taken away, dressed up and quite transformed. I remember that Joe was a tiger, Eilidh a Geisha girl, Nicky a Hussar, Darren a clown, David a hedgehog, Mark a cook and Tamas a little girl. The children moved about as independently as they could and thoroughly enjoyed the party. It was a most enjoyable event that ended the month perfectly.

The snow still lay thickly on the pavements and side streets. In Vaci Utca, a pedestrianised shopping area, men with shovels were hard at work clearing the ground. They would lift the beautifully patterned brass manhole covers and push the snow in, presumably to the sewers. Ice floes of varying sizes travelled down the Danube making a very attractive picture.

Towards the end of the last week, I was called into Agnes's office and she asked: *"Are you pleased with Eilidh's progress? What do you think?"* I simply turned the question around – was she pleased? *"Yes,"* she replied.

"This time was much better." She seemed pleased that Eilidh worked well on her own, that she was standing better and that her attitude had improved. I assured her that I'd do as much as I possibly could and she said that we could return for a month between May and June.

Gyula drove us to the airport on the last day of January. It was a bitterly cold day and the windows of the plane were steamed up. There were armed police on guard and a shiver ran up my spine. But we boarded the plane and flew without further ado, or so I thought. Having disembarked at Heathrow, we boarded the flight to Inverness in the rosy assurance that our luggage would accompany us. The lady who checked it in at Budapest Airport had assured us that it would go right through. I did not question her, because on previous occasions it had been checked in for both flights. This time, however, it wasn't! By the time that it was finally retrieved some four days later, it had gone full circle – to Budapest and back. One case looked as if it had been in a 12 round fight and lost. Luckily the contents were intact.

Home at Last

Arriving back home to Ron, Linsey and Andrew was wonderful. It seemed we all appreciated each other and wondered how on earth we could possibly ever quarrel, be inconsiderate, selfish or rude. Absence definitely makes the heart grow fonder, for a while at least.

Much to everyone's surprise Eilidh immediately settled very quickly into school; it was as if she'd never been away. Everyone there was amazed by the difference in her balance and growing confidence. They were very keen to learn what they could do to help maintain her progress. With Eilidh attending school for a full day it was difficult to fit in her full programme of exercises. However, I did work with her when she came back from school, doing part of her plinth programme and we increased the amount of walking she did at home compared to before. We practised standing from a sitting position, standing against a wall or standing holding onto the sink top. Her right arm and hand were loosening up somewhat and we practised switching off the light, flushing the loo and picking up coins and pencils.

The pain that I'd experienced in January was investigated and found to be gallstones. I was prescribed painkillers in case I should suffer a further attack. Many years later I had my gallbladder removed by microsurgery.

The extension to our house was causing chaos and we had become accustomed to a nomadic type of life. All of us had developed the habit of leaving things lying around. Linsey and Andrew justified this dreadful deed by saying: *"Well everything is in a mess anyway."* Though it didn't excuse them, they were absolutely right.

Interest in Conductive Education was growing so I was asked to talk to the Society of Paediatric Nurses in the recreation room at Raigmore Hospital, about the benefits of Conductive Education in Eilidh's case. This was mainly because Eilidh had been born in Raigmore Hospital and had stayed in the Special Care Baby Unit there for 12 weeks. From time to time we'd pop in to see the people who had cared for her. The nurses who attended my talk were very interested and afterwards they asked a huge variety of questions. They seemed very open minded about what I told them and not in the least dismissive. Of course they were clearly interested in knowing more about the possible outcomes for the babies they'd tenderly cared for. Later we had a lovely supper and I was given a box of sweets.

I also discovered at this meeting that Dr Hari and Julia Horvath from the Peto Intezete, as well as Andrew Sutton, who had written a book about Conductive Education, were going to be talking in Edinburgh on April 3rd. The day after that they were due to talk at a conference in Coventry organised by Rapid Action for Conductive Education (RACE).

This organisation began in Coventry as a result of some parents' dissatisfaction with what the British system had to offer. After the BBC's screening of the documentary Standing up for Joe and the ensuing publicity, RACE gained momentum. People who'd never previously heard of Conductive Education wrote off for information packs and contacted the Peto Intezete about having their children assessed. This culminated in an Early Day Motion and a Parliamentary Lobby in October 1986, apparently the largest of its kind, asking for the system of Conductive Education to be adopted in Britain. Many parents were publicly questioning the whole system and arguing for the Hungarian philosophy as opposed to ours. Their belief in what is possible united parents who were fed, being constantly told what was impossible.

I decided to attend the conference in Edinburgh. So we went to Dundee and took Linsey, Andrew and Eilidh to stay with Ron's Mum. The following day Ron and I went to the conference. We were very sad, disheartened and disappointed by the awkward questions and quite rude behaviour of some of the delegates, many of whom worked either in Special Education or the Health Service. I recall that many of the questions and comments were very dismissive of the Hungarian method. I felt most ashamed of my fellow Scots and was upset that I didn't get the opportunity to make a comment. I prayed sincerely that Dr Hari wouldn't leave with a bad impression. Suffice to say that when the trio went to Coventry the following day they had a rapturous reception. This time the audience mainly comprised of parents and friends of the motor disordered.

I did at least have the opportunity at the Edinburgh conference to talk with Andrew Sutton. He was the Birmingham University research fellow who had helped to develop a method whereby the Hungarians would train some British conductors while he worked to find funding for this ambitious project. This began in 1986 when the Foundation for Conductive Education was established in Birmingham under his leadership. In September of the following year a group of ten young British teachers, together with ten youngsters with cerebral palsy began training in both Birmingham and Budapest. Future plans were made for more children to join the class and a unit was set up for those adults with Parkinson's Disease. A few years later a similar project was set up in Cumbernauld Scotland, when the Craighalbert Centre, that was to practise the principles of Conductive Education, was built.

Our Third Trip to Budapest

Once the children returned to school after the Easter holidays, I began the task of filling the freezer with home-made ready meals, doing extra household chores that I thought Ron would never get round to and organising everything that Eilidh and I would need for a month's stay in Budapest. Although Eilidh was working as hard as possible on her exercises, I felt that she was at the point at which she needed to return for both of our sakes – she to build on foundations already laid and me to get a bit of encouragement and moral support in doing her exercises. This time our home was to be in Bertalan Lajos, not a stone's throw from the River Danube. It was also conveniently situated by the No 18 tram stop. Its terminus was at the bottom of Kutvolgyi Utca about 700 metres from the Peto Intezete.

Once again, Granny Wynton was there to look after Linsey, Andrew and Ron. She arrived the day before we left and Eilidh returned jubilantly from school armed with homework to take with her. We spent part of the evening packing after which poor Linsey and Andrew reluctantly went off to bed. Early the next morning we crept out quietly leaving them and Granny to sleep on undisturbed. It was becoming even harder to leave each time as the guilt seemed to get worse. I felt torn between two lives and two sets of priorities.

After two good flights we arrived and were met by friends John Kempton, who taught English to the conductors, and Bodis Edit, a Hungarian who taught English at the International School. The next day we had to register with the police and, because it was Sunday, we went to the zoo.

Next morning we were on the way to school by 7.30am. Lifting Eilidh and balancing her against my legs while I folded the buggy, I was greeted by: *"Segith etek?"* This means: *"May I help you?"* I nodded gratefully adding *"koszonom"* or *"thank you"* and confidently boarded the tram. After 11 stops, we were at the terminus and again I heard the phrase: *"Segith etek"*. This was to become very familiar to me. The walk up Kutvolgyi Utca left me panting and sincerely wishing that the terminus had been outside the Intezete rather than at the bottom of the hill. However, once upstairs I forgot my fatigue. The group we were in was entirely English speaking and we spent time renewing old acquaintances and making new ones.

Eilidh worked hard and several times that week I was asked to *"go away"*. Apparently she worked hard on her own with another conductor helping when necessary. During the second week, as was custom, Agnes and Eva asked me how I felt Eilidh was progressing and if she'd learned anything new while at home. I explained that we were trying to build on what she'd already learned and were concentrating hard on her right hand: she could now pick up 20p pieces and put them in a jar. They seemed pleased, so I explained my increasing worries as to Eilidh's rapid rate of growth that would, if it continued, leave her towering above me and still unable to walk. Together Agnes and Eva held a hurried conversation then Agnes said: *"We would like to help you."* She went down to the 4th floor and returned with Julia Horvath, the floor leader, who said that Eilidh could go to her floor for the whole of the next term, either residentially or as an outpatient. This floor was for older children and because she'd been working well on her own it was felt that she'd manage. I was overwhelmed.

Since our flat had a telephone, I called Ron that evening to tell him the news. He was very pleased and while he felt that although Linsey, who was 12 and would undoubtedly miss me, she'd be all right. However, he felt that Andrew, who was ten wouldn't fare so well. He'd been unwell a few times as a result of tummy upsets and Ron thought that he really missed us quite a lot. I well remember Ron's words to me: *"I can't be the good guy and the bad guy!"* When we'd come home after our second visit and I said we'd been invited to return for a month in May, Andrew said: *"Oh not again Mum."* My new euphoria melted and after I put down the receiver, I wondered what to do next. In a flash I knew what I was going to do – take him with me. What a wonderful opportunity it would be for him. He'd never been out of Britain before.

We'd been asked to return at the end of August until Christmas of that year, so I set about flat hunting. Since Andrew was coming with us, we needed accommodation with a proper bedroom as well as a bed settee in the living room. My friend Edit helped me find exactly what was needed. It was cheap, conveniently situated for trams and shops, had a communal garden and was in a quiet residential area. Quite by chance it was just round the corner from her flat and since the Horseley family lived further up the road, we would be able to share lifts. Even better was the fact that I had enough Hungarian money to pay the first month's rent in advance.

Eilidh and I very much enjoyed our summer month in Budapest. There was harmony in the group, all of the children strove to please and some made tremendous progress. One day Chris Buckley and her son Andrew arrived just as we'd finished the stick programme. This involved the children sitting on small chairs or stools and holding a stick that was about 30 centimetres long horizontally in both hands. When the conductor prompted them, they began to sing and raise the stick as high above their heads as possible. As the music continued the stick was lowered and raised several times. The children learned to wait until every child managed to do it to the best of their abilities.

Chris sat down and little Andrew held onto the side of the chair. Then he was off – walking! He tottered forward for a few steps, my gaze riveted on him. It was amazing to see him take his first few steps. I called out to Chris and to Agnes: *"Look!"* Of course they'd seen too, as had

226

everyone else. I must confess to having a lump in my throat while Andrew, unaware of his tremendous feat, promptly went onto his knees and crawled away only to be put once more into an upright position.

Happily the weather was quite a contrast from our last visit in January and we were able to go on various excursions. Our group leaders arranged a tour of Budapest, including a walk round Margaret Island which is an island in the middle of the Danube that is home to an extensive park with a small zoo housing goats, rabbits, guinea pigs and parrots. There is also a wonderful outdoor swimming pool heated naturally by the warm sulphur springs. In addition, there are many statues of famous people, such as the Hungarian composers Franz Lizst and Zoltan Kodaly.

One sunny Saturday we all set out for Esztergom, the former Hungarian capital, where kings had once been crowned. Later several brave souls ventured to the top of the basilica, which is the largest church and tallest building in Hungary. I didn't count the steps but I thought they would never end. Photographs were taken as we viewed the then Czechoslovakia from the Danube bend.

Many of us went inside the Basilica to see the altarpiece with the picture of the Assumption of the Blessed Virgin Mary which is the largest painting in the world, painted on a single piece of canvas. We ate a picnic lunch on the riverbank before visiting Visegrad on the way back to Budapest. This town is home to a medieval citadel and here we marvelled at the spectacular views of mountains, the river Danube and lush green fields. On the way home Darren and Eilidh sat holding hands on the bus.

Another Sunday we spent a happy time with Lise, Mike, Joe and Edit. We drove into the countryside where we had drinks at an inn. Later we swam in the river, sunbathed and were barked at by what Lise called a Rastafarian dog. On the return journey we ate the wild cherries that we'd bought from a roadside stall.

Having visited the castle on the group bus tour, Eilidh and I decided to return on Sunday and visit St Matthias Basilica with Louise, an Irish lady from our group, and her small son Mark. By ten o'clock the Sunday stalls arranged around the Fisherman's Bastion were already bustling and when we entered the cool, dim church the service had already started. People were everywhere – the pews were packed and others stood at the sides. Ethereal music from the choir soared upwards to the vaulted roof. The contrast to the mêlée outside was incredible. Louise lifted Mark out of his buggy and, as she held him in her arms, he turned his little face towards her and a smile of pure joy, trust and love spread across it. I think that all four of us gained peace and tranquility from that experience.

I must confess that I had given up on going to church for a while after what had happened to Eilidh. I was not sure why God had allowed that to happen to her. But this experience renewed my faith and my confidence.

The month drew to its inevitable close and we all prepared to leave to go our separate ways, pleased with what we'd achieved and been offered. All of us were going to return at future dates, some for a few weeks, others for a full term. Addresses were exchanged, goodbyes said – it was a very emotional time. Edit had promised to see us off and faithful Gyula was coming to take us to the airport. My great fear was that I'd oversleep, but I double checked my alarm and used my Dad's failsafe method of gently tapping my head with my knuckle the required number of times: in this instance I had to tap five times for 5 o'clock.

Edit arrived first, bringing a few presents for us and ten minutes later Gyula's taxi stopped outside the door. I was touched that on the way to the airport Gyula and Edit spoke in English. All too soon we arrived at Budapest's Ferihegy, or airport. Gyula unloaded the luggage and we bid him *"viszontlatasra" (till the next time).* Flying is a wonderful mode of transport. It seemed incredible that only a few hours later we'd be some 1,600 miles away.

A Busy Summer

Ron, Linsey and Andrew met us at Inverness airport. It was lovely to see them though the two elder Wynton children spent most of the journey home in altercation. I didn't care about this sibling rivalry as the pure joy of being home, breathing in the sea air and having all of my family together was a very precious thing indeed.

As on previous occasions, Eilidh settled down in school as if she'd never left, though in truth the summer holidays were only some 12 days off. I continued to walk her everywhere as far as possible with my hands supporting her under her arms. I also did as much of her plinth programme as I could fit into the day. At last the house extension was finished and her new bedroom was complete. We'd previously done her exercises in the living room holding onto the bottom spar of her ladder-back chair. But now we could do these in her lovely new bedroom.

At the front was a small window that looked out to sea. At the side was a patio door that led out onto the balcony, overlooking the fields, woodland and a couple of hills. There was also an en suite with a low-level toilet, washbasin and shower. Ron had fitted a wardrobe, shelves and made a plinth and wall bars for her exercises. She was a very lucky little girl indeed.

Before the summer exodus from school, I decided to ask the local education authority if they'd be prepared to contribute towards Eilidh's Intezete fees. So Ron and I met with the depute director, who promised that it would be considered by some members of the education committee. If there was a positive outcome then that would be good.

We discussed Andrew joining Eilidh and me on our next visit, at length as a family and concluded that it was in everyone's interests if he came too. He seemed quite happy and I felt sure that I was doing the right thing. However, Andrew's Headteacher was unhappy and told me that she *"would not sanction it"*. Her reason was that he'd not be attending school, but working on his own being supervised by myself. I pointed out that I was a trained and experienced primary teacher. It did sow a seed of doubt in my mind, but after further discussions with Ron, several close friends and other professionals, I decided that my worries were unfounded. If truth be told, few children at that time had the opportunity of spending four months of their lives in a foreign country. I felt that that would be an education in itself. When we returned Janet MacDonald, his class teacher, commented: *"His English has really come on."*

And Linsey? Well since she was leaving Avoch Primary and transferring to Fortrose Academy, I didn't want to disrupt this new routine. Linsey loved her horses and her freedom and I felt that she might feel hemmed in if she was away with us in a small flat for four months. I also knew that Ron and she would spend some precious and quality time together.

The summer holidays began and Eilidh's class gerbils came to us for the duration, as did a Shetland pony called Tigger, who belonged to

229

Anne Tidmarsh. We even had Pepsi, the minister's black Labrador while he was on holiday. The Wilson children stayed for a few days and so Sarah and Linsey went horse riding, the two Andrews went camping in the woods and I did regular exercises with Eilidh and as much walking practice as possible. Somehow Ron and I kept sane, though it wasn't easy.

When Stuart and Val Wilson returned to take Sarah and Andrew back home they kindly invited Linsey and Andrew to stay with them in Almondbury because they wanted to give us all a bit of a break and thought that it would be nice for them to have a holiday on their own. Linsey and Andrew were keen to go and Ron drove down the following week to collect them.

The education authority granted Eilidh's school fees and we were given two complimentary air tickets to London from the then airline Dan-Air. Their cargo manager, a member of the Round Table, whose organisation had given us some money towards our summer trip, arranged this. We were extremely lucky in being given more than £2,000 in donations in total. We received nearly £900 from the Education Department for payment of Eilidh's school fees as well as money from the cubs and scouts, who had done a sponsored obstacle course in the grounds of nearby Raddery School, the congregation of St Andrew's Church which I had started attending and the rest had been given by friends, including Mrs Swan who gave us £100 from her B&B takings in a new black leather purse. Apart from the money from the Education Department, we hadn't asked for any of it.

If I Could Walk 500 Miles

Like all good things holidays have to end and all too soon it was time for the children to return to school and Ron to work. By this time Ron was working as the Assistant Head of the Technical Department at Millburn Academy in Inverness. Only ten days remained before the 29th August, when we were due to fly back to Budapest. I was apprehensive about returning for four months. While I hoped that Eilidh would greatly benefit from the intensive education, I wondered how I could cope being away from Ron and Linsey for so long. Much of the remaining time was spent in contemplating the situation and trying to stifle some of my emotions. One day that week Ron came home with a telescopic fishing rod for Andrew. *"You're the best Dad in the world,"* was Andrew's delighted response.

D-Day dawned. Even though we were leaving at 6am Linsey was determined to come and *"see us off"*. And just as well as she had no choice: Granny Wynton wasn't coming to look after her and her Dad this time. All too soon, we arrived at Dalcross airport and I found myself unable to control the tears that were coursing down my cheeks. I hugged both of these precious people for a long time then shepherded Andrew and Eilidh through the departure gate and out to the tarmac, looking and waving through the huge glass window innumerable times. Both the children were eagerly anticipating their aeroplane journey. Poor Linsey and poor

Ron – why was I doing this? Knowing that I was at the point of no return, I had no choice but to relax.

Funnily enough at this time the Fife band, The Proclaimers, rose to fame with the song If I Could Walk 500 Miles. It was only a third of the distance between Budapest and the Black Isle as the crow flies, but Linsey and Ron say that this is the anthem that most reminds them of that time. I think they actually quite enjoyed themselves as they had a strong bond. Ron cooked a lot of fry-ups and bought a lot of cakes and many friends and neighbours invited them over for meals.

Andrew, who'd never previously flown, seemed to enjoy the journey to Heathrow, apart from the landing. It was so good having an extra pair of hands to help with bags and several times I found myself wondering how on earth I had ever managed to cope on previous trips without him. As we waited in the departure lounge Andrew perfected his yo-yoing skills. When the flight was called, not only could he pull his yo-yo up and down vertically he could also do it horizontally, much to the amusement of other passengers.

At Ferihegy airport in Budapest my taxi driver friend Gyula was waiting for us in the hall. He was delighted to meet Andrew. That afternoon his taxi had been used for a wedding and Gyula had left the floral wreaths and sprays of beautiful fresh flower decorations for us to see. Twenty minutes later we arrived at Romer Floris Utca 16 to find Gita the landlady waiting to greet us. She insisted on showing us everything again, even though I had seen her place on my previous visit. Just as I thought she was planning to stay the night, she decided to leave us to it.

This flat had a washing machine, spin drier, black and white television and telephone. It was wonderful knowing that we could regularly talk to Ron and Linsey. Although the television programmes were all in Hungarian, Andrew thoroughly enjoyed watching Around the World with Willy Fogg. This was a cartoon based on the story of Jules Verne's fictitious explorer character Phileas Fogg. The introductory music became so much of an earworm that I hear it each time I reminisce about Budapest.

Luckily we had two days before Eilidh had to be at the Intezete to spend sight seeing and registering with the police of course. I took him to Buda Castle, Gellert Hill and to the outdoor swimming pool on Margaret Island. To his credit Andrew walked for miles without complaint. He even corrected me when I was about to take a wrong turning. Children seem to have an inbuilt sense of direction, which was just as well, as I am not the best map-reader.

Palatinus Strand on Margaret Island
in Budapest.

Eilidh settled well on the Zoldszint Emelet, or the 4ᵗʰ floor. Initially her class comprised a small group of 12 children. Some of them, like Eilidh, came for a term, while several others came for shorter periods of between two and five weeks. I found it very strange to ask for information as to her progress since on the three previous occasions I'd worked with her and found it very satisfying. If she'd had a good day, I was on cloud nine whereas if she hadn't I felt deflated. However, I busied myself with Andrew and put it out of my mind, resolving to go into the group when it was mutually convenient so I could see for myself how the programme varied with what I already knew.

If I had wondered at any time as to how we were going to spend the intervening hours then I needn't have worried. By mutual agreement we decided to work at home during part of the morning then enjoy the fresh air and go exploring for the rest of the day. A weekly target was set and Andrew more or less kept to it. I had absolutely no apprehensions about teaching my son, since both of us knew from the outset what was expected. He brought various Maths, English and recreational reading books with him and faithfully documented the daily events in his diary. He made a lovely scrapbook of miscellaneous articles, leaflets and photographs and avidly read my copy of H E Bates The Darling Buds of May, which I must admit was my favourite television programme at the time; a nice lighthearted escape. Andrew also read many of the books in the children's section of the British Embassy library. We went swimming in the naturally hot outdoor pool on Margaret Island, travelled up the funicular railway. He used his new rod to fish in the Danube (although he did not catch anything) and we travelled by tram and underground to all sorts of museums, the Roman ruins and both the pool and luxurious café in the sumptuous thermal Gellert Hotel. We also took the train to the lovely wee town of Szentendre (St Andrews) and enjoyed visiting the wonderful traditionally thatched cottages at the nearby Magyar village museum. (see below)

I think that Andrew, who is really interested in history, thoroughly enjoyed exploring the city and finding out about the famous people who had lived there.

Most of the British families who came to the Intezete brought their other children with them. They were generally either at the nursery or early years stage of education. One morning after we arrived at school, one of the dads asked me if I'd be interested in teaching some of them. Although I felt very pleased and touched to be asked to do this, I immediately declined. It was completely out of the question. Even if I'd been on my own it would have been too much of a commitment.

Four months certainly seemed like an eternity in the beginning. But the weeks simply slipped by. Lots of folk wrote to us and I experienced such a feeling of exhilaration when the mailbox was opened revealing a letter. We used to either rip open the envelope eagerly devouring the contents there and then or else sit down with a drink after carefully slitting it open and savouring every word of its contents. It made a pleasant change not to receive bills or circulars.

Most of September and October was warm and sunny, unlike the unsettled spells that start during the autumn at home. In Budapest you could go swimming outdoors and several times a week found us at Palatinus Strand on Margaret Island where, for a few Hungarian forints, you could swim, sunbathe, relax in a thermal bath and have a picnic. There was also a series of water chutes and a swimming pool with a wave machine. I thoroughly enjoyed spending this rare one to one quality time with Andrew.

Andrew fishing in the Danube

The opening of MacDonalds fast food restaurant coincided with that visit and sometimes we went there for a snack. Now there was competition for the City Grill fast food chain. Sometimes we went for cake in the Gerbaud café in Vorosmarty Ter. One day we found a café that had a window from where a man made and sold waffles. There was a wide selection of topping but our favourite was chocolate.

My friend Edit had spent the summer in England returning to Hungary in mid-September. She arranged Hungarian lessons for those of us who wished to learn and this proved very useful. I found the language very difficult since it seemed to be unrelated to any other apart from Finnish and Estonian. But that apart, it is beautifully expressive and extremely musical to the ear. Thoughtful Edit asked us if we'd any specific words categories we would like to learn, for example for shopping, restaurants or transport. We would go over the pronunciation, which I realised, once learned, never varies, unlike in our mother tongue. Each Wednesday a "posse", as Andrew referred to us, would head for Edit's flat, climb the 96 stairs and sink into her comfy chairs. One afternoon Andrew and I joined her children's class at the Language School. I know that it was quite interesting for both parties and he really enjoyed the visit.

Although I longed to go in to see Eilidh's progress, I was told to wait until later. Since I'd worked with her on each previous occasion, I expected that the group leader felt that I had a fairly good idea as to what she was doing. One evening when I went to collect her, there was great excitement. They had tried her out walking with a stick in her left hand while she held on to the ladder-back chair with her right. She was ebullient and even more so when Barbely Agnes, her conductor, said she could take a spare stick home with her in order to practise standing. Eilidh took the stick to bed with her and when she was fast asleep, I removed it lest she should hurt herself. What progress.

One night my friend Cherry phoned. She was really upset. This was her second visit and this time she had come alone with her sons Tom, age six, and Mark, who had cerebral palsy and was age 8. Her husband David, who was a self-employed electrician, was at home in England. Tom was ill and needed to go to hospital. Gyula was going to take Tom and her there and she wondered if she could bring Mark round to stay overnight. Mark stayed with us and I made up a bed for him on the settee. He settled quickly and soon fell asleep. Poor Tom was quite ill as his throat had closed up and he was struggling to breathe. He spent the night in hospital and was discharged the following day with some antibiotics. Next morning Gyula came and he and Andrew helped me to take Mark and Eilidh to school.

On our previous visit I'd asked Dr Hari as to the possibility of joining the six-week interest course on Conductive Education. She told me that she'd consider my application but that I knew as much as was necessary. It was an information course and lots of others had also applied. My application was successful, but since Andrew was with me, I felt I had to turn the opportunity down.

The warm sunny days turned autumnal and very quickly the temperature dropped. All too soon December arrived. We did our Christmas shopping, wrote and posted all of the cards and then it was time to return home. Eilidh was invited to return the following year at a time that suited us. She was due to have an operation in order to correct a strabismus (squint) in her right eye and she also had orthopaedic appointments both in Inverness and Edinburgh.

Home for Christmas

We left Budapest the week before Christmas hoping to get to Inverness Airport in Inverness in the late afternoon. However, Inverness was enveloped in a thick blanket of fog and the plane was diverted to RAF Kinloss. The passengers were bussed for the last part of the journey. Instead of her planned spiel in Hungarian, Eilidh's first words of greeting to Ron were: *"Hi Dad, I've been sick."* There had been a bit of turbulence during the descent and thankfully Andrew was none the worse. I hugged Ron and Linsey so very tightly and thanked God for our safe return. Among the luggage was Eilidh's stick that she was so proud of! It was an amazing achievement and she had worked so hard to earn this wooden mobility trophy.

The next day I let Linsey stay off school to spend time with us. She was delighted with a pair of black leather ankle boots I had brought back for her and wore them everywhere.

Just before Christmas our GP Dr Sandy MacGregor arranged an orthopaedic appointment for Eilidh and to everyone's delight the X-ray showed a great improvement in the left hip. It was wonderful news and a lovely Christmas present.

However, a few weeks later when we returned to the hospital in Edinburgh a further X-ray told a different story. I clearly remember the paediatrician Keith Brown asking me: *"What have you done?"* He then manipulated Eilidh's hip back into place. It was sublaxed (partially out of joint). It may have been that because she had been sitting in the car for a few hours that that had caused her hip to sublax. In the meantime, he told me that the hip would be monitored and a further appointment made for a later date.

1988 seemed a busy year. Eilidh had her eye operation in January. On her 9th birthday we were invited to take part in a television discussion about Conductive Education on a programme called The Time and the Place. Eilidh and I travelled to Glasgow by train and stayed in the nearby Holiday Inn. There were a variety of participants: a hospital consultant, a physiotherapist, occupational therapist, a speech and language therapist, the Headteacher of Corseford (a special school for children with cerebral palsy) and some parents, including me. The debate focused on the advantages of adopting Conductive Education here. Like all debates, points were made for and against. I remember being asked about the cost of going to Budapest and replying that it was not so expensive as some people might think.

Not long afterwards I was also offered some voluntary work as a home tutor for adults with learning disabilities. I thoroughly enjoyed working with a few folk helping them solve their literacy difficulties. In July, Andrew left Avoch Primary and started at Fortrose Academy the following month. Then a letter arrived inviting us to return to Budapest for a month in November. This time I asked Linsey if she'd like to come with us. She was absolutely delighted. Her German teacher Sheena Munro had organised some pen friends for the class and when she knew that Linsey was going to Hungary she paired her with Fozo Emese, a Hungarian teenager.

Our Final Visit to Hungary

Linsey, Eilidh and I arrived in Budapest one cold crisp winter's day to be met once more by our good friend Gyula. He was delighted to meet Linsey and see Eilidh. He then took us to a lovely apartment quite near the Intezete.

Eilidh settled quickly and certainly benefited from the intensity of the now familiar programmes. Agnes cautioned me that: *"You must do something about Eilidh's hip then come back and we will work very hard."* I promised that I would, although at the time I felt that if Eilidh experienced no pain then it might be wise just to leave well alone.

Spending a month in Budapest ignited Linsey's appetite for travel and almost three decades later I have lost count of how many countries she has visited. We packed so much into that month, because, like Ron, she

Maggie and Eilidh in Budapest

is always on the go. Like Andrew she took schoolwork with her and assiduously wrote an account of each day's events in her diary. She also made a scrapbook, in which to keep her precious mementoes. Roisin one of the Mums from Ireland, who was a Maths teacher, would sometimes help her solve any difficulties she encountered with that subject. This was a relief as quadratic equations were never my strong point.

Linsey by the Danube

We visited Linsey's pen friend Emese and her family. It was much too cold to swim outside but we visited the thermal pool at the beautiful Gellert Hotel overlooking the Danube. We also visited the lovely old town of Szentendre and the nearby Magyar village museum, complete with thatched roofed cottages. We would regularly travel around the city by tram stopping at the Parliament, the Fisherman's Bastion, St Matthias Cathedral, Margaret Island and of course Gerbaud's café.

Once we went to a photography exhibition of black and white photographs documenting the life of a man who worked on the railways. It was a real insight into what was a tough life: in Britain you might have expected this lifestyle at a different time in history. But this was Eastern bloc communism and at that time the iron curtain remained in place: though I do remember the rising popularity of the reformist Russian leader Mikhail Gorbachev and having a Gorbachev badge. The foods were so basic still and we would eat a lot of grilled chicken and salad and go to the City Grill or McDonald's for a treat. I remember one day seeing oranges on a market stall. We were going to buy some, when Linsey said we shouldn't because the Hungarian people probably did not get to have them very often.

Linsey met lots of British, Hungarian and Irish people and was fascinated to hear about their lives. On reflection this was a coming of age moment for her. She had found her wings. I did not realise at the time, but within five years she would fly the nest for good.

The night before we left for home Cherry, David, Mark and Tom came to see us. They had just arrived and wanted to see us before we left. It was so good to see them again and I was disappointed that we wouldn't be able to spend any time together. Linsey had imbibed every single drop and cried a lot the night before we left. Maybe she sensed that it would be our last trip to the Peto Intezete.

Re-Rooting at Home

In the days that followed I thought long and hard about my future. I was very aware that I had not done any work other than voluntary in the 14 years since Linsey was born. After the Christmas holidays I applied to have my name added to the primary teachers' supply list and was lucky enough to be given some work in a few local schools. Shortly after that I noticed an advertisement in the local paper for a four-month temporary post in a special class within a primary school, Park Primary in Invergordon. *"I'd love that job,"* I thought.

I applied and to my great delight was interviewed and got the job. I felt so lucky. The post was from the beginning of March until the end of June and was a wonderful experience. During the Easter holiday Linsey and Andrew came with me to the school where we painted the windows and put up a few decorations to brighten up the classroom.

There were six children with very diverse needs in my class. Support was provided by two lovely classroom assistants. At the beginning of each day we made breakfast: cereal, toast and tea or juice. The children helped in the preparation of this. They were encouraged to spread their toast independently and they helped to clear up afterwards.

Since there was a bathroom, I asked the Mum of one child who had cerebral palsy if he could have a bath after his breakfast. She was delighted and this was built into his daily programme. I had brought some sage from Budapest, so the combination of the warm water with the sage helped relax and reduce his spasticity. Then we could do his exercises that the physiotherapist, who visited weekly, suggested. We did reading, writing and number work during the morning and in the afternoon we did craft work, cooking, PE and always went out. We'd regularly go to the local fruit shop where I'd give them a small sum of money to buy some fruit. This taught them to work out what they could buy and patiently wait their turn in the queue.

Meanwhile Eilidh had another appointment for an orthopaedic assessment at the Princess Margaret Rose Hospital in Edinburgh. During that time the consultant, the physiotherapist and occupational therapist assessed her. Because of the problems she was having with her hip clicking in and out of joint, her legs continued to scissor and when she walked with her rollator she always veered to the right: she found it impossible to move in a straight line. Mr Robb, the orthopaedic consultant, suggested that she could have another tenotomy (a tendon release like she'd had three years previously) and this time the plasters would be on for only four days instead of the previous three weeks. Once they were removed, she would have a course of intense physiotherapy. Thanking them, I explained that in order to make a decision I needed to discuss this option with Ron and the consultant in Inverness.

Soon afterwards I went to see the consultant in Inverness and explained what had been suggested. He told me that in his opinion a tenotomy alone would not solve the problem. He suggested a femoral varus derotation osteotomy adductor tenotomy and psoas muscle lengthening. Using a skeletal hip joint he demonstrated how he would cut Eilidh's femur (thigh bone), reposition the hip joint and join the two pieces of the femur together with two steel plates. He would also lengthen her psoas muscle and do another tenotomy. He felt that this option would be preferable as it would keep her hip joint in place, thus reducing the potential for pain in the future. When I explained that there was no way I would send Eilidh to school with plasters and also about my temporary job, he suggested doing the surgery at the beginning of the summer holiday. Although Eilidh experienced no pain at this time, we felt that there was always that potential later in life. After a great deal of discussion and thought and for the best of reasons, we made the decision to choose that option. I will always wonder if it was the right decision.

Chapter 10: Learning to Fly

Leo and me

I never wanted to get a second dog, but I have to admit I grew to love Leo dearly. He was a back Labrador cross Spaniel who had spent time living on the streets prior to becoming our pet. When Ron and I went on holiday, Andrew offered to look after Leo. At this time Andrew worked as a policeman and would take Leo to the police station with him so he would not be lonely at home.

A holiday like Nun Other

Just before her 10th birthday, my younger daughter Eilidh was invited on a trip to Lourdes with a group of disabled youngsters. Many children with disabilities go on annual pilgrimages to this holy French town, many hoping they will be cured. I had no such illusions about Eilidh. All I ever hoped for was that she would have the chance to walk and that she would become as independent as possible.

I had doubted my faith in God when Eilidh was diagnosed with cerebral palsy as a baby. Although this had recently been renewed on a trip to St Matthias Basilica in Budapest, I concluded that a holiday would benefit Eilidh. She would gain more independence. In addition, Ron and I would have a break and some rare quality time with our older children, Linsey and Andrew.

Eilidh was really excited when she showed me the letter at the beginning of March 1989 about the trip during the Easter holidays. Shortly afterwards we met Mr and Mrs Lamont who were organising the trip. They came to our house to meet us, as did two of the volunteers Gerry Finnegan, who was a PE teacher at Ron's school, and Kathleen, his wife, who was a nurse. They were so kind and positive and no one other than me had any hesitations. I was very protective of Eilidh and a bit apprehensive – especially after she had come back from her first school trip to Glasgow with measles. But though she could not walk, Eilidh was finding her wings.

So, with her belongings packed into a small maroon coloured vinyl leather suitcase, she set off with Ron to Inverness to catch the bus that would take her to Prestwick Airport. From there she would fly to the Pyrenees town of Lourdes, where the Virgin Mary was said to have appeared in 1858. She would have the chance to be bathed in the holy water from the Grotto of Massabielle.

While Eilidh was away Linsey and Andrew asked if I could take them to the Landmark adventure centre near Carrbridge. This allowed us to have a wonderful time climbing in a network of ladders in the treetops. I know now that Andrew and Linsey really enjoyed not having to consider Eilidh's needs for a short time, because there were many things we could not do as a family since Eilidh was unable to participate. I never realised at the time how much they craved just a bit of time as an ordinary family, without having to put her needs before theirs.

They were now quite independent and had been going out on their bikes and the horses on their own for years and Ron had always taken them out and about. I was quite single-minded about Eilidh and had tended to stay at home with her doing her exercises, cooking and tidying up. Ron had always told me that I was the expert so I never asked him to do it, despite how drained I sometimes felt. But on that trip to Landmark I had such a great time with my older two. Linsey says now that I really came to life in a way she had not seen before, as if the child in me came out.

I remember we were looking after a collie called Kyle who belonged to Linsey's friend Rhiannon, so we went on lots of nice walks and enjoyed our week of freedom.

One of the reasons I felt a bit guilty was that Eilidh was spending her 10th birthday away from home. But when she returned she told us she had got a lovely cake. She brought back several souvenirs including a lovely candle, a prayer sheet and a St Christopher necklace. But she confessed she was quite scared at the sight of the nuns. She would never have seen such outfits before. After all she had been a child who was always apprehensive when she saw Santa (for years).

Summer Days, Drifting Away

I was glad she had had a nice Easter holiday because poor Eilidh spent the whole school summer holiday that year in a plaster cast up to her waist.

Her surgery had involved cutting Eilidh's thigh-bone, repositioning her hip joint and joining her sliced thigh bone with two steel plates. Her psoas muscle was lengthened and her tendons trimmed with the aim of ensuring her left hip did not come out of the socket and that she could maintain a more upright posture. Her legs had been crossing like scissors and she needed help to unlock them. When she stood up with support she would lean quite heavily to the left. We hoped the surgery would rectify these issues and give her the best chance of walking with a Rollator (which is a little like a Zimmer frame on wheels).

When the letter arrived giving the date for Eilidh's operation, I decided not to mention it to her. I knew she would be anxious. There didn't seem to be any point in upsetting her for any longer than necessary. So I decided just to tell her the day before. Of course, she started to cry, so I distracted her by telling her that Granny Wynton would be coming and we would be going to the station to meet her.

Eilidh was pleased that Granny came to hospital with us. Once she was a little more settled, Ron collected his Mum and took her home. I knew I would be in hospital for a few days so Granny had kindly offered to help Ron with the cooking and cleaning.

I spent the night sleeping fretfully in the chair beside Eilidh's bed. In the morning she had pre-med cream rubbed on her hands. This relaxed her, then Ron brought Andrew in because Eilidh had asked if he'd go up to the theatre with her until everything was ready. He stayed in the little anteroom while I went in with Eilidh until the anaesthetic took effect. *"Hello young lady,"* said the consultant as she was given an injection. We managed to count to five before sleep overtook her and she was wheeled off. I had a huge lump in my throat and prayed I was doing the right thing.

When Andrew and I returned to the ward I got a big row from the sister on the ward for taking him upstairs. She said that it would have upset him. It was not particularly helpful to do this in front of him, however. Memories flooded back of the big fuss that my Stepmother Margaret had made after her brother John died. (I'd inadvertently looked in the open door of the front room where his coffin lay.) As far as I was concerned Andrew suffered no ill effects. He had had minor surgery himself and we treated this as a routine event that siblings of disabled children have to go through. Andrew and Eilidh were quite close because Andrew had had that extra time at home with her before he started school as well as those four months in Hungary two years previously.

After a longer than expected time, Eilidh duly returned: she'd been holding her breath in the recovery room. Maybe she wanted to sleep for a bit longer. A medical student, who'd been observing, came to tell me that everything had gone well and the consultant confirmed this later. As with her previous surgery, two sticks were positioned at her ankles and knees to facilitate easy lifting for when she needed the toilet, transferring her to a different seat and getting her in and out of bed. The plasters were up to her waist, but her bottom was exposed so she would have to wear baggy dresses that could be pulled over her head.

Eilidh coped very well indeed, although I remember her screaming in pain the day after when the nurses sat her up in bed: one bit of the plaster cast was a bit high and was digging into her. It was soon trimmed and extra soft padding inserted. Thankfully she was only in hospital for a few days after. Ron's Mum stayed for another couple of weeks, which was invaluable. Eilidh's splinted legs made it impossible for her to use the toilet and so we used a bedpan instead.

Dear Eilidh was pretty much housebound and I spent much of my time at home that summer with her. Just before she had gone into hospital, we bought Linsey a mint green racing bike and Andrew a yellow mountain bike. With these and the ponies, they had lots of adventures.

Linsey got to go on another foreign trip – this time to Denmark with the Guides – and her Hungarian pen friend Emese came to stay with us for a month. I remember Ron taking them and Andrew to Dundee for a family wedding and I think the girls had a few swigs of martini. Eilidh and I missed out, but despite her summer confinement, she stayed in good spirits. When they were at home, Linsey and Emese's favourite pastime seemed to be painting a mural on Linsey's bedroom wall with Linsey's friend Kath, who was (and still is) a great cartoonist. They also spent a lot of time listening to Aha, Guns 'n' Roses and Dépêche Mode. I was pleased that Linsey was soon to be singing something more upbeat as she took part in the school musical Grease wearing a big netted spotty skirt that I made.

My three and a half months of supply work in the special unit at Park Primary School in Invergordon, ended as the summer holiday began. I was delighted to be offered another temporary job, in the same small town. This time it was teaching a Primary 5 class at South Lodge Primary School.

This proved difficult because the first week coincided with Eilidh returning to hospital for a week to have her plasters removed and a course of intensive physiotherapy before she returned to school. Ron used to visit her at lunchtimes and I went in each evening. We were all very relieved when she was discharged and life returned to some semblance of normality, or as much as it can for a family with a disabled member.

We hoped that Eilidh would be able to attend weekly hydrotherapy sessions after she came out of hospital. This seemed the ideal way to ease her stiff joints and muscles into making the movements they needed to in the lovely warm water. So we were bitterly disappointed that our request for hydrotherapy after her surgery was turned down despite letters of support from both the consultant and our local GP. The reason given was that the physiotherapist would have to spend a considerable amount of time in the water with Eilidh. Even though I offered to sign a disclaimer to say that I would go in the water with her, the request was still refused. I was told I was not qualified. No matter that I had been her Mum for ten years. Luckily Ron found out that Eilidh would be able to attend weekly hydro-therapy sessions at the Nairn County Hospital pool. We were told she was making an excellent recovery from the surgery and that it had been a success.

Since Ron's Mum had been here for part of the holidays when Eilidh's legs were in plaster, we felt that she needed a holiday herself! Over the last few years she had come up a number of times to help out while Eilidh and I were in Hungary and while Eilidh had been in hospital. It wasn't hard to persuade her to go on holiday to Spain with her great friend May. They'd met many years previously when both of them worked in a florist's shop. Granny was a real sun-worshipper and hadn't been to Spain since Grandpa Wynton died. She and May had a ball and it was the first of several Spanish holidays for them.

I thought a great deal about going back to Budapest to the Peto Intezete. The methods of Conductive Education practised there were becoming more widely known about and I sometimes wondered if the growing numbers of children who were attending the Intezete from across Europe, Israel and America, were coming at the expense of Hungarian children.

The more I thought about it the more reasons I found for not returning. I wrote to the Intezete to tell them that Eilidh had had her surgery and I'd let them know in due course what we thought we should do.

Eilidh returned to Cauldeen School for another two years. But this time she had a new taxi driver. The bid had been put out to tender and Charlie Fraser, who owned the garage at Munlochy, bid successfully for this. And so it came to pass that Graham MacLeod, also known as Rocker, was appointed as Eilidh's chauffeur. Not only did this personable, red-haired young man drive the taxi, he also drove one of Charlie's buses for the school pupils. In between he used his mechanic's skills to service and repair a variety of vehicles. He and Eilidh soon became firm friends. He'd play the latest music from the charts, which they'd sing along to at the tops of their voices, he'd buy Eilidh crisps, and once she told me he had opened the window to discard the empty packets. If for any reason she was feeling a bit sad, Graham would always cheer her up. I remember one time when Eilidh was having her hair cut at a friend's house after school, Graham carried her in and sat her down. He certainly was one of these outgoing positive people who definitely went the extra mile just to make her feel like anyone else and not a hassle.

During this time Linsey and Andrew went on a school trip to France, Belgium and Holland. There they saw the battlefields of the Somme, the Menin Gate and the war memorial in Ypres. Although I later discovered that Linsey and her friends had a few sneaky alcoholic beverages, I remember the profound effect seeing the trenches and the fields of mass graves had on both her and Andrew. The rows of white headstones, many to unnamed soldiers, the memorials bearing so many names of men robbed of their lives. Linsey and Andrew's responses were unequivocal that life is precious and war is pointless. Andrew has always been really interested in history and after that trip I know he felt quite relieved that he was born in the 1970s and not any earlier.

A Set Back

The following summer Eilidh and I attended the annual clinic appointment at the Royal Hospital for Sick Children in Edinburgh for a check up. After being thoroughly examined I was curtly told by the Registrar: *"Since you've already had surgery, Eilidh will be discharged."* It was the first time that I doubted the decision we'd made the previous year to have a more extensive surgery in Inverness as opposed to having a second tenotomy (tendon lengthening), as had been suggested on our last visit to Edinburgh.

I felt uncomfortable, as if we were being criticised for what we'd done. The choice had been ours and we had opted for the more complex procedure offered in Inverness as we thought it would be most effective.

Perhaps they felt that we shouldn't have doubted their opinion, perhaps they felt that their opinion was superior. Or, on reflection, maybe their suggestion was part of a process of operations that Eilidh would go through – if the tendon lengthening was not enough, then further surgery would have been suggested. Who knows? I guess I should have contacted them after the alternative suggestion was made in Inverness to ensure that we knew the exact implications. BUT I didn't and there's no point in living life with regrets.

Meanwhile, all seemed well. Eilidh sat straight, she exercised on the plinth which Ron had made and hinged on her bedroom wall, and she managed to walk, wearing supportive splints (Ankle Foot Orthotics or AFOs) and holding on to two parallel bars.

However a few months later I took her from school to her appointment at the hospital's combined clinic. Inside, I transferred her from her wheelchair and onto the floor. At this point I had noticed a slight tilt in her left hip, but on this occasion it seemed so obvious that her left leg appeared shorter. The consultant seemed surprised as to how this had happened. Then I remember Anne, the physiotherapist, and her colleague disagreeing as to whether or not the sole of Eilidh's left boot should be raised. This would compensate for the slight difference in length. I remember Anne saying that if her boot was raised it would cause her hip to dislocate more. However because of the disagreement no decision was reached at that time.

The consultant offered to repeat the surgery, but I immediately and flatly refused to consider this and afterwards reflected long and hard on what the outcome might have been if we'd opted for the simpler surgery offered by the consultants in Edinburgh or indeed if Eilidh had had nothing else done. We really had made the decision for the very best of reasons but as Eilidh's posture continued to deteriorate over the years, I was haunted by thoughts as to whether or not I had made the right decision. I remember asking the consultant on several occasions what the outcome might have otherwise been. He would generally reply that the potential for future pain was a factor and that, had Eilidh not had the surgery, then she would otherwise have been in a worse state, or that she might have been in her current state sooner.

What I've learned over the years, and what I always urged other parents of disabled children to do, is to seek as much advice and to do independent research beforehand. While Eilidh was growing up, I believe that surgery was the only option to treat spasticity. It was not until a good few years later that Botox became an alternative as it could prolong the need for surgery; a number of the children with whom I worked and who had spasticity had and seemed to benefit from this treatment in hospital in Glasgow. I remember long after Eilidh's operation that Linsey showed me a newspaper article about an Australian man who had been paralysed as a result of an accident. Botox was used as part of the treatment in his rehabilitation programme and he was now able to walk. It was incredible and I remember asking the rehabilitation consultant if Eilidh might benefit from this treatment. I was told that Botox was only given to those adults whose legs were so stiff that they could not part them at all. At least Eilidh could do this.

Secondary School

Linsey had started Fortrose Academy in 1987 and Andrew joined her in 1988. But when Eilidh was due to transfer to secondary school in 1991, we felt their school with its stairs and lack of lift, was not suitable. The best option for her seemed to be the special unit at Alness Academy, some 18 miles away. Since Eilidh would need considerable support in school, the job of a PSA (Pupil Support Assistant) was advertised. Anne Flett, who had been a PSA in another school, was appointed. Towards the end of the holidays Eilidh and I went to meet her at the café in the local distillery.

After the holidays Eilidh joined the class of children aged between 12 and 16. The teacher was Mrs Adam and there were two pupil support assistants including Anne Flett. Often, Bronwen the school nurse, would join the class. Just as when Eilidh attended the special unit at Cauldeen Primary School, she travelled by taxi. She would leave the house about 8.15am and return about 4.30pm. Although it was a longer journey than the one to Inverness, Eilidh always seemed reasonably happy. Her taxi driver also had a selection of music, but the premier choice was always the rousing March of the Toreadors from Bizet's opera Carmen.

The school had its own swimming pool, so the children from the special unit were able to use it twice weekly. Eilidh definitely benefited from this. Anne, her PSA, carried out all the exercises suggested by Anne the physiotherapist. Eilidh quickly made friends, not only with her classmates, but with others who were in the mainstream classes. Two girls in particular, Jill Hoseason and Sonya Barrett, were firm favourites and were often invited here for tea.

Eilidh could be quite a fussy eater and though we didn't eat out a great deal she did enjoy eating at such fast food restaurants as The Little Chef. Linsey and Andrew got a bit fed up with this on a family holiday to Yorkshire. However, they didn't complain too much as Ron and I had hired two chalets next door to each other and they each brought a friend with them. Kay MacRury and Graeme Grant and Linsey and Andrew got up to quite a lot of mischief and silliness I believe. I do recall they wrote a sign for the window reading: "If you must stare, please smile." They were fed up with people staring at Eilidh and felt it was really unfair on her. We even passed the hotel I had worked at in Scarborough on an outing. Boy was I glad my days there were behind me.

My New Vocation

During the summer holidays of 1989, I remember scanning the local Ross-shire Journal and seeing a job advert and thinking: *"That's the job I'd love."* I was sitting with Eilidh at the time and she was curious to know what it was. I read her the ad, which advertised a new service being set up in four areas of the Highlands for teachers to visit pre-school children with special needs in their homes.

I applied, was interviewed and was lucky enough to get the job in my area of Ross-shire and South Sutherland. I firmly believe that part of the reason I got the job was because of my experience of Eilidh's disability. I felt elated – it was wonderful to think that I could put all my hands-on learning into practice to help other families in similar circumstances.

At that time there were only a few nurseries and playgroups that were able to support children with special needs, because of a lack of funding to pay for extra support. To me, my main job was to provide support in as many ways as I possibly could, focusing on the child's learning and development. I knew that I would be able to empathise rather than sympathise. I had also learned on our trips to the Peto Intezete in Budapest the importance of positivity and consistent focus and I hoped to pass this on.

At the time of my interview, I'd been asked if I intended to return to Budapest. I remember the Divisional Officer saying, *"These families will be depending on you."*

I'd thought long and hard about this beforehand and knew in my mind that in all conscience I couldn't go back to Hungary. Eilidh was growing taller, and as a consequence heavier and with the issues with her left hip, this would have been difficult for me to manage. At least I had learned such a great deal in Budapest and Eilidh was having regular physiotherapy. Anne Chambers visited the school every week to work with her and advise Anne Flett who regularly carried out the exercise programme. In addition Eilidh was now able to have weekly swimming sessions. Most Saturdays I took her to the hydrotherapy pool in Nairn and continued to do her leg stretches on Sundays and during the holidays.

More importantly Linsey and Andrew were growing fast. Linsey was already a teenager and Andrew was not far behind. In fact, Linsey only had four years left at school and Andrew five. Though I had striven to give them as much attention as I could, Eilidh always had more because of her condition. Now they weren't children any more and I had lost that precious time with them. However now they were older we could at least sit up at night chatting about our lives and what was going on in the world. Despite Eilidh not being able to walk, she had gained some independence going on those two trips to Glasgow and Lourdes and commuting to school each day and over the last year or so I felt free of some of the ties I felt I'd been constrained by.

Although I would continue to do my best for her, reality had dawned and I had gradually learned to adjust my expectations. A few years later I read an article by Claire Tomalin in The Independent, questioning how effective Conductive Education was as children grew into adults. She summed up how I felt. She wrote: "Those who take their children to Lourdes expecting a miracle, for instance, often come back convinced that there has been one, although no one else can see any change. What has changed is their attitude."

I'd initially gone to Budapest because I wanted to see Conductive Education first-hand and I was not disappointed. The holistic, repetitive and consistent approach throughout the day meant that the participants made some progress even though some would never ever be able to walk. I had given my daughter a chance, but her dream of walking had died. Her hip had got the better of us and now I needed to focus on making her life in a wheelchair as positive as possible.

Just before I started my new job we booked a chalet holiday in Crieff to celebrate. One morning I awoke to an almighty crash and fits of laughter. Andrew and Eilidh had been sharing a room and Eilidh's favourite toy, Roland Rat, had fallen out of bed. Eilidh had tried to grab him and fallen out of bed too.

I remember making a similar mistake myself. We'd gone to the swimming pool and I'd plonked Eilidh on the side and jumped in only to realise I could not put my feet down. I had to gently push her along the edge towards the shallow end. The phrase *"look before you leap"* springs to mind. Excitingly for Andrew he and his Dad went fishing and he caught his first fish. Ron took a photograph of him with it – just like the one his own Dad took of him when he caught his first fish, only Andrew's one was in colour, not black and white.

Straight afterwards I started my new job in October 1989. I was given a compact office in the Education Centre in Dingwall where I was part of the team of Psychological Services. Initially I worked in Ross-shire and South Sutherland, visiting the equivalent of a class of children every fortnight. Linsey and Andrew always got home from school before Eilidh and they would walk her with their hands under her arms from her taxi then take her to the toilet, get her a snack and play with her or let her watch her favourite TV programmes until Ron and I got home.

Sometimes the journeys were lengthy: destinations including Scourie, Shieldaig and Applecross took approximately two hours to reach, while Ullapool took just over an hour. But the scenery was spectacular! One of my favourite journeys was to Applecross on the West Coast. Here was a tiny village of just a couple of hundred people, a jewel of a peninsula whose shores were lapped by the sparkling waters of the Inner Sound and could only be accessed by the coast road from Shieldaig or by the spectacular Bealach Na Ba (the pass of the cattle – the road on which the crofters used to drive their cattle.) This narrow single-track road with its backdrop of mountains and hairpin bends rises high above Loch Kishorn and through amazing scenery. It's Scotland's 3rd highest road, rising to 626 metres and is impassible in winter, but when I ventured there I used to think that I was climbing up to heaven each time that I drove on it. It was as if I too had found my wings – to fly away free from the responsibility of Eilidh, at least for a while each day.

The journey to Achiltibuie, some 25 miles north of Ullapool, was equally glorious. Just before the village is Achnahaird beach. It is the most beautiful crescent of sand that seems to stretch endlessly. This brilliant white sand contrasts with the wonderful shades of blue and turquoise in the ocean and on a clear day the distinctive mountains of Suilven, Ben More, Canisp, Ben Mor Assynt, Ben Mor Coigach and Staic Pollaidh can be seen. Every time I travelled to these places I thanked God for choosing me and also for giving me the privilege of being paid to visit there – even on the day that I went to use the toilet at the crossroads and was confronted inside by a large blackface sheep!

The response from the children and their families made it all worthwhile. It was the first time that these parents had had pre-school input from a teacher. The remit of the job was to offer support to the families, engage with the children and help them to manage their situation in the best possible way. While occupational therapists, physiotherapists, speech and language therapists and community nurses visited, they couldn't always go fortnightly like I did. This is because, in addition to home visits, they ran clinics, such as those in the hospital's Child Development Unit.

For me, an additional bonus was that when I visited families in or around Ullapool then I would always call on my Aunt Margaret. We'd have a welcome cuppa and a natter before I went back to my office in Dingwall. A few years later Aunt Margaret had cardiac surgery and since she was no longer able to manage the stairs at home, the council allocated her a small pensioner's house opposite Ullapool Primary School. So she sold her cottage, the extra furniture and things she no longer needed and moved in with the help of Ron, Andrew and friends Jim and Barbara Beck.

What I most enjoyed about my job was being able to support and empower fellow parents of children with special needs. Usually these children had been referred to the service because of their medical needs or concerns about their development. Initially I would generally visit each family with the educational psychologist. The range of disabilities included Down's Syndrome, Autistic Spectrum Disorders, Cerebral Palsy, visual impairment, as well as some rare conditions. I found that my own personal experience with Eilidh helped me enormously because I was acutely aware of parents' worries, fears and hopes. Had Eilidh been able-bodied I doubt if I'd *ever* have considered teaching outwith the primary classroom.

It was a great privilege to share in the joy and sadness of these families. It didn't take long for me to be accepted by both the children and their parents and the level of support I offered varied depending on the needs of the family and their disabled child.

Ron often made equipment. These items included shape sorters and chunky form-boards (boards into which matching shapes could be fitted). I regularly made animal puppet gloves for children and finger puppets, which I used for story telling. Along with other colleagues I helped to make All About Me communication books for the children, so others, including other professionals, would be able to learn about each child as a person. On one occasion when I made a return visit to a wee lad I found that his wonderful Mum had made this book herself using the template that I'd previously shown her. The book was made up of twelve pages of A4 paper folded in half and each page gave information on family members as well as a list of things that her son liked and disliked and a list of things he was good at. It also contained photos and information about his extended family.

She had also made him a picture timetable with symbols that could be stuck on a strip of card to prompt him with routines. When one routine was finished the symbol could then be posted in a finished box. This Mum would also make or buy any equipment like mine that had proved successful. Every year at Christmas she still brings me round a card and a box of sweets. It is quite touching because I realise that I made a real difference to their lives. Quite a number of parents still keep in touch by sending Christmas cards.

During my years in this job, the first word or sign used by a child who had previously been silent seemed like a miracle. It was so satisfying for myself and parents when a child managed independent play with a cause and effect toy, when previously co-active help (hand over hand) was necessary. Over the years and often for the first time, I watched children making eye contact, smiling, laughing and engaging in co-operative play. These actions may seem so basic, so simple, but for these children they were truly amazing achievements.

Sometimes parents did not know where to begin in order to help their child. Some lived in isolated places and others did not have a lot of help and support from family. I used to encourage parents to turn off the TV during our play sessions and was delighted once I'd achieved this goal. I vividly remember the day I visited two wee girls, one of whom had severe communication difficulties. When I arrived they were both in high chairs eating porridge. They both looked up and waved their spoons. They had so much porridge on them that they looked as if they'd been rendered. Once they'd finished, their Mum and I washed it off them and we began our play session.

There was one wee lad who always sucked on a dummy and eventually when I visited he'd hand it to me. I'd put it on the mantelpiece while we played and afterwards he'd use sign language to indicate to me that he wanted it back. One day, as I was leaving, he went through to the kitchen to have a drink. His Mum poured him a cup of milk. This was promptly rejected. Shaking his head vigorously, he pointed to the bottles of Coke and Irn Bru that were on top of the fridge. *"What will I do?"* asked his Mum. *"Don't buy them, or else hide them,"* I replied. I always tried to empower parents by saying, *"You're the Mammy, you're in charge!"*

Another time when I'd visited, I found him and his brother sitting on the floor in the corner of the room eating their cereal. There were more Rice Crispies on the floor around them than in their mouths. *"Did your children make a mess like this Maggie?"* she asked, while I helped clear up. *"Oh yes,"* I replied. *"And what did you do?"* she asked *"Well, they sat at the table,"* I replied. By the time I visited again she'd bought a second hand table. I was ELATED.

Inevitably, as a result of working with these children, there were also really sad times too. I remember a wee boy who had to go for the cardiac surgery that was deemed necessary to improve his future quality of life. The day before his operation, he was happily running around. But the dear wee lad never woke from the anaesthetic.

I also attended the funeral of another little boy, who was a twin and suffered a severe disability as a result of a birth injury. I remember after his funeral going back to the family's house with a box of Duplo for his twin and his big brother. They were both on the upstairs landing when I arrived and called out in unison: *"Hello Maggie, have you come to play with us?"* They added: *"That star in the sky is our brother."* How my heart broke as I managed to stem the tears that were pricking my eyes.

Besides discovering the best way to help the children learn through play, I helped parents who were struggling under the pressure it takes to raise a child with a disability, especially if you have other children too. I ended up helping to wash, dress, change and feed children and even kindle fires in the depths of winter. I also wrote applications to charities for specialist equipment and household goods and completed Disability Living Allowance forms and applications for respite care for children, because usually these were a minefield for overwhelmed parents. Although none of these tasks that I undertook had been in the job specification, to me they were a very necessary part. Parents needed to take their children to regular appointments with various agencies and so it was crucially important to have extra money to cover the cost. I firmly believe that while every parent benefits from some *"me time"*, when children are disabled then that is even more important as the pressures and stresses are often greater especially on siblings who might well feel *they* didn't count so much. I'd learned this the hard way and through *my* own experience because I'm certain that Linsey and Andrew felt that their needs weren't so important to me as those of their sister because of the amount of time I convinced myself that I needed to spend with her. On reflection I really should have delegated more. At times my friend Denise's words from years ago would echo back, *"I'd have looked after Eilidh more often Maggie but I felt that you preferred to do it yourself."* I therefore did my utmost to encourage these parents to take up the offer of respite when they felt able to.

Naturally over the years the job evolved and eventually there were seven teachers covering the Highland area. In time, playgroups were given the necessary funding to support children with special needs. Part-time nursery education was provided initially for all four-year-olds and shortly afterwards also for three-year-olds including those with special needs. I helped parents find a suitable playgroup or nursery for morning or afternoon sessions for their child. When children became old enough to go to school I worked with the educational psychologists to help parents decide whether to opt for mainstream school, a special unit at a mainstream school or a special school. Eventually the policy became mainstream education for all children, unless their needs would be best met in a special school.

In 1994 I decided to enhance my initial teaching qualifications by doing an Advanced Diploma in Special Educational Needs with the Open University and I completed this course three years later.

Tough Times and a Special Bonus

The year after I started working was an eventful one. Sadly we lost Tina our Shetland pony. To add to this, Tara died the following year. When Linsey saw Tara's lifeless white figure collapsed as a result of peritonitis and twisted intestines, she was hysterical. She just screamed and cried and could not go to school for two days. Strangely this affected her worse than the deaths of people. I think this was because Linsey had had ponies for six years and during all this time I was so busy with Eilidh, her ponies had been there for her.

We later grew concerned that Toyah, our Icelandic pony, was lonely. Because Linsey had to crack down at school and focus on her studies, we decided to sell her to Linsey's school friend Melissa Grant and her Mum Marjorie. There were four girls in the family and they already had one pony named Misty. Toyah was incredibly popular with them all and Linsey was able to visit her regularly.

Then in 1991 Ron's Mum died. She had been on her way out to the Sunshine Hour at the church and had collapsed in the street. Moira phoned to tell us that she'd been taken to hospital as a result of a heart attack. Ron drove down to visit her. It was so very sad because she never regained consciousness and died a few days later. Ron came home before her funeral then returned to Dundee with Linsey to attend her cremation and wake.

Andrew and Eilidh said that they didn't want to go and so they stayed at home with me. Naturally we were all deeply shocked especially Ron.

You only have one Mum. Granny Wynton had been the children's last surviving grandparent. Granny had been such a rock to me since I had

had my children. Because she had had four kids of her own she really understood my situation. And because I did not have a Mum of my own, I relied on her help, which had been invaluable to me many times in the 16 years since I had had my children.

When I think of Granny, I remember her builder's tan. Like Ron she always had a weathered glow to her face, neck and arms because she was always out gallivanting or in her garden. There she would tend to her roses, and collect their petals to make perfume with the girls. I remember her poor hands, which she burnt in a chip pan fire. From then on she always baked potato croquettes and oven chips! Her chocolate truffles were a favourite of the children and their friends (it was probably the sherry that did it) and I regretted that she never wrote down the recipe to pass on.

There were, of course, times when she drove me mad. When she visited, she would sometimes follow me even when I went to the loo, to tell me stories about growing up during the war, leaving school at 14 to work in a fish shop or bargain hunting trips she had been on round the markets in Dundee. Despite this, she was never judgmental and always full of funny stories, such as the time Ron and his two brothers had converted Moira's dolls' pram into a wagon train from where they fired their toy rifles. Another time their Granny brought them plastic mouth organs and trumpets. The boys swooped on them and made so much noise that their exasperated Mum hid them in the first place she could find – the oven! That night there was pie for tea and so she switched the oven on to preheat it completely forgetting about the instruments inside. Imagine the collective horror when she opened the door and saw the melted toys. There was also the time the three boys had dissected Moira's new watch that she had got from their Aunty Chris. This, of course, was not at all funny for Moira and it wasn't until years later I realised how hard it must have been to be the big sister to three boys, who were the apples of Granny's eyes.

My favourite Granny Wynton story had to be the time Ron's Dad got a new Fiat 124. At the time this seemed a bit of a luxury car with a miscellany of buttons and switches. Granny would always accompany Grandpa when he went fishing, telling him she liked to be there in case he fell into the water while engaged in his pastime and possibly not realising that perhaps he wanted a bit of peace. But she had a point, since Grandpa had sometimes fallen in. Ever curious, on one occasion, Granny decided to test a particular switch in the car that seemed unfamiliar. *"What's that for?"* she asked while pressing it. Before her husband could stop her, her seat back had flown backwards. Luckily she told so many stories we can still think of her with laughter.

Until Granny Wynton's death, Mrs Swan had been a surrogate granny to Linsey, Andrew and Eilidh in all but name. Now seemed to them an appropriate time to "adopt" her. Ron and I thought it was a good idea too, but said that they needed to ask Mrs Swan if she was willing. They duly did so and Mrs Swan was overcome with delight and from then on she was known as Granny Swan.

Granny Wynton's death had not come at a good time for Ron who had had the most horrendous dispute with our neighbour. It started with Ron asking him to remove the ragwort that was growing prolifically in his field. Ragwort is a weed that is highly poisonous to horses. But instead of complying with regulations this man went off on holiday for three months. When he returned, for the next couple of years we suffered 23 incidents, including the deaths of two of our ponies, the stable being burned down and trees being damaged. It was a painful time and eventually Ron ended up in court charged with taking some power tools from the man's shed. Of course this was a complete fabrication and, though Ron was found not guilty, it deeply affected him not to mention the rest of us.

Wheels

Ron was by this time working in the Technical Department at Millburn Academy. After working for an initial two years at both Inverness Royal Academy and Millburn, he had been promoted to the post of Assistant Principal Teacher at IRA, and had worked there for ten years before transferring to Millburn. The aspect of his job he most enjoyed was arranging work experience placements for the fourth year pupils. Ron thought it was really important that these young people went out to see what the world of work involved. Some were not academic at all, others were. But the aim was to help them focus on what they wanted to do and he got some great feedback from enthused pupils.

He was also involved in the schools road safety programme. This was carried out using a small moped to ensure young people were prepared for the hazards we face on the roads, on which we depend so much in the Highlands. Over the years Ron managed to acquire a miscellany of school items that were no longer required including old fashioned wooden desks with lids and little wooden chairs, a BBC computer, and a few pairs of skis and canoes no longer needed for outdoor sports. So when the moped came to be replaced at school, I knew where it was going to be re-housed.

Linsey and Andrew were overjoyed at having the chance to ride this motorised banger in the fields along with the quad bike and the bright orange 4 wheel drive Lada jeep. Because they had been out on the roads so much from a young age on their bikes and ponies, their road safety awareness was good. So, when Linsey turned sixteen, Ron suggested we buy her a better moped. She regularly babysat for a couple of families and he argued that this way she would be able to get herself there and back. Because he'd had a scooter and he trusted Linsey, he went off to town one day and bought a Kawasaki 50cc moped. I was not best pleased. But Linsey was excited and Ron arranged lessons for her with his colleague and friend, Graham Murdoch, who was a part-time motorcycle instructor.

The plan was for her to drive with her L-plates for a year and then go on to do driving lessons. However, one day she gave her friend Kay a backie and was spotted by a local policeman. Somehow they got away with it by telling him they had been studying so hard for their exams that they must have suffered a memory lapse. He told them he was sure that they had learned their lesson. Memories of Ron taking me home on the back of his scooter when he had not passed his test came flooding back. In Linsey's case it was always "like father, like daughter".

Linsey passed her test in Nairn shortly afterwards. Graham accompanied her all the way back to Fortrose (about 30 miles). She was elated and over time my fears evaporated. She had her independence and would be off visiting friends and working at her Saturday supermarket job in Safeway. The next year she learned to drive and Andrew inherited the moped.

She and her brother had actually learned to drive Ron's orange Lada in the field. This was a car in which they would not be seen in public. During the time Ron had it, if he gave them a lift somewhere, they would jump out before their destination! Ron however, thought the 4 by 4 Soviet invention was fabulous. He and I took turns to teach them. Ron was a lot better than I was. After all he had been a driving instructor years ago. I was always nervous they would damage my Peugeot, which I relied on for work and I would nitpick about them switching from say fourth to second gear at a junction, as I had always been taught to go down through each gear individually. After taking lessons with a local instructor, Linsey passed her test, like me, first time. Andrew, like his Dad, passed on his second attempt. This did not stop me worrying about them and both had minor incidents on the very steep hill down from our house, but luckily were not injured.

Before Linsey left school we went on what would be our last holiday as a whole family to Paris. I remember Linsey traipsing round lots of art galleries seeing the artwork of the Impressionist painters she was studying at school. Ron, who had not previously been abroad, was not impressed by the French standard of driving. When he would try to cross the road with Eilidh in her wheelchair he was heard shouting *"stupedo"* to offending drivers. It was some time since he had studied French.

Three New Starts and a milesone reached

In 1993 Eilidh went on her third independent holiday. This time she was lucky enough to go on a seaside trip to Cullen with PHAB (Physically Handicapped and Able Bodied). It was here that she made friends with Sharon, another wheelchair user. Sharon attended Corseford Residential School, in Lanarkshire, which was run by the then Spastic's Society (now named Capability Scotland). By the end of the holiday Eilidh had made her mind up: she wanted to transfer to Corseford too.

While Eilidh was very happy at Alness Academy in the special unit, Ron and I felt she'd benefit from a peer group of other wheelchair users. I

255

had previously visited Corseford in the spring of 1990 as part of a training course. During the visit, the Head Teacher asked me if I'd consider enrolling Eilidh. I remember shaking my head. At the time Eilidh was still at primary school. I shuddered at the thought of her attending a residential school at such a young age.

But when she came home, Eilidh talked about wanting to go to Corseford a great deal. So we agreed to visit. Afterwards, Eilidh remained steadfast – she really liked it. I think she just wanted to be with other young people like her and it must have been amazing for her to feel the same instead of different. I don't think that she fully comprehended the enormity of her decision as she was only 14 and a half, but it certainly was the catalyst for us thinking about life after school.

She was excited on the day she started and chatted happily during the three-hour journey. I, however, was full of trepidation. The school catered for youngsters of nursery age through to school leavers. All nursery and some primary aged pupils attended daily while others like Eilidh were residents. The school, set in its own spacious grounds, had a play area equipped with swings, sand pits and other play equipment. We settled Eilidh and then, when she was busy, we left. I was wracked with many mixed emotions. On one hand I knew that it would be good for everyone, but I couldn't help feeling guilty about her attending a residential setting, which meant that when she was there we now had time to pursue other hobbies and interests. However, Corseford was actually Eilidh's choice and Eilidh was happy there.

She shared a room with three other girls, all of whom she became good friends with. It was spacious and there was pin boarding to put up pictures and posters. She had a wardrobe and chest of drawers for her clothes and a shelf for her radio and cassette player. She asked staff if her Dad would be allowed put up a border frieze to decorate the wall. This was readily given and the girls were absolutely delighted when this happened.

She spent the next four years at Corseford. She flew home every third weekend arriving on Friday morning and returning on Monday evening. At these times, Ron met her at the airport, brought her home and my neighbour Val would look after her until I got home from work. Although she enjoyed school, she found saying goodbye to us tough – when I recall how I felt going to Budapest with her all these times, I realise that *she* was a chip off the old block. When it was time to return, Ron always took her back to the airport because she almost always got upset. Ron was much better at distracting her than I was! I would just start to cry too!

One of the first things that Eilidh was given was a power wheelchair. This meant that she could move around independently. By this time she'd grown quite tall and her hip, which had previously clicked in and out was now sublaxed (partially dislocated). As a consequence her left leg appeared a bit shorter than before and her windswept pattern became more pronounced because of the tilt of her pelvis. The physiotherapist had told me earlier that some of the pupils had hips that clicked in and out and some had had similar surgery to Eilidh. This innocent statement did fuel my quest to discover whether or not I'd made the best decision on Eilidh's behalf about the surgery we opted for. I thought about the wonderful progress she'd made in Budapest, her improved balance when she was walking pushing the ladder-back chair AND that stick! It was sad that she had not achieved her dream to walk. But she had certainly improved as a result of her visits to Budapest in terms of the use of her right hand for picking up items and standing and walking with help.

Eilidh made many friends at Corseford. Two I particularly remember were Mark Gardner and Gillian Grieve. Regular therapy was provided and built into the school day by the speech and language therapist, occupational therapist and physiotherapist, using a multi-disciplinary approach. The classes were small and each pupil had an individualised education plan. In addition to the teaching staff, there were several housemothers who exuded warmth and comfort. I particularly remember Helen Millar, one of the housemothers. She was a warm, friendly person who instinctively knew when someone was homesick and needed a cuddle. In the evenings there were group activities such as the Scouts, Guides, quizzes, clubs and outings to places like Largs, Rouken Glen and the zoo. Sometimes there were discos during the evenings at weekends for the pupils who were staying. Some children actually stayed there all term, only returning home at the holidays. Sadly some of their families just could not cope or did not want to know them. I remember that in her last year at Corseford, Eilidh arranged her 18th birthday party herself at school, including food and a disco with support from the staff.

Eilidh going to school in Corseford was particularly tough for Ron and me because it coincided with Linsey leaving home to go to university. She'd looked at Glasgow, Edinburgh, Stirling and Aberdeen and we thought she'd probably go to Glasgow. She wanted to study English and Politics because she wanted to become a journalist. This had a lot to do with being Eilidh's sister and seeing how one article and one television documentary had had such a life changing effect on our lives. She felt it was vital to tell people information that they might not otherwise know. Her sister had been the feature of so many articles during our time in Budapest that Linsey had written to various news editors and arranged work experience at the Inverness Courier. I remember her being in her element getting to talk to all sorts of people, attending the court for a murder trial, and even getting her photograph on the front page pointing out a spelling mistake in a street sign. This was topped off when they had champagne on a Friday to celebrate one of the reporter's birthdays.

Her ambition was burning and I remember sitting with her just a few months after she had come back from Hungary, watching the Berlin Wall coming down. It was Brian Hanrahan's report on the then BBC Nine O' Clock news and Linsey just said she wished she could be there. She was glued to the television news during the fall of communism in Eastern Europe and the exposure of the orphanages in Romania, and she was fascinated when she met a friend of her then boyfriend who travelled there, taking supplies out to help those abandoned children. Many of these children were disabled and unwanted because of the social stigma attached to this.

After a lot of agonising, Linsey opted for Aberdeen University as she would have the chance to study Film and Creative Writing as part of the English course and International Relations as part of her Politics course. I remember clearing out the boot of my red Peugeot estate car, which was always full of toys and equipment for work, and filling it with all of her belongings. I was glad that Linsey had made her choice, though it felt as if another door was closing. Although she would come home and we would visit, she was flying the nest. During the journey to Aberdeen, I reminisced about my journey from my home in Fife to college in Dundee almost 30 years before. I comforted myself with the fact that Linsey was a resourceful young woman and she was only a two and a half hour car journey away. Quite a number of her friends from school had also opted for Aberdeen so I was certain that she'd manage. Also she would have a lot of FUN!

From having five of us, we suddenly just had three people at home. Andrew was not particularly focused about what he wanted to do. He got through his last year of school and left aged seventeen. He had a variety of jobs including working in a fish factory, working at the car auction, selling double-glazing, working with The Builder's Centre, working as a manager in Wickes and then joining the police. To be honest he was just like his Dad in that regard. I often described and compared his progress to climbing a ladder because, with each new job, Andrew climbed another rung as new opportunities beckoned.

The house was quite empty without our girls, though we were glad that they were making the most of their respective opportunities. Then in late November of 1994 Ron decided to take early retirement from his job. He was only 50, but for various reasons he felt he had done his bit and had enough. He quickly filled his time researching the family tree managing to trace family back hundreds of years, teaching Advanced Driving, going fishing, keeping fit at Scottish Country dancing classes, turning wood on his lathe to make all sorts of weird and wonderful household objects and presents, volunteering by teaching curling to disabled people at Inverness ice rink and creating a lovely garden with a folly and poly-tunnel in which he grows all sorts of fruit and vegetables through a hydroponic system.

I remember Eilidh's first Christmas home from Corseford in 1994. She had greeted me a few weeks before with the question: *"Can Gillian come to stay with us at Christmas. She doesn't have anywhere else to go?"* My heart melted and told me, *"Yes, of course she can",* I said smiling and wondering how I was going to manage two girls in wheelchairs.

Although initially I felt very daunted, it was an extremely enjoyable holiday and we all had great fun having Gillian to stay. On top of this, Mrs Swan, who was by now 94, also came to stay. We went to the cinema, out for meals and I took Gillian to be fitted for her first bras. Gillian slept in

Eilidh's room and Ron set up the internet for her. She was a very easily managed young woman and it was a great pleasure to have her to stay. Eilidh was so incredibly happy and it was lovely for her to have her friend around, just like Linsey and Andrew often did. When the holiday was over and it was time to return to school with Gillian, dear Eilidh still broke down as usual.

A few years later poor Gillian tragically died. Eilidh was devastated. Sadly, and like many physically disabled young people, she has had to get used to quite a few of her friends passing away over the years. She also lost her other firm friend from Corseford, Mark Gardner, who was during her school days, her boyfriend.

While Andrew was quite a homebody in those days, Linsey was anything but. During the spring of 1994 she decided that she'd really like to do her second year in America. She'd got the idea from Eilidh's able-bodied friend Jill, whom Eilidh met at Alness Academy. Jill was a year older than Linsey and was studying in Glasgow and had spent her second year in Florida. At the last minute Linsey had found out about an exchange scheme to the States, so ran to the relevant department to fill out an application and got it in just in the nick of time. Not long afterwards she was accepted to spend her second year at Bloomsburg University in Pennsylvania.

Having been bitten by the travel bug, she had also decided to travel to Greece that summer with one of her university friends. I had hoped that she would stay at home and continue working in Safeway, where she'd worked during her last years of school part-time and in the school holidays. Linsey assured us she would get a job in a bar in Greece. I remember crying as I put her on the bus to Edinburgh. The driver was Willie, the Dad of one of the children with whom I used to work. *"Don't cry,"* he said. *"She's not going away for a year."* I sobbed: *"She is."* I knew that when Linsey got back she would just have a couple of weeks before she was off again to America.

She came home much browner than her self-named *"blue"* Scottish skin had ever been, just in time to help us celebrate our 25th wedding anniversary dinner at the Royal Hotel in Cromarty, where we danced the night away after consuming good food and alcohol. We had a right houseful with Ron's sister Moira and her husband Douglas in Linsey's room, Ron's brother Graham in Andrew's room, Mrs Swan and Eilidh in her room and Linsey and Andrew and their friends Kay and Mark sleeping in sleeping bags in the living room.

All too soon came the cold, rainy Saturday morning in September when Ron and I took her to Dalcross Airport in Inverness. It brought back all those memories of trips to Hungary when we had crept out of bed, in the wee small hours, leaving Linsey and Andrew to sleep. I expected she might suffer a turmoil of emotions, but Linsey did not seem phased at all. I vividly remember watching her walk confidently through the departure gate and out onto the tarmac. Ron and I held on to each other as we watched our firstborn climb the steps. We waited to see the plane taxi down the runway and take off, then watched as it climbed through the clouds high into the sky becoming smaller and smaller. Only when it completely disappeared did we leave the airport. This time she'd really gone. She wasn't just 120 miles away in Aberdeen and I knew I would not see her for a long time. I felt hollow.

It was only just after 7am, none of the shops were open at that time and so we parked down by the Ness Islands and walked in the rain. At least that disguised our tears. Much, much later we had a phone call to say that she'd arrived safely in Philadelphia from the mother of another student with whom Linsey was spending the weekend. After that I relaxed knowing that she was safe. I lay for ages thinking about all of the things that she'd achieved in her 19 years. I felt very proud. But I was also incredibly sad that my Mum had never known her. I firmly believe that Linsey has spent her life trying to make up for the time my Mum lost and the things her sister cannot do. She is independent because she has always had to be since her sister was born.

Now Country and Western music is definitely not my first choice, but during the time that Linsey spent in America, I borrowed Ron's cassette as he is a devotee of that genre. He would often drive me mad singing the first few snatches of Charlie Pride's Crystal Chandelier. The song I associated with Linsey was Rhinestone Cowboy. The lyrics, sung by Glen Campbell, made me feel as if she was there beside me. As I would drive down single track roads in Wester Ross surrounded by mountains and lochs I would sing at the top of my voice:

"Like a Rhinestone Cowboy
Riding out on a horse at a star spangled rodeo...

"And I dream of the things that I'll do
With a subway ticket and a dollar tucked inside my shoe.
There'll be a load of compromisin'
On the way to my horizon
But I'm gonna be where the lights are shinin' on me."

She had a whale of a time in America, making friends easily with people because of their fascination with her accent. She spent a weekend with friends in New York, visited Montreal in Canada on Thanksgiving weekend and spent her Christmas holiday travelling with a friend as far as LA on a Greyhound bus! Eilidh had wanted to go to Disneyland for years, so we took the opportunity to visit Linsey with her in Easter 1995 and combine this with a trip to Florida. Andrew stayed at home and celebrated his 18th birthday in the house with his friends.

I remember hiring a car and Ron getting lost driving round New York and Linsey taking over and driving across the Brooklyn Bridge. Ron nearly got arrested for taking a photograph of the then Prime Minister John Major, who was visiting the then President, Bill Clinton. And despite her excitement, poor Eilidh cried when she saw the larger than life Disney characters up close and personal.

After Linsey's return she was always on the move. She spent her second summer of university in Glasgow staying with friends and working in bars and volunteering with Irish traveller children. Her third summer of university was spent in Romania, volunteering with children, then revisiting Budapest with her friends.

During her four years at Corseford, Eilidh experienced small classes and best of all the Glasgow banter and craic were hilarious. I remember one time another pupil deliberately threw something on the floor. *"I don't want to see you doing that again,"* said the housemother. *"Och jist close yer een* (eyes) *then,"* came the reply. It was very difficult to suppress a giggle.

Carole McKinnon, the physiotherapist, and Katrina Brunton, the occupational therapist, always paid joint visits to all of the pupils during the summer holiday and we eagerly looked forward to them coming. One time I remember Eilidh helping to make nut roast and tomato puree using some of Ron's homegrown tomatoes and courgettes, as both Carole and Katrina were vegetarians.

Each year, the school put on musicals including Joseph and Oliver. Once Mrs Swan and I travelled to see Eilidh performing in Oliver. Eilidh has always loved music and singing. She was so proud to show her surrogate Granny around the school and Mrs Swan said the performance was MARVELLOUS. I remember that Eilidh was wearing bright pink lipstick and had a sparkly scarf around her neck and I still have a video of the performance.

During her last year at Corseford Eilidh and three other girls from her class spent a lovely holiday at the Kielder Outdoor Centre near Hexham. This centre is a wonderful place for families or groups with disabled members. The ambience is so positive and those who work there ensure that the participants have a memorable time. Accommodation is provided in either the main building or chalets. Guests can opt for either self-catering or full board. There are a wide number of activities on offer, including abseiling, archery, horse riding, swimming, sailing and fishing. Eilidh and her friends thoroughly enjoyed many of these and she had such a good time that we took her back on three other occasions. She especially enjoyed going out on a fishing expedition with her Dad, although she didn't catch anything.

In the November of Eilidh's last year at Corseford I turned 50 – half a century. Three weeks previously Ron had also reached this momentous age. Linsey and Andrew avowed that this occasion definitely needed to be marked and decided to arrange a party. Unbeknown to either Ron or me, our address book was carefully examined for the contact details of our friends and family who were all invited. Andrew made sandwiches and Mrs Swan contributed to the cost of the party food and drinks. Eilidh was home for that weekend and Linsey and Andrew booked a lovely meal for the three of us in the Indian restaurant in Beauly. We arrived home in darkness, fumbled the key in the lock and entered our house. As we switched on the living room light the collective shout of "Happy Birthday" rang out and people poured out through the kitchen door. We were happily astonished. It was a truly wonderful evening and I was so touched that Linsey and Andrew had gone to the trouble of arranging this for us. We certainly had a ball.

Although annual X-rays taken at hospital in Inverness, indicated that the condition and position of Eilidh's hip seemed stable, she had developed scoliosis (curvature of her spine). This had deteriorated over the years because the pull of her muscles affected the position of her left hip. In turn this had a knock on effect on her posture: her rib cage, once straight, had gradually rotated. The right hand part of the front section of her ribs seemed out of position. I was concerned that this would affect her vital organs and so I decided to contact Mr Robb, the consultant in Edinburgh. He had assessed her all those years ago and had suggested a second tenotomy instead of the more complex surgery she eventually had in Inverness. Although I had rejected this option, he readily agreed to see Eilidh again. In order to progress my request he said that I would need a letter of referral from our GP.

After I got this, an appointment was made for the clinic during the Easter holidays. Poor Eilidh was apprehensive, although everyone had tried to reassure her. We duly visited and Eilidh had her spine X-rayed. I remember him saying that although it didn't look good, it would be *"crazy to do anything"*. I hadn't asked for anything to be done, but he reassured me that nothing was pressing on Eilidh's vital organs. When I told him that her pelvis would likely be X-rayed at the Inverness clinic, he said that he wouldn't X-ray that part because it wasn't good to have too many X-rays.

He told me that about half of his patients had similar surgery to Eilidh's but I have no idea how many were successful. I'd hoped to have my worries put to rest but I left feeling that the consultation hadn't really done this. I told myself: *"Don't look back Maggie. There's nothing you can do. It's all water under the bridge now."*

Despite Eilidh's physical condition, her confidence and self-esteem grew steadily during her time at Corseford. When it came time for her to leave school, she visited various colleges near Glasgow as well as Beaumont College in Lancaster. But she made up her mind that she wanted to move to Red Cross House in Inverness rather than live at home. She had been there in the past on two occasions to offer us respite and this also gave her the chance to see if she would really like to go to live there.

The Best of Both Worlds

Red Cross House had been built in the 1960s for those people who were ambulant, some of whom were recovering from accidents. Each of the 30 residents had their own room. There were two sitting rooms, a dining room, a workshop and a room for the physiotherapist, who was employed there for half of the week. In addition, there was also a fully adapted purpose-built flat within the building that provided the residents with opportunities to work towards independent living. Linsey said it was basically like students' halls and thought it was great that Eilidh would have a chance to experience this like she had. During the daytime there were classes such as woodwork and crafts for the young people to take part in. They were also taught independent living skills, such as laundry and cooking.

After the school summer holiday of 1997 Eilidh took up residence in Red Cross House. By this time, there were a number of residents who used wheelchairs. There were also residents with other physical and learning disabilities who could walk but needed support in the skills, such as cooking, laundry and personal care. I felt she was going to have another great opportunity to socialise with other young people, just like her.

"Eilidh's bedroom's quite shabby," I said to Ron just after Eilidh moved in. *"It could do with a bit of sprucing up."* Despite buying some cheery flat pack furniture and new bedding and curtains, the room most definitely needed some decoration. Eilidh helped choose some paint and we soon freshened up the walls. *"What a difference Dad",* said Eilidh and looked in the direction of the room opposite where one of her friends stayed. *"Absolutely not",* I said. *"Some things are not possible."* Not long after that Eilidh was given another room that was en suite and needless to say that also needed to be freshened up.

Because Ron had recently taken early retirement, voluntary work beckoned. So when Eilidh went to live at Red Cross House, he ran a woodwork class in the workshop. This was a good arrangement because it meant that he could see for himself how Eilidh was settling in, as well as using his skills to teach young people with disabilities. He found this incredibly satisfying. He helped them make whatever they wanted and this included shelving for their rooms. I recall Cherry, one of the support workers, asking him if he would make a Chinese bridge for her garden. The group had great fun designing and helping Ron to make this. Apart from some expected hiccups, he reported back that Eilidh was doing well. She had the best of both worlds, socialising with her new friends in the week and returning home to us each weekend and all of the holidays.

Eilidh thoroughly enjoyed gardening and was delighted when she was offered a place in a gardening group in Dingwall. Ron used to transport her there and back. She happily filled flowerpots for the re-potting of plants, most particularly enjoying the craic in the poly-tunnel and the tea break. She enrolled in the local college where she studied first aid and fabric and fashion courses. Although she was not independent enough to venture out alone, each week a volunteer took her out to the local shops or a cafe. Another volunteer paid weekly visits to help her complete two modules in computing skills. Eilidh also joined Ron's woodwork class where she thoroughly enjoyed sorting out nails and screws and hoovering up the wood shavings and sawdust.

While she was at Red Cross House, Ron and I decided that Eilidh should take advantage of the Motability scheme. This allowed users to rent a vehicle for five years if it was adapted for a wheelchair and three years if not. We collectively decided that at that point in time she didn't need a WAV (Wheelchair Accessible Vehicle) but instead chose one where a swivel seat could be fitted. This seat swivelled into two positions – 90/180 degrees – thus allowing her to be transferred easily from her wheelchair and position herself onto the front passenger seat. She was then swivelled 90 degrees around to face forwards fairly effortlessly.

Leo the First

"Dad should get another dog Mum," said Andrew. *"Linsey agrees. He enjoys going for walks and another dog would be great company for him."* I didn't share these sentiments because I felt that this would be quite a tie, especially when we went on holiday. *"Dad can offer to take someone else's dog for walks if he wants to,"* I countered, thinking that was the end of the matter. How wrong I was. Andrew clearly decided that we did not go on that many holidays and took his Dad to Munlochy Animal Aid where Ron chose Leo, a black mongrel, who was part Labrador, part Spaniel.

The following Saturday Ron persuaded me to go there to collect this beast. Leo and I stared at each other. *"That dog has been in a fight,"* I said. *"How do you know that?"* asked Ron. *"Just look at his ear."* I replied. Leo's left ear had a small mouse hole shaped nick in it. Iona, the owner of Animal Aid, clipped on the lead that Ron had brought, led Leo out of his enclosure and handed him to Ron. Leo gazed adoringly at his new master and happily trotted to the car. When the door was opened he leapt in and settled himself comfortably on the back seat.

On the way home Ron told me that Leo had been allowed to roam the streets of Inverness where he'd been picked up by the dog warden and taken to Munlochy Animal Aid several times. On the last occasion, his owner had said that she would just have to tie him to a bollard to stop him running off. As she got out her purse to pay for his keep, Iona told her to keep her money. She told her that she would re-home the dog. *"We are the third owners,"* continued Ron. *"Another family chose him but they couldn't cope and returned him within a few days."* I didn't know whether to laugh or cry. All I could think was: *"Well there may be another family after us."*

But dear Leo lived happily with us for six years. Iona was unsure as to his age but reckoned he was about five or six. Ron and he went for long walks to the beach or along the golf course path. The first time Leo went to the beach he leapt into the water and began to swim out. *"Oh my, maybe he's heading back to Inverness,"* thought Ron. But no, Leo swam parallel to the beach, carefully negotiating the rocks, and when Ron whistled, he obediently came out, ran towards him and vigorously shook himself all over his new master.

Leo loved company, was great with children and would join in games any time the opportunity arose. He enjoyed eating and once stole a sandwich from a golfer. He explored the gorse and whin bushes on the golf course, often emerging with a golf ball in his mouth. Obviously he was not popular with the golf club members and on one occasion he stole a ball from the fairway before Ron could stop him.

I remember one of the times that we had some guests round for Sunday dinner. Leo barked as they rang the doorbell and, as I went to answer it, the cheeky hound stole a cooked joint of roast beef from which I'd cut three slices – he ignored these in favour of the whole joint! As there was not enough left to go round, I had to get some salmon en croute out of the freezer.

Sometimes Leo would disappear down the woods and return looking very smug. We later found out that he'd been taking afternoon tea with a neighbour. She told us that he was particularly fond of cream buns. On the few occasions that he was left alone in the house and in the back hall, rather than sleep in his dog bed, he pulled Ron's jacket down and made a nest of it.

Another time Andrew, who was a policeman at the time, looked after him when we were on holiday. He'd taken Leo to work and shut him in an upstairs room. Leo strongly objected to this and dragged Andrew's civilian clothes into a pile and made a nest for himself. When Andrew returned, he remonstrated with Leo, tidied everything up and then, to the dog's dismay, abandoned him again. By this time Leo had had enough and once more repeated his misdemeanors. For his efforts he was incarcerated in the back of the car where he spent the rest of Andrew's shift.

Although I had never wanted him in the first place, I loved him dearly. I remember one summer's morning when Ron had taken him to the beach. Leo had displayed his customary road rage barking when Ron stopped the car to let a cyclist cross at the pedestrian crossing. He had spent the afternoon basking in the sun outside the workshop while Ron pottered on his lathe. Then Leo went exploring in the woods. He was unusually slow eating his dinner and after a few mouthfuls went over to the corner of the room where he lay down and began shaking uncontrollably. I telephoned the vet who advised us to bring him in. While Ron went off for a blanket in which to carry him, I stroked his head but within minutes he'd left this life for the happy hunting ground.

I phoned all the children. We were completely devastated. All of Leo's misdeeds were forgotten as we thought of the carefree animal who'd lived his life to the full and had had a good death. We put him in his basket in the back hall. Eilidh came over the next afternoon and watched while her Dad wrapped him in his blanket and buried him in the woods. Ron carved his name on a small headstone.

Another Great Loss

By this time Linsey had graduated from Aberdeen University with a 2:1 in English and Politics. Ron and Eilidh and I spent graduation day with her. And we celebrated with an Indian meal, always a favourite for Ron, Linsey and me. Eilidh had by now also developed a taste for curries and eagerly

tucked into her meal. After lunch we visited Eilidh's boyfriend Mark
Gardner as his family lived in Aberdeen; Eilidh stayed with Mark while Ron
and I went to the evening ceremony. I turned a blind eye to Linsey
sneaking an alcopop in the ceremony, concealed in the sleeve of her gown.

Linsey had applied for a place on her dream course: a Post
Graduate Diploma in Newspaper Journalism at City University in London. I
have to be honest and say I was a wee bit disappointed when she was
accepted. I rather wished she had taken up a place on a similar course at
Glasgow University. But our intrepid traveller was not to be stopped. She
spent the summer juggling about five jobs to save up enough for the move.
Then she and her boyfriend at the time presented Ron with a Monkey
Puzzle tree for the front garden, before heading off in search of their
fortune.

My Great Aunt Margaret was now over 80 and her health was
failing. She'd had several spells in hospital and Ron, Andrew and I visited
her regularly. One of these times was just after Christmas when Linsey
was up for the holidays from London. She visited her several times before
she left knowing in her heart that it was highly unlikely that Aunt Margaret
would be there when she returned. Linsey told me Aunt Margaret seemed
at peace, her skin was warm and pink and she looked snug in her hospital
bed when she left her. Closing the door quietly, she looked at her sleeping
Aunt through the glass window one last time.

Each time we visited there was a noticeable change in Aunt
Margaret's appearance and we knew that she was slipping away. I felt so
sad knowing that she wasn't going to be part of my life any more. She was
sleeping peacefully the last time I visited. As I left I looked back through
the glass window in the door of her room and I fancied that I saw a slight
smile play on her lips. She was awake when Ron visited her later. He gave

her a drink, then left when sleep once more overtook her. We had a call from the hospital a short time later to say that she'd passed away.

A few weeks after her funeral we held a wake in the Ceilidh Place in Ullapool. This had been one of Aunt Margaret's favourite haunts over the years, where we had often dropped in to have tea and a scone or a bowl of homemade soup. It was packed with her many local friends who hadn't been able to make the journey to the crematorium in Inverness. It was wonderful to celebrate the life and times of my surrogate Mum's life. I had made up an album of photographs of Aunt Margaret at different stages of her life and Ron made the following speech about her.

Aunt Margaret's eulogy, by Ron, February 1997

"Welcome, particularly on such a dreich night, when the temptation to sit by your own fireside is so great. It's nice to see you all.

"Firstly I think it appropriate to offer my wife's and my thanks to the good people of Ullapool for all of the friendship, kindness, services and care that Margaret enjoyed over the years, be it from shops, hotels, restaurants, hairdressers, tradesmen, medical services (including hospital cars), ambulances, doctors, nurses, home helps and dog walkers. You all made Margaret very happy and content to remain in Ullapool.

"I first met Margaret some 30 years ago when my then fiancée brought me up "for inspection purposes" by Aunt Margaret. I have to admit that we hit it off immediately, her kindness, her openness, her sense of fun, her keen intellect, her wide interest in all that was happening at the time, but most of all her warmth made her an easy person to love.

"Although Margaret was actually Maggie's father's cousin, she became my Aunt Margaret too. When Maggie was a toddler, her mother died, and Aunt Margaret took little Margaret under her wing and was a great support to her throughout her life.

"Aunt Margaret had a habit of taking all sorts of folk under her wings, be they girls who used to work at the telephone exchange who boarded with her, or Patrick and Vernon who used to rent her cottage; she was so much more than just their landlady. Over the years there were lots of youngsters who became Youngsters with a capital Y as in her surname and who benefited from her kindness, care and wisdom.

"When Barbara Beck, who started work at the age of 16, came to know Aunt Margaret they remained devoted friends throughout her life, despite the obvious age difference. In case there are any mathematicians present, I'll not give away the number of years so you'll have to continue guessing as to Barbara's age. When Barbara married Jim and later had Nicole and Douglas, they too came under Aunt Margaret's wings. She had BIG wings.

"Now these wings may have contributed to her free spirit because at a time when women were not supposed to have spirit, let alone free spirit, Aunt Margaret did her own thing. She jumped at the chance of early retirement from the Civil Service, moved up to Moss, bought the VW camper

van and she, Aunt Susan and many of her friends would pile in for days or weeks at a time, touring favourite beauty spots in the Highlands, camping on windswept seashores or as far up mountainsides as the camper van would go, enjoying the peace, beauty and splendour that is Scotland.

"Margaret had a big, warm and generous heart. It eventually let her down but to my certain knowledge, Margaret never let anyone down. She was constant, dependable and generous. Even in death she was generous leaving 14 individual bequests; the bulk of the remainder is going to 3 national charities – the Highland Hospice, the Royal School for the Blind in Edinburgh and the Association of Guide Dogs for the Blind.

"Please join me in offering thanks for the life of Margaret Young."

On a wet cold afternoon, Ron and I together with Jim and Barbara Beck scattered her ashes in the river that ran in front of her former home. Although that final goodbye was tinged with sadness, I felt that she would always live on there where she'd been so happy and contented. She'd taught me so much about life and I'm certain that my Mum would have been very pleased knowing that she had.

My Aunt Margaret

Tall, plump and homely,
       Brown wispy hair, blue twinkling eyes,
Rosy apple cheeks
       And a smile that lit up the room

Brown wispy hair, blue twinkling eyes
       Wobbly hips and a comfy lap
And a smile that lit up the room
       Hugging arms and an ample bosom

Wobbly hips and a comfy lap
       To sit on lots of times.
Hugging arms and an ample bosom
       That made me feel secure.

Our Battle for Care in the Community

Four years after Eilidh moved to Red Cross House, it was decided that it should be demolished! It was not up to date with regulations stating that all residents must have their own en suite bathrooms. Nevertheless, Eilidh and many other residents would have been very happy to remain there.

At this time the Government policy of Care in the Community had come into place. Although admirable in principle, I really wondered if the community would care about local disabled people. I thought many would be more secure living together among the joy and laughter that bound Red Cross House together. There were quite a few of the residents who really didn't want to move into independent living. Whether it was fear of the unknown or that they didn't know any different, I don't know. Loneliness never seemed to be an issue in Red Cross House, though it certainly would be out in the community.

The policy seemed to me short-sighted and not cost effective. If Eilidh and her disabled peers had been able to stay at Red Cross House, they would have been able to share care. They wouldn't each need someone to cook them a meal – someone could cook for a large group.

Meanwhile, activities were gradually phased out, including physiotherapy sessions. We were aghast. Having made extensive enquiries, we realised that it was extremely difficult to access physiotherapy for adults. By some stroke of luck Ron arranged for Eilidh to have this treatment at the MS Centre each week and, sixteen years later, she still attends each Tuesday morning.

Understandably Eilidh experienced a miscellany of mixed emotions about this new venture away from her friends and support workers, who were a second family to her but, once she got used to the idea of having her own home, her apprehension began gradually to diminish.

The Social Work Department assessed the needs of all residents and gave all of them their own tenancies in rented accommodation. However, it seemed that many of these disabled adults were not going to be given appropriate support. After all it would be more expensive to offer this in different dwelling places, as opposed to collectively under one roof. I wondered how on earth they were going to manage to look after themselves, let alone be able to get out and visit friends?

In principle, the idea was that each resident would be provided with the appropriate support package to enable them to live as independently as possible. In reality those with parents who could argue for their needs had a monumental battle on their hands.

We had two crucial tasks at hand: firstly to find a suitable wheelchair accessible ground floor home for Eilidh; and, secondly and (just as importantly) to ensure she had a care package tailored to her specific needs as a young person with a severe physical disability and learning difficulties, who had never lived alone. Finding the home was much easier than sorting out the care package.

During the summer of 2001 Eilidh was offered a newly built flat, but when we went to view it, though lovely, it was totally unsuitable because the corridor was not wide enough for her wheelchair to turn in at right angles to the bathroom or bedroom. In addition, the internal doors were not hinged against the wall, so this just added another obstruction.

Shortly afterwards, a newly planned housing development had been approved with wheelchair accessible accommodation suitable for Eilidh. Her Social Worker said that she would put the wheels in motion so that this could happen. The flat was completed and available for occupation from the 19th December. We had signed the necessary tenancy, electricity, gas and house insurance agreements: all conditions of the tenancy agreement. Since Eilidh was in residential care, once the fees for Red Cross House were paid from her state benefits, all that she and others in similar circumstances were left with was £14. How was she supposed to pay? Since she wasn't occupying the house she could claim neither housing nor transitional housing benefit.

During this time we had been doing our utmost to ensure that Eilidh's support package was tailored to her needs. This was eventually achieved, though not without considerable hassle and effort. We strenuously argued that Eilidh required 24-hour care. Although she can hold a conversation, speak on the phone and feed herself, she needs assistance with cooking, bathing and toileting, dressing and undressing, getting in and out of bed as well as getting out and about. To Ron and me there was no question of her *not* having a 24-hour support package, but there was the question of *how* this was going to be provided.

Because of her learning disability Eilidh was functioning with the abilities of a teenager, who you certainly would not leave unattended at night and for a variety of reasons. She would have been positively terrified at the prospect of being on her own and her sleep pattern would undoubtedly have been disturbed. We were concerned about what would happen if she took ill at night, or if there was a fire or a break in, etc. She would not be able to get herself out of bed because of her physical disability. Nor could she access an alarm for similar reasons and she would not be able to see without her glasses, which she does not wear to bed. We just did not want to leave her high and dry as sadly so many vulnerable people have been, with a support worker rushing in to get her up, make her three quick meals a day while Eilidh sat plonked in front of the TV, then put to bed at night. We knew that sort of "life" would result in her becoming depressed.

These points were made to Social Work, but fell on deaf ears. So the war of attrition began. We wrote to councillors, MPs, and MSPs highlighting our case. The replies that we received from Social Work were: that there was a support package in place; there were questions over the funding; and, that the Complex Needs Assessment was a grey area. (The Complex Needs Assessment is the tool on which care/support packages are based. It assesses all aspects of a person's needs using information from the relevant agencies – social workers, community nurses from the Learning Disabilities Team, speech and language therapists, occupational therapists and physiotherapists).

Subsequent letters, emails and meetings proved to be fruitless. It turned out that Ross-shire Social Work Department was planning to provide a 24-hour care package mainly with Independent Living Fund (ILF) funding. The ILF, which was set up in 1993, is a fund that administers regular moneys to people in order to help them to be able to live in their own homes. However, it cannot be used *instead* of council funding as that would absolve the council of its statutory duty of care. Ross-shire Social Work seemed therefore to be trying to provide a support package almost entirely with ILF funding with a contribution of £200 per month from its Gateway Committee (a social work committee that

270

approves funding requests from the Area Managers). But this would have covered only a small percentage of the costs.

At the initial meeting, which Ron attended with Eilidh and Noemia, her key worker from Red Cross House, the Social Work manager was very vague as to what was being offered. He adamantly refused to specify what was on offer, refused to let us see the assessment, refused to say when it had been done and by whom, refused to specify how many hours of care Eilidh would receive and made statements such as: *"We'll get someone to get you up in the morning and to put you to bed at night, and it can be reviewed in 6 month's time."*

We however, thought that those with similar needs to Eilidh whohad been used to communal living would have benefited from a 24-hour support package for the initial six months after which it could then have been reviewed.

Ron's points about Eilidh being used to always having someone around were curtly dismissed. The Social Work Manager belligerently and continually demanded that Eilidh sign the document there and then. Ron felt that what the manager was offering was serious neglect that would have a detrimental effect on her health and well-being, not to mention her confidence. Because of the raised tones of voice and the fact that she couldn't understand the arguments, Eilidh became extremely upset and had to be taken out by Noemia on several occasions. Several times she asked, *"When can I move into my house?"*

But the manager persisted and advised that Eilidh: *"Just sign and we'll finalise it later."* But Ron told him in no uncertain terms: *"She can neither read nor understand this, so is signing nothing!"* Next day the manager sent a young Social Worker to Red Cross House, with the same documents and it was only by good luck that Eilidh's key worker, Noemia, saw her, challenged her and sent her away.

The next few months were spent going round in circles, with meetings, letters, emails and we arranged for our own assessment of Eilidh's needs to be done by a private company. The nurse who carried it out said that what was on offer was wholly inadequate.

I phoned the Director of Social Work and arranged a meeting, at which we presented the Convener of the council and the Director of Social Work with copies of this assessment. Arrangements were subsequently made to re-assess Eilidh by another experienced Social Worker of our choosing.

By March Eilidh had received a rent demand for her three months unpaid rent. An official letter of complaint was then sent to the Chief Executive of Highland Council making the following points: there was a total lack of policy of uniform assessment in Highland,
Social Work had had six month's advance notice of the need for such a care package. A number of Social Work staff involved had shown unprofessional behaviour, Eilidh had incurred unnecessary expense due entirely to delays by Social Work.

Almost immediately Eilidh had a new care manager and a 24-hour support package. We had a full and unreserved apology from the Director, the Convener and the Chief Executive of Highland Council. They agreed to pay all of Eilidh's costs. They set up a committee on the Single Shared Assessment to which Ron was invited to contribute. The Single Shared Assessment (SSA) was designed to gather basic information from both health and social services regarding a disabled person's circumstances and needs. Its aim was to assess the type and amount of support that someone required to help them live as independently as possible.

They also set up an equalities group that he was invited to join and the Director arranged a meeting for Social Work staff so that they might reflect on their handling of the situation and to take the appropriate action to ensure such a situation would not recur in the future. Although we had won the battle it left us both completely physically and mentally drained. Our older daughter Linsey was also really concerned about our stress levels.

At last! a Home of her Own for Eilidh

Eilidh's first flat seemed perfect. It was in a new building development and had been specially designed for a wheelchair user. We all took a great deal of pleasure in helping her set up her new home. Ron and Andrew laid laminate flooring in the hall, kitchen and living room, Calum, our carpet fitter, laid carpets in the bedroom and Fiona, who had made our curtains, created Eilidh's curtains too. Eilidh had great fun choosing all of her furniture and kitchen appliances, although later the gas hob proved faulty and resulted in the whole of the building being evacuated and made safe by the Gas Board.

She opted for pine furniture for the bedrooms, a blue leather settee and pine dresser for the living room. Ron made her a small stepped unit with drawers – she'd admired one but couldn't quite decide and when we returned to the shop it had been sold. He also made wheelchair accessible flower troughs for her little garden. She loves plants and flowers and with these adapted troughs she would be able to help to plant flowers and pull out weeds.

In April 2002 Eilidh's house was ready and waiting for her. She had been so excited while she was busy choosing everything but, as the time for moving grew nearer, her anxiety increased and emotions welled up. There was that fear of the unknown. She is exactly like me in this regard and I was at a loss as to what more I could do to reassure her.

She knew two of the ladies who were going to provide support, as they had worked at Red Cross House. But she worried about who else was going to support her. She also worried about missing her friends. Her sleep pattern, usually so untroubled, became disturbed, she would regularly break down and cry inconsolably and she lost her appetite. At these times our dog Leo would sit beside her and push his wet nose into her lap. Ron and I told her that when she moved into her house we'd go and stay with her for the first week and I arranged leave of absence from work in order to do this.

During that time the support staff would come in regularly to see her. The arrangement was that staff would each work a twenty-four hour shift, staying overnight with Eilidh and swapping at 3.30pm pm each day. She would have about three or four regular support workers, who would get to know her needs. They would be required to help her with everything from personal care to cooking to taking her out and about. I demonstrated the methods that I used to move and handle Eilidh and explained the importance of preserving her existing mobility by giving her opportunities to stand for transfer from her wheelchair into her comfy chair, etc. I also stressed the importance of encouraging and reminding her to sit up because she tends to lean forward and to her right hand side

Eilidh soon settled into independent living and thoroughly enjoyed her new flat. She entertained lots of visitors, including family and friends, and folk from Red Cross House.

Unfortunately some of the tenants were not others with disabilities, but people who were hard to house because of problems with drugs and alcohol and such like. Regular anti-social incidents occurred. These included excessive noise such as shouting and swearing, doors often being slammed, lighted cigarette butts being dropped from the upstairs window of the top floor flat, discarded needles in the garden next door and occasional pools of vomit in the communal hall. There was at times a sea of rubbish covering the car park because some tenants were either too lazy or forgetful to remember to put out their bins. When they did, they were full to the brim and the excess was placed beside them in black plastic sacks. The bin men wouldn't take anything that wasn't in the bin. Consequently roving seagulls found them easy pickings and would peck at the bags, leaving everything from dirty nappies to used needles, strewn over the ground.

During the four years that Eilidh stayed there, I applied to various other housing associations for an alternative tenancy. It seemed easier for a good tenant to move, than for the housing association to evict and re-house an anti-social tenant. We knew that Eilidh was safe because of her wonderful and dedicated support staff and we did not want her to give up her tenancy and bring her home. That seemed like a backward step and we felt we would be making a rod for our own backs. Plus, if we had, in all likelihood she would have lost her support package.

Residential school and Red Cross House had paved the way for independent living for Eilidh and without the experiences of both places I think that she would have been reluctant to leave home. While I could not see into the future, I couldn't think of anything worse than struggling to support her as we both grew older. I baulked at the thought of becoming ill and dying and her having to go almost immediately into an alien setting until an appropriate place was made available. I wanted to know she was safe and happy so that I could grow old in peace.

There is a saying: *"The darkest hour is just before the dawn".* And so it came to pass that in May 2006 Eilidh was offered a shared ownership cottage – she would own a part of it and rent the remainder. We arranged to view it and Eilidh immediately fell in love with it, so we decided to buy her a quarter share with the money from an insurance policy that we'd taken out for her when she was very young. There was almost enough to pay for that and settle the legal fees.

The house had needed a complete makeover, new flooring, a new kitchen, a wet wall in the bathroom, a replacement patio door and decoration throughout. Ron laid the flooring, Calum the carpets and Fiona made new curtains for the living room and Roman blinds for the kitchen and bathroom as not all Eilidh's old ones were the right size. Ron and I assembled the kitchen units and Andrew and his future wife Mary fitted them. Andrew tiled the walls and Linsey helped with the painting and framing pictures for Eilidh. Eilidh just loved the craic and being part of it all. In November, when the renovations were completed, she moved in and made a Will. I felt very proud of her.

By this time Linsey was working as a journalist in London – she first worked in newspapers and then in television. And Andrew had decided to move to Ireland. After a trip there with his Irish colleague Pat, he met Mary, whom he later married. We were extremely sad at the prospect of him going, but Ron and I knew instinctively that he would be happy. When I thought about him going, I was reminded about my move with Ron, almost three decades previously, to the Highlands. I had moved away from my Dad, not really knowing how tough that separation would be.

The night before Andrew left, I had said my goodbyes to him because I was going to be leaving early for work the next day. Andrew and I have a lot in common, including a love of history and music, and like me he can be quite fastidious. He is the only other person I know who will thoroughly rinse all the crockery and cutlery before it goes into the dishwasher.

That aside, most of all, I treasure the conversations we used to have. At times we would sit up late having a right good chinwag. Andrew is a great listener and he is also very, very funny. His repertoire of accents never ceases to have me in stitches. Ron helped pack Andrew's car with the luggage he was taking on the ferry and we were so relieved when he phoned later that evening to say that he'd arrived safely. I was just so glad to hear that: he'd spread his wings.

The End of an Era

At this point our old friend Mrs Swan was, incredibly, in her 107th year. She'd lived a very full and independent life for more than 99 years, but eventually needed more help than a daily visit from a support worker could provide. She spent her remaining years in a wonderful care home in

Inverness overlooking the River Ness, where she was an extremely valued resident. She passed away peacefully in April 2007 and just three months shy of her 107th birthday.

Later that year I decided to retire from my job. I was now almost 61 and my health was not as good as it had been. I felt working full time was a bit much. I did, however, start working as a part-time supply teacher at St Duthus special school in Tain, where I thoroughly enjoyed teaching life skills to children with learning difficulties, some of whom I'd taught as toddlers, for quite a number of years.

During this time I often wished for a glimpse into the future and once had a tarot reading hoping I would get some idea of what might happen to Eilidh. In this regard, it was quite vague.

Over the years I have agonised and wrestled as to whether we made the right decision regarding Eilidh's hip operation in 1989. I often wondered if we should have left the dislocated hip alone or just had the tetonomy instead of opting for the more invasive surgery. As if in answer to a prayer, I finally met Reverend Dr Barbara Chandler, a wonderful rehabilitation consultant. She arranged a meeting a few months ago and I was able to tell her every single one of my worries and gain something near to closure on this.

What I can rest assured about is that ten years after moving to her own home, Eilidh's thoroughly enjoying her life. Everyone who supports her is well aware of the importance of giving her lots of opportunities to stand, be properly and comfortably seated so that her existing mobility is preserved. She has a settled team of wonderful support staff who often comment that: *"It doesn't feel like a job."* Eilidh goes out most days. She attends the L'Arche community workshop on Monday, Wednesday and Thursday afternoons. Here she helps grow plants in the polytunnel and enjoys the craft group where she helps to make decorated mirrors and candles. She also thoroughly enjoys colouring pictures and playing board games with her friends there.

This L'Arche group stems from a group that was set up in 1964 in Trosly-Breuil in France by the philosopher and teacher Jean Vanier, who is now 84. He had become acutely aware of the plight of people with disabilities. He bought a small house, which he called L'Arche (the Ark), and invited Raphael Simi and Philippe Seux, two men with disabilities, to leave the institution in which they were staying and share his home. Jean firmly believed that whatever their strengths, all people are bound together by common humanity. The idea spread and over 50 years later there are L'Arche communities all over the world.

Eilidh is lucky enough to also receive both massage and physiotherapy at the MS Centre on Tuesday mornings and to go to wheelchair curling in the afternoons between September and March with her Dad. On Friday afternoons we exercise and swim at the hydrotherapy pool, while each weekend she gets out and about in her wheelchair accessible vehicle, to the shops and the cinema or lunch with Ionutsa, her friend from L'Arche. Ionutsa, who was adopted by her wonderful family from a Romanian orphanage, comes for tea quite often. Eilidh also enjoys visits from family, including Ron's sister Moira and her husband Douglas. She also enjoys going out for dinner and visiting our old neighbour Cathy in Glenurquhart. She is so lucky that she just does not have much time to be bored and stuck in front of the TV, as so many people with disabilities are. Over the years frequent attempts have been proposed to make cuts to her support package. We have had to argue strenuously to counter this. As a consequence, we have often been utterly drained, because this left us feeling very concerned about her future well-being and security. However we are feeling more relaxed about her future now because at her last review the recommendation was *"no change"*. Andrew, her dedicated social worker, told me beforehand that Eilidh was *"getting older, so trying to trim any hours would be counter productive."* She is extremely settled and happy and her house has just had a ten-year makeover!

As for her brother and sister, Andrew now works as a loss adjuster in Ireland. He and his wife Mary now have four lovely children Iona, Callum, Christopher and Lewis. Linsey and her husband Alex have three lovely boys Raphy and identical twins Luca and Leo. When Leo and Luca were born almost twelve weeks prematurely we were totally devastated. Painful memories of Eilidh's stormy birth arose, leaving me feeling so very raw and emotional. I thought of the twins I'd known during the time in my job, how often one child had been left disabled and sometimes both of them. How I hoped and prayed that Luca and Leo wouldn't have a similar outcome to Eilidh.

Leo and Luca's prematurity was entirely unrelated to their Aunty Eilidh's. It was just an unnerving coincidence. They were diagnosed with acute and severe Twin to Twin Transfusion Syndrome at 24 weeks and required urgent surgery to separate the blood vessels in their shared placenta, giving each their own blood supply. Linsey's consultant explained that after the surgery each boy would have only a 30% chance of survival and, if that happened, there would then be a 15% chance of each boy having a disability. She was given a chance to decide whether she wanted to have surgery within 24 hours and take these risks, or let fate take its course. Knowing how tough it is to raise a disabled child, Linsey opted for surgery, determined to try to achieve the best outcome for her babies.

As Eilidh's sister, for Linsey this was her worst fear and the reason she had been terrified at the prospect of having a baby. She knows only too well that not only does this mean you spend all your life fighting for your child and that life is so much tougher for the child with the disability as well as their brothers and sisters.

Linsey's twins miraculously survived. They were born just hours into their 29th week and spent eight weeks in special care. After coming home, they had to attend regular health and developmental check ups. During their first year I was certain they were fine, because they met each developmental milestone, but Linsey was not convinced. She longed for a glimpse into the future to know that they would be OK.

That moment came one summer day when they were just over a year old and when she looked through the kitchen window at them in the garden playing happily with their big brother.

I have always told Eilidh that she was a pioneer and it's because of her and others like her that positive outcomes in medical advances are made. When Linsey's boys were in the special care baby unit, some 32 years after their Aunty Eilidh, Mums were asked to express and freeze breast milk for them and to hold them on their chests, offering them skin-to-skin contact. These things did not happen when Eilidh was tiny. Eilidh's birth at 28 weeks was fairly sudden, but Linsey had a warning five weeks before Luca and Leo's birth that they would likely be premature. This gave her the chance to eat as much protein as she could in an effort to get their birth weights up. They were born at the same stage of pregnancy as Eilidh, but weighing 2lb 10oz – 8oz more than she did. And for that I am truly grateful. Although Linsey's friends were horrified when they heard the boys' birth weights, I actually remarked that they were great weights for twins at that gestation.

Though Eilidh's life is not the life that any parent would choose for their child, it is certainly the best that we can give her. The most important thing is that she is happy, which, really sadly, many able-bodied people aren't. I wish so much that my Mum could have met her and that she could have been there for me through all these trials and tribulations that life has thrown at me. But each day I think of her and feel glad that at least she was my Mum.

Eilidh was over for a meal on Mother's Day. We'd had a lovely time and as she was leaving her parting shot summed it all up. *"I'm not coming over again Mum, the access is rubbish!"* This was in response to Ron accidently bumping her over the front door frame. That statement stayed with me as I stood at the door waving her off and I smiled wistfully as I thought of the wee girl who was so very shy and lacking in confidence. Over the years she has steadily grown in confidence and though she'll always be dependant on others for many aspects of her life, with appropriate support and guidance she is well able to make choices, decisions and speak up for herself.

I believe that children are gifts. But they are gifts that we cannot keep forever. All I ever wanted was to be around while my children were growing up, because I would have loved to have had my Mum around. My job was to grow from my roots and to give my own children good wings to travel on their own chosen routes through life.

Each night I thank God for my family and for all of the other people who have helped and influenced me throughout my life.
Maggie Wynton June 2017

Looking forward to the future

The Wynton Family including Mary Andrew's wife

Alex Linsey's husband with Eilidh at Andrew and Mary's wedding

Callum, Christopher, Iona and Lewis Andrew and Mary's children

Lewis's Christening

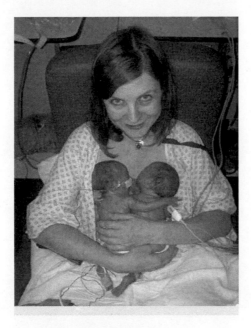

Linsey with twins
Luca and Leo

Linsey with Luca, Leo and Raphy

Eilidh having a lovely time at Pat and Tracy's
wedding with Maggie and Raphy behind

**Letters from my Mum during
World War II and after.**

Edinburgh

10th May 1944

Dear Bob

How are you getting on? I am fine. I didn't have my head dressed today (A relief). They have been doing a spot of cleaning in the ward and it does smell nice. I had a get well card from Mrs Dunn (Alison Peace). It was good of her eh?

There were three people got home today, oh how I envied them. I'm bucking myself up with all the good times I'm going to have when I do get out. Well honey please don't work too hard and look after yourself till I get home. All my love darling. Some letter eh?

Ann

Wednesday

10th May 1944

Dear Bob

How are you getting on now? I've just had a bed bath so feel grand and clean. I didn't have my ear dressed today so that's something to look forward to tomorrow. I hope you're not working too hard, as we are going to play hard when I get out of here. Other two got out today. Mrs Thomson next bed and I are the only two in bed, all the others are up. I had a card from Ina Cameron yesrerday also a card and letter from our Janet. Let her come over some day Bob, maybe she could come next time. Kit's coming as Lizzie says she is going to start my cleaning. Well honey I must close now give my regards to all, and all my love to you.

Ann xxxx

I'd have you before anyone else coming in – selfish eh? Well my darling cheerio for now and please pray for me to get home soon.

All my love

 Ann xxxxx

Ward 38
R.I.E.
May 1944

Dearest Bob

This is Sunday night and I'm feeling ok again. It's you that always does it to me. I miss you so much whenever I see you I could start in fact even writing this has started me off again. The tall patient with the white hair Mrs Murphy was down so she told me to keep weeping if I could that the tears were a reaction and the more I wept the sooner I'll get over it. Supposing I'm crying I feel ok. Oh Bob I wish I was beside you again we have so much to make up. You'll never know how I miss you. Last night I just imagined you and me listening to the play. Oh dear I'll have to stop, Theatre nurse has come in . She wants me to do some swabs for her. When she saw me crying it started her too. Her mother is very ill. We're a pair sitting blabbing here. Well my darling Good night remember your prayers. I'll finish this after my dressing tomorrow.

Well honey here it is Tuesday and my dressing over (Thank God) Sister said when she started, "Well dear, I'll try not to hurt you" so I knew what to expect. OH boy she didn't let me down.

There are five going out today and fancy Bob, Mrs Thomson across the ward is getting up today. I think she looks worse that me don't you. The post has just been and I had a nice long letter from Jenny Fernie.

Well Bob remember don't you worry about me. I'm just a bubble and could kick myself after you go away. You're the only one I shed tears for. I hope they're all pulling their wait at the office and helping you out.

Saturday seems a long time away, however I guess it will soon wear round. You know don't you Bob I'd have you before anyone else coming in selfish eh?

Well my darling cheerio for now and please pray for me to get home soon.

All my love
Ann xxxxx

over

Tell Jessie her parcel was lovely that I enjoyed my tea a hundred per cent. Tell anybody we know I'm asking for them.

Love
Ann

Darling

This is Monday night and the blackouts will soon be going up 8 o'clock. Did you get my letter? Marion Brown got home today so she promised to drop it in the letter box. I've felt grand today. In the afternoon I was darning for the Infirmary nurse asked me to do it. I sat up and did that from dinner time till tea time. My bottom had to get rubbed after it. The thing that amazes me, Mrs Thomson is never asked to do anything. I was cutting swabs for the Theatre nurse last night. These are jobs one must be able to sit up and do, and yet Mrs Thomson gets up. I don't however I'm not really fussy. I'll maybe be all the stronger when I do get up.

Tomorrow is operating day again. We have four patients just now but we'll probably get some tomorrow. I'm going to try to write you a few lines every night, then finish it next morning after my dressing. Well honey goodnight and God bless, this is another day nearer home.

Well Honey here it is Tuesday and my dressing has been done again. Oh Bob it was hell. My ear has been bleeding a lot so it has been packed in the inside. Sister just hauls the paper out and you know how it is all tender and stitching. Then she packs and presses it again. One can hardly bear a touch on the ear let alone anything else. However that's another one over. She always tells me, "You've been very good." I never say a word when she's there but this morning after she'd finished, the tears were running, even the nurses were sorry for me. There I go again giving you all the sore bits Bob. I was always the same wasn't I? Please don't worry about it. I suppose Mrs Brown will be in on Friday. I forgot to let you know that I got my stitches out. I can bear that ok, it's not too bad, but the pack!

I'm reading George's book, it's very good. If Lizzie comes over this week Bob, if my own dressing gown is presentable I'd prefer it. I've never had Jessie's on and would rather not. Well Honey, this is operating day there'll be some poor souls. I pray I don't have to go back.

What do you think of the sirens going. They are very loud here. Just puts one of sleep. I'm sleeping better now. I haven't had tablets for a few nights (touch wood)

Night nurse is away home to Birmingham for three nights. Staff nurse (the one who always talks to you) is going away for a fortnight in three days wish it had been sister.

Well angel goodbye for now another day nearer.

All my love

Ann xxxxx

I missed you a lot today somehow Bob

Dear Bob
Here it is Tuesday and I'm still not stitched. They kept me lying here till 1.15pm thinking that I was going to Theatre, and then brought me my dinner and told me I wasn't being done today. I can honestly tell you I was very disappointed because it just means I've all the suspense to go through again, however it can't be helped. I had it all counted up, stitched today, and get them out on Monday (maybe) then I'd probably get out on the Thursday or Friday but I suppose they thought 2 days wouldn't make any difference to me. Little do they know how I'm dying to get home. Oh Bob can you just imagine it you and me together again. I lie here nights on end and imagine it. It helps to keep me happy. Roll on Saturday. There is nothing more I can say. I only wanted to tell you what they'd done to me.

All my love

Ann xxx

Ward 38
R.I.E.
24th May 1944

My darling

What news I have for you tonight. I'm to get up for 10 mins. Sister came in and said, "How long is it since this girlie had her first operation?" I at once answered 3 weeks tomorrow sister to which she paid absolutely no attention. She next took down my chart and started to count. The staff nurse was with her. Then she said, "21 days. I think we'll have her u tomorrow." Changed her mind and said, "Couldn't we get her up today." Staff nurse said, "How about when we make her bed?" so it was agreed on. I'll tell you I had to stop because I've been up for 10 minutes./ I feel fine. When I got up I was helped by two nurses across to a chair which was smothered in blankets. I felt pains shoot right up through me starting at my soles, however I felt much better coming back. By the time I got back to bed both nurses let go of me and I stood quite steady. I'll admit I'm glad to be in bed again but that's always a start eh? I'll get up for half an hour tomorrow all going well.

Margaret (think it was my stepmother) was in today. She brought me a1/4 choc pep creams. I was very happy to get them but I half expected something for my tea, however don't tell her will you.

Mrs Campbell and Mrs Brown will be over tomorrow I expect. When you come on Saturday bring my navy coat, my costume jacket (best one) and a scarf or something for my head. Remember Bob about the socks from Mrs Bernard. Also I spoke to Margaret about the stockings for sister. Lizzie will pick out a pair of fully fashioned stockings from the same drawer as your socks are in. I'll give sister two pairs of stockings. How much will we give the nurses? We'll give the chief some cigarettes along with the socks eh? He came in to see me at dinner time and here was I sound asleep. He must have had a quiet smile for the patient in the next bed said he came up and looked over me and just walked out of the ward again. Actually I'm his only patient here, and you know how doctors are if you're not their patient they don't hold the same interest in you. I'm really getting to like his quiet manner, and he always seems so pleased with my progress.

I forgot to tell you, remember my shoes, my coolees (don't know what they were), also two suspender buttons lying around somewhere. I'll tell you what Bob, bring out our case that stands in the byre and you'll get this wee one home with you. Oh I forgot, bring my curlers and a coat hanger. This is all I can remember tonight sweetheart but I'll finish this after my dressing tomorrow. Goodnight my darling and God bless. I've got an awful idea I'll only be another week or 10 days. Im praying very hard anyway.

Well Bob here it is and my dressing over again. I spoke too quick yesterday. She gave me 'hell" today again, also she put some stuff like red ink in and am I dripping, right from my ear to my neck. I'm alright now after I've had my weep.

Mrs Macfarlane next bed was weeping after her dressing and she's very brave. Mrs Thomson has to go to Theatre to have her ear scraped. Poor soul I feel for her. Well Honey the post has been and I've had a letter from Isa Cameron. I think I must close now, the people have started to come in to have their operations today.

All my love darling. Write soon

Ann xxxxx

If I'd come from Edinburgh I'd have been home

Ward 38
R.I.E.
May 1944

My darling

Here is Tuesday night again and I feel just grand. Lizzie and Kit were over, and I got you letter just before they came in. I was so pleased to get it Bob. I've read it again and again.

Fancy Will Moyes's wife, poor soul what a blow that must be. Two wee girls left too.

I also had a letter from Margaret today. She's so very pleased about the engagement, says she'll try to make Frank very happy and a whole lot of other things. I'll keep the letter and you can read it.

Mrs Campbell shouldn't bother coming on Tuesday, no doubt I'll be glad to see her but still it takes too much out of her.

Two of my favourite nurses left today. I'm sorry to see them go. Remember the wee one on Sunday well she's one of hem.\Lizzie brought a bottle of orange juice today and fillet steak and some biscuits. Kit had made some things 2 rhubarb tarts and fruit scones. They were lovely.

Well my darling here goes again for another night. Goodnight and God bless. You'll never know how much I miss you.

All my love

Till Wednesday

Well Bob here it is and my dressing over again and I can hardly believe it myself it was quite bearable today. She gave me "hell" yesterday so when she came in to the ward she said, "Did I do you yesterday?" to which I replied (thinking that I wasn't being let off today) , "Yes sister." Then with a smile on her face she replied, "Well I'll do you today again." I nearly passed out but she was more gentle today the inside of the ear didn't seem so bad, wasn't too tender. The post has just been so I got a letter from Frank. I love getting letters. This is all for now. I'm not up yet.

All my love darling

Ann xxxxx

If I'd come from Edinburgh I'd have been home

Ward 38

Darling

Am I not the big bubbling fool. When you come I always wish I could get back with you not that I'm discontented. I'm not that in fact I'm very happy and I really think I'll shed tears when I leave.

Tell Jessie her sandwiches and baking were grand. I enjoyed my tea very much. I was back in bed at 5.30pm. That was from 9.30am so I did fine didn't I? I felt very tired because I walked nearly all the time. I'm lying down writing this hence the reason for the scrawl. Nurse Sillitoe was telling me just now Nurse Maxwell and she were talking about my walking and they had been saying 3 weeks ago they couldn't have even visions of my doing it. You know Bob the more they talked to me about it, the more I realize how much I have to be thankful for. Remember to thatnk God every night will you? I do anyway.

After I write this I'll write Mrs Bernard. It's only 8 o'clock yet so I've an hour. Night nurses don't come on till nine on Sunday night.

When I come into Dunfermline Bob we'll try to make it a real holiday. I'm started to look forward to it already picturing all the things we'll do. I'll make this do for tonight and finish it in the morning.

All my love darling sleep well, I'm thinking of you all the time.

Ann

Tell Lizzie to bring a scarf that I may wear like a turban and this one's too big.

This is Monday morning Sister dressed me today and she actually said, "Where do you live Mrs Campbell?" That means something. If I'd lived in Edinburgh bet I'd been out tomorrow, however another day or two of this and I'll be ok. I've written Mrs Bernard. I think I'll drop old Mrs Bernard a line too. Well Honey this is all for now. One of the nurses fainted this morning while sister was dressing Mrs Thomson. When she came to another nurse was asked to take her out. When they were going out the ward 'old mother sister ' shouts, "Stick her head between her knees." Have you ever seen anybody walking like that?"

Love
Ann xxxxx

R.I.E.

30th May 1944

Dear Bob

How are you tonight. I am fine and what do you think, I've been out all day. I had a walk round the Infirmary then sat in the sun for ages. The staff nurse made me get to bed at five since I'd been out so long. I'd never have believed I was so stiff, the backs of my legs are aching, but I know a big difference in myself.

I got a nice chance of sister today, so I gave her the things. She was delighted, this afternoon I nearly laughed out at her. Five of us were sitting just after dinner-time. She came up pointed an accusing finger at me and said, "You get out in the sun." Her way of showing affection. When she singles anybody out for attention it's because she's trying to be nice and it's just not in her. Her brother is Lord Leitch. I've never heard of him, have you/

I had to borrow this paper so I must close now and leave a space for morning.

Well Bob this is morning. Dressing over again. It was ok. Lizzie will be in today. I forgot you would not get my letter in time for the wee scarf. Kit is bringing the hood tomorrow, and I have got this into a pixie. I never wakened from 9o'clock till 5am, Not bad eh? My legs are needing massaged. Dr Russell from ward 33 sent his kindest regards with Nurse Maxwell. Fancy him remembering me. I'll tell you what he said after.

All my love darling

Ann xxxxx

Letters from my Dad during World War II and after.

LUMPHINNANS No X1 COLLIERY PITHEAD BATHS

R. Campbell
Secretary

Please sign the enclosed letter and have it posted. Jessie will do it

Kelty
16th May 1944

My Dear Ann
Received your welcome letter day from Janet. She tells me that Kate did
not turn up, something must have come in her way at the last moment. I
expect you would be very pleased to see Janet today, I was waiting on her
tonight to hear about you. I was so sorry that they didn't "do" you today
and that you must think about Thursday now. Never mind Fud after
Thursday you'll be as good as new again, and I'll be waiting on you. Don't
mind if you don't get out as early as you want to think you will. When you
come home I want you to be fit and well. I know you, if you get out too
quick you'll be thinking to spring clean the house all over again.
Lizzie is doing well she has done the living room, front room and bedroom,
also bathroom and scullery. She is now at the byre and I've suggested to
her that she leaves my den alone.
When you come home all you'll have to do is sit at the fire and stoke up.
Everybody is very kind and are asking for you. You know I think you
should stand at the next store quarterly meeting, you'd be a cinch to get on.
Jessie and Isa will be across to see you tomorrow (Wednesday) I expect
they'll arrive before this letter. Mrs Campbell will be on Thursday to see
you. Father must have lost one of the tickets on Saturday and I had a letter
from Margaret tonight saying she has looked everywhere she can think of
but can't find it.
It is possible to get another, you might enquire and also see about the
sweetie coupon.
Well honey I'll say goodnight now and wish you pleasant dreams. Iw as
thinking of you today and all I'm thinking about now is Saturday and
Sunday. In future I'm keeping Sunday for you and me only.

Yours
Bob x

I might give this letter to Jessie for you

R. Campbell   Kelty
Secretary   24th May 1944

My Dear Ann

Received your welcome letter this morning and derived very much pleasure in learning that you were feeling grand. I'm very sorry that the dressing is so very painful but you're tough and can take it supposing it's hell.

I'll bring your dressing gown on Saturday. Lizzie washed it some time ago and it turned out very nice. Can you get Jessie's for me and I will bring it home. I had forgotten all about it and she may require it. was up at old Mrs Bernard's tonight and saw her, Belle Gregory and Annie Stevenson and they are all asking for you. Belle says she'll see you when you come home. Mrs Bernard hasn't been keeping too well of late but is now feeling better. She tells me she is almost 80. She is not knitting as much either but I managed to get a nice pair of socks from her and will bring them over on Saturday and then you can give them to the doctor.

By the time you get this letter, it will only be 2 days till Saturday and then we'll see each other again. I expect Father to be there also. I always feel sorry for him as it always seems to upset him.

Meg Ferguson will have been in today to see you. How is the romance going? Frank hasn't written to me yet. Mrs Brown will be in on Thursday, please give her my apologies.

Jean McCabe started in Rosyth on Monday last. I saw her tonight, she is getting along fine, tells me she's been lucky and has landed in an office, where funny enough according to her she writes all day. Mr Bald has got started at Cowdenbeath on part time. I was speaking to him on the phone today. He also enquired for you.

Things I think are getting better at the office and I'm beginning to see daylight again.

Well Fud I'll close now. Remember to keep your chin up in the grand old Fotheringham manner. Goodnight.

Yours truly,
Bob x

R. Campbell   Kelty
Secretary   25th May 1944

My Dear Ann

I received your welcome letter again this morning. Helen Bernard is on the post again for two months and she gives it to Ina Cameron in the morning. Helen is replacing big Sandy Swinby who is away on observation duties with minesweepers or trawlers for two months. My guess is as good as the next one and if he second front starts Sandy maybe not get back for a long time. I wonder how Isa is managing during his absence. Well Ann that the "store" business all set for another week. Fancy during my absence from two Board meetings they agreed to part-time workers in the grocery branches. I had a good dig at them tonight about it. "Oh Boy." Belle Gregory was telling me last night that she is fed up working. She is employed full time in the Bakehouse and I think has made up her mind to leave at the holidays.

Can you guess who her successor is likely to be Jean Phelp.

I tried in vain tonight to make this a part time job and employ two women, thus giving Belle a part time job. Again I was unsuccessful as Jean was willing to take full time.

Well Ann everything is fairly quiet and settled in Kelty except that Andrew Phelp was at court today for not having his identity card on him when challenged. I haven't seen him tonight to see how he got on.

His Father and Mother went to England to see his brother Bob who has arrived in this country from America and is in the American Army.

I asked "wet blanket's" sister if she could mend the frayed cuff of my working suit. She agreed but couldn't do it till after July. So very busy you know.

I must say goodnight and pleasant dreams as it's now past my bed time.

Yours
Bob

See you on Saturday

LUMPHINNANS No X1 PITHEAD BATHS

R. Cambell   Kelty
 Secretary   30th May 1944

My Dear Ann
Received your welcome letter this morning (had to stop and change the nib) and glad to know that you are getting on first class. I saw Lizzie this morning. She came up for the card. I forgot to leave it on Sunday night. Lizzie came up tonight after returning from Edinburgh and told me how well you are getting on and that you were out yesterday and today again. Lizzie thinks you are getting along nicely and sees a big improvement in you since she saw you last week.
I am pleased to know that you are not discontented and even supposing you are in for anther week or fortnight what does that matter as long as you come out well and strong again.
When you get out what arrangements are you going to make about the treatment to your ear? It will be very unsuitable if we go to Dunfermline and you have to travel to Kelty every day to have it done. Think it over and we'll discuss it on Saturday when we see each other again.
Did you give the hospital staff the gifts you had for them and also the donation. I'm all on edge to know what the sister said about hers, or haven't you plucked up sufficient courage to give it to her. You should have plenty courage in you after what you've been through. You're a regular hero.
Remember and write old Mrs Bernard and thank her for the socks. I didn't tell her they were for your doctor, I just let her think they were for myself. Here I am troubling you about finance, ask Frank to send me a note authorizing me to draw £15 from his account. I will have to square the "Store Book" this weekend have you many purchases on your own number do you know. Sorry Ann to bother you with these details. Well I'll close now, hoping to see you in the pink on Saturday.

Yours, Bob x

` LUMPHINNANS No X1 COLLIERY PITHEAD BATHS

R. Campbell   Kelty
Secretary   1st June 1944

My Dear Ann

Here I am again, have just come from Jessie's and she tells me that you are
getting on excellently and hoping to get home soon. I also saw Janet (Mrs
Lawson) this morning and she too thinks you are looking wonderfully well.
She tells me Janet Hughes was with her yesterday when she visited you.
You would have a lot of visitors yesterday, Kit and Nancy (my stepmother's
younger sister) also. Meg Ferguson (my stepmother) whom I saw on
Tuesday night is suffering from a rheumatic in the foot. I expect Nancy
would tell you all about it.
Both Jessie and Janet tells me the big chief is to see you tomorrow. I bet
you hope he says you can get home. I'll keep my fingers crossed for you.
But remember and keep your chin up if he says he would like you to stay
on a little longer.
Received a nice letter of thanks and receipt for our donation to the
Infirmary Funds. Makes you feel good when you read it.
Lizzie has been up working and washing today and the weather's been
terrible. You'd better get your thinking cap on in operation again and
consider what we'll give Lizzie in return for all her goodness and work.
Well Annie by the time this letter reaches you it will almost be Saturday
again and almost Sunday again.
I will close now and wish you goodnight and pleasant dreams and hope
that the doctor and God answer your wishes tomorrow.

Yours

Bob x

Later letters

Kelty
Sunday 4th August 1946

Dear Bob

How are you now? I hope you landed safe and sound. This morning it was pouring buckets of rain and this lasted well into the afternoon. I thought if it was like that in Inverness you'd not get the tent down, however maybe it wasn't like that there.

Tommy Philbin and Bob Paterson came up for the urns around eleven. You might have heard Philbin up there.   Kept saying, "Did you ever see it any better for the Peewit Gala Day" (the Peewit was a coal mine and all of the mines had a Gala Day for the families of those who worked for them) Then he asked how I was keeping so he must know.

Well honey enjoy yourself as much as possible for it will be a long time before you get away on your own again. Hadn't I a carry on yesterday when you were leaving. I just couldn't help myself then I was quite mad at sending you away and me with tears in my eyes. I'm a big bubble. I bawled for ages after it, but was ok when Lizzie came. Today Sunday we've been out and in bed all day, we've had a holiday alright.

Well goodnight my darling try to come home Saturday or at latest early Sunday. Funny Bob, I think I must be more in love with you than ever. I miss you so very much. Kept saying to myself all day, that's one sleep over maybe just another six now. I hope so anyway.

We went to Kelty Goth (cinema) last night, just to pass the time that was all it did. All going well you'll take two people for a nice fortnight next year so make the most of your freedom.

All my love

Ann xxxxx

Ps Tell brother (Frank) I'll post on a post card to him also to behave himself and not promise any more rings (not sure if that was when my stepmother and he ended their engagement)

Scotty (the dog) is missing you both a whole lot. She slept in the bedroom last night and didn't go to her chair until I took her at 2.20am. Poor wee soul when I was bawling yesterday, she laid her head on my knee and kept staring at me with her big eyes. Then she brought her ball for me to play with she couldn't understand what ws wrong. 11 o'clock.

Ann
xxxxxx

Dear Mrs Somerville

As I write the date I realise this is the first letter I've written this year. Will you please cancel our fish. I may be away from Kinneddar for quite a time. If I'm spared to come home I'm going to live with friends. Bob was telling me he forgot to come for the fish on Friday, this was a pity but quite understandable under the circumstances. On Friday night, Bob was like me fish was furthest from our minds.

These last two days have been lovely so I trust you've been able to enjoy them. Regards to Mr Somerville. Thanking you again for all you did for me.

Sincerely yours

Ann Campbell

Ward 33
R.I.E.
10-1-49

Dear Bob
This is Monday. Nothing much happened today. The lady doctor tested
my blood. Took it from my arm same as the clinic. Everything is as cheery
as ever here. I'm certain there's a patient, the one who was put into the
bed where the woman who died on Saturday came out of just died.
There's a great stir on anyway and you could hear a pin drop.
How did you get on with my letter to Cath Sorry (I think she was referring
to her letter to Mrs Somerville but I don't think that my Dad delivered it.
Instead he'd likely have gone round in person to apologise and explain)
I wonder how Margaret is poor wee soul? I bet you miss her Bob. I don't
seem to be able to think up anything else only that I'm ok and quite happy.
I told the sister about the pain. She told the doctor so I know not what will
happen. They've been having the same talk as last time, "Ever been
abroad. Are you sure you've never had malaria?" Think I must have a
germ of some kind about me.
All my love and roll on Saturday

Ann xxxxx

Ward 33
R.I.E.
12-1-49

Dear Bob

Here is Wednesday. I've just got your letter and feel very happy about it. We'll go out in the Spring Ha1 Ha! I know that you mean Margaret and I might but I can't see daddy, he'll always have either office or canteen work to do and well you know it Robin.

How is the office going. Work at Comrie should go with a swing these days. The cashier (my Dad) will be there morning, noon and night.

Do you know who was in last night to see me? My old pal of 1944 Dr Russell and fancy he remembered the whole thing and said he'd have to look back my old records. He said he'd have to have me put right and, " I remember that night when I brought in the other doctors, you know Mrs C you were very very ill."

He was house doctor then but is now next to the chief. What a difference on him and he's now a moustache which makes him older looking. When he went away he said, "Well I'll be back again to see you", and when young Dr Gardiner came up he said, "Mrs Campbell's an old friend of mine doctor," and they both laughed.

I keep wishing it was Saturday again as I always seem to have more to tell you than any of the others. Janet brought a lot of nice things. Gran will be today, hope it's not too much for her.

I had a Pakistani doctor from 9 o'clock till 1.30pm yesterday. It was part of a big exam he was sitting, apparently trying to be a professor. When he left I wished him the best of luck and he was very pleased. Part of his exam the chief came in with some X ray photos! This doctor had to explain to the chief about them. Oh you should have heard him Bob he certainly knew his stuff, so I thought anyway, and the chief seemed quite pleased. I sat with my fingers X all the time he was answering the chief. He always started , "Well Sir." I said to him I kept my fingers crossed for you he said, "Thankyou very much Mrs C"

Well Bob my darling I've rambled enough so am finishing now but will write tomorrow. Miss my two darlings ever so much and certainly wish we were all together again.

xxxxxxxxxx for M and you Love Ann

Dear Bob

How are you today? There has still been nothing much done but more pills, and stuff called Bemax. Have you been doing a lot of late work? as if I needed to ask.

I had 3 letters this morning one from Kit, one from Billy and one from poor wee Frank. I hope he has it done ere this. I've thought about him all morning. How's our wee lamb getting on? It always brings tears to my eyes when I think of the wee soul. She says, "Hurry home from the Infirmary mummy." I said, "Be a good girl darling" and she said, "Yes." I'm glad I slept with her the night before. I must have kissed her all night, kissed and cried timed about, there that's enough I'm going all sentimental. It looks a nice day outside. Then how about your old pal Tommy Handley? Gave everybody quite a shock it did. Poor soul I believe he was really good.

How did you get on with Mrs Cath Somerville. I get angry every time I think about her.

Well darling I must say cheerio now but keep well and write soon. All my love to daddy and Margaret.

Xxxxxxx Ann

Dear Bob

This will be some letter as I'm on my back to write it. I'm back from X Ray 5 o'clock and I've been there since 2.30pm. Believe me Bob I'm exhausted. They took my chest as well as my tummy. Oh God I pray there is nothing wrong with my lungs too. There is definitely something wrong with my liver. I don't like to write this Bob, but I've cried for Margaret and you (the only two I've got to live for) all day. I do wish we were together again. Please pray for me to get well soon as I pray as hard as I know how.

Is Willie Paris up tonight? (He was a friend and work colleague of Dad's) The two of you will have a fine pow wow or are you too busy.

This has been a nice day but very windy here. I've just had my tea the first I've eaten since tea time last night. ½ slice toast – 1 cup tea it's awful. Janet will be here tomorrow and Kit and Aitch (a friend Aitchison) Wednesday. I'm so depressed today that I'll be better Tuesday surely. Don't bother about what I've written as I've taken a shaken. I feel awful and of course can only pour my heart out to you. Roll on Saturday and I hope we may be more decided about something then.

I believe this wondering is having a bad effect on me. I've pictured myself with all sorts of trouble silly eh? Fancy I feel brighter even now. Did you have a nice mea at the canteen? Look after yourself Bob as I don't want you ill.

I've read this over and wonder if I should post it but can't be bothered writing another so excuse me this.

Goodnight my darlings and please write me soon.

All my love to my darlings.

xxxxx

Ann

Ward 33
E.R.I.
19-1-49

Dearest Bob

I am writing just now as I feel in a sort of good humour. I really thought shame after I wrote the last letter but believe me Bob I'd been through it. If you can imagine me running around in a wee shirt 3 inches above my knees and a pair of hospital socks it was awful. I had this special X Ray called Barium Enema. I had a nozzle pushed up my back passage and white fluid sprayed in. This they had to try to get to the bowel. He massaged and massage and had me like I could pass urine at any minute and there I was bursting and holding it at the same time. He got that plate then I had to empty the bowel if you had heard that white stuff come splashing out and it run for ages. Up on the table again, the machine on me again and there was still something in the bowel. Away I had to trot in my wee white shirt and socks out to the lavvy, however I managed the second time. Then I'd to go to another part and have my stomach done and before all this I'd had my chest done, that was when I was silly enough to write you, but I knew if I'd waited I wouldn't have been able to write you and that would have worried you.

Dr R Russell was in at me last night again. I wish I saw more of him as he gives me such a lot of confidence. He gave me a good examination, but wouldn't tell me what he thought he said, "We'll wait till the plates come back." He said, "Now why are you letting this temperature of yours go up and down." I said I couldn't understand it. Then her smiled and said, "tell me do you remember what your temp. was like last time you were in." I of course said, "no." He said, "I'll tell you it was right off the chart altogether and that's over 106.

Well Bob I suppose I'll get Kit and Aitch in half an hour. Poor souls what a day for them. This is all for now only write soon.

All my love to my two darlings.

Ann
xxxxx

Dear Bob

This is just going to be a short scribble. I had the surgeon can't spell it in yesterday with 6 of his henchmen. My tummy was examined and examined until I could have seen them far enough. I believe it will be an operation but I'm to have another X Ray first. If it's not a barium enema I don't mind and after that they'll decide.

The surgeon's name is Mr Jardin and one of the nurses told me he was one of the best in the country. He's a principal in the Royal College of Surgeons.

Anyway when I saw him he satisfied me and if he'd said "Come and I'll operate now" I'd have gone gladly.

We've all been happier here this day or two and Mrs Randolph has christened her across from me hungry Horace and believe me it suits her. She could shame a navy with what she eats. It chaws (upsets) me with the helpings I get, bet Margaret gets more.

I expect Aunt Belle will be in today. I'll be pleased to see her.

How are you getting on at the office? Have you made up your Balance Sheet yet? How's Willie Paris these days and Bunty too?

My bottom's sore so I'm not writing any more just wanted to do this so Aunt Belle could bring it back as I know you'll go down.

Well dear this is all for now so write soon.

All my love

Ann
Keep praying
xxxxxxx

The Tay Bridge Disaster

Beautiful Railway Bridge of the Silv'ry Tay,
Alas! I am very sorry to say,
That ninety lives have been taken away,
On the very last Sabbath day of 1879,
Which will be remember'd for a very long time.

'Twas about seven o'clock at night,
And the wind blew with all its might,
And the rain came pouring down,
And the dark clouds seemed to frown,
And the Demon of the air seem'd to say,
"I'll blow down the Bridge of Tay.

When the train left Edinburgh,
The passengers hearts were light, and felt no sorrow,
But Boreas blew a terrific gale,
Which made their hearts for to quail
And many of the passengers with fear did say,
"I hope God will send us safe across the Bridge of Tay"

But when the train came near to Wormit Bay,
Boreas he did loud and angry bray,
And shook the central girders of the Bridge of Tay,
On the last Sabbath day of 1879,
Which will be remembered for a very long time.

So the train sped on with all its might,
And Bonnie Dundee soon hove in sight,
And the passengers' hearts felt light,
Thinking they would enjoy themselves on the New Year,
With their friends at home they lov'd most dear,
And wish them all a Happy New Year.

So the train mov'd slowly along the Bridge of Tay,
Until it was about midway,
Then the central girders with a crash gave way,
And down went the train and passengers into the Tay!
The Storm fiend did loudly bray,
Because ninety lives had been taken away,
On the last Sabbath day of 1879,
Which will be remember'd for a very long time.

As soon as the catastrophe came to be known,
The alarm from mouth to mouth was blown,
And the cry rang out o'er all the town,
Good Heavens! The Tay Bridge is blown down,
And a passenger train from Edinburgh,
Which filled the peoples' hearts with sorrow,
And made them for to turn pale,
Because none of the passengers were sav'd to tell the tale,
How the disaster happen'd on the last Sabbath day of 1879,
Which will be remember'd for a vey long time.

It must have been an awful sight,
To witness in the dusky moonlight,
While the Storm Fiend did laugh and bray,
Along the Railway Bridge of the Silv'ry Tay,
Oh! Ill-fated Bridge of the Silv'ry Tay,
I must now conclude my lay,
By telling the world fearlessly, without the least dismay,
That your central girders would not have given way,
At least many sensible men do say,
Had they been supported on each side with buttresses,
At least many sensible man confesses,
For the stronger we our houses do build,
The less chance we have of being killed.